FROM INQUIRY TO ACADEMIC WRITING

A Practical Guide

FROM INQUIRY TO ACADEMIC WRITING

A Practical Guide

FOURTH EDITION

Stuart Greene
University of Notre Dame

April Lidinsky
Indiana University South Bend

bedford/st.martin's
Macmillan Learning

Boston | New York

For Bedford/St. Martin's

Vice President, Editorial, Macmillan Learning Humanities: Edwin Hill
Senior Program Director for English: Leasa Burton
Program Manager: John E. Sullivan III
Executive Marketing Manager: Joy Fisher Williams
Director of Content Development: Jane Knetzger
Senior Developmental Editor: Mara Weible
Associate Editor: Stephanie Thomas
Editorial Assistant: Aubrea Bailis
Senior Content Project Manager: Ryan Sullivan
Senior Workflow Project Manager: Lisa McDowell
Production Supervisor: Robert Cherry
Media Project Manager: Rand Thomas
Editorial Services: Lumina Datamatics, Inc.
Composition: Lumina Datamatics, Inc.
Photo Editor: Angela Boehler
Photo Researcher: Richard Fox, Lumina Datamatics, Inc.
Permissions Manager: Kalina Ingham
Senior Art Director: Anna Palchik
Cover Design: William Boardman
Cover Art: Mina De La O/Getty Images
Printing and Binding: LSC Communications

Manufactured in the United States of America.

2   1   0   9   8   7
f   e   d   c   b   a

For information, write: Bedford/St. Martin's, 75 Arlington Street, Boston, MA 02116

ISBN 978-1-319-07124-0

Acknowledgments
Text acknowledgments and copyrights appear at the back of the book on pages 413–15, which constitute an extension of the copyright page. Art acknowledgments and copyrights appear on the same page as the art selections they cover.

Preface for Instructors

Academic writing can be a challenging hurdle for students entering college. They must learn new habits of writing, reading, and even thinking. That's where *From Inquiry to Academic Writing* comes in. It addresses the challenges of academic writing, offering a clear, methodical approach to meeting those challenges. Our students, and many others, have told us that our approach demystifies academic writing, while helping them to see that its skills carry over to civic participation and life issues beyond their college years.

Specifically, *From Inquiry to Academic Writing: A Practical Guide* is a composition rhetoric that introduces students to college-level inquiry, analysis, and argument. It is based on a first-year composition course in which we guide students to produce essays that use evidence and sources in increasingly complex ways. In this book, as in our classes, we present academic writing as a collaborative conversation, undertaken to pursue new knowledge. We teach students to see that academic writing is a social act that involves working responsibly with the ideas of others. At the same time, we encourage students to see themselves as makers of knowledge who use sources to advance arguments about important academic and cultural issues.

This fourth edition encompasses an even greater range of academic habits and skills than the third, with more support for synthesis and analysis. A third of the readings are new and explore issues that have become more prominent in academia and public life over the past few years. This edition of *From Inquiry to Academic Writing* is available with LaunchPad, including the complete text and interactive materials in a flexible course space that you can tailor to the needs of your course and students. Read on for details about what's new to the text.

HOW *FROM INQUIRY TO ACADEMIC WRITING* IS ORGANIZED

The book starts by addressing academic thinking and proceeds through academic reading and research, integrating academic writing throughout. Yet the chapters are freestanding enough to be taught in any order that suits your course. What unites them is our constant emphasis on the recursive nature of these skills and the centrality of the writing process. We punctuate every chapter with short readings and activities that prompt students to practice what we teach.

Chapter 1 is an overview of academic writing as a process motivated by inquiry, and it introduces academic habits of mind. Chapter 2 encourages students to practice writerly reading—the rhetorical analysis of other writers' decisions — to learn appropriate strategies for their own writing. Chapter 3 is new and provides students with opportunities to practice basic skills of summary and paraphrase, while learning to write themselves into an academic conversation that entails representing others' ideas accurately. While Chapters 2–6 address the essentials of getting started on writing, from how to mark a text to forming questions and developing a working thesis, we recognize that this process is rarely linear and that it benefits from conversation with invested readers. Chapters 6 and 7 help students develop and support their theses by providing strategies for finding and working with sources. Chapter 8 focuses on synthesis and includes a new set of readings encouraging students to see their everyday lives in and out of school through the lens of civic engagement. Chapter 9 again links writerly reading with readerly writing—this time with writing that reflects rhetorical appeals and strategies of structure and development. Chapter 10 provides new support for visual analysis, including strategies to help students effectively analyze visual rhetoric and incorporate maps, photographs, tables, and graphs to support and enrich their writing. Chapter 11 provides students with strategies for writing introductions and conclusions.

Chapter 12 presents revision in the context of peer groups. The responses of classmates can help students determine when they might need to read additional material to shape more effective research questions, or when they might need more evidence to support an argument. Our supporting materials for peer workshops foster productive group interaction at every stage of the peer review process. Finally, in Chapter 13, we provide students with updated strategies for conducting original research and working with human subjects. This material builds upon earlier chapters about using personal experience and writing a researched argument.

The book concludes with an Appendix that introduces the basics of documentation in current MLA and APA styles.

Although the process of developing an academic argument can be unruly, the structured, step-by-step pedagogy in the rhetoric text supports students during each stage of the process. Several readings are followed by "Reading as a Writer" questions that send students back into the reading to respond to the rhetorical moves writers make. "Steps to" boxes summarize the major points about each stage of thinking, reading, and writing, offering quick references that bring key information into focus for review. "Practice Sequences" ask students to try out and build on the strategies we have explained or demonstrated. We also provide templates, formulas, and worksheets that students may use to organize information as they read and write.

Your students should feel further supported and encouraged by the abundance of student writing (annotated to highlight the rhetorical moves students make) that we use as examples in the rhetoric text, side by side with examples of professional writing.

WHAT'S NEW IN THE FOURTH EDITION?

Among many smaller revisions, we made the following additions in response to numerous comments by instructors:

- **New emphasis on reflection.** Chapter 1 now offers a series of key reflection prompts to help students take control of their own learning.
- **More support for critical reading and analysis, including multimodal texts.** Chapter 4, on analyzing arguments, helps students read critically and detect causal and definition claims. The new Chapter 10 guides students through analyzing the variety of visuals they encounter in multimodal texts and helps them apply that thinking to their own multimodal projects.
- **New advice on summarizing, now earlier in the book.** The authors discuss summary in a new Chapter 3—earlier and in more detail than before—to give students a head start with this foundational academic skill.
- **Extended coverage of synthesizing sources.** Chapter 8 uses new readings focused on civic engagement to help students grasp the process and value of successfully synthesizing sources.

AVAILABLE IN STANDALONE E-BOOK FORMATS

From Inquiry to Academic Writing is available as an e-Book in a variety of electronic formats. Online at a value price, e-Books are available from a variety of vendors. You can find more information at **macmillanlearning .com/ebooks** or contact your Bedford/St. Martin's representative for more details.

AVAILABLE WITH AN ANTHOLOGY OF READINGS

From Inquiry to Academic Writing is available in an alternative version that appends an extensive collection of readings to its text chapters. The longer version, *From Inquiry to Academic Writing: A Text and Reader*, Fourth Edition, includes an additional thirty-five readings organized in chapters focusing on issues in the fields of education, sociology, media studies, psychology and biology, sustainability and environmental studies, and economics. Selections from scholarly works, public intellectuals, and even best-selling authors reveal that the topics, issues, and rhetorical moves of academia are as relevant outside the university as they are within it.

AN INSTRUCTOR'S MANUAL IS AVAILABLE FOR DOWNLOAD

We have prepared an instructor's manual, *Resources for Teaching From Inquiry to Academic Writing: A Practical Guide*, Fourth Edition. The manual addresses every step of the process of academic writing we set forth in the rhetoric. Not only do we discuss many of the issues involved in taking our rhetorical approach to academic argument— problems and questions students and instructors may have—but we also suggest background readings on the research informing our approach. The instructor's manual can be downloaded from **macmillanlearning.com**. Visit the instructor resources tab for *From Inquiry to Academic Writing*.

ACKNOWLEDGMENTS

We would first like to thank the many reviewers who commented on the proposal, the manuscript, and the first edition, as well as the reviewers of the second and third editions in both their full and compact iterations. Invariably their comments were useful, and frequently helpful and cheering as well. The list of reviewers includes Andrea Acker, Seton Hill University; Angela Adams, Loyola University–Chicago; Steve Adkison, Idaho State University; Kay Ames, University of Mount Olive; Teresa Fernandez Arab, University of Kansas; Jonathan Arnett, Kennesaw State University; Brian Artese, Kennesaw State University; Yesho Atil, Asheville-Buncombe Technical Community College; Anthony Atkins, University of North Carolina, Wilmington; Paula Bacon, Pace University–Pleasantville; Susan Bailor, Front Range Community College; Mary Ellen Bertolini, Middlebury College; Laurel Bollinger, University of Alabama–Huntsville; Rebecca Boncal, John Tyler Community College; Margaret Bonesteel,

Syracuse University; Elizabeth Brewer, Central Connecticut State University; James Brill, University of California, Chico; Laurie Britt-Smith, St. Louis University; Christina Riley Brown, Mercyhurst University; Siobhan Brownson, Winthrop University; William Brugger, Brigham Young University Idaho; Lise Buranen, California State University–Los Angeles; Keely Byars-Nichols, University of Mount Olive; Robin Caine, Montclair State University; Bettina Caluori, Mercer County Community College; Jeffrey Cebulski, Kennesaw State University; Kathleen Chriest, Mercyhurst University; Marie Coffey, San Antonio College; Carolyn Cole, Oklahoma Baptist University; Tami Comstock-Peavy, Arapahoe Community College; Emily Cosper, Delgado Community College; Karen Cox, City College of San Francisco; Donna Craine, Front Range Community College; Ryan Crider, Missouri State University; Virginia Crisco, California State University–Fresno; Bonnie Cross, Community College of Allegheny; Calum Cunningham, Fanshawe College–London; Sarah Dangelantonio, Franklin Pierce University; Alexis Davis, University of Mount Olive; J. Madison Davis, University of Oklahoma–Norman; Anne DeMarzio, University of Scranton; Erin Denney, Community College of San Francisco; Jason DePolo, North Carolina A&T State University; Brock Dethier, Utah State University; Clark Draney, College of Southern Idaho; Eugenia C. Eberhart, Garden City Community College; Lisa Egan, Brown University; Ed Eleazer, Francis Marion University; Brant Ellsworth, Penn State Harrisburg; Larry Eson, Front Range Community College; Jennifer Fletcher, University of Phoenix; Elaine Fredericksen, University of Texas–El Paso; Hannah Furrow, University of Michigan–Flint; Christine A. Geyer, Cazenovia University; Zan Goncalves, Franklin Pierce University; Rhoda Greenstone, Long Beach City College; Rima Gulshan, George Mason University; Sinceree Gunn, University of Alabama–Huntsville; Clinton Hale, Blinn College; Juli E. Hale, King College; Jane Hammons, University of California, Berkeley; Amy Hankins, Blue River Community College; Ann Hartney, Fort Lewis College; Beth Hedengren, Brigham Young University; Tara Hembrough, Southern Illinois University, Carbondale; Virginia Scott Hendrickson, Missouri State University; Zachery Hickman, University of Miami; Wilbur Higgins, University of Massachusetts Dartmouth; Monica Hogan, Johnson County Community College; Shelli Homer, University of Missouri–Columbia; Jean Incampo, Gateway Community College; Karen Keaton Jackson, North Carolina Central University; Dennis Jerz, Seton Hill University; T. Christine Jesperson, Western State College of Colorado; Margaret Johnson, Idaho State University; Therese Jones, Lewis University; Laura Katsaros, Monmouth University; Michael Kaufmann, Indiana University–Purdue and University Fort Wayne; Trevor Kearns, Greenfield Community College; Howard Kerner, Polk Community College; Lynn Kilpatrick, Salt Lake Community College; Jeff Klausman, Whatcom Community College; Marcel Kristel, Ohlone College; Tamara Kuzmenkov, Tacoma Community College; Michelle LaFrance, UMass Dartmouth; Thomas Lapointe, Bergen

Community College; Erin Lebacqz, University of New Mexico; Lindsay Lewan, Arapahoe Community College; April Lewandowski, Front Range Community College–Westminster; Meredith Love-Steinmetz, Francis Marion University; Robert Lundergan, Fullerton College; Renee Major, Louisiana State University; Diane L. Maldonado, Point Park University; Michael Manis, Indiana University; Brenna Manuel, Franklin Pierce University; Gina Maranto, University of Miami; Loren Loving Marquez, Salisbury University; Carola Mattord, Kennesaw State University; Mark McBeth, John Jay College; Megan McGee-Yinger, Pennsylvania State University–Harrisburg; Timothy McGinn, Northwest Arkansas Community College; Craig Medvecky, Loyola University; Erica Messenger, Bowling Green State University–Main; Keri Mikulski, Rowan University; Alyce Miller, Indiana University; Deborah Miller, University of Georgia; Lamata Mitchell, Rock Valley College; Robert Mohrenne, University of Central Florida; Whitney Myers, University of New Mexico; Nela Navarro, Rutgers University; Erin Nelson, Blinn College; Teddy Norris, St. Charles Community College; Lolly J. Ockerstrom, Park University; Judy Olson, California State University, Los Angeles; Jill Onega, University of Alabama–Huntsville; Jill Parrott, Eastern Kentucky University; Robert Peltier, Trinity College; Valeries L. Perry, Lewis University; Jeanette Pierce, San Antonio College; Christian Pyle, Eastern Kentucky University; Mary Jo Reiff, University of Tennessee; Tonya Ritola, Georgia Gwinnett College; Mary Roma, New York University; Claudia Rubner, Mercer County Community College; David Ryan, University of San Francisco; Amanda McGuire Rzicznek, Bowling Green State University; Daniel Schenker, University of Alabama–Huntsville; Roy Stamper, North Carolina State University; Jeannine Stanko, Community College of Allegheny; Scott Stevens, Western Washington University; Sarah Stone, University of California–Berkeley; Joseph Sullivan, Marietta College; Mark Todd, Western State Colorado University; Gretchen Treadwell, Fort Lewis College; Tisha Turk, University of Minnesota, Morris; Raymond M. Vince, University of Tampa; Tonya Warden, East Tennessee State University; Charles Warren, Salem State College; Patricia Webb, Arizona State University; Susan Garrett Weiss, Goucher College; Worth Weller, Indiana University–Purdue University–Fort Wayne; Jackie White, Lewis University; Edward Whitelock, Gordon State College; Audrey Wick, Blinn College; and Rodney Zink, Pennsylvania State University.

We are also grateful to the many people at Bedford/St. Martin's, starting with Edwin Hill, vice president, editorial, Macmillan Learning Humanities; senior program director for English Leasa Burton; and program manager John Sullivan. Since the first edition, senior executive editor Steve Scipione has been a terrific collaborator, reading our work carefully and offering sage advice every step of the way. We are especially grateful to Mara Weible, senior editor, who has guided us through the fourth edition. Executive media editor Adam Whitehurst and associate editor Stephanie Thomas were invaluable advisors who helped us develop the new LaunchPad. We are grateful to executive marketing manager Joy Fisher Williams for her wise and imaginative marketing efforts, assisted by Andie Aiken. The talented production department steered the manuscript through a demanding schedule to create the book you hold. We thank Elise Kaiser, Michael Granger, Lisa McDowell, and especially Ryan Sullivan, the book's accommodating and masterly production editor. Kalina Ingham, Angie Boehler, Richard Fox, and Arthur Johnson negotiated the complicated process of permissions acquisition. Thanks also to William Boardman for the striking cover design.

Stuart Greene writes: I wish to thank the many students and faculty with whom I have worked over the years. Specifically, I would like to thank Kelly Kinney, Stephen Fox, Rebecca Nowacek, and Katherine Weese, who served as my assistant directors in the past and who taught me a great deal about the teaching of writing. I would also like to thank Robert Kachur, who contributed a great deal to our early iterations of this book. And I will always appreciate the many discussions I have had with John Duffy during these many years, and with Connie Mick, a tireless and innovative teacher of writing. Susan Ohmer provided much insight into my understanding of media and student culture. A special thanks to Mike Palmquist, with whom I taught writing as "conversation" over thirty years ago and who gave this book direction. Finally, thanks to Denise Della Rossa, who has listened to me rehearse these ideas for years. I dedicate this book to her.

April Lidinsky writes: I am grateful for the superb pedagogical mentorship I received from Lou Kelly at the University of Iowa. I thank Kurt Spellmeyer, Hugh English, and Ron Christ at Rutgers, the State University of New Jersey, for my training in both hermeneutical and rhetorical approaches to teaching writing. My colleagues and graduate student instructors at the University of Notre Dame, especially Julie Bruneau, Connie Mick, Marion C. Rohrleitner, Misty Schieberle, and Scott T. Smith, inspired early versions of this text. Thanks to Joshua Wells, Mara Weible, and Ollie Lidinsky-Smith for their suggestions for readings for this fourth edition. My students continue to challenge and sharpen my teaching and especially my own learning. Finally, I am indebted to my parents, JoElla Hunter and Tom Lidinsky, for their model of lifelong reading and learning, and to Ken Smith, Ollie Lidinsky-Smith, and Miriam Lidinsky-Smith for ensuring every day is filled with wit and wisdom.

WE'RE ALL IN. AS ALWAYS.

Bedford/St. Martin's is as passionately committed to the discipline of English as ever, working hard to provide support and services that make it easier for you to teach your course your way.

Find **community support** at the Bedford/St. Martin's English Community (**community.macmillan.com**), where you can follow our *Bits* blog for new teaching ideas, download titles from our professional resource series, and review projects in the pipeline.

Choose **curriculum solutions** that offer flexible custom options, combining our carefully developed print and digital resources, acclaimed works from Macmillan's trade imprints, and your own course or program materials to provide the exact resources your students need.

Rely on **outstanding service** from your Bedford/St. Martin's sales representative and editorial team. Contact us or visit **macmillanlearning .com** to learn more about any of the options below.

■ LaunchPad for *From Inquiry to Academic Writing*: Where Students Learn

LaunchPad provides engaging content and new ways to get the most out of your book. Get an interactive e-Book combined with assessment tools in a fully customizable course space; then assign and mix our resources with yours.

- LaunchPad for *From Inquiry to Academic Writing* includes **reading comprehension quizzes** and interactive **"Reading as a Writer" prompts** and **"Practice Sequences."**

- **Diagnostics** provide opportunities to assess areas for improvement and assign additional exercises based on students' needs. Visual reports show performance by topic, class, and student as well as improvement over time.

- **Pre-built units**—including readings, videos, quizzes, and more—are easy to adapt and assign by adding your own materials and mixing them with our high-quality multimedia content and ready-made assessment options, such as **LearningCurve** adaptive quizzing and Exercise Central.

- Use LaunchPad on its own or **integrate it** with your school's learning management system so that your class is always on the same page.

LaunchPad for *From Inquiry to Academic Writing* can be purchased on its own or packaged with the print book at a significant discount. An activation code is required. To order LaunchPad for *From Inquiry to Academic Writing* with the print book, use ISBN 978-1-319-14719-8. For more information, go to **launchpadworks.com.**

■ Choose from Alternative Formats of *From Inquiry to Academic Writing*

Bedford/St. Martin's offers a range of formats. Choose what works best for you and your students. For details on our e-Book partners, visit **macmillanlearning.com/ebooks**.

■ Select Value Packages

Add value to your text by packaging any Bedford/St. Martin's resource, such as *Writer's Help 2.0* or *LaunchPad Solo for Readers and Writers*, with *From Inquiry to Academic Writing* at a significant discount. Contact your sales representative for more information.

LaunchPad Solo for Readers and Writers allows students to work on what they need help with the most. At home or in class, students learn at their own pace, with instruction tailored to each student's unique needs. *LaunchPad Solo for Readers and Writers* features:

- **Pre-built units that support a learning arc.** Each easy-to-assign unit is comprised of a pre-test check, multimedia instruction and assessment, and a post-test that assesses what students have learned about critical reading, writing process, using sources, grammar, style, and mechanics. Dedicated units also offer help for multilingual writers.

- **Diagnostics that help establish a baseline for instruction.** Assign diagnostics to identify areas of strength and areas for improvement and to help students plan a course of study. Use visual reports to track performance by topic, class, and student as well as improvement over time.

- **A video introduction to many topics.** Introductions offer an overview of the unit's topic, and many include a brief, accessible video to illustrate the concepts at hand.

- **Twenty-five reading selections with comprehension quizzes.** Assign a range of classic and contemporary essays, each of which includes a label indicating Lexile level to help you scaffold instruction in critical reading.

- **Adaptive quizzing for targeted learning.** Most of the units include LearningCurve, game-like adaptive quizzing that focuses on the areas in which each student needs the most help.

- **Additional reading comprehension quizzes.** *From Inquiry to Academic Writing* includes multiple-choice quizzes, which help you quickly gauge your students' understanding of the assigned reading. These are available in *LaunchPad Solo for Readers and Writers*.

Order ISBN 978-1-319-19230-3 to package *LaunchPad Solo for Readers and Writers* with *From Inquiry to Academic Writing* at a significant discount.

Students who rent or buy a used book can purchase access and instructors may request free access at **macmillanlearning.com/readwrite**.

Writer's Help 2.0 is a powerful online writing resource that helps students find answers, whether they are searching for writing advice on their own or as part of an assignment.

- **Smart search.**   Built on research with more than 1,600 student writers, the smart search in *Writer's Help 2.0* provides reliable results even when students use novice terms, such as *flow* and *unstuck*.

- **Trusted content from our best-selling handbooks.**   Choose *Writer's Help 2.0, Hacker Version*, or *Writer's Help 2.0, Lunsford Version*, and ensure that students have clear advice and examples for all of their writing questions.

- **Diagnostics that help establish a baseline for instruction.**   Assign diagnostics to identify areas of strength and areas for improvement and to help students plan a course of study. Use visual reports to track performance by topic, class, and student as well as improvement over time.

- **Adaptive exercises that engage students.**   *Writer's Help 2.0* includes LearningCurve, game-like online quizzing that adapts to what students already know and helps them focus on what they need to learn.

- **Reading comprehension quizzes.**   *From Inquiry to Academic Writing* includes multiple-choice quizzes, which help you quickly gauge your students' understanding of the assigned reading. These are available in *Writer's Help 2.0*.

Student access is packaged with *From Inquiry to Academic Writing* at a significant discount. Order ISBN 978-1-319-19194-8 to package the text with *Writer's Help 2.0, Hacker Version*, or ISBN 978-1-319-19236-5 to package the text with *Writer's Help 2.0, Lunsford Version*, to ensure your students have easy access to online writing support. Students who rent or buy a used book can purchase access and instructors may request free access at **macmillanlearning.com/writershelp2**.

INSTRUCTOR RESOURCES

You have a lot to do in your course. We want to make it easy for you to find the support you need—and to get it quickly.

Resources for Teaching From Inquiry to Academic Writing: A Practical Guide, **Fourth Edition,** is available as a PDF that can be downloaded from **macmillanlearning.com**. Visit the instructor resources tab for *From Inquiry to Academic Writing*. In addition to chapter overviews and teaching tips, the instructor's manual includes sample syllabi, commentaries on all the readings, and classroom activities.

Brief Contents

Contents

 Starting with Inquiry
Habits of Mind of Academic Writers   1

6 From Formulating to Developing a Thesis   141

7 From Finding to Evaluating Sources   165

8 From Synthesis to Researched Argument   187

9 From Ethos to Logos

Appealing to Your Readers   247

How This Book Supports WPA Outcomes for First-Year Composition

Note: This chart aligns with the latest **WPA** Outcomes Statement, ratified in July 2014.

WPA OUTCOMES	RELEVANT FEATURES OF *FROM INQUIRY TO ACADEMIC WRITING: A PRACTICAL GUIDE*, FOURTH EDITION
Rhetorical Knowledge	
Learn and use key rhetorical concepts through analyzing & composing a variety of texts.	A full range of rhetorical concepts is presented throughout the text. For example, see: • the treatment of rhetorical analysis in Chapter 2, "From Reading as a Writer to Writing as a Reader" • the treatment of argument in Chapter 4, "From Identifying Claims to Analyzing Arguments" • the treatment of rhetorical appeals in Chapter 9, "From Ethos to Logos"
Gain experience reading and composing in several genres to understand how genre conventions shape and are shaped by readers' and writers' practices and purposes.	A wide range of genres is represented in the text for analysis and composition. • See the literacy narratives that conclude Chapter 1 and the Practice Sequence that follows (pp. 19–37). • Chapter 2 presents rhetorical context as a tool for analysis. • Throughout the text, all student essays are annotated to indicate particular practices for particular purposes.

WPA Outcomes	Relevant Features of *From Inquiry to Academic Writing: A Practical Guide*, Fourth Edition
Develop facility in responding to a variety of situations and contexts, calling for purposeful shifts in voice, tone, level of formality, design, medium, and/or structure.	Throughout the text, students are instructed to attend to situations and contexts and given strategies for recognizing and responding to them in their composing. For example: • Chapter 6 shows how to establish a context for a thesis. • Chapter 9 shows analysis and modulation of appeals, and Chapter 10 includes examples of visual appeals.
Understand and use a variety of technologies to address a range of audiences.	The range of texts and technologies in the print text and available through LaunchPad help students understand and analyze different technologies they can use in their own composing. • Chapter 10 provides new coverage of visual and multimodal analysis, along with new texts for students to analyze.
Match the capacities of different environments (e.g., print & electronic) to varying rhetorical situations.	The rhetorical and analytical instruction in the text helps students match the capacities of different composing technologies to different rhetorical situations, including words-only and multimodal examples.

Critical Thinking, Reading, and Composing

Use composing and reading for inquiry, learning, thinking, and communicating in various rhetorical contexts.	• Chapter 1 sets the stage for academic writing as a form of inquiry. • Chapters 2–5 show critical reading in action. • Chapters 6 and 8 show how to generate texts and compositions from reading in various rhetorical contexts.
Read a diverse range of texts, attending especially to relationships between assertion and evidence, to patterns of organization, to interplay between verbal and nonverbal elements, and how these features function for different audiences and situations.	• Chapter 4 offers instruction in identifying claims and assertions and relating them to evidence. • Chapter 6 presents thesis statements as ways of developing claims and using evidence depending on the situation. • Chapter 11 shows how to shape a composition via different patterns of organization.
Locate and evaluate primary and secondary research materials, including journal articles, essays, books, databases, & informal Internet sources.	• Chapter 7, "From Finding to Evaluating Sources," presents instruction in locating and evaluating primary and secondary research materials, including journal articles, essays, books, databases, and informal Internet sources. • Chapter 13, "Other Methods of Inquiry," helps students do primary research via interviews and focus groups.

WPA Outcomes	Relevant Features of *From Inquiry to Academic Writing: A Practical Guide*, Fourth Edition
Use strategies—such as interpretation, synthesis, response, critique, and design/redesign—to compose texts that integrate the writer's ideas with those from appropriate sources.	Chapter 8, "From Synthesis to Researched Argument," helps students compose texts that integrate the writer's ideas with those from appropriate sources.

Processes

Develop a writing project through multiple drafts.	• Chapters 1–13 provide instruction in the various stages of developing writing projects. • Within chapters, the "Practice Sequences" often present compound activities for chapter-specific writing projects, such as comparing arguments in Chapter 4 (pp. 112–13) and developing a synthesis in Chapter 8 (p. 218).
Develop flexible strategies for reading, drafting, reviewing, collaboration, revising, rewriting, rereading, and editing.	• Chapters 2 and 4 offer flexible strategies for rhetorical reading and inventive reading, such as reading to extend the ideas of others. • Chapters 11 and 12 feature concrete strategies on drafting, collaborating, revising, and editing.
Use composing processes and tools as a means to discover and reconsider ideas.	• Throughout the text, the importance of rereading and rewriting to discover and reconsider ideas is emphasized. • Chapter 6 teaches the importance of revising a thesis in light of new evidence.
Experience the collaborative and social aspects of writing processes.	• The habits of mind of academic writing set forth in Chapter 1 emphasize the importance of collaboration and the idea of academic writing as conversation. • Chapter 12, "From Revising to Editing: Working with Peer Groups," presents collaboration and revision as essential components of academic writing.
Learn to give and act on productive feedback to works in progress.	Chapter 12 includes sample documents and worksheets for the various stages of productive feedback readers can give writings.
Adapt composing processes for a variety of technologies and modalities.	Chapter 10's coverage of visual analysis fosters an awareness of how rhetorical concepts function across various technologies and modalities.
Reflect on the development of composing practices and how those practices influence their work.	Practice Sequence assignments often encourage students to reflect on their composing practices and how those practices influence their work.

Knowledge of Conventions

Develop knowledge of linguistic structures, including grammar, punctuation, and spelling, through practice in composing and revising.	Chapters 11 and 12, on drafting, revising, and editing, help students develop knowledge of linguistic structures, including grammar, punctuation, and spelling.

WPA OUTCOMES	RELEVANT FEATURES OF *FROM INQUIRY TO ACADEMIC WRITING: A PRACTICAL GUIDE*, FOURTH EDITION
Understand why genre conventions for structure, paragraphing, tone, and mechanics vary.	The overarching emphasis on rhetorical context and situation in the text fosters critical thinking about genre conventions.
Gain experience negotiating variations in genre conventions.	Critical reading of the variety of formats and genres represented by the multidisciplinary selections in the text imparts experience negotiating variations in genre conventions.
Learn common formats and/or design features for different kinds of texts.	• Annotated texts such as the student essays impart awareness of common formats and/or design features for difference kinds of texts. • The Appendix on documentation styles gives specific instruction in formats and design.
Explore the concepts of intellectual property (such as fair use and copyright) that motivate documentation conventions.	• A "Practice Sequence" in Chapter 8 concerns critical thinking about copyright and intellectual property (p. 246). • The Appendix on documenting sources (specifically MLA and APA formats) raises issues of different documentation conventions.
Practice applying citation conventions systematically in their own work.	The Appendix enables students to apply citation conventions of MLA and APA styles systematically in their own work.

FROM INQUIRY TO ACADEMIC WRITING

A Practical Guide

Starting with Inquiry
Habits of Mind of Academic Writers

WHAT IS ACADEMIC WRITING?

In the strictest sense, *academic writing* is what scholars do to communicate with other scholars in their fields of study, their *disciplines*. It's the research report a biologist writes, the interpretive essay a literary scholar composes, the media analysis a film scholar produces. At the same time, *academic writing* is what you have to learn so that you can participate in the different disciplinary conversations that take place in your courses. You have to learn to *think* like an academic, *read* like an academic, *do research* like an academic, and *write* like an academic—even if you have no plans to continue your education and become a scholar yourself. Learning these skills is what this book is about.

Fair warning: It isn't easy. Initially you may be perplexed by the vocabulary and sentence structure of many of the academic essays you read. Scholars use specialized language to capture the complexity of an issue or to introduce specific ideas from their discipline. Every discipline has its own vocabulary. You probably can think of words and phrases that are not used every day but that are necessary, nevertheless, to express certain ideas precisely. For example, consider the terms *centrifugal force*, *Oedipus complex*, and *onomatopoeia*. These terms carry with them a history of study; when you learn to use them, you also are learning to use the ideas they represent. Such terms help us describe the world specifically rather than generally; they help us better understand how things work and how to make better decisions about what matters to us.

Sentence structure presents another challenge. The sentences in academic writing are often longer and more intricate than the sentences in popular magazines. Academics strive to go beyond what is quick, obvious, and general. They ask questions based on studying a subject from multiple points of view, to make surprising connections that would not occur to someone who has not studied the subject carefully. It follows that academic writers are accustomed to extensive reading that prepares them to examine an issue, knowledgeably, from many different perspectives, and to make interesting intellectual use of what they discover in their research. To become an adept academic writer, you have to learn these practices as well.

Academic writing will challenge you, no doubt. But hang in there. Any initial difficulty you have with academic writing will pay off when you discover new ways of looking at the world and of making sense of it. Moreover, the habits of mind and core skills of academic writing are highly valued in the world outside the academy.

Basically, academic writing entails making an **argument**—a text that is crafted to persuade an audience—often in the service of changing people's minds and behaviors. When you write an academic essay, you have to

- define a situation that calls for some response in writing;
- demonstrate the timeliness of your argument;
- establish a personal investment;
- appeal to readers whose minds you want to change by understanding what they think, believe, and value;
- support your argument with good reasons; and
- anticipate and address readers' reasons for disagreeing with you, while encouraging them to adopt your position.

Academic argument is not about shouting down an opponent. Instead, it is the careful expression of an idea or perspective based on reasoning and the insights gathered from a close examination of the arguments others have made on the issue.

Making academic arguments is also a social act, like joining a conversation. When we sit down to write an argument intended to persuade someone to do or to believe something, we are never really the first to broach the topic about which we are writing. Thus, learning how to write a researched argument is a process of learning how to enter conversations that are already going on in written form. This idea of writing as dialogue—not only between author and reader but between the text and everything that has been said or written about its subject beforehand—is crucial. Writing is a process of balancing our goals with the history of similar kinds of communication, particularly others' arguments that have been made on the same subject. The conversations that have already been going on about a subject are the subject's historical context.

WHAT ARE THE HABITS OF MIND OF ACADEMIC WRITERS?

The chapters in the first part of this book introduce you to the habits of mind and core skills of academic writing. By **habits of mind**, we mean the patterns of thought that lead you to question assumptions and opinions, explore alternative opinions, anticipate opposing arguments, compare one type of experience to another, and identify the causes and consequences of ideas and events. These forms of **critical thinking** demand an inquiring mind that welcomes complexities and seeks out and weighs many different points of view, a mind willing to enter complex conversations both in and out of the academy. We discuss academic habits of mind in the rest of Chapter 1 and refer to them throughout this book.

Such habits of mind are especially important today, when we are bombarded with appeals to buy this or that product and with information that may or may not be true. For example, in "106 Science Claims and a Truckful of Baloney" (*The Best American Science and Nature Writing*, 2005), William Speed Weed illustrates the extent to which the claims of science vie for our attention alongside the claims of advertising. He notes that advertisers often package their claims as science, but wonders whether a box of Cheerios really can reduce cholesterol.

As readers, we have a responsibility to test the claims of both science and advertising in order to decide what to believe and act upon. Weed found that "very few of the 100 claims" he evaluated "proved completely true" and that "a good number were patently false." Testing the truth of claims—learning to consider information carefully and critically and to weigh competing points of view before making our own judgments—gives us power over our own lives.

The habits of mind and practices valued by academic writers are probably ones you already share. You are behaving "academically" when you comparison shop, a process that entails learning about the product in the media and on the Internet and then looking at the choices firsthand before you decide which one you will purchase. You employ these same habits of mind when you deliberate over casting a vote in an election. You inform yourself about the issues that are most pressing; you learn about the candidates' positions on these issues; you consider other arguments for and against both issues and candidates; and you weigh those arguments and your own understanding to determine which candidate you will support.

Fundamentally, academic habits of mind are *analytical*. When you consider a variety of factors before making a shopping choice—the quality and functionality of the item you plan to buy, how it meets your needs, how it compares to similar items—you are conducting an **analysis**. That is, you are pausing to examine the reasons why you should buy something, instead of simply handing over your cash and saying, "I want one of those."

To a certain extent, analysis involves breaking something down into its various parts and then reflecting on how the parts do or don't work together. For example, when you deliberate over your vote, you may consult one of those charts that newspapers often run around election time: A list of candidates appears across the top of the chart, and a list of issues appears on the side. With a chart from a credible news source in hand, you can scan the columns to see where each candidate stands on the issues, and you can scan the rows to see how the candidates compare on a particular issue. The newspaper editors have performed a preliminary analysis for you. They've asked, "Who are the candidates?" "What are the issues?" and "Where does each candidate stand on the issues?"; and they have presented the answers to you in a format that can help you make your decision.

But you still have to perform your own analysis of the information before you cast your ballot. Suppose no candidate holds your position on every issue. Whom do you vote for? Which issues are most important to you? Or suppose two candidates hold your position on every issue. Which one do you vote for? What characteristics or experience are you looking for in an elected official? And you may want to investigate further by visiting the candidates' Web sites or by talking with your friends to gather their thoughts on the election.

As you can see, analysis involves more than simply disassembling or dissecting something. It is a process of continually asking questions and looking for answers. Analysis reflects, in the best sense of the word, a *skeptical* habit of mind, an unwillingness to settle for obvious answers in the quest to understand why things are the way they are and how they might be different.

This book will help you develop the questioning, evaluating, and conversational skills you already have into strategies that will improve your ability to make careful, informed judgments about the often conflicting and confusing information you are confronted with every day. With these strategies, you will be in a position to use your writing skills to create change where you feel it is most needed.

The first steps in developing these skills are to recognize the key academic habits of mind and then to refine your practice of them. We explore five key habits of mind in the rest of this chapter:

1. inquiring,
2. seeking and valuing complexity,
3. understanding that academic writing is a conversation,
4. understanding that writing is a process, and
5. reflecting.

ACADEMIC WRITERS MAKE INQUIRIES

Academic writers usually study a body of information so closely and from so many different perspectives that they can ask questions that may not occur to people who are just scanning the information. That is, academic writers learn to make **inquiries**. Every piece of academic writing begins with a question about the way the world works, and the best questions lead to rich, complex insights that others can learn from and build on.

You will find that the ability to ask good questions is equally valuable in your daily life. Asking thoughtful questions about politics, popular culture, work, or anything else—questions like, What exactly did that candidate mean by "Family values are values for all of us," anyway? What is lost and gained by bringing Tolkien's *Lord of the Rings* trilogy to the screen? What does it take to move ahead in this company?—is the first step in understanding how the world works and how it can be changed.

Inquiry typically begins with **observation**, a careful noting of phenomena or behaviors that puzzle you or challenge your beliefs and values (in a text or in the real world). Observers attempt to understand phenomena by **asking questions** (Why does this exist? Why is this happening? Do things have to be this way?) and **examining alternatives** (Maybe this doesn't need to exist. Maybe this could happen another way instead.).

For example, Steven Pearlstein, a professor of public affairs at George Mason University, *observes* that only a small percentage of the students he teaches are enrolled as majors in the humanities. This prompts him to *ask* why this is the case, particularly because students express their appreciation for the opportunity to read popular works of history. In his essay "Meet the Parents Who Won't Let Their Children Study Literature," he also points out that faculty at other universities, including Harvard, share his concern that fewer and fewer students are majoring in English or history. He wonders why this is the case and finds that parents, the media, and politicians all advise students to steer clear of the liberal arts. He wonders further why parents in particular would adopt such a view, and he *examines different explanations* such as parents' anxieties over debt, the trends toward professionalism, and parents' own interests. Parents, he concludes, want to see a "direct line" between what their children study and a job. This, Pearlstein argues, is unfortunate since the available data show that students completing a major in the humanities have many job opportunities. In the end, he *asks* what happens to students who major in fields to please their parents and who lack the motivation to study what they are passionate about. For that matter, what will happen if fewer and fewer students learn "discipline, persistence, and how to research, analyze, communicate clearly and think logically"?

In her reading on the American civil rights movement of the 1950s and 1960s, one of our students *observed* that the difficulties many immigrant groups experienced when they first arrived in the United States are not acknowledged as struggles for civil rights. This student of Asian descent *wondered why* the difficulties Asians faced in assimilating into American culture are not seen as analogous to the efforts of African Americans to gain civil rights (Why are things this way?). In doing so, she *asked* a number of relevant questions: What do we leave out when we tell stories about ourselves? Why reduce the struggle for civil rights to black-and-white terms? How can we represent the multiple struggles of people who have contributed to building our nation? Then she *examined alternatives*—different ways of presenting the history of a nation that prides itself on justice and the protection of its people's civil rights (Maybe this doesn't need to exist. Maybe this could happen another way.). The academic writing you will read—and write yourself—starts with questions and seeks to find rich answers.

Steps to Inquiry

1 **Observe.** Note phenomena or behaviors that puzzle you or challenge your beliefs and values.

2 **Ask questions.** Consider why things are the way they are.

3 **Examine alternatives.** Explore how things could be different.

A Practice Sequence: Inquiry Activities

The activities below will help you practice the strategies of observing, asking questions, and examining alternatives.

1 Find an advertisement for a political campaign, and write down anything about what you observe in the ad that puzzles you or that challenges your beliefs and values. Next, write down questions you might have (Do things have to be this way?). Finally, write down other ways you think the ad could persuade you to vote for this particular candidate (Maybe this could happen another way instead.).

2 Locate and analyze data about the students at your school. For example, you might research the available majors and determine which departments have the highest and lowest enrollments. (Some schools have fact books that can be accessed online; and typically the registrar maintains a database with this information.) Is there anything that puzzles you? Write down any questions you have (Why are things the way they are?). What alternative explanations can you provide to account for differences in the popularity of the subjects students major in?

ACADEMIC WRITERS SEEK AND VALUE COMPLEXITY

Seeking and valuing complexity are what inquiry is all about. As you read academic arguments (for example, about school choice), observe how the media work to influence your opinions (for example, in political ads), or analyze data (for example, about candidates in an election), you will explore reasons why things are the way they are and how they might be different. When you do so, we encourage you not to settle for simple either/or reasons. Instead, look for multiple explanations.

When we rely on **binary thinking**—imagining there are only two sides to an issue—we tend to ignore information that does not fall tidily into one side or the other. Real-world questions (How has the Internet changed our sense of what it means to be a writer? What are the global repercussions of fast-food production and consumption? How do we make sense of terrorism?) don't have easy for-or-against answers. Remember that an **issue** is open to dispute and can be explored and debated. Issue-based questions, then, need to be approached with a mind open to complex possibilities. (We say more about identifying issues and formulating issue-based questions in Chapter 5.)

If we take as an example the issue of terrorism, we would discover that scholars of religion, economics, ethics, and politics tend to ask very different questions about terrorism and to propose very different approaches for addressing this worldwide problem. This doesn't mean that one approach is right and the others are wrong; it means that complex issues are likely to have multiple explanations, rather than a simple choice between A and B.

In her attempt to explain the popularity of hip-hop culture, Bronwen Low, a professor of education, provides a window on the steps we can take to examine the complexity of a topic. In the introductory chapters of her book, *Slam School: Learning Through Conflict in the Hip Hop and Spoken Word Classroom,* she begins with the observation that hip-hop "is the single-most influential cultural force shaping contemporary urban youth culture in the United States, and its international reach is growing." She then defines what she means by hip-hop culture, distinguishing it from "rapping," and helps readers understand hip-hop culture as encompassing graffiti art and "a whole culture of style," including "fashion" and "sensibility." Motivated by a sense of curiosity, if not puzzlement, Low asks questions that guide her inquiry: What is it that makes hip-hop culture so compelling to young people across such a wide spectrum of race, culture, and gender? Further, how can social, cultural, and literary critics better understand the evolution of new forms of language and performance, such as spoken-word poetry, in "youth-driven popular culture"? Notice that she indicates that she will frame her inquiry using the multiple perspectives of social, cultural, and literary critics. In turn, Low explains that she began to answer these questions by giving herself a "hip-hop education." She attended spoken-word poetry festivals ("slams") across the United States, listened to the music, and read both "academic theory and journalism" to see what others had to say about "poetry's relevance and coolness to youth."

In still another example, one of our students was curious about why her younger brother struggled in school and wondered if boys learn differently than girls. She began her inquiry by reading an article on education, "It's a Boy Thing (or Is It?)," and realized that researchers have begun to study the question that she was curious about. However, rather than presenting a clear-cut answer, the author of this article, Sara Mead, pointed out that researchers have generated a number of conflicting opinions. Mead's article motivated our student to deepen her inquiry by examining different perspectives in the disciplines of cognitive theory, education, counseling psychology, and sociology. She was able to refine her question based on an issue that puzzled her: If educators are aware that boys have difficulty in school despite receiving more attention than girls receive, how can research explain what seems like a persistent gap between the achievement of boys and girls? In looking at this issue-based question, the student opened herself up to complexity by resisting simple answers to a question that others had not resolved.

Steps to Seeking and Valuing Complexity

1. **Reflect on what you observe.** Clarify your initial interest in a phenomenon or behavior by focusing on its particular details. Then reflect on what is most interesting and least interesting to you about these details, and why.

2. **Examine issues from multiple points of view.** Imagine more than two sides to the issue, and recognize that there may well be other points of view, too.

3. **Ask issue-based questions.** Try to put into words questions that will help you explore why things are the way they are.

A Practice Sequence: Seeking and Valuing Complexity

These activities build on the previous exercises we asked you to complete.

1. Look again at the political ad you selected earlier. Think about other perspectives that would complicate your understanding of how the ad might persuade voters.

2. Imagine other perspectives on the data you found on the students in your school. Let's say, for example, that you've looked at data on student majors. How did you explain the popularity of certain majors and the unpopularity of others? How do you think other students would explain these discrepancies? What explanations would faculty members offer?

ACADEMIC WRITERS SEE WRITING AS A CONVERSATION

Another habit of mind at the heart of academic writing is the understanding that ideas always build on and respond to other ideas, just as they do in the best kind of conversations. Academic conversations are quite similar to those you have through e-mail and social media: You are responding to something someone else has written (or said) and are writing back in anticipation of future responses.

Academic writing also places a high value on the belief that good, thoughtful ideas come from conversations with others, *many* others. As your exposure to other viewpoints increases, as you take more and different points of view into consideration and build on them, your own ideas will develop more fully and fairly. You already know that to get a full picture of something, often you have to ask for multiple perspectives. When you want to find out what "really" happened at an event when your friends are telling you different stories, you listen to all of them and then evaluate the evidence to draw conclusions you can stand behind—just as academic writers do.

Theologian Martin Marty starts a conversation about hospitality in his book *When Faiths Collide* (2004). *Hospitality* is a word he uses to describe a human behavior that has the potential to bring about real understanding among people who do not share a common faith or culture. As Marty points out, finding common ground is an especially important and timely concern "in a world where strangers meet strangers with gunfire, barrier walls, spiritually land-mined paths, and the spirit of revenge." He believes that people need opportunities to share their stories, their values, and their beliefs; in doing so, they feel less threatened by ideas they do not understand or identify with.

Yet Marty anticipates the possibility that the notion of hospitality will be met with skepticism or incomprehension by those who find the term "dainty." Current usage of the term—as in "hospitality suites" and "hospitality industries"—differs from historical usage, particularly biblical usage. To counter the incredulity or incomprehension of those who do not immediately understand his use of the term *hospitality*, Marty gives his readers entrée to a conversation with other scholars who understand the complexity and power of the kind of hospitality shown by people who welcome a stranger into their world. The stranger he has in mind may simply be the person who moves in next door, but that person could also be an immigrant, an exile, or a refugee.

Marty brings another scholar, Darrell Fasching, into the conversation to explain that hospitality entails welcoming "the stranger . . . [which] inevitably involves us in a sympathetic passing over into the other's life and stories" (cited in Marty, p. 132). And John Koenig, another scholar Marty cites, traces the biblical sources of the term in an effort to show the value of understanding those we fear. That understanding, Marty argues, might lead to peace among warring factions. The conversation Marty begins on the page helps us see that his views on bringing about peace have their source in other people's ideas. In turn, the fact that he draws on multiple sources gives strength to Marty's argument.

The characteristics that make for effective oral conversation are also in play in effective academic conversation: empathy, respect, and a willingness to exchange and revise ideas. **Empathy** is the ability to understand the perspectives that shape what people think, believe, and value. To express both empathy and respect for the positions of all people involved in the conversation, academic writers try to understand the conditions under which each opinion might be true and then to represent the strengths of that position accurately.

For example, imagine that your firm commitment to protecting the environment is challenged by those who see the value of developing land rich with oil and other resources. In challenging their position, it would serve you well to understand their motives, both economic (lower gas prices, new jobs that will create a demand for new houses) and political (less dependence on foreign oil). If you can demonstrate your knowledge of these factors, those committed to developing resources in protected areas will listen to you. To convey empathy and respect while presenting your own point of view, you might introduce your argument this way:

> Although it is important to develop untapped resources in remote areas of the United States both to lower gas prices and create new jobs and to eliminate our dependence on other countries' resources, it is in everyone's interest to use alternative sources of power and protect our natural resources.

As you demonstrate your knowledge and a sense of shared values, you could also describe the conditions under which you might change your own position.

People engaging in productive conversation try to create change by listening and responding to one another rather than dominating one another. Instead of trying to win an argument, they focus on reaching a mutual understanding. This does not mean that effective communicators do not take strong positions; more often than not they do. However, they are more likely to achieve their goals by persuading others instead of ignoring them and their points of view. Similarly, writers come to every issue with an agenda. But they realize that they may have to compromise on certain points to carry those that mean the most to them. They understand that their perceptions and opinions may be flawed or limited, and they are willing to revise them when valid new perspectives are introduced.

In an academic community, ideas develop through give and take, through a conversation that builds on what has come before and grows stronger from multiple perspectives. You will find this dynamic at work in your classes when you discuss your ideas: You will build on other people's insights, and they will build on yours. As a habit of mind, paying attention to academic conversations can improve the thinking and writing you do in every class you take.

Steps to Joining an Academic Conversation

1 **Be receptive to the ideas of others.** Listen carefully and empathetically to what others have to say.

2 **Be respectful of the ideas of others.** When you refer to the opinions of others, represent them fairly and use an evenhanded tone. Avoid sounding scornful or dismissive.

3 **Engage with the ideas of others.** Try to understand how people have arrived at their feelings and beliefs.

4 **Be flexible in your thinking about the ideas of others.** Be willing to exchange ideas and to revise your own opinions.

A Practice Sequence: Joining an Academic Conversation

The following excerpt is taken from Thomas Patterson's *The Vanishing Voter* (2002), an examination of voter apathy. Read the excerpt and then complete the exercises that follow.

> Does a diminished appetite for voting affect the health of American politics? Is society harmed when the voting rate is low or in decline? As the *Chicago Tribune* said in an editorial, it may be "humiliating" that the United States, the oldest continuous democracy, has nearly the lowest voting rate in the world. But does it have any practical significance? . . .
>
> The increasing number of nonvoters could be a danger to democracy. Although high participation by itself does not trigger radical change, a flood of new voters into the electorate could possibly do it. It's difficult to imagine a crisis big and divisive enough to prompt millions of new voters to suddenly flock to the polls, especially in light of Americans' aversion to political extremism. Nevertheless, citizens who are outside the electorate are less attached to the existing system. As the sociologist Seymour Martin Lipset observed, a society of nonvoters "is potentially more explosive than one in which most citizens are regularly involved in activities which give them some sense of participation in decisions which affect their lives."
>
> Voting can strengthen citizenship in other ways, too. When people vote, they are more attentive to politics and are better informed about issues affecting them. Voting also deepens community involvement, as

the philosopher John Stuart Mill theorized a century ago. Studies indicate that voters are more active in community affairs than nonvoters are. Of course, this association says more about the type of person who votes as opposed to the effect of voting. But recent evidence, as Harvard University's Robert Putnam notes, "suggests that the act of voting itself encourages volunteering and other forms of government citizenship."

1   In this excerpt, Patterson presents two arguments: that increasing voter apathy is a danger to democracy and that voting strengthens citizenship. With which of these arguments do you sympathize more? Why? Can you imagine reasons that another person might not agree with you? Write them down. Now do the same exercise with the argument you find less compelling.

2   Your instructor will divide the class into four groups and assign each group a position—pro or con—on one of Patterson's arguments. Brainstorm with the members of your group to come up with examples or reasons why your group's position is valid. Make a list of those examples or reasons, and be prepared to present them to the class.

3   Your instructor will now break up the groups into new groups, each with at least one representative of the original groups. In turn with the other members of your new group, take a few moments to articulate your position and the reasons for it. Remember to be civil and as persuasive as possible.

4   Finally, with the other members of your new group, talk about the merits of the various points of view. Try to find common ground ("I understand what you are saying; in fact, it's not unlike the point I was making about . . ."). The point of this discussion is not to pronounce a winner (who made the best case for his or her perspective) but to explore common ground, exchange and revise ideas, and imagine compromises.

ACADEMIC WRITERS UNDERSTAND THAT WRITING IS A PROCESS

Academic writing is a process of defining issues, formulating questions, and developing sound arguments. This view of writing counters a number of popular myths: that writing depends on inspiration, that writing should happen quickly, that learning to write in one context prepares you to write in other contexts, and that revision is the same as editing. The writing process addresses these myths. First, choosing an idea that matters to you is one way to make your writing matter. And there's a better chance that writing you care about will contribute in a meaningful way to the conversation going on about a given issue in the academic community. Second, writers who invest time in developing and revising their ideas will improve the quality of both their ideas and their language—their ability to be specific and express complexity.

There are three main stages to the writing process: collecting information, drafting, and revising. We introduce them here and expand on them throughout this book.

■ Collect Information and Material

Always begin the process of writing an essay by collecting *in writing* the material—the information, ideas, and evidence—from which you will shape your own argument. Once you have read and marked the pages of a text, you have begun the process of building your own argument. The important point here is that you start to put your ideas on paper. Good writing comes from returning to your ideas on your own and with your classmates, reconsidering them, and revising them as your thinking develops. This is not something you can do with any specificity unless you have written down your ideas. The following box shows the steps for gathering information from your reading, the first stage in the process of writing an academic essay. (In Chapter 2, these steps are illustrated and discussed in more detail.)

Steps to Collecting Information and Material

1 **Mark your texts as you read.** Note key terms; ask questions in the margins; indicate connections to other texts.

2 **List quotations you find interesting and provocative.** You might even write short notes to yourself about what you find significant about the quotations.

3 **List your own ideas in response to the reading or readings.** Include what you've observed about the way the author or authors make their arguments.

4 **Sketch out the similarities and differences among the authors whose work you plan to use in your essay.** Where would they agree or disagree? How would each respond to the others' arguments and evidence?

■ Draft, and Draft Again

The next stage in the writing process begins when you are ready to think about your focus and how to arrange the ideas you have gathered in the collecting stage. Writers often find that writing a first draft is an act of discovery, that their ultimate focus emerges during this initial drafting process. Sometimes it is only at the end of a four-page draft that a writer says, "Aha! This is what I really want to talk about in this essay!" Later revisions of an essay, then, are not simply editing or cleaning up the grammar of a first draft. Instead, they truly involve *re*vision, seeing the first draft again to establish the clearest possible argument and the most persuasive evidence. This means that you do not have to stick with the way a draft turns out the first time. You can—and must!—be willing to rewrite a substantial amount of a first draft if the focus of the argument changes, or if in the process of writing new ideas emerge that enrich the essay. This is why it's important not to agonize over wording in a first draft: It's difficult to toss out a paragraph you've sweated over for hours. Use the first draft to get your ideas down on paper so that you and your peers can discuss what you see there, with the knowledge that you (like your peers) will need to stay open to the possibility of changing an aspect of your focus or argument.

Steps to Drafting

1 **Look through the materials** you have collected to see what interests you most and what you have the most to say about.

2 **Identify what is at issue** and what is open to dispute.

3 **Formulate a question** that your essay will respond to.

4 **Select the material you will include,** and decide what is outside your focus.

5 **Consider the types of readers** who might be most interested in what you have to say.

6 **Gather more material** once you've decided on your purpose—what you want to teach your readers.

7 **Formulate a working thesis** that conveys the point you want to make.

8 **Consider possible arguments** against your position and your response to them.

▪ Revise Significantly

The final stage, revising, might involve several different drafts as you continue to sharpen your insights and the organization of what you have written. As we discuss in Chapter 12, you and your peers will be reading one another's drafts, offering feedback as you move from the larger issues to the smaller ones. It should be clear by now that academic writing is done in a community of thinkers: That is, people read other people's drafts and make suggestions for further clarification, further development of ideas, and sometimes further research. This is quite different from simply editing someone's writing for grammatical errors and typos. Instead, drafting and revising with real readers, as we discuss in Chapter 12, allow you to participate in the collaborative spirit of the academy, in which knowledge making is a group activity that comes out of the conversation of ideas. Importantly, this process approach to writing in the company of real readers mirrors the conversation of ideas carried on in the pages of academic books and journals.

Steps to Revising

1 **Draft and revise the introduction and conclusion.**

2 **Clarify any obscure or confusing passages** your peers have pointed out.

3 **Provide details and textual evidence** where your peers have asked for new or more information.

4 **Make sure you have included opposing points of view** and have addressed them fairly.

5 **Consider reorganization.**

6 **Make sure that every paragraph contributes clearly to your thesis or main claim** and that you have included signposts along the way, phrases that help a reader understand your purpose ("Here I turn to an example from current movies to show how this issue is alive and well in pop culture.").

7 **Consider using strategies you have found effective in other reading** you have done for class (repeating words or phrases for effect, asking rhetorical questions, varying your sentence length).

ACADEMIC WRITERS REFLECT

Reflection entails pausing and taking note of what you are doing—finding answers to complex questions about why unemployment persists or solving a problem to ensure that schools can be safe places where all kids can learn—and observing yourself for a moment. For example, as you are skimming articles to find answers to questions or searching for possible solutions, it's valuable to *monitor* what you feel you are learning, particularly if you are accustomed to doing research in an online environment where it's easy to get distracted. Monitoring entails asking yourself a few questions: What did I just read? Did I comprehend the writer's argument? Do I need to go back and reread the argument? It's equally useful to *evaluate* what you are learning and what you still want or need to know to ensure that you discuss an issue in complex ways that avoid binary thinking. Try to *formulate strategies*, based on your own self-assessment, to address any challenges, such as comprehending a technical argument. What other sources of information can you consult? Whom can you ask for additional help? Finally, *apply what you learn about your own learning* by compiling a repertoire of strategies that can guide you in the reading, writing, and problem solving that you are doing in different classes.

Reflection is essentially having an awareness of our own thought processes. What do I want to accomplish? Is this the right question to ask? What other questions could I be asking? Where should I look for answers? What steps should I take? Why? Educator Jackie Gerstein developed the following cycle of questions for taking control of our own learning:

- Was I resourceful in terms of finding information, resources, and materials?
- Did I ask other people for feedback and information; to collaborate?
- Did I share my work and findings with others?
- Did I learn something new?
- Did I try to either make something better or create something new, rather than just copy something that already exists?
- Did I approach learning as an open-ended process, open to new and all possibilities?
- Did I accept failure as part of the process and use it to inform my learning?

—Jackie Gerstein

Gerstein is insistent when she explains, "If we don't create a process of reflecting . . . then we are leaving learning up to chance."

Reflection in writing can focus on different types of knowledge: (1) the *content* of an issue, such as how economic resources are distributed in different neighborhoods and schools or trade policies that affect employment; (2) the *strategies* one might use to write an essay to persuade readers that immigration policies do not affect opportunities in employment as much as trade policies do; (3) the *procedures* for developing an argument, such as using stories of people affected by unemployment or the failures of providing safe environments for kids in and out of school; and (4) the *conditions* under which certain kinds of strategies might work in one context or another. That is, stories might be a powerful way to raise an issue for a class in sociology or education, but some hard data might be more appropriate in developing a persuasive argument in economics. Making decisions like this one emphasizes the role of reflection—monitoring, evaluating, developing strategies, and taking control over your own learning.

Finally, reflection is an important habit of mind because the act of thinking and questioning encourages us to critically examine our own lived experiences. In his memoir *Between the World and Me*, Ta-Nehisi Coates writes about a moment in his life when he first became literate, and he explains in the following passage how literacy—reading and writing— opened up a world that he wanted to know more about. Here Coates, recipient of a MacArthur Foundation "Genius Grant," addresses his son, as he does throughout his memoir, to tell a story of a time when his mother would make him write when he was in trouble. For us, the story he conveys is about the power of reflection that comes from writing—the significance of writing to make thinking visible, to ask questions that prompt Coates to consider his actions in the present, and to envision future actions based on what he has learned.

> Your grandmother taught me to read when I was only four. She also taught me to write, by which I mean not simply organizing a set of sentences into a series of paragraphs, but organizing them as a means of investigation. When I was in trouble at school (which was quite often) she would make me write about it. The writing had to answer a series of questions: *Why did I feel the need to talk at the same time as my teacher? Why did I not believe that my teacher was entitled to respect? How would I want someone to behave while I was talking? What would I do the next time I felt the urge to talk to my friends during a lesson?* [Our emphasis].

Coates admits that his mother's assignment never really taught him to "curb" his behavior, but these early lessons were a powerful source of learning to "interrogate" the world. Reflecting on the past, present, and future drew Coates into "consciousness," as he puts it. "Your grandmother was not teaching me how to behave in class. She was teaching me how to ruthlessly interrogate the subject that elicited the most sympathy and rationalizing—myself."

Researchers are consistent in describing the importance of encouraging us to think critically on our own lived experiences before we begin to think about how we can participate in a project, take action, and create meaningful change in our surroundings. The following steps can help you pause and make sure learning is actually happening.

Steps to Reflection

1 **Monitor.** Pause and ask yourself some questions: Did I comprehend the writer's argument? Do I need to go back and reread the argument?

2 **Evaluate.** Assess what you are learning and what you still want or need to know to ensure that you discuss an issue in complex ways that avoid binary thinking.

3 **Formulate strategies.** Identify some next steps, based on your own self-assessment, for addressing any challenges, such as comprehending a technical argument, solving a problem you have formulated, or answering a question you have posed. What other sources of information can you consult? Whom can you ask for additional help?

4 **Apply what you learn about your own learning.** Write down some of the challenges you have faced in writing—formulating a question, collecting materials, drafting, or revising, for example. How have you dealt with those challenges? How would you apply what you have learned to completing other academic writing assignments?

A Practice Sequence: Reflection Activities

The activities that follow will give you an opportunity to practice monitoring your work, evaluating what you are learning, formulating strategies, and documenting how you will apply what you learned.

1   Reflect upon and write about the steps you are taking to collect information for what you are writing, to draft your essay, and to revise your work.

- Pause and consider the approach you are taking and whether this is the best way to fulfill your goals as a writer and reach your audience.

- Assess what you are learning about taking a process approach to writing.

- Formulate some next steps for your writing.

- What have you learned so far about writing that you can apply to this and other kinds of academic tasks? That is, if you have faced some uncertainties, what did you do to address these moments? Did you talk to others in your writing group? Were they helpful? Or did you seek other forms of help to get what you needed?

2   Earlier we suggested that you might find a political advertisement or data about majors at your school to analyze. Choose one of these two areas of inquiry.

- As you try to find information, monitor the steps you are taking by pausing for a moment. How is the process going for you? Are you getting what you need? Why or why not?

- Assess what you are learning from your search for relevant information and data.

- Formulate next steps if you are having trouble finding what you want.

- Write down what you have learned about locating information and what you still need to know in order to find relevant, timely information in an efficient way.

The five academic habits of mind we have discussed throughout this chapter—making inquiries, seeking and valuing complexity, understanding writing as a conversation, understanding writing as a process, and reflecting—are fundamental patterns of thought you will need to cultivate as an academic writer. The core skills we discuss through the rest of the book build on these habits of mind.

Moreover, the kind of writing we describe in this chapter may challenge some models of writing that you learned in high school, particularly the five-paragraph essay. The five-paragraph essay is a **genre**, or kind, of writing that offers writers a conventional formula for transmitting information to readers. Such a formula can be useful, but it is generally too limiting for academic conversations. By contrast, academic writing is a genre responsive to the role that readers play in guiding writing and the writing process. That is, academic writing is about shaping and adapting information for the purpose of influencing how readers think about a given issue, not simply placing information in a conventional organizational pattern. We expect academic readers to critically analyze what we have written and anticipate writers' efforts to address their concerns. Therefore, as writers, we need to acknowledge different points of view, make concessions, recognize the limitations of what we argue, and provide counterarguments. Reading necessarily plays a prominent role in the many forms of writing that you do, but not necessarily as a process of simply gathering information. Instead, as James Crosswhite suggests in his book *The Rhetoric of Reason*, reading "means making judgments about which of the many voices and encounters can be brought together into productive conversation."

BECOMING ACADEMIC: THREE NARRATIVES

In the following passages, three writers describe their early experiences as readers. A well-known journalist and writer, Ta-Nehisi Coates reflects upon his growing sense of curiosity at Howard University, which he refers to as Mecca, the site where he is motivated to learn about the history of black people and where he learns to formulate questions to help him better understand who he is as an individual. The passage we include here is taken from his award-winning book *Between the World and Me*, and is addressed to his son. Coates makes many references to authors he has read and public figures he admires. We invite you to do some research to learn about who these people are and their significance in the ways Coates writes about his education. Richard Rodriguez and Gerald Graff are well known outside the academy. In this excerpt from *Hunger of Memory*, Rodriguez describes what it was like growing up as a bookish bilingual "scholarship boy" in a Spanish-speaking household. In the other excerpt, from *Beyond the Culture Wars*, Graff narrates how he disliked reading books, especially literature and history books, well into his undergraduate years as an English major. Both of their narratives turn around moments of recognition triggered by exposure to the ideas of others. As you read the selections, consider these questions:

- Where are the turning points in each narrative? What are the most important things the writers seem to learn?

- What incidents or insights did you find most interesting in the narratives? Why?

- What seem to be the key ideas in each narrative? Do these ideas strike you as being potentially useful in your own work as a thinker and writer?

- Do you find that the writers exhibit academic habits of mind (making inquiries, seeking and valuing complexity, seeing writing as a kind of conversation, and reflecting)? If so, where?

TA-NEHISI COATES

Between the World and Me

A journalist, educator, and writer, Ta-Nehisi Coates received the 2015 National Book Award for *Between the World and Me*, from which the following excerpt is taken. He has also written a memoir, *The Beautiful Struggle: A Father, Two Sons, and an Unlikely Road to Manhood*, and he is a regular contributor to *The Atlantic*, where he writes about culture, politics, race, and the persistence of racial inequality in the United States. His writings have appeared in the *Washington Post*, *The New York Times Magazine*, *Time*, and the *Village Voice*. Most recently, he has been working on an eleven-issue series of *Black Panther* for Marvel. When the Black Panther character debuted in an issue of *Fantastic Four* in 1966, he was the first black superhero in mainstream American comics.

■ ■ ■

When I came to Howard, Chancellor Williams's *Destruction of*   *1*
Black Civilization was my Bible. Williams himself had taught at Howard. I read him when I was sixteen, and his work offered a grand theory of multi-millennial European plunder. The theory relived me of certain troubling questions—this is the point of nationalism—and it

gave me my Tolstoy. I read about Queen Nzinga, who ruled in Central Africa in the sixteenth century, resisting the Portuguese. I read about her negotiating with the Dutch. When the Dutch ambassador tried to humiliate her by refusing her a seat, Nzinga had shown her power by ordering one of her advisers to all fours to make a human chair of her body. That was the kind of power I sought, and the story of our own royalty became for me weapon. My working theory then held all black people as kings in exile, a nation of original men severed from our original names and our majestic Nubian culture. Surely this was the message I took from gazing out on the Yard. Had any people, anywhere, ever been as sprawling and beautiful as us?

I needed more books. At Howard University, one of the greatest collections of books could be found in the Moorland-Spingarn Research Center, where your grandfather once worked. Moorland held archives, papers, collections, and virtually any book ever written by or about black people. For the most significant portion of my time at The Mecca, I followed a simple ritual. I would walk into the Moorland reading room and fill out three call slips for three different works. I would take a seat at one of these long tables. I would draw out my pen and one of my black-and-white composition books. I would open the books and read, while filling my composition books with notes on my reading, new vocabulary words, and sentences of my own invention. I would arrive in the morning and request, three call slips at a time, the works of every writer I had heard spoken of in classrooms or out on the Yard: Larry Neal, Eric Williams, George Padmore, Sonia Sanchez, Stanley Crouch, Harold Cruse, Manning Marable, Addison Gayle, Carolyn Rodgers, Etheridge Knight, Sterling Brown. I remember believing that the key to all life lay in articulating the precise difference between "the Black Aesthetic" and "Negritude." How, specifically, did Europe underdevelop Africa? I must know. And if the Eighteenth Dynasty pharaohs were alive today, would they live in Harlem? I had to inhale all the pages.

I went into this investigation imagining history to be a unified narrative, free of debate, which, once uncovered, would simply verify everything I had always suspected. The smokescreen would lift. And the villains who manipulated the schools and the streets would be unmasked. But there was so much to know—so much geography to cover—Africa, the Caribbean, the Americas, the United States. And all of these areas had histories, sprawling literary canons, fieldwork, ethnographies. Where should I begin?

The trouble came almost immediately. I did not find a coherent tradition marching lockstep but instead factions, and factions within factions. Hurston battled Hughes, Du Bois warred with Garvey, Harold Cruse fought everyone. I felt myself at the bridge of a great ship that I could not control because C.L.R. James was a great wave and Basil

Davidson was a swirling eddy, tossing me about. Things I believed merely a week earlier, ideas I had taken from one book, could be smashed to splinters by another. Had we retained any of our African inheritance? Frazier says it was all destroyed, and this destruction evidences the terribleness of our capturers. Herskovitz says it lives on, and this evidences the resilience of our African spirit. By my second year, it was natural for me to spend a typical day mediating between Frederick Douglass's integration into America and Martin Delany's escape into nationalism. Perhaps they were somehow both right. I had come looking for a parade, for a military review of champions marching in ranks. Instead I was left with a brawl of ancestors, a herd of dissenters, sometimes marching together but just as often marching away from each other.

I would take breaks from my reading, walk out to the vendors who   5
lined the streets, eat lunch on the Yard. I would imagine Malcolm, his body bound in a cell, studying the books, trading his human eyes for the power of flight. And I too felt bound by my ignorance, by the questions that I had not yet understood to be more than just means, by my lack of understanding, and by Howard itself. It was still a school, after all. I wanted to pursue things, to know things, but I could not match the means of knowing that came naturally to me with the expectations of professors. The pursuit of knowing was freedom to me, the right to declare your own curiosities and follow them through all manner of books. I was made for the library, not the classroom. The classroom was a jail of other people's interests. The library was open, unending, free. Slowly, I was discovering myself. The best parts of Malcolm pointed the way. Malcolm, always changing, always evolving toward some truth that was ultimately outside the boundaries of his life, of his body. I felt myself in motion, still directed toward the total possession of my body, but by some other route which I could not before then have imagined.

I was not searching alone. I met your uncle Ben at The Mecca. He   6
was, like me, from one of those cities where everyday life was so different than the Dream that it demanded an explanation. He came, like me, to The Mecca in search of the nature and origin of the breach. I shared with him a healthy skepticism and a deep belief that we could somehow read our way out. Ladies loved him, and what a place to be loved—for it was said, and we certainly believed it to be true, that nowhere on the Earth could one find a more beautiful assembly of women than on Howard University's Yard. And somehow even this was part of the search—the physical beauty of the black body was all our beauty, historical and cultural, incarnate. Your uncle Ben became a fellow traveler for life, and I discovered that there was something particular about journeying out with black people who knew the length of the road because they had traveled it too.

I would walk out into the city and find other searchers at lectures, book signings, and poetry readings. I was still writing bad poetry. I read this bad poetry at open mics in local cafes populated mostly by other poets who also felt the insecurity of their bodies. All of these poets were older and wiser than me, and many of them were well read, and they brought this wisdom to bear on me and my work. What did I mean, *specifically*, by the loss of my body? And if every black body was precious, a one of one, if Malcolm was correct and you must preserve your life, how could I see these precious lives as simply a collective mass, as the amorphous residue of plunder? How could I privilege the spectrum of dark energy over each particular ray of light? These were notes on how to write, and thus notes on how to think. The Dream thrives on generalization, on limiting the number of possible questions, on privileging immediate answers. The Dream is the enemy of all art, courageous thinking, and honest writing. And it became clear that this was not just for the dreams concocted by Americans to justify themselves but also for the dreams that I had conjured to replace them. I had thought that I must mirror the outside world, create a carbon copy of white claims to civilization. It was beginning to occur to me to question the logic of the claim itself. I had forgotten my own self-interrogations pushed upon me by my mother, or rather I had not yet apprehended their deeper, lifelong meaning. I was only beginning to learn to be wary of my own humanity, of my own hurt and anger—I didn't yet realize that the boot on your neck is just as likely to make you delusional as it is to ennoble.

The art I was coming to love lived in this void, in the not yet knowable, in the pain, in the question. The older poets introduced me to artists who pulled their energy from the void—Bubber Miley, Otis Redding, Sam and Dave, C. K. Williams, Carolyn Forché. The older poets were Ethelbert Miller, Kenneth Carroll, Brian Gilmore. It is important that I tell you their names, that you know that I have never achieved anything alone. I remember sitting with Joel Dias-Porter, who had not gone to Howard but whom I found at The Mecca, reviewing every line of Robert Hayden's "Middle Passage." And I was stunned by how much Hayden managed to say without, seemingly, saying anything at all—he could bring forth joy and agony without literally writing the words, which formed as pictures and not slogans. Hayden imagined the enslaved, during the Middle Passage, from the perspective of the enslavers—a mind-trip for me, in and of itself; why should the enslaver be allowed to speak? But Hayden's poems did not speak. They conjured:

> You cannot stare that hatred down
> or chain the fear that stalks the watches

I was not in any slave ship. Or perhaps I was, because so much of what I'd felt in Baltimore, the sharp hatred, the immortal wish, and the

7

8

9

timeless will, I saw in Hayden's work. And that was what I heard in Malcolm, but never like this—quiet, pure, and unadorned. I was learning the craft of poetry, which really was an intensive version of what my mother had taught me all those years ago—the craft of writing as the art of thinking. Poetry aims for an economy of truth—loose and useless words must be discarded, and I found that these loose and useless words were not separate from loose and useless thoughts. Poetry was not simply the transcription of notions—beautiful writing rarely is. I wanted to learn to write, which was ultimately, still, as my mother had taught me, a confrontation with my own innocence, my own rationalizations. Poetry was the processing of my thoughts until the slag of justification fell away and I was left with the cold steel truths of life.

These truths I heard in the works of other poets around the city. They   *10* were made of small hard things—aunts and uncles, smoke breaks after sex, girls on stoops drinking from mason jars. These truths carried the black body beyond slogans and gave it color and texture and thus reflected the spectrum I saw out on the Yard more than all of my alliterative talk of guns or revolutions or paeans to the lost dynasties of African antiquity. After these readings, I followed as the poets would stand out on U Street or repair to a café and argue about everything—books, politics, boxing. And their arguments reinforced the discordant tradition I'd found in Moorland, and I began to see discord, argument, chaos, perhaps even fear, as a kind of power. I was learning to live in the disquiet I felt in Moorland-Spingarn, in the mess of my mind. The gnawing discomfort, the chaos, the intellectual vertigo was not an alarm. It was a beacon.

RICHARD RODRIGUEZ

Scholarship Boy

Richard Rodriguez was born into a Mexican immigrant family in San Francisco, California, and spoke only Spanish until age six. He had a formidable education, receiving a BA from Stanford University and an MA from Columbia University; studying for a PhD at the University of California, Berkeley; and attending the Warburg Institute in London on a Fulbright fellowship. Instead of pursuing a career in academia, he became a journalist. He is perhaps best known for his contributions to PBS's *The NewsHour with Jim Lehrer* and for his controversial opposition to affirmative action and bilingual education. His books include *Hunger of Memory: The Education of Richard Rodriguez* (1981), *Mexico's Children* (1990), *Days of Obligation: An Argument with My Mexican Father* (1992), and *Brown: The Last Discovery of America* (2002).

■ ■ ■

I stand in the ghetto classroom—"the guest speaker"—attempting to lecture on the mystery of the sounds of our words to rows of diffident students. "Don't you hear it? Listen! The music of our words. '*Sumer is i-cumen in. . . .*' And songs on the car radio. We need Aretha Franklin's voice to fill plain words with music—her life." In the face of their empty stares, I try to create an enthusiasm. But the girls in the back row turn to watch some boy passing outside. There are flutters of smiles, waves. And someone's mouth elongates heavy, silent words through the barrier of glass. Silent words—the lips straining to shape each voiceless syllable: "*Meet meee late errr.*" By the door, the instructor smiles at me, apparently hoping that I will be able to spark some enthusiasm in the class. But only one student seems to be listening. A girl, maybe fourteen. In this gray room her eyes shine with ambition. She keeps nodding and nodding at all that I say; she even takes notes. And each time I ask a question, she jerks up and down in her desk like a marionette, while her hand waves over the bowed heads of her classmates. It is myself (as a boy) I see as she faces me now (a man in my thirties). *1*

The boy who first entered a classroom barely able to speak English, twenty years later concluded his studies in the stately quiet of the reading room in the British Museum. Thus with one sentence I can summarize my academic career. It will be harder to summarize what sort of life connects the boy to the man. *2*

With every award, each graduation from one level of education to the next, people I'd meet would congratulate me. Their refrain always the same: "Your parents must be very proud." Sometimes then they'd ask me how I managed it—my "success." (How?) After a while, I had several quick answers to give in reply. I'd admit, for one thing, that I went to an excellent grammar school. (My earliest teachers, the nuns, made my success their ambition.) And my brother and both my sisters were very good students. (They often brought home the shiny school trophies I came to want.) And my mother and father always encouraged me. (At every graduation they were behind the stunning flash of the camera when I turned to look at the crowd.) *3*

As important as these factors were, however, they account inadequately for my academic advance. Nor do they suggest what an odd success I managed. For although I was a very good student, I was also a very bad student. I was a "scholarship boy," a certain kind of scholarship boy. Always successful, I was always unconfident. Exhilarated by my progress. Sad. I became the prized student—anxious and eager to learn. Too eager, too anxious—an imitative and unoriginal pupil. My brother and two sisters enjoyed the advantages I did, and they grew to be as successful as I, but none of them ever seemed so anxious about their schooling. A second-grade student, I was the one who came home *4* and corrected the "simple" grammatical mistakes of our parents. ("Two negatives make a positive.") Proudly I announced—to my family's startled silence—that a teacher had said I was losing all trace of a Spanish accent. I was oddly annoyed when I was unable to get parental help with a homework assignment. The night my father tried to help me with an arithmetic exercise, he kept reading the instructions, each time more deliberately, until I pried the textbook out of his hands, saying, "I'll try to figure it out some more by myself."

When I reached the third grade, I outgrew such behavior. I became   5
more tactful, careful to keep separate the two very different worlds of my day. But then, with ever-increasing intensity, I devoted myself to my studies. I became bookish, puzzling to all my family. Ambition set me apart. When my brother saw me struggling home with stacks of library books, he would laugh, shouting: "Hey, Four Eyes!" My father opened a closet one day and was startled to find me inside, reading a novel. My mother would find me reading when I was supposed to be asleep or helping around the house or playing outside. In a voice angry or worried or just curious, she'd ask: "What do you see in your books?" It became the family's joke. When I was called and wouldn't reply, someone would say I must be hiding under my bed with a book.

(How did I manage my success?)   6

What I am about to say to you has taken me more than twenty years   7
to admit: *A primary reason for my success in the classroom was that I couldn't forget that schooling was changing me and separating me from the life I enjoyed before becoming a student.* That simple realization! For years I never spoke to anyone about it. Never mentioned a thing to my family or my teachers or classmates. From a very early age, I understood enough, just enough about my classroom experiences to keep what I knew repressed, hidden beneath layers of embarrassment. Not until my last months as a graduate student, nearly thirty years old, was it possible for me to think much about the reasons for my academic success. Only then. At the end of my schooling, I needed to determine how far I had moved from my past. The adult finally confronted, and now must publicly say, what the child shuddered from knowing and could never admit to himself or to those many faces that smiled at his every success. ("Your parents must be very proud. . . .")

At the end, in the British Museum (too distracted to finish my disser-   8
tation) for weeks I read, speed-read, books by modern educational theorists, only to find infrequent and slight mention of students like me. (Much more is written about the more typical case, the lower-class student who barely is helped by his schooling.) Then one day, leafing through Richard Hoggart's *The Uses of Literacy*, I found, in his description of the scholarship boy, myself. For the first time I realized that there

were other students like me, and so I was able to frame the meaning of my academic success, its consequent price—the loss.

Hoggart's description is distinguished, at least initially, by deep understanding. What he grasps very well is that the scholarship boy must move between environments, his home and the classroom, which are at cultural extremes, opposed. With his family, the boy has the intense pleasure of intimacy, the family's consolation in feeling public alienation. Lavish emotions texture home life. *Then*, at school, the instruction bids him to trust lonely reason primarily. Immediate needs set the pace of his parents' lives. From his mother and father the boy learns to trust spontaneity and nonrational ways of knowing. *Then*, at school, there is mental calm. Teachers emphasize the value of a reflectiveness that opens a space between thinking and immediate action.

Years of schooling must pass before the boy will be able to sketch the cultural differences in his day as abstractly as this. But he senses those differences early. Perhaps as early as the night he brings home an assignment from school and finds the house too noisy for study.

> He has to be more and more alone, if he is going to "get on." He will have, probably unconsciously, to oppose the ethos of the hearth, the intense gregariousness of the working-class family group. Since everything centers upon the living-room, there is unlikely to be a room of his own; the bedrooms are cold and inhospitable, and to warm them or the front room, if there is one, would not only be expensive, but would require an imaginative leap—out of the tradition—which most families are not capable of making. There is a corner of the living-room table. On the other side Mother is ironing, the wireless is on, someone is singing a snatch of song or Father says intermittently whatever comes into his head. The boy has to cut himself off mentally, so as to do his homework, as well as he can.[1]

The next day, the lesson is as apparent at school. There are even rows of desks. Discussion is ordered. The boy must rehearse his thoughts and raise his hand before speaking out in a loud voice to an audience of classmates. And there is time enough, and silence, to think about ideas (big ideas) never considered at home by his parents.

Not for the working-class child alone is adjustment to the classroom difficult. Good schooling requires that any student alter early childhood habits. But the working-class child is usually least prepared for the change. And, unlike many middle-class children, he goes home and sees in his parents a way of life not only different but starkly opposed to that of the classroom. (He enters the house and hears his parents talking in ways his teachers discourage.)

---

[1] All quotations in this selection are from Richard Hoggart, *The Uses of Literacy* (London: Chatto and Windus, 1957), chapter 10.

Without extraordinary determination and the great assistance of others—at home and at school—there is little chance for success. Typically most working-class children are barely changed by the classroom. The exception succeeds. The relative few become scholarship students. Of these, Richard Hoggart estimates, most manage a fairly graceful transition. Somehow they learn to live in the two very different worlds of their day. There are some others, however, those Hoggart pejoratively terms "scholarship boys," for whom success comes with special anxiety. Scholarship boy: good student, troubled son. The child is "moderately endowed," intellectually mediocre, Hoggart supposes—though it may be more pertinent to note the special qualities of temperament in the child. High-strung child. Brooding. Sensitive. Haunted by the knowledge that one *chooses* to become a student. (Education is not an inevitable or natural step in growing up.) Here is a child who cannot forget that his academic success distances him from a life he loved, even from his own memory of himself.

Initially, he wavers, balances allegiance. ("The boy is himself [until he reaches, say, the upper forms] very much of *both* the worlds of home and school. He is enormously obedient to the dictates of the world of school, but emotionally still strongly wants to continue as part of the family circle.") Gradually, necessarily, the balance is lost. The boy needs to spend more and more time studying, each night enclosing himself in the silence permitted and required by intense concentration. He takes his first step toward academic success, away from his family.

From the very first days, through the years following, it will be with his parents—the figures of lost authority, the persons toward whom he feels deepest love—that the change will be most powerfully measured. A separation will unravel between them. Advancing in his studies, the boy notices that his mother and father have not changed as much as he. Rather, when he sees them, they often remind him of the person he once was and the life he earlier shared with them. He realizes what some Romantics also know when they praise the working class for the capacity for human closeness, qualities of passion and spontaneity, that the rest of us experience in like measure only in the earliest part of our youth. For the Romantic, this doesn't make working-class life childish. Working-class life challenges precisely because it is an *adult* way of life.

The scholarship boy reaches a different conclusion. He cannot afford to admire his parents. (How could he and still pursue such a contrary life?) He permits himself embarrassment at their lack of education. And to evade nostalgia for the life he has lost, he concentrates on the benefits education will bestow upon him. He becomes especially ambitious. Without the support of old certainties and consolations, almost mechanically, he assumes the procedures and doctrines of the classroom. The kind of allegiance the young student might have given his mother and father only days earlier, he transfers to the teacher, the new figure of authority. "[The scholarship boy] tends to make a father-figure of his form-master," Hoggart observes.

But Hoggart's calm prose only makes me recall the urgency with   16
which I came to idolize my grammar school teachers. I began by imitating their accents, using their diction, trusting their every direction. The very first facts they dispensed, I grasped with awe. Any book they told me to read, I read—then waited for them to tell me which books I enjoyed. Their every casual opinion I came to adopt and to trumpet when I returned home. I stayed after school "to help"—to get my teacher's undivided attention. It was the nun's encouragement that mattered most to me. (She understood exactly what—my parents never seemed to appraise so well—all my achievements entailed.) Memory gently caressed each word of praise bestowed in the classroom so that compliments teachers paid me years ago come quickly to mind even today.

The enthusiasm I felt in second-grade classes I flaunted before both   17
my parents. The docile, obedient student came home a shrill and precocious son who insisted on correcting and teaching his parents with the remark: "My teacher told us. . . ."

I intended to hurt my mother and father. I was still angry at them for   18
having encouraged me toward classroom English. But gradually this anger was exhausted, replaced by guilt as school grew more and more attractive to me. I grew increasingly successful, a talkative student. My hand was raised in the classroom; I yearned to answer any question. At home, life was less noisy than it had been. (I spoke to classmates and teachers more often each day than to family members.) Quiet at home, I sat with my papers for hours each night. I never forgot that schooling had irretrievably changed my family's life. That knowledge, however, did not weaken ambition. Instead, it strengthened resolve. Those times I remembered the loss of my past with regret, I quickly reminded myself of all the things my teachers could give me. (They could make me an educated man.) I tightened my grip on pencil and books. I evaded nostalgia. Tried hard to forget. But one does not forget by trying to forget. One only remembers. I remembered too well that education had changed my family's life. I would not have become a scholarship boy had I not so often remembered.

Once she was sure that her children knew English, my mother would   19
tell us, "You should keep up your Spanish." Voices playfully groaned in response. "¡Pochos!" my mother would tease. I listened silently.

After a while, I grew more calm at home. I developed tact. A fourth-   20
grade student, I was no longer the show-off in front of my parents. I became a conventionally dutiful son, politely affectionate, cheerful enough, even—for reasons beyond choosing—my father's favorite. And much about my family life was easy then, comfortable, happy in the

rhythm of our living together: hearing my father getting ready for work; eating the breakfast my mother had made me; looking up from a novel to hear my brother or one of my sisters playing with friends in the back-yard; in winter, coming upon the house all lighted up after dark.

But withheld from my mother and father was any mention of what most mattered to me: the extraordinary experience of first-learning. Late afternoon: In the midst of preparing dinner, my mother would come up behind me while I was trying to read. Her head just over mine, her breath warmly scented with food. "What are you reading?" Or, "Tell me all about your new courses." I would barely respond, "Just the usual things, nothing special." (A half smile, then silence. Her head moving back in the silence. Silence! Instead of the flood of intimate sounds that had once flowed smoothly between us, there was this silence.) After dinner, I would rush to a bedroom with papers and books. As often as possible, I resisted parental pleas to "save lights" by coming to the kitchen to work. I kept so much, so often, to myself. Sad. Enthusiastic. Troubled by the excitement of coming upon new ideas. Eager. Fascinated by the promising texture of a brand-new book. I hoarded the pleasures of learning. Alone for hours. Enthralled. Nervous. I rarely looked away from my books—or back on my memories. Nights when relatives visited and the front rooms were warmed by Spanish sounds, I slipped quietly out of the house.

It mattered that education was changing me. It never ceased to matter. My brother and sisters would giggle at our mother's mispronounced words. They'd correct her gently. My mother laughed girlishly one night, trying not to pronounce *sheep* as *ship*. From a distance I listened sullenly. From that distance, pretending not to notice on another occasion, I saw my father looking at the title pages of my library books. That was the scene on my mind when I walked home with a fourth-grade companion and heard him say that his parents read to him every night. (A strange-sounding book—*Winnie the Pooh*.) Immediately, I wanted to know, "What is it like?" My companion, however, thought I wanted to know about the plot of the book. Another day, my mother surprised me by asking for a "nice" book to read. "Something not too hard you think I might like." Carefully I chose one, Willa Cather's *My Ántonia*. But when, several weeks later, I happened to see it next to her bed unread except for the first few pages, I was furious and suddenly wanted to cry. I grabbed up the book and took it back to my room and placed it in its place, alphabetically on my shelf.

"Your parents must be very proud of you." People began to say that to me about the time I was in sixth grade. To answer affirmatively, I'd smile. Shyly I'd smile, never betraying my sense of the irony: I was not proud of my mother and father. I was embarrassed by their lack

21

22

23

of education. It was not that I ever thought they were stupid, though stupidly I took for granted their enormous native intelligence. Simply, what mattered to me was that they were not like my teachers.

But, "Why didn't you tell us about the award?" my mother demanded, *24* her frown weakened by pride. At the grammar school ceremony several weeks after, her eyes were brighter than the trophy I'd won. Pushing back the hair from my forehead, she whispered that I had "shown" the *gringos*. A few minutes later, I heard my father speak to my teacher and felt ashamed of his labored, accented words. Then guilty for the shame. I felt such contrary feelings. (There is no simple roadmap through the heart of the scholarship boy.) My teacher was so soft-spoken and her words were edged sharp and clean. I admired her until it seemed to me that she spoke too carefully. Sensing that she was condescending to them, I became nervous. Resentful. Protective. I tried to move my parents away. "You both must be very proud of Richard," the nun said. They responded quickly. (They were proud.) "We are proud of all our children." Then this afterthought: "They sure didn't get their brains from us." They all laughed. I smiled.

GERALD GRAFF

Disliking Books

Gerald Graff received his BA in English from the University of Chicago and his PhD in English and American literature from Stanford University. In his distinguished academic career, he has taught at numerous universities and is currently a professor of English and education at the University of Illinois at Chicago. He is probably best known for his pedagogical theories, especially "teaching the controversies," an approach he argues for most famously in his book *Beyond the Culture Wars: How Teaching the Conflicts Can Revitalize American Education* (1993), from which this excerpt is taken. His other well-known books include *Literature Against Itself: Literary Ideas in Modern Society* (1979), *Professing Literature: An Institutional History* (1987), and *Clueless in Academe: How Schooling Obscures the Life of the Mind* (2003).

I like to think I have a certain advantage as a teacher of literature *1* because when I was growing up I disliked and feared books. My youthful aversion to books showed a fine impartiality, extending across the whole spectrum of literature, history, philosophy, science, and what by then (the late 1940s) had come to be called social studies. But had I been forced to choose, I would have singled out literature and history as the reading I disliked most. Science at least had some discernible practical use, and you could have fun solving the problems in the textbooks with their clear-cut answers. Literature and history had no apparent application to my experience, and any boy in my school who had cultivated them—I can't recall one who did—would have marked himself as a sissy.

As a middle-class Jew growing up in an ethnically mixed Chicago   2
neighborhood, I was already in danger of being beaten up daily by rougher working-class boys. Becoming a bookworm would have only given them a decisive reason for beating me up. Reading and studying were more permissible for girls, but they, too, had to be careful not to get too intellectual, lest they acquire the stigma of being "stuck up."

In *Lives on the Boundary*, a remarkable autobiography of the mak-   3
ing of an English teacher, Mike Rose describes how the "pain and confusion" of his working-class youth made "school and knowledge" seem a saving alternative. Rose writes of feeling "freed, as if I were untying fetters," by his encounters with certain college teachers, who helped him recognize that "an engagement with ideas could foster competence and lead me out into the world."[1] Coming at things from my middle-class perspective, however, I took for granted a freedom that school, knowledge, and engagement with ideas seemed only to threaten.

My father, a literate man, was frustrated by my refusal to read any-   4
thing besides comic books, sports magazines, and the John R. Tunis and Clair Bee sports novels. I recall his once confining me to my room until I finished a book on the voyages of Magellan, but try as I might, I could do no better than stare bleakly at the pages. I could not, as we would later say, "relate to" Magellan or to any of the other books my father brought home—detective stories, tales of war and heroism, adventure stories with adolescent heroes (the *Hardy Boys*, *Hans Brinker*, or *The Silver Skates*), stories of scientific discovery (Paul de Kruif's *Microbe Hunters*), books on current events. Nothing worked.

It was understood, however, that boys of my background would go   5
to college and that once there we would get serious and buckle down. For some, "getting serious" meant prelaw, premed, or a major in business to prepare for taking over the family business. My family did not own a business, and law and medicine did not interest me, so I drifted by default into the nebulous but conveniently noncommittal territory of the liberal arts. I majored in English.

At this point the fear of being beaten up if I were caught having any-   6
thing to do with books was replaced by the fear of flunking out of college if I did not learn to deal with them. But though I dutifully did my

[1] Mike Rose, *Lives on the Boundary* (New York: Free Press, 1989), pp. 46–47.

homework and made good grades (first at the University of Illinois, Chicago branch, then at the University of Chicago, from which I graduated in 1959), I continued to find "serious" reading painfully difficult and alien. My most vivid recollections of college reading are of assigned classics I failed to finish: *The Iliad* (in the Richmond Lattimore translation); *The Autobiography of Benvenuto Cellini*, a major disappointment after the paperback jacket's promise of "a lusty classic of Renaissance ribaldry"; E. M. Forster's *Passage to India*, sixty agonizing pages of which I managed to slog through before giving up. Even Hemingway, Steinbeck, and Fitzgerald, whose contemporary world was said to be "close to my own experience," left me cold. I saw little there that did resemble my experience.

Even when I had done the assigned reading, I was often tongue-tied and embarrassed when called on. What was unclear to me was what I was supposed to *say* about literary works, and why. Had I been born a decade or two earlier, I might have come to college with the rudiments of a literate vocabulary for talking about culture that some people older than I acquired through family, high school, or church. As it was, "cultured" phrases seemed effete and sterile to me. When I was able to produce the kind of talk that was required in class, the intellectualism of it came out sounding stilted and hollow in my mouth. If *Cliffs Notes* and other such crib sheets for the distressed had yet come into existence, with their ready-to-copy summaries of widely taught literary works, I would have been an excellent customer. (As it was, I did avail myself of the primitive version then in existence called *Masterplots*.) 7

What first made literature, history, and other intellectual pursuits seem attractive to me was exposure to critical debates. There was no single conversion experience, but a gradual transformation over several years, extending into my first teaching positions, at the University of New Mexico and then Northwestern University. But one of the first sparks I remember was a controversy over *Adventures of Huckleberry Finn* that arose in a course during my junior year in college. On first attempt, Twain's novel was just another assigned classic that I was too bored to finish. I could see little connection between my Chicago upbringing and Huck's pre–Civil War adventures with a runaway slave on a raft up the Mississippi. 8

My interest was aroused, however, when our instructor mentioned that the critics had disagreed over the merits of the last part of the novel. He quoted Ernest Hemingway's remark that "if you read [the novel] you must stop where the nigger Jim is stolen by the boys. This is the real end. The rest is cheating." According to this school of thought, the remainder of the book trivializes the quest for Jim's freedom that has motivated the story up to that point. This happens first when Jim becomes an object of Tom Sawyer's slapstick humor, then when it is 9 revealed that unbeknownst to Huck, the reader, and himself, Jim has already been freed by his benevolent owner, so that the risk we have assumed Jim and Huck to be under all along has been really no risk at all.

Like the critics, our class divided over the question: Did Twain's end-   *10* ing vitiate the book's profound critique of racism, as Hemingway's charge of cheating implied? Cheating in my experience up to then was something students did, an unthinkable act for a famous author. It was a revelation to me that famous authors were capable not only of mistakes but of ones that even lowly undergraduates might be able to point out. When I chose to write my term paper on the dispute over the ending, my instructor suggested I look at several critics on the opposing sides, T. S. Eliot and Lionel Trilling, who defended the ending, and Leo Marx, who sided with Hemingway.

Reading the critics was like picking up where the class discussion had   *11* left off, and I gained confidence from recognizing that my classmates and I had had thoughts that, however stumbling our expression of them, were not too far from the thoughts of famous published critics. I went back to the novel again and to my surprise found myself rereading it with an excitement I had never felt before with a serious book. Having the controversy over the ending in mind, I now had some issues *to watch out for* as I read, issues that reshaped the way I read the earlier chapters as well as the later ones and focused my attention. And having issues to watch out for made it possible not only to concentrate, as I had not been able to do earlier, but to put myself in the text—to read with a sense of personal engagement that I had not felt before. Reading the novel with the voices of the critics running through my mind, I found myself think-ing of things that I might say about what I was reading, things that may have belonged partly to the critics but also now belonged to me. It was as if having a stock of things to look for and to say about a literary work had somehow made it possible for me to read one.

One of the critics had argued that what was at issue in the debate   *12* over *Huckleberry Finn* was not just the novel's value but its cultural significance: If *Huckleberry Finn* was contradictory or confused in its attitude toward race, then what did that say about the culture that had received the novel as one of its representative cultural documents and had made Twain a folk hero? This critic had also made the intriguing observation—I found out only later it was a critical commonplace at that time—that judgments about the novel's aesthetic value could not be separated from judgments about its moral substance. I recall taking in both this critic's arguments and the cadence of the phrases in which they were couched; perhaps it would not be so bad after all to become the sort of person who talked about "cultural contradictions" and the "inseparability of form and content." Perhaps even mere literary-critical talk could give you a certain power in the real world. As the possibility dawned on me that reading and intellectual discussion might actually have something to do with my real life, I became less embarrassed about using the intellectual formulas.

The Standard Story

It was through exposure to such critical reading and discussion over a *13* period of time that I came to catch the literary bug, eventually choosing the vocation of teaching. This was not the way it is supposed to happen. In the standard story of academic vocation that we like to tell ourselves, the germ is first planted by an early experience of literature itself. The future teacher is initially inspired by some primary experience of a great book and only subsequently acquires the secondary, derivative skills of critical discussion. A teacher may be involved in instilling this inspiration, but a teacher who seemingly effaces himself or herself before the text. Any premature or excessive acquaintance with secondary critical discourse, and certainly with its sectarian debates, is thought to be a corrupting danger, causing one to lose touch with the primary passion for literature. . . .

The standard story ascribes innocence to the primary experience of *14* literature and sees the secondary experience of professional criticism as corrupting. In my case, however, things had evidently worked the other way around: I had to be corrupted first in order to experience innocence. It was only when I was introduced to a critical debate about *Huckleberry Finn* that my helplessness in the face of the novel abated and I could experience a personal reaction to it. Getting into immediate contact with the text was for me a curiously triangular business; I could not do it directly but needed a conversation of other readers to give me the issues and terms that made it possible to respond.

As I think back on it now, it was as if the critical conversation I *15* needed had up to then been withheld from me, on the ground that it could only interfere with my direct access to literature itself. The assumption was that leaving me alone with literary texts themselves, uncontaminated by the interpretations and theories of professional critics, would enable me to get on the closest possible terms with those texts. But being alone with the texts only left me feeling bored and helpless, since I had no language with which to make them mine. On the one hand, I was being asked to speak a foreign language—literary criticism—while on the other hand, I was being protected from that language, presumably for my own safety.

The moral I draw from this experience is that our ability to read *16* well depends more than we think on our ability to *talk well* about what we read. Our assumptions about what is "primary" and "secondary" in the reading process blind us to what actually goes on. Many literate people learned certain ways of talking about books so long ago that they have forgotten they ever had to learn them. These people therefore fail to understand the reading problems of the struggling students who have still not acquired a critical vocabulary.

How typical my case was is hard to say, but many of the students I teach seem to have grown up as the same sort of nonintellectual, nonbookish person I was, and they seem to view literature with some of the same aversions, fears, and anxieties. That is why I like to think it is an advantage for a teacher to know what it feels like to grow up being indifferent to literature and intimidated by criticism and what it feels like to overcome a resistance to talking like an intellectual.

17

A Practice Sequence: Composing a Literacy Narrative

A *literacy narrative*—a firsthand, personal account about reading or composing—is a well-established genre that is popular both inside and outside the academy. Coates's, Rodriguez's, and Graff's, autobiographical stories dealing with aspects of how they became literate and their relationship with reading and writing are literacy narratives. Coates's narrative is part of *Between the World and Me*, a memoir that examines racial identity and the politics of race in the United States. Rodriguez's narrative is part of *Hunger of Memory: The Education of Richard Rodriguez*, a memoir that explores the politics of language in American culture. Graff's narrative is embedded in his *Beyond the Culture Wars: How Teaching the Conflicts Can Revitalize American Education*, which, as the subtitle suggests, presents arguments and proposals for altering educational practices.

We would like you to write your own literacy narrative. The following practice sequence suggests some strategies for doing so.

1   Reflect on your experiences as a reader. Spend some time jotting down answers to these questions (not necessarily in this order) or to other related questions that occur to you as you write.

- Can you recall the time when you first began to read?

- What are the main types of reading you do? Why?

- How would you describe or characterize yourself as a reader?

- Is there one moment or event that encapsulates who you are as a reader?

- What are your favorite books, authors, and types of books? Why are they favorites?

- In what ways has reading changed you for the better? For the worse?

- What is the most important thing you've learned from reading?

- Have you ever learned something important from reading, only to discover later that it wasn't true or sufficient? Explain.

2 Write your literacy narrative, focusing on at least one turning point, at least one moment of recognition or lesson learned. Write no fewer than two pages but no more than five pages. See where your story arc takes you. What do you conclude about your own "growing into literacy"?

3 Then start a conversation about literacy. Talk with some other people about their experiences. You might talk with some classmates—and not necessarily those in your writing class—about their memories of becoming literate. You might interview some people you grew up with—a parent, a sibling, a best friend—about their memories of you as a reader and writer and about their own memories of becoming literate. Compare their memories to your own. Did you all have similar experiences? How were they different? Do you see things the same way? Then write down your impressions and what you think you may have learned.

4 Recast your literacy narrative, incorporating some of the insights you gathered from other people. How does your original narrative change? What new things now have to be accounted for?

5 Like Graff, who takes his own experience as a starting point for proposing new educational policies, can you imagine your insights having larger implications? Explain. Do you think what you've learned from reading Coates's, Rodriguez's, and Graff's literacy narratives has implications for the ways reading is taught in school?

2

From Reading as a Writer
to Writing as a Reader

Reading for class and then writing an essay might seem to be separate tasks, but reading is the first step in the writing process. In this chapter we present methods that will help you read more effectively and move from reading to writing your own college essays. These methods will lead you to understand a writer's purpose in responding to a situation, the motivation for asserting a claim in an essay and entering a particular conversation with a particular audience.

Much if not all of the writing you do in college will be based on what you have read. This is the case, for example, when you summarize a philosopher's theory, analyze the significance of an experiment in psychology, or, perhaps, synthesize different and conflicting points of view in making an argument about race and academic achievement in sociology.

As we maintain throughout this book, writing and reading are inextricably linked to each other. Good academic writers are also good critical readers: They leave their mark on what they read, identifying issues, making judgments about the truth of what writers tell them, and evaluating the adequacy of the evidence in support of an argument. This is where writing and inquiry begin: understanding our own position relative to the scholarly conversations we want to enter. Moreover, critical readers try to understand the strategies that writers use to persuade readers to agree with them. At times, these are strategies that we can adapt in advancing our arguments.

READING AS AN ACT OF COMPOSING: ANNOTATING

Leaving your mark on the page—**annotating**—is your first act of composing. When you mark the pages of a text, you are reading critically, engaging with the ideas of others, questioning and testing those ideas, and inquiring into their significance. **Critical reading** is sometimes called *active reading* to distinguish it from memorization, when you just read for the main idea so that you can "spit it back out on a test." When you read actively and critically, you bring your knowledge, experiences, and interests to a text, so that you can respond to the writer, continuing the conversation the writer has begun.

Experienced college readers don't try to memorize a text or assume they must understand it completely before they respond to it. Instead they read strategically, looking for the writer's claims, for the writer's key ideas and terms, and for connections with key ideas and terms in other texts. They also read to discern what conversation the writer has entered, and how the writer's argument is connected to those he or she makes reference to.

When you annotate a text, your notes in the margins might address the following questions:

- What arguments is this author responding to?
- Is the issue relevant or significant?
- How do I know that what the author says is true?
- Is the author's evidence legitimate? Sufficient?
- Can I think of an exception to the author's argument?
- What would the counterarguments be?

Good readers ask the same kinds of questions of every text they read, considering not just *what* a writer says (the content), but *how* he or she says it given the writer's purpose and audience.

The marks you leave on a page might indicate your own ideas and questions, patterns you see emerging, links to other texts, even your gut response to the writer's argument—agreement, dismay, enthusiasm, confusion. They reveal your own thought processes as you read and signal that you are entering the conversation. In effect, they are traces of your own responding voice.

Developing your own system of marking or annotating pages can help you feel confident when you sit down with a new reading for your classes. Based on our students' experiences, we offer this practical tip: Although wide-tipped highlighters have their place in some classes, it is more useful to read with a pen or pencil in your hand, so that you can do more than draw a bar of color through words or sentences you find important. Experienced readers write their responses to a text in the margins, using personal codes (boxing key words, for example), writing out definitions of words they have looked up, drawing lines to connect ideas on facing pages, or writing notes to themselves ("Connect this to Edmundson on consumer culture"; "Hirsch would disagree big time—see his ideas on memorization in primary grades"; "You call THIS evidence?!"). These notes help you get started on your own writing assignments.

Annotating your readings benefits you twice. First, it is easier to participate in class discussions if you have already marked passages that are important, confusing, or linked to specific passages in other texts you have read. It's a sure way to avoid that sinking feeling you get when you return to pages you read the night before but now can't remember at all. Second, by marking key ideas in a text, noting your ideas about them, and making connections to key ideas in other texts, you have begun the process of writing an essay. When you start writing the first draft of your essay, you can quote the passages you have already marked and explain what you find significant about them based on the notes you have already made to yourself. You can make the connections to other texts in the paragraphs of your own essay that you have already begun to make on the pages of your textbook. If you mark your texts effectively, you'll never be at a loss when you sit down to write the first draft of an essay.

Let's take a look at how one of our students marked several paragraphs of Douglas Massey and Nancy Denton's *American Apartheid: Segregation and the Making of the Underclass* (1993). In the excerpt below, the student underlines what she believes is important information and begins to create an outline of the authors' main points.

1. racist attitudes

2. private behaviors

3. & institutional practices lead to ghettos (authors' claim?)

Ghetto = "multistory, high-density housing projects." Post-1950

The spatial isolation of black Americans was achieved by a conjunction of racist attitudes, private behaviors, and institutional practices that disenfranchised blacks from urban housing markets and led to the creation of the ghetto. Discrimination in employment exacerbated black poverty and limited the economic potential for integration, and black residential mobility was systematically blocked by pervasive discrimination and white avoidance of neighborhoods containing blacks. The walls of the ghetto were buttressed after 1950 by government programs that promoted slum clearance and relocated displaced ghetto residents into multi-story, high-density housing projects.   1

I remember this happening where I grew up, but I didn't know the government was responsible. Is this what happened in There Are No Children Here?

Authors say situation of "spatial isolation" remains despite court decisions. Does it?

In theory, this self-reinforcing cycle of prejudice, discrimination, and segregation was broken during the 1960s by a growing rejection of racist sentiments by whites and a series of court decisions and federal laws that banned discrimination in public life. (1) The Civil Rights Act of 1964 outlawed racial discrimination in employment, (2) the Fair Housing Act of 1968 banned discrimination in housing, and (3) the *Gautreaux* and *Shannon* court decisions prohibited public authorities from placing housing projects exclusively in black neighborhoods. Despite these changes, however, the nation's largest black communities remained as segregated as ever in 1980. Indeed, many urban areas displayed a pattern of intense racial isolation that could only be described as hypersegregation.   2

Although the racial climate of the United States im-   3
proved outwardly during the 1970s, <u>racism still restricted
the residential freedom of black Americans</u>; it just did so in
less blatant ways. In the aftermath of the civil rights revolution, few whites voiced openly racist sentiments; realtors no
longer refused outright to rent or sell to blacks; and few local
governments went on record to oppose public housing projects because they would contain blacks. This lack of overt
racism, however, did not mean that prejudice and discrimination had ended.

*Subtler racism, not
on public record.*

*Lack of enforce-
ment of Civil Rights
Act? Fair Housing
Act? Gautreaux
and Shannon? Why?
Why not?*

Notice how the student's annotations help her understand the argument the authors make.

1. She numbers the three key factors (racist attitudes, private behaviors,
   and institutional practices) that influenced the formation of ghettos in
   the United States.

2. She identifies the situation that motivates the authors' analysis: the
   extent to which "the spatial isolation of black Americans" still exists
   despite laws and court decisions designed to end residential segregation.

3. She makes connections to her own experience and to another book she
   has read.

By understanding the authors' arguments and making these connections, the student begins the writing process. She also sets the stage for her
own research, for examining the authors' claim that residential segregation still exists.

READING AS A WRITER: ANALYZING A TEXT RHETORICALLY

When you study how writers influence readers through language, you
are analyzing the **rhetoric** (available means of persuasion) of what you
read. When you identify a writer's purpose for responding to a situation
by composing an essay that puts forth claims meant to sway a particular audience, you are performing a rhetorical analysis. Such an analysis
entails identifying the features of an argument to better understand how
the argument works to persuade a reader:

- how the writer sees the situation that calls for a response in writing
- the writer's purpose for writing
- intended audience
- kinds of claims
- types of evidence

We discuss each of these elements as we analyze the following preface from E. D. Hirsch's book *Cultural Literacy: What Every American Needs to Know* (1987). Formerly a professor of English, Hirsch has long been interested in educational reform. That interest developed from his (and others') perception that today's students do not know as much as students did in the past. Although Hirsch wrote the book decades ago, many observers still believe that the contemporary problems of illiteracy and poverty can be traced to a lack of cultural literacy.

Read the preface. You may want to mark it with your own questions and responses, and then consider them in light of our analysis (following the preface) of Hirsch's rhetorical situation, purpose, claims, and audience.

E. D. HIRSCH JR.

Preface to *Cultural Literacy*

E. D. Hirsch Jr., a retired English professor, is the author of many acclaimed books, including *The Schools We Need and Why We Don't Have Them* (1996) and *The Knowledge Deficit* (2006). His book *Cultural Literacy* was a best seller in 1987 and had a profound effect on the focus of education in the late 1980s and 1990s.

■ ■ ■

Rousseau points out the facility with which children lend themselves to our false methods: . . ."The apparent ease with which children learn is their ruin."

—JOHN DEWEY

There is no matter what children should learn first, any more than what leg you should put into your breeches first. Sir, you may stand disputing which is best to put in first, but in the meantime your backside is bare. Sir, while you stand considering which of two things you should teach your child first, another boy has learn't 'em both.

—SAMUEL JOHNSON

To be culturally literate is to possess the basic information needed   *1* to thrive in the modern world. The breadth of that information is great, extending over the major domains of human activity from sports to science. It is by no means confined to "culture" narrowly understood as an acquaintance with the arts. Nor is it confined to one social class. Quite the contrary. Cultural literacy constitutes the only sure avenue of opportunity for disadvantaged children, the only reliable way of combating the social determinism that now condemns them to remain in the same social and educational condition as their parents. That children from poor and illiterate homes tend to remain poor and illiterate is an unacceptable failure of our schools, one which has occurred not because our teachers are inept but chiefly because they are compelled to teach a fragmented curriculum based on faulty educational theories. Some say that our schools by themselves are powerless to change the cycle of poverty and illiteracy. I do not agree. They *can* break the cycle, but only if they themselves break fundamentally with some of the theories and practices that education professors and school administrators have followed over the past fifty years.

Although the chief beneficiaries of the educational reforms advocated in this book will be disadvantaged children, these same reforms will also enhance the literacy of children from middle-class homes. The educational goal advocated is that of mature literacy for *all* our citizens.

The connection between mature literacy and cultural literacy may already be familiar to those who have closely followed recent discussions of education. Shortly after the publication of my essay "Cultural Literacy," Dr. William Bennett, then chairman of the National Endowment for the Humanities and subsequently secretary of education in President Ronald Reagan's second administration, championed its ideas. This endorsement from an influential person of conservative views gave my ideas some currency, but such an endorsement was not likely to recommend the concept to liberal thinkers, and in fact the idea of cultural literacy has been attacked by some liberals on the assumption that I must be advocating a list of great books that every child in the land should be forced to read.

But those who examine the Appendix to this book will be able to judge for themselves how thoroughly mistaken such an assumption is. Very few specific titles appear on the list, and they usually appear as words, not works, because they represent writings that culturally literate people have read about but haven't read. *Das Kapital* is a good example. Cultural literacy is represented not by a *prescriptive* list of books but rather by a *descriptive* list of the information actually possessed by literate Americans. My aim in this book is to contribute to making that information the possession of all Americans.

The importance of such widely shared information can best be understood if I explain briefly how the idea of cultural literacy relates to currently prevailing theories of education. The theories that have dominated American education for the past fifty years stem ultimately from Jean Jacques Rousseau, who believed that we should encourage the natural development of young children and not impose adult ideas upon them before they can truly understand them. Rousseau's conception of education as a process of natural development was an abstract generalization meant to apply to all children in any time or place: to French children of the eighteenth century or to Japanese or American children of the twentieth century. He thought that a child's intellectual and social skills would develop naturally without regard to the specific content of education. His content-neutral conception of educational development has long been triumphant in American schools of education and has long dominated the "developmental," content-neutral curricula of our elementary schools.

In the first decades of this century, Rousseau's ideas powerfully influ-   6
enced the educational conceptions of John Dewey, the writer who has the most deeply affected modern American educational theory and practice. Dewey's clearest and, in his time, most widely read book on education, *Schools of Tomorrow*, acknowledges Rousseau as the chief source of his educational principles. The first chapter of Dewey's book carries the telling title "Education as Natural Development" and is sprinkled with quotations from Rousseau. In it Dewey strongly seconds Rousseau's opposition to the mere accumulation of information.

> Development emphasizes the need of intimate and extensive personal acquaintance with a small number of typical situations with a view to mastering the way of dealing with the problems of experience, not the piling up of information.

Believing that a few direct experiences would suffice to develop the   7
skills that children require, Dewey assumed that early education need not be tied to specific content. He mistook a half-truth for the whole. He placed too much faith in children's ability to learn general skills from a few typical experiences and too hastily rejected "the piling up of information." Only by piling up specific, communally shared information can children learn to participate in complex cooperative activities with other members of their community.

This old truth, recently rediscovered, requires a countervailing the-   8
ory of education that once again stresses the importance of specific information in early and late schooling. The corrective theory might be described as an anthropological theory of education, because it is based on the anthropological observation that all human communities are founded upon specific shared information. Americans are different from Germans, who in turn are different from Japanese, because each group possesses specifically different cultural knowledge. In an anthropological perspective, the basic goal of education in a human community is acculturation, the transmission to children of the specific information shared by the adults of the group or polis.

Plato, that other great educational theorist, believed that the specific   9
contents transmitted to children are by far the most important elements of education. In *The Republic* he makes Socrates ask rhetorically, "Shall we carelessly allow children to hear any casual tales which may be devised by casual persons, and to receive into their minds ideas for the most part the very opposite of those which we shall wish them to have when they are grown up?" Plato offered good reasons for being concerned with the specific contents of schooling, one of them ethical: "For great is the issue at stake, greater than appears—whether a person is to be good or bad."

Time has shown that there is much truth in the durable educational *10* theories of both Rousseau and Plato. But even the greatest thinkers, being human, see mainly in one direction at a time, and no thinkers, however profound, can foresee the future implications of their ideas when they are translated into social policy. The great test of social ideas is the crucible of history, which, after a time, usually discloses a one-sidedness in the best of human generalizations. History, not superior wisdom, shows us that neither the content-neutral curriculum of Rousseau and Dewey nor the narrowly specified curriculum of Plato is adequate to the needs of a modern nation.

Plato rightly believed that it is natural for children to learn an adult *11* culture, but too confidently assumed that philosophy could devise the one best culture. (Nonetheless, we should concede to Plato that within our culture we have an obligation to choose and promote our best traditions.) On the other side, Rousseau and Dewey wrongly believed that adult culture is "unnatural" to young children. Rousseau, Dewey, and their present-day disciples have not shown an adequate appreciation of the need for transmission of specific cultural information.

In contrast to the theories of Plato and Rousseau, an anthropologi- *12* cal theory of education accepts the naturalness as well as the relativity of human cultures. It deems it neither wrong nor unnatural to teach young children adult information before they fully understand it. The anthropological view stresses the universal fact that a human group must have effective communications to function effectively, that effective communications require shared culture, and that shared culture requires transmission of specific information to children. Literacy, an essential aim of education in the modern world, is no autonomous, empty skill but depends upon literate culture. Like any other aspect of acculturation, literacy requires the early and continued transmission of specific information. Dewey was deeply mistaken to disdain "accumulating information in the form of symbols." Only by accumulating shared symbols, and the shared information that the symbols represent, can we learn to communicate effectively with one another in our national community.

Now let's take a look at the steps for doing a rhetorical analysis.

■ Identify the Situation

The **situation** is what moves a writer to write. To understand what motivated Hirsch to write, we need look no further than the situation he identifies in the first paragraph of the preface: "the social determinism that now condemns [disadvantaged children] to remain in the same social and educational condition as their parents." Hirsch wants to make sure his readers are aware of the problem so that they will be motivated to read his argument (and take action). He presents as an urgent problem the situation of disadvantaged children, an indication of what is at stake for the writer and for the readers of the argument. For Hirsch, this situation needs to change.

The urgency of a writer's argument is not always triggered by a single situation; often it is multifaceted. Again in the first paragraph, Hirsch identifies a second concern when he states that poverty and illiteracy reflect "an unacceptable failure of our schools, one which has occurred not because our teachers are inept but chiefly because they are compelled to teach a fragmented curriculum based on faulty educational theories." When he introduces a second problem, Hirsch helps us see the interconnected and complex nature of the situations authors confront in academic writing.

■ Identify the Writer's Purpose

The **purpose** for writing an essay may be to respond to a particular situation; it also can be what a writer is trying to accomplish. Specifically, what does the writer want readers to do? Does the writer want us to think about an issue, to change our opinions? Does the writer want to make us aware of a problem that we may not have recognized? Does the writer advocate for some type of change? Or is some combination of all three at work?

Hirsch's main purpose is to promote educational reforms that will produce a higher degree of literacy for all citizens. He begins his argument with a broad statement about the importance of cultural literacy: "Cultural literacy constitutes the only sure avenue of opportunity for disadvantaged children, the only reliable way of combating the social determinism that now condemns them to remain in the same social and educational condition as their parents" (para. 1). As his argument unfolds, his purpose continues to unfold as well. He identifies the schools as a source of the problem and suggests how they must change to promote literacy:

> Some say that our schools by themselves are powerless to change the cycle of poverty and illiteracy. I do not agree. They *can* break the cycle, but only if they themselves break fundamentally with some of the theories and practices that education professors and school administrators have followed over the past fifty years. (para. 1)

The "educational goal," Hirsch declares at the end of paragraph 2, is "mature literacy for *all* our citizens." To reach that goal, he insists, education must break with the past. In paragraphs 5 through 11, he cites the influence of Jean-Jacques Rousseau, John Dewey, and Plato, tracing what he sees as the educational legacies of the past. Finally, in the last paragraph of the excerpt, Hirsch describes an "anthropological view, . . . the universal fact that a human group must have effective communications to function effectively, that effective communications require shared culture, and that shared culture requires transmission of specific information to children." It is here, Hirsch argues, in the "transmission of specific information to children," that schools must do a better job.

■ Identify the Writer's Claims

Claims are assertions that authors must justify and support with evidence and good reasons. The **thesis**, or **main claim**, is the controlling idea that crystallizes a writer's main point, helping readers track the idea as it develops throughout the essay. A writer's purpose clearly influences the way he or she crafts the main claim of an argument, the way he or she presents all assertions and evidence.

Hirsch's main claim is that "cultural literacy constitutes the only sure avenue of opportunity for disadvantaged children, the only reliable way of combating the social determinism that now condemns them to remain in the same social and educational condition as their parents" (para. 1). Notice that his thesis also points to a solution: making cultural literacy the core of public school curricula. Here we distinguish the main claim, or thesis, from the other claims or assertions that Hirsch makes. For example, at the very outset, Hirsch states that "to be culturally literate is to possess the basic information needed to thrive in the modern world." Although this is an assertion that requires support, it is a **minor claim**; it does not shape what Hirsch writes in the remainder of his essay. His main claim, or thesis, is really his call for reform.

■ Identify the Writer's Audience

A writer's language can help us identify his or her **audience**, the readers whose opinions and actions the writer hopes to influence or change. In Hirsch's text, words and phrases like *social determinism, cycle of poverty and illiteracy, educational reforms, prescriptive,* and *anthropological* indicate that Hirsch believes his audience is well educated. References to Plato, Socrates, Rousseau, and Dewey also indicate the level of knowledge Hirsch expects of his readers.

Finally, the way the preface unfolds suggests that Hirsch is writing for an audience that is familiar with a certain **genre**, or type, of writing: the formal argument. Notice how the author begins with a statement of the situation and then asserts his position. The very fact that he includes a preface speaks to the formality of his argument. Hirsch's language, his references, and the structure of the document all suggest that he is very much in conversation with people who are experienced and well-educated readers.

More specifically, the audience Hirsch invokes is made up of people who are concerned about illiteracy in the United States and the kind of social determinism that appears to condemn the educationally disadvantaged to poverty. Hirsch also acknowledges directly "those who have closely followed recent discussions of education," including the conservative William Bennett and liberal thinkers who might be provoked by Bennett's advocacy of Hirsch's ideas (para. 3). Moreover, Hirsch appears to assume that his readers have achieved "mature literacy," even if they are not actually "culturally literate." He is writing for an audience that not only is well educated but also is deeply interested in issues of education as they relate to social policy.

Steps to Analyzing a Text Rhetorically

1. **Identify the situation.** What motivates the writer to write?

2. **Identify the writer's purpose.** What does the writer want readers to do or think about?

3. **Identify the writer's claims.** What is the writer's main claim? What minor claims does he or she make?

4. **Identify the writer's audience.** What do you know about the writer's audience? What does the writer's language imply about the readers? What about the writer's references? The structure of the essay?

Hirsch's writings on cultural literacy have inspired and provoked many responses to the conversation he initiated decades ago. Eugene F. Provenzo's book *Critical Literacy: What Every American Needs to Know*, published in 2005, is a fairly recent one. Provenzo examines the source of Hirsch's ideas, his critiques of scholars like John Dewey, the extent to which Hirsch's argument is based on sound research, and the implications of Hirsch's notion of cultural literacy for teaching and learning. Despite its age, Hirsch's book remains relevant in discussions about the purpose of education, demonstrating how certain works become touchstones and the ways academic and cultural conversations can be sustained over time.

A Practice Sequence: Analyzing a Text Rhetorically

To practice the strategies of rhetorical analysis, read "Hirsch's Desire for a National Curriculum," an excerpt from Eugene F. Provenzo's book, using these questions as a guide:

- What motivates Provenzo as a writer?
- What does he want readers to think about?

- What is Provenzo's main point?
- Given the language Provenzo uses, who do you think his main audience is?

EUGENE F. PROVENZO JR.

Hirsch's Desire for a National Curriculum

Eugene F. Provenzo Jr. is a professor in the Department of Teaching and Learning in the School of Education at the University of Miami in Coral Gables, Florida. His career as a researcher has been interdisciplinary in nature. Throughout his work, his primary focus has been on education as a social and cultural phenomenon. One of his prime concerns has been the role of the teacher in American society. He is also interested in the impact of computers on contemporary children, education, and culture. He is author or coauthor of numerous books, including *Teaching, Learning, and Schooling: A Twenty-First Century Perspective* (2001); *Internet and Online Research for Teachers* (Third Edition, 2004); and *Observing in Schools: A Guide for Students in Teacher Education* (2005).

■ ■ ■

To a large extent, Hirsch, in his efforts as an educational reformer, wants to establish a national curriculum.

> Our elementary schools are not only dominated by the content-neutral ideas of Rousseau and Dewey, they are also governed by approximately sixteen thousand independent school districts. We have viewed this dispersion of educational authority as an insurmountable obstacle to altering the fragmentation of the school curriculum even when we have questioned that fragmentation. We have permitted school policies that have shrunk the body of information that Americans share and these policies have caused our national literacy to decline.

This is an interesting argument when interpreted in a conservative political context. While calling for greater local control, Hirsch and other conservatives call for a curriculum that is controlled not at the state and local level, but at the national level by the federal government.

Putting contradictions like this aside, the question arises as to whether or not Hirsch even has a viable curriculum. In an early review of Hirsch's *Cultural Literacy*, Hazel Whitman Hertzberg criticized the book and its list of 5,000 things every American needs to know for its fragmentation. As she explained:

Hirsch's remedy for curricular fragmentation looks suspiciously like more fragmentation. Outside of the dubious claim that his list represents what literate people know, there is nothing that holds it together besides its arrangement in alphabetical order. Subject-matter organization is ignored. It is not hard to imagine how Hirsch's proposal would have been greeted by educational neoconservatives had it been made by one of those professors of education who he charges are responsible for the current state of cultural illiteracy.

Hertzberg wonders what Hirsch's "hodgepodge of miscellaneous, arbitrary, and often trivial information" would look like if it were put into a coherent curriculum.

In 1988 Hirsch did in fact establish the Core Knowledge Foundation, which had as its purpose the design of a national curriculum. Called the "Core Knowledge Sequence," the sequence offered a curriculum in six content areas: history, geography, mathematics, science, language arts, and fine arts. Hirsch's curriculum was intended to represent approximately half of the total curriculum for K–6 schools. Subsequent curriculum revisions include a curriculum for grades seven and eight as well as one at the preschool level.   3

Several hundred schools across the United States currently use Hirsch's model. A national conference is held each year, which draws several thousand people. In books like *What Your First Grader Needs to Know* (1991) as well as *A First Dictionary of Cultural Literacy: What Our Children Need to Know* (1989) and *The Dictionary of Cultural Literacy* (1993), along with the Core Knowledge Sequence, one finds a fairly conservative but generally useful curriculum that conforms to much of the content already found in local school systems around the country.   4

Hirsch seems not to recognize that there indeed is a national curriculum, one whose standards are set by local communities through their acceptance and rejection of textbooks and by national accreditation groups ranging from the National Council of Teachers of Mathematics to the National Council for Social Studies Teachers and the National Council of Teachers of English. One need only look at standards in different subject areas in school districts across the country to realize the extent to which there is indeed a national curriculum.   5

Whether the current curriculum in use in the schools across the country is adequate is of course open to debate. Creating any curriculum is by definition a deeply political act, and is, or should be, subject to considerable negotiation and discussion at any level. But to act as though there is not a de facto national curriculum is simply inaccurate. First graders in most school districts across the country learn about   6 the weather and the seasons, along with more basic skills like adding and subtracting. Students do not learn to divide before they learn how to add or multiply. Local and state history is almost universally introduced for the first time in either third or fourth grade. It is reintroduced in most states at the seventh or eighth grade levels. Algebra is typically taught in the ninth grade. Traditions, developmental patterns of students, textbook content, and national subject standards combine to create a fairly uniform national curriculum.

Hirsch's complaint that there is no national curriculum is not 7 motivated by a desire to establish one but rather a desire to establish a curriculum that reflects his cultural and ideological orientation. It is a sophisticated assault on more inclusive and diverse models of curriculum and culture—one that represents a major battle in the culture wars of the last twenty years in the United States.

WRITING AS A READER: COMPOSING A RHETORICAL ANALYSIS

One of our favorite exercises is to ask students to choose a single paragraph or a brief section from a text they have read and to write a rhetorical analysis. We first ask our students to identify the writer's key claims and ideas to orient them to the main points they want to make in their analysis. We then ask our students to consider such features as the situation that calls for a response in writing and the writer's purpose, intended audience, kinds of claims, and types of evidence. In their rhetorical analyses, we encourage our students to analyze the ways writers develop their ideas and the extent to which these strategies succeed. That is, we ask our students to consider how writers express their ideas, develop their points of view, respond to a given situation, and use evidence to persuade readers. Once you are able to identify *how* writers make arguments, look critically at what works and what doesn't in making a persuasive argument; then you will be able to make use of their strategies in your own writing.

For example, one of our students wrote a rhetorical analysis of an excerpt from David Tyack's book on education, *Seeking Common Ground: Public Schools in a Diverse Society* (2004). In his book, Tyack examines the extent to which the purpose of education in American schools has developed out of and reflected the political, economic, and moral concerns of the nation. His analysis begins with the emergence of public schools in the nineteenth century and demonstrates a sense of continuity in twenty-first-century education, particularly in light of contemporary debates around national standards, teacher evaluation, social justice, equity, civic engagement, and the common good. This continuity is best represented in the quest for a common denominator of political and moral truths, often evidenced in textbooks that point to the progress of history and American democracy, the focus on great men who understood the grandeur of America's destiny, and the importance of individual character in building a strong nation founded on shared values. For Tyack, history textbooks have served as a significant source of civic education—that is, "what adults thought children should learn about the past"—and assimilation. However, the search for common values in official histories (what he calls "stone monuments") has not been without dissent, given their focus on white, male, Protestant ideology. Tyack also writes about the ways in which educators have dealt with questions of social and educational diversity, particularly race, immigration and ethnicity, and gender; efforts to establish models of educational governance to meet the needs of a pluralistic society; and the implications of opening public education to a free market.

Note that in the following passage, Tyack assesses the state of American history textbooks by citing a number of writers, sometimes generally and at other times more specifically, to address ways to solve the problems he identifies (for example, Patricia Nelson Limerick's proposal for a "pluralistic model of history").

As you read the Tyack passage, take notes on the rhetorical situation, purpose, main claim, audience, and language. You may want to underline passages or circle words and phrases where the writer makes the following points explicit:

- the situation that motivates his writing,
- the purpose of his analysis and argument,
- his main claim or thesis, and
- who he believes his audience is.

DAVID TYACK

Whither History Textbooks?

David Tyack was the Vida Jacks Professor of Education and Professor of History, Emeritus, at Stanford University. In addition to writing *Seeking Common Ground*, he authored *The One Best System: A History of American Urban Education* (1974) and coauthored *Tinkering Toward Utopia: A Century of Public School Reform* (1997), *Law and the Shaping of Public Education, 1785–1954* (1991), *Learning Together: A History of Coeducation in American Public Schools* (1992), and *Public Schools in Hard Times: The Great Depression and Recent Years* (1984).

A history textbook today is hardly the republican catechism that Noah Webster appended to his famous speller. It is more like pieces of a sprawling novel with diverse characters and fascinating subplots waiting for an author to weave them into a broader narrative. Now a noisy confusion reigns about what stories the textbooks should tell. Special-interest groups of the right and left pressure publishers to include or drop topics, especially in big states such as California or Texas. Worries abound about old truths betrayed and new truths ignored. Many groups want to vet or veto what children learn, and it is unclear what roles teachers, parents, ethnic groups, religious activists, historians, and others should play. Tempers rise. In New York debates over a multicultural curriculum, Catherine Cornbleth and Dexter Waugh observed, "both sides engaged in a rhetoric of crisis, doom, and salvation."

In the United States, unlike most other nations, private agencies — publishing companies — create and sell textbooks. Thus commerce plays an important part in deciding which historical truths shall be official. To be sure, public agencies usually decide which textbooks to adopt (about half of the states delegate text adoption to local districts, and the rest use some form of state adoption). For all the conventionality of the product, the actual production and sale of textbooks is still a risky business. It's very expensive to create and print textbooks, and the market (the various agencies that actually decide which to adopt) is somewhat unpredictable. In addition, at any time some citizens are likely to protest whatever messages the texts send. Textbook adoption can be a free-for-all.

Thus it is not surprising that textbooks still beget textbooks. To control risk, companies find it wise to copy successes. Old icons (Washington) remain, but publishers respond to new demands by multiplying new state-approved truths. It has been easier to add those ubiquitous sidebars to the master narrative than to rethink it, easier to incorporate new content into a safe and profitable formula than to create new accounts. American history textbooks are enormous — 888 pages, on average — in part because publishers seek to neutralize or anticipate criticisms by adding topics. The result is often not comprehensive coverage but a bloated book devoid of style or coherence.

The traditional American fear of centralized power, salient today in debates over national standards and tests, has resulted in a strange patchwork of agencies and associations — textbook companies, state and local governments, lobby groups of many persuasions, individuals who want to play Grand Inquisitor — to choose and monitor the public truths taught in the texts. One of the most rapid ways of changing what students learn in American schools is to transform the textbooks, but the present Rube Goldberg system of creating and selecting textbooks makes such a change very difficult (though fine history textbooks have on occasion appeared).

What are some strategies to cope with the cross-cutting demands on history textbooks? Three possible ones are these: muddling through with modest improvements; turning over the task of writing textbooks to experts; or devising texts that depart from the model of state-approved truths and embrace instead the taking of multiple perspectives. Each of these has some advantages and faults that are worth contemplating. *5*

Muddling through may seem sensible to people who believe that there is a vast gap between superheated policy talk about the defects of textbooks and the everyday reality teachers face in classrooms. Is all the debate over bad textbooks a dust-devil masquerading as a tornado? For many teachers, the big challenge is to prepare students for high-stakes tests they must take for graduation, and textbooks are a key resource in that task. *6*

Teachers tend to find the status quo in textbooks more bearable than do the critics. When a sample of classroom teachers was asked their opinion of the textbooks they used, they generally said that the books are good and getting better. Teachers rely heavily on textbooks in their instruction, employing them for about 70 percent of class time. *7*

A commonsense argument for muddling through, with gradual improvement of textbooks, is that pedagogical reforms rarely work well if they are imposed on teachers. Study after study has shown that teachers tend to avoid controversy in teaching American history (indeed, being "nonpartisan" is still judged a virtue, as it was in the past). And parents and school board members, like teachers, have their own ideas about what is "real history." Too sharp a turn in the historical highway might topple reform. So some teachers argue that the best way to improve education is to keep the old icons and welcome the newcomers in the textbooks. And hope that the students in fact *do read* the textbooks! Common sense—that's the way to cope amid all the confusion. *8*

An alternate approach to reform of textbooks is to set good state or local standards for history courses and turn the writing of textbooks over to experts—an approach used in many nations and sometimes advocated in the United States today. Muddling through just maintains the status quo and guarantees incoherence in textbooks and hence in learning. In the current politics and commerce of text publishing, "truth" becomes whatever the special interests (left or right) pressure textbook companies to say. Current textbooks are often victims of commercial timidity, veto groups, and elephantiasis (888 pages!). *9*

What is missing, proponents of this view argue, is a clear set of national standards about what students should know and a vivid and cogent text that engages students in learning. Those who call for *10* expertise suggest that history is too important *not* to be left to the historians.

But this response to the faults of history texts presents its own problems. Calling in the experts doesn't eliminate disputes; PhDs love to differ among themselves. Teachers are adept at sabotaging reforms dropped on them from above. And amid all the commercialism and special interests now rife in the process of selecting textbooks, the public still deserves some say in deciding what American students learn about the past, expert or not. *11*

Patricia Nelson Limerick, professor of history at the University of Colorado, suggests a pluralistic model of history that contrasts with both muddling through and textbooks by experts. She recently suggested that the Little Bighorn Battlefield, where Sioux and Cheyenne fought George Armstrong Custer, needed not two monuments, one in honor of the Indians and one to recognize Custer and his soldiers, but "a different kind of memorial—one in which no point of view dominates." She imagines visitors walking among memorials to the warriors and Custer, but also to the enlisted men dragooned into the slaughter, to Custer's widow, to the families of the white soldiers, and to the children and wives of the Indian warriors. *12*

Such perspective-taking lies at the core of historical understanding of a socially diverse nation. Pluralistic history can enhance ethnic self-respect and empathy for other groups. Parallel to the monuments Limerick proposes, texts for a pluralistic civic education might have not one master narrative but several, capturing separate identities and experiences. *13*

But the history of Americans in their separate groups would be partial without looking as well at their lives in interaction. Our society is pluralistic in character, and so should be the history we teach to young citizens. But alongside that *pluribus* citizens have also sought an *unum*, a set of shared political aspirations and institutions. One reason there have been so many textbook wars is that group after group has, in turn, sought to become part of a common story told about our past. The *unum* and the *pluribus* have been in inescapable tension, constantly evolving as Americans struggled to find common ground and to respect their differences. *14*

AN ANNOTATED STUDENT RHETORICAL ANALYSIS

Now read our student's rhetorical analysis about David Tyack's discussion of history textbooks in "Whither History Textbooks?" We have annotated the student's analysis to point out how he identifies the author's situation, purpose, argument, and audience.

Collie 1

Quentin Collie

A Rhetorical Analysis of
"Whither History Textbooks?"

In my analysis, I will focus on "Whither History Textbooks?"
which serves as a conclusion to David Tyack's chapter on American
history textbooks in his book *Seeking Common Ground*. In this
section, Tyack explains the state of history textbooks in American
schools today, the causes and influences that result in what he sees
as a problem with trying to cover too many topics without much
depth, and possible ways in which history textbooks can be changed
and improved. In advocating for a pluralistic account of history,
Tyack use specific words and phrases that convey his impatience
with American history textbooks and presents a number of options
to make his discussion appear fair.

Tyack points out that today's textbooks are, for the most
part, bulky and disjointed. Many storylines and historic figures
are pieced together without any all-encompassing narrative flow
or style. Textbooks have come to take this form because of two
significant influences. On one hand, nearly every interest group
argues for certain events, figures, or issues to be included in the
history curriculum. On the other hand, in a more economical sense,
textbooks that present the traditional and generic American narrative
have been the most successful. As a result, textbook authors and
producers attempt to intersperse the variety of new pieces into the
original American narrative. This results in the heavy and boring
textbooks that students use in the classroom today. Tyack offers
three possibilities for how to navigate through the demands and
difficulties involved in history textbook production: continuing the
use of current textbooks with moderate additions and improvements,
delegating the writing of textbooks to experts, and embracing a new
style of textbook which emphasizes the multiple perspectives of
Americans.

In this particular section of the book, Tyack's purpose seems
to be a call for change. In describing the current types of textbooks,
he implies his personal stance through his word choice. Tyack's
use of vivid imagery throughout this part of his book allows him to
delve into the textbook problem by appealing to the emotions of

The student provides an overview of the author's argument.

The student explains the author's argument in more detail and, specifically, the source of what the author sees as a problem in teaching history. This is the situation that calls for some response in writing: that textbooks have become "heavy" and "boring." The student then describes three possible approaches that the author takes to address the problem he identifies in teaching history in school.

1

2

3

Collie 2

The student underscores the author's purpose. He then shows how language reflects the author's point of view. In addition, the student helps us see that the situation the author responds to is not only about how textbooks are written, but how educators choose to adopt textbooks.

the reader. For instance, Tyack explains that the average American history textbook is 888 pages long and laments this length as the reason that most of today's history books are "bloated" and "devoid of style or coherence" (para. 3). He also alludes to anarchy when he claims that "textbook adoption can be a free-for-all" (para. 2), establishing his skeptical perspective on the decision processes of textbook writers as well as of those who buy them. Another way Tyack explains his views on the methodology behind buying and selling textbooks is through an allusion to a "Rube Goldberg system" (para. 4) in his description of how textbooks are created and sold. This reference implies that our current method has become unnecessarily complex and has rendered making changes in history textbooks difficult or impossible.

He points out the author's strategy for developing the argument, one that forces knowledgeable readers to draw their own conclusions.

Tyack does not advocate for just any change, but, rather, a particular change and ideal type of textbook. He does not make an outright statement of support for a particular plan. Instead, he presents an examination of possibilities that leads the audience to decide which one option is superior. The possibilities include using the same format with slight changes, having experts write the textbooks, and departing from the regular model of textbooks to include new truths and multiple perspectives. He makes a point to state that each option has both pros and cons to be considered.

4

The student points to the author's concession that not everyone agrees that the quality of textbook writing is a problem. The student again demonstrates how word choice conveys an author's point of view and that the author does not find this first solution tenable.

Tyack writes that teachers, in general, do not have a large problem with the current types of textbooks, and pedagogical reforms rarely work if imposed on teachers. This evidence argues in favor of using the same types of textbooks. The discussion of this particular option, however, ends with its success resting on a "hope that the students in fact *do read* the textbooks!" (para. 8). This statement carries a tone of sarcasm, leaving the reader with a feeling that Tyack believes that students will not read this type of textbook, so this particular plan of action is not likely to improve the schools. In addition, Tyack's exact phrasing for this possibility is "muddling through with modest improvements" (para. 5). From word choice alone, the reader can see that Tyack discredits this idea. The verb *muddle* is associated with things being confused, messed up, and unclear, so his choice of this word implies that he thinks using the current format for textbooks results in teachers and students having

5

Collie 3

a confused and incorrect view of American history. Eventually, he concludes that "muddling through just maintains the status quo and guarantees incoherence in textbooks and hence learning" (para. 9).

He presents the author's second possible solution to the problem but explains why the author is not sympathetic to that position.

His next suggested approach is using textbooks written by experts. This option could set clear national standards about what students should be learning about history by those most informed. This option, however, also has its faults as Tyack argues that the experts differ in their opinions. Furthermore, the public does deserve some input about material to be taught to its children, which this option would take away.

Although it would seem that the author lets readers draw their own conclusions, the student explains how Tyack uses research to give credence to this last solution to the problem.

Tyack's final option is "a pluralistic model of history that contrasts with both muddling through and textbooks by experts" (para. 12). Tyack argues that "such perspective-taking lies at the core of historical understanding of a socially diverse nation. Pluralistic history can enhance ethnic self-respect and empathy for other groups" (para. 13). Tyack supports this point of view with quotations from a professor of history, which gives credibility to this option. In addition, Tyack does not discuss any possible difficulties in pursuing this type of textbook, even though he stated earlier that each option has both benefits and faults. In this, Tyack appears to be considering multiple possibilities for textbook reform, but, at the same time, he dismisses two of the options and advocates for a particular course of action through his writing strategy.

6

7

WRITING A RHETORICAL ANALYSIS

By now you should have a strong sense of what is involved in rhetorical analysis. You should be ready to take the next steps: performing a rhetorical analysis of your own and then sharing your analysis and the strategies you've learned with your classmates.

Read the next text, "The Flight from Conversation" by Sherry Turkle, annotating it to help you identify her situation, purpose, thesis, and audience. As you read, also make a separate set of annotations — possibly with a different color pen or pencil, circled, or keyed with asterisks — in which you comment on or evaluate the effectiveness of her essay. What do you like or dislike about it? Why? Does Turkle persuade you to accept her point of view? What impressions do you have of her as a person? Would you like to be in a conversation with her?

SHERRY TURKLE

The Flight from Conversation

Sherry Turkle—the Abby Rockefeller Mauzé Professor of the Social Studies of Science and Technology in the Program in Science, Technology, and Society at the Massachusetts Institute of Technology—is a licensed clinical psychologist with a joint doctorate in sociology and personality psychology from Harvard University. Director of the MIT Initiative on Technology and Self, she is the author or editor of many books, including *The Second Self: Computers and the Human Spirit* (1984), *Life on the Screen: Identity in the Age of the Internet* (1995), *Simulation and Its Discontents* (2009), and *Alone Together: Why We Expect More from Technology and Less from Each Other* (2011). "The Flight from Conversation" appeared in the April 12, 2012, issue of *The New York Times Magazine*.

We live in a technological universe in which we are always communicating. And yet we have sacrificed conversation for mere connection.

At home, families sit together, texting and reading e-mail. At work executives text during board meetings. We text (and shop and go on Facebook) during classes and when we're on dates. My students tell me about an important new skill: It involves maintaining eye contact with someone while you text someone else; it's hard, but it can be done.

Over the past fifteen years, I've studied technologies of mobile connection and talked to hundreds of people of all ages and circumstances about their plugged-in lives. I've learned that the little devices most of us carry around are so powerful that they change not only what we do, but also who we are.

We've become accustomed to a new way of being "alone together." Technology-enabled, we are able to be with one another, and also elsewhere, connected to wherever we want to be. We want to customize our lives. We want to move in and out of where we are because the thing we value most is control over where we focus our attention. We have gotten used to the idea of being in a tribe of one, loyal to our own party.

Our colleagues want to go to that board meeting but pay attention only to what interests them. To some this seems like a good idea, but we can end up hiding from one another, even as we are constantly connected to one another.

A businessman laments that he no longer has colleagues at work. He doesn't stop by to talk; he doesn't call. He says that he doesn't want to interrupt them. He says they're "too busy on their e-mail." But then he pauses and corrects himself. "I'm not telling the truth. I'm the one who doesn't want to be interrupted. I think I should. But I'd rather just do things on my BlackBerry."

A 16-year-old boy who relies on texting for almost everything says almost wistfully, "Someday, someday, but certainly not now, I'd like to learn how to have a conversation." 7

In today's workplace, young people who have grown up fearing conversation show up on the job wearing earphones. Walking through a college library or the campus of a high-tech start-up, one sees the same thing: We are together, but each of us is in our own bubble, furiously connected to keyboards and tiny touch screens. A senior partner at a Boston law firm describes a scene in his office. Young associates lay out their suite of technologies: laptops, iPods, and multiple phones. And then they put their earphones on. "Big ones. Like pilots. They turn their desks into cockpits." With the young lawyers in their cockpits, the office is quiet, a quiet that does not ask to be broken. 8

In the silence of connection, people are comforted by being in touch with a lot of people—carefully kept at bay. We can't get enough of one another if we can use technology to keep one another at distances we can control: not too close, not too far, just right. I think of it as a Goldilocks effect. 9

Texting and e-mail and posting let us present the self we want to be. This means we can edit. And if we wish to, we can delete. Or retouch: the voice, the flesh, the face, the body. Not too much, not too little—just right. 10

Human relationships are rich; they're messy and demanding. We have learned the habit of cleaning them up with technology. And the move from conversation to connection is part of this. But it's a process in which we shortchange ourselves. Worse, it seems that over time we stop caring, we forget that there is a difference. 11

We are tempted to think that our little "sips" of online connection add up to a big gulp of real conversation. But they don't. E-mail, Twitter, Facebook, all of these have their places—in politics, commerce, romance, and friendship. But no matter how valuable, they do not substitute for conversation. 12

Connecting in sips may work for gathering discrete bits of information or for saying, "I am thinking about you." Or even for saying, "I love you." But connecting in sips doesn't work as well when it comes to understanding and knowing one another. In conversation we tend to one another. (The word itself is kinetic; it's derived from words that mean to move, together.) We can attend to tone and nuance. In conversation, we are called upon to see things from another's point of view. 13

Face-to-face conversation unfolds slowly. It teaches patience. When we communicate on our digital devices, we learn different habits. As we ramp up the volume and velocity of online connections, we start to 14 expect faster answers. To get these, we ask one another simpler questions; we dumb down our communications, even on the most important matters. It is as though we have all put ourselves on cable news. Shakespeare might have said, "We are consum'd with that which we were nourish'd by."

And we use conversation with others to learn to converse with ourselves. So our flight from conversation can mean diminished chances to learn skills of self-reflection. These days, social media continually asks us what's "on our mind," but we have little motivation to say something truly self-reflective. Self-reflection in conversation requires trust. It's hard to do anything with 3,000 Facebook friends except connect.

As we get used to being shortchanged on conversation and to getting by with less, we seem almost willing to dispense with people altogether. Serious people muse about the future of computer programs as psychiatrists. A high school sophomore confides to me that he wishes he could talk to an artificial intelligence program instead of his dad about dating; he says the AI would have so much more in its database. Indeed, many people tell me they hope that as Siri, the digital assistant on Apple's iPhone, becomes more advanced, "she" will be more and more like a best friend—one who will listen when others won't.

During the years I have spent researching people and their relationships with technology, I have often heard the sentiment "No one is listening to me." I believe this feeling helps explain why it is so appealing to have a Facebook page or a Twitter feed—each provides so many automatic listeners. And it helps explain why—against all reason—so many of us are willing to talk to machines that seem to care about us. Researchers around the world are busy inventing sociable robots, designed to be companions to the elderly, to children, to all of us.

One of the most haunting experiences during my research came when I brought one of these robots, designed in the shape of a baby seal, to an elder-care facility, and an older woman began to talk to it about the loss of her child. The robot seemed to be looking into her eyes. It seemed to be following the conversation. The woman was comforted.

And so many people found this amazing. Like the sophomore who wants advice about dating from artificial intelligence and those who look forward to computer psychiatry, this enthusiasm speaks to how much we have confused conversation with connection and collectively seem to have embraced a new kind of delusion that accepts the simulation of compassion as sufficient unto the day. And why would we want to talk about love and loss with a machine that has no experience of the arc of human life? Have we so lost confidence that we will be there for one another?

We expect more from technology and less from one another, and seem increasingly drawn to technologies that provide the illusion of companionship without the demands of relationship. Always-on/ always-on-you devices provide three powerful fantasies: that we will always be heard; that we can put our attention wherever we want it to be; and that we never have to be alone. Indeed our new devices have turned being alone into a problem that can be solved.

When people are alone, even for a few moments, they fidget and   *21* reach for a device. Here connection works like a symptom, not a cure, and our constant, reflexive impulse to connect shapes a new way of being.

Think of it as "I share, therefore I am." We use technology to define   *22* ourselves by sharing our thoughts and feelings as we're having them. We used to think, "I have a feeling; I want to make a call." Now our impulse is, "I want to have a feeling; I need to send a text."

So, in order to feel more, and to feel more like ourselves, we connect.   *23* But in our rush to connect, we flee from solitude, our ability to be separate and gather ourselves. Lacking the capacity for solitude, we turn to other people but don't experience them as they are. It is as though we use them, need them as spare parts to support our increasingly fragile selves.

We think constant connection will make us feel less lonely. The oppo-   *24* site is true. If we are unable to be alone, we are far more likely to be lonely. If we don't teach our children to be alone, they will know only how to be lonely.

I am a partisan for conversation. To make room for it, I see some first,   *25* deliberate steps. At home, we can create sacred spaces: the kitchen, the dining room. We can make our cars "device-free zones." We can demonstrate the value of conversation to our children. And we can do the same thing at work. There we are so busy communicating that we often don't have time to talk to one another about what really matters. Employees asked for casual Fridays; perhaps managers should introduce conversational Thursdays. Most of all, we need to remember—in between texts and e-mails and Facebook posts—to listen to one another, even to the boring bits, because it is often in unedited moments, moments in which we hesitate and stutter and go silent, that we reveal ourselves to one another.

I spend the summers at a cottage on Cape Cod, and for decades I   *26* walked the same dunes that Thoreau once walked. Not too long ago, people walked with their heads up, looking at the water, the sky, the sand and at one another, talking. Now they often walk with their heads down, typing. Even when they are with friends, partners, children, everyone is on their own devices.

So I say, look up, look at one another, and let's start the conversation.   *27*

A Practice Sequence: Writing a Rhetorical Analysis

1   Write a brief rhetorical analysis of Sherry Turkle's essay, referring to your notes and citing passages where she indicates her situation, purpose, main claim, and audience.

2   An option for group work: As a class, divide into three or more groups. Groups should answer the following questions in response to Turkle's essay:

> *Group 1*: Identify the situation(s) motivating Turkle to write. Then evaluate: How well does her argument function as a conversation with other authors who have written on the same topic?

> *Group 2*: Analyze the audience's identity, perspectives, and conventional expectations. Then evaluate: How well does the argument function as a conversation with the audience?

> *Group 3*: Analyze the writer's purpose. Then evaluate: Do you believe Turkle achieves her purpose in this essay? Why or why not?

Then, as a class, share your observations:

- To what extent does the author's ability as a conversationalist— that is, her ability to enter into a conversation with other authors and her audience—affect your evaluation of whether she achieves her purpose in this essay?

- If you were to meet this writer, what suggestions or advice would you give her for making her argument more persuasive?

3

From Writing Summaries and Paraphrases to Writing Yourself into Academic Conversations

Reading like a writer and writing like a reader help you understand how texts work rhetorically. When you start to use those texts to build your own arguments, there are certain strategies for working with the words and ideas of others that you will have to learn. Often you can quote the words of an author directly; but just as often you will restate (paraphrase) and condense (summarize) the arguments of others to educate your reader about the issues in a particular academic conversation. Indeed, many academic essays begin with a **literature review**—a roundup that summarizes important arguments and perspectives in such a conversation—as a prelude to the writer setting forth his or her own arguments on an issue. In this chapter, we will present methods of paraphrase and summary. Learning to paraphrase and summarize helps you understand texts and convey that understanding to other participants in the conversation.

SUMMARIES, PARAPHRASES, AND QUOTATIONS

In contrast to quotations, which involve using another writer's exact words, paraphrases and summaries are both restatements of another writer's ideas in your own words, but they differ in length and scope:

- A paraphrase is frequently about the same length as the original passage.

- A summary generally condenses a significantly longer text, conveying the argument not only of a few sentences but also of entire paragraphs, essays, or books.

In your own writing, you might paraphrase a few sentences or even a few paragraphs, but you certainly would not paraphrase a whole essay (much less a whole book). In constructing your arguments, however, you will often have to summarize the main points of the lengthy texts with which you are in conversation.

Both paraphrasing and summarizing are means to inquiry. That is, the act of recasting someone else's words or ideas into your own language, to suit your argument and reach your readers, forces you to think critically: What does this passage really mean? What is most important about it for my argument? How can I best present it to my readers? It requires making choices, not least of which is determining the best way to present the information—through paraphrase, summary, or direct quotation. In general, the following rules apply:

- *Paraphrase* when all the information in the passage is important, but the language is not key to your discussion, or if it may be difficult for your readers to understand.

- *Summarize* when you need to present only the key ideas of a passage (or an essay or a book) to advance your argument.

- *Quote* when the passage is so effective—so clear, so concise, so authoritative, so memorable—that you would be hard-pressed to improve on it.

WRITING A PARAPHRASE

A **paraphrase** is a restatement of all the information in a passage in your own words, using your own sentence structure and composed with your own audience in mind to advance your argument.

- When you paraphrase a passage, start by identifying key words and phrases, and think of other ways to state them. You may have to reread what led up to the passage to remind yourself of the context. For example, did the writer define terms earlier that he or she uses in the passage and now expects you to know?

- Continue by experimenting with word order and sentence structure, combining and recombining phrases to convey what the writer says without replicating his or her style. As you consider how best to state the writer's idea in your own words, you should come to a much better understanding of what the writer is saying. By thinking critically, then, you are clarifying the passage for yourself as much as for your readers.

Let's look at a paraphrase of a passage from science fiction writer and scholar James Gunn's essay "Harry Potter as Schooldays Novel"*:

ORIGINAL PASSAGE

The situation and portrayal of Harry as an ordinary child with an extraordinary talent make him interesting. He elicits our sympathy at every turn. He plays a Cinderella-like role as the abused child of mean-spirited foster parents who favor other, less-worthy children, and also fits another fantasy role, that of changeling. Millions of children have nursed the notion that they cannot be the offspring of such unremarkable parents; in the Harry Potter books, the metaphor is often literal truth.

PARAPHRASE

According to James Gunn, the circumstances and depiction of Harry Potter as a normal boy with special abilities captivate us by playing on our empathy. Gunn observes that, like Cinderella, Harry is scorned by his guardians, who treat him far worse than they treat his less-admirable peers. And like another fairy-tale figure, the changeling, Harry embodies the fantasies of children who refuse to believe that they were born of their undistinguished parents (146).

In this paraphrase, the writer uses his own words to express key terms (*circumstances and depiction* for "situation and portrayal," *guardians* for "foster parents") and rearranges the structure of the original sentences. But the paraphrase is about the same length as the original and says essentially the same things as Gunn's original.

Now, compare the paraphrase with this summary:

SUMMARY

James Gunn observes that Harry Potter's character is compelling because readers empathize with Harry's fairy tale–like plight as an orphan whose gifts are ignored by his foster parents (146).

The summary condenses the passage, conveying Gunn's main point without restating the details. Notice how both the paraphrase and the summary indicate that the ideas are James Gunn's, not the writer's — "According to James Gunn," "James Gunn observes" — and signal, with page references, where Gunn's ideas end. *It is essential that you acknowledge your sources*, a subject we come back to in our discussion of plagiarism on page 228. The

---

*Gunn's essay appears in *Mapping the World of Harry Potter: An Unauthorized Exploration of the Bestselling Fantasy Series of All Time*, edited by Mercedes Lackey (Dallas: BenBella, 2006).

point we want to make here is that borrowing from the work of others is not always intentional. Many students stumble into plagiarism, especially when they are attempting to paraphrase. Remember that it's not enough to change the words in a paraphrase; you must also change the structure of the sentences and cite your source.

You may be wondering: "If paraphrasing is so tricky, why bother? What does it add? I can see how the summary of Gunn's paragraph presents information more concisely and efficiently than the original, but the paraphrase doesn't seem to be all that different from the source and doesn't seem to add anything to it. Why not simply quote the original or summarize it?"

Good questions. The answer is that you paraphrase when the ideas in a passage are important but the language is not key to your discussion or it may be difficult for readers to understand. When academics write for their peers, they draw on the specialized vocabulary of their disciplines to make their arguments. By paraphrasing, you may be helping your readers, providing a translation of sorts for those who do not speak the language.

Consider this paragraph by George Lipsitz from his academic book *Time Passages: Collective Memory and American Popular Culture* (1990), and compare the paraphrase that follows it:

ORIGINAL PASSAGE

The transformations in behavior and collective memory fueled by the contradictions of the nineteenth century have passed through three major stages in the United States. The first involved the establishment and codification of commercialized leisure from the invention of the telegraph to the 1890s. The second involved the transition from Victorian to consumer-hedonist values between 1890 and 1945. The third and most important stage, from World War II to the present, involved extraordinary expansion in both the distribution of consumer purchasing power and in both the reach and scope of electronic mass media. The dislocations of urban renewal, suburbanization, and deindustrialization accelerated the demise of tradition in America, while the worldwide pace of change undermined stability elsewhere. The period from World War II to the present marks the final triumph of commercialized leisure, and with it an augmented crisis over the loss of connection to the past.

PARAPHRASE

Historian George Lipsitz argues that Americans' sense of the past is rooted in cultural changes dating from the 1800s and has evolved through three stages. In the first stage, technological innovations of the nineteenth century gave rise to widespread commercial entertainment. In the second stage, dating from the 1890s to about 1945, attitudes toward the consumption of goods and services changed. Since 1945, in the third stage, increased consumer spending and the growth of the mass media have led to a crisis in which Americans find themselves cut off from their traditions and the memories that give meaning to them (12).

Notice that the paraphrase is not a word-for-word translation of the original. Instead, the writer has made choices that resulted in a slightly briefer and more accessible restatement of Lipsitz's thinking. (Although this paraphrase is shorter than the original passage, a paraphrase can also be a little longer than the original if extra words are needed to help readers understand the original.)

Notice too that several specialized terms and phrases from the original passage—the "codification of commercialized leisure," "the transition from Victorian to consumer-hedonist values," "the dislocations of urban renewal, suburbanization, and deindustrialization"—have disappeared. The writer not only looked up these terms and phrases in the dictionary but also reread the several pages that preceded the original passage to understand what Lipsitz meant by them.

The paraphrase is not meant to be an improvement on the original passage—in fact, historians would most likely prefer what Lipsitz wrote—but it may help readers who do not share Lipsitz's expertise understand his point without distorting his argument.

Now compare this summary to the paraphrase:

SUMMARY

Historian George Lipsitz argues that technological, social, and economic changes dating from the nineteenth century have culminated in what he calls a "crisis over the loss of connection to the past," in which Americans find themselves cut off from the memories of their traditions (12).

Which is better, the paraphrase or the summary? Neither is better or worse in and of itself. Their correctness and appropriateness depend on how the restatements are used in a given argument. That is, the decision to paraphrase or summarize depends entirely on the information you need to convey. Would the details in the paraphrase strengthen your argument? Or is a summary sufficient? In this case, if you plan to focus your argument on the causes of America's loss of cultural memory (the rise of commercial entertainment, changes in spending habits, globalization), then a paraphrase might be more helpful. But if you plan to define *loss of cultural memory*, then a summary may provide enough context for the next stage of your argument.

Steps to Writing a Paraphrase

1 **Decide whether to paraphrase.** If your readers don't need all the information in the passage, consider summarizing it or presenting the key points as part of a summary of a longer passage. If a passage is clear, concise, and memorable as originally written, consider quoting instead of paraphrasing. Otherwise, and especially if the original was written for an academic audience, you may want to paraphrase the original to make its substance more accessible to your readers.

2 **Understand the passage.** Start by identifying key words, phrases, and ideas. If necessary, reread the pages leading up to the passage, to place it in context.

3 **Draft your paraphrase.** Replace key words and phrases with synonyms and alternative phrases (possibly gleaned from the context provided by the surrounding text). Experiment with word order and sentence structure until the paraphrase captures your understanding of the passage, in your own language, for your readers.

4 **Acknowledge your source.** Protect yourself from a charge of plagiarism and give credit for ideas you borrow.

A Practice Sequence: Writing a Paraphrase

1   In one of the sources you've located in your research, find a sentence of some length and complexity, and paraphrase it. Share the original and your paraphrase of it with a classmate, and discuss the effectiveness of your restatement. Is the meaning clear to your reader? Is the paraphrase written in your own language, using your own sentence structure?

2   Repeat the activity using a short paragraph from the same source. You and your classmate may want to attempt to paraphrase the same paragraph and then compare results. What differences do you detect?

WRITING A SUMMARY

As you have seen, a **summary** condenses a body of information, presenting the key ideas and acknowledging the source. A common activity or assignment in a composition class is to *summarize* a text. You may be asked to read a text, reduce it to its main points, and convey them, without any details or examples, in a written summary. The goal of this assignment is to sharpen your reading and thinking skills as you learn to distinguish between main ideas and supporting details. Being able to distill information in this manner is crucial to critical thinking.

However, summarizing is not an active way to make an argument. While summaries do provide a common ground of information for your readers, you must shape that information to support the purposes of your researched argument with details that clarify, illustrate, or support their main ideas for your readers.

We suggest a method of summarizing that involves

1. describing the author's key claims,
2. selecting examples to illustrate the author's argument,
3. presenting the gist of the author's argument, and
4. contextualizing what you summarize.

We demonstrate these steps for writing a summary following Clive Thompson's article "On the New Literacy."

CLIVE THOMPSON

On the New Literacy

A print journalist at *New York Magazine*, Clive Thompson started his blog, Collision Detection, in September 2002, when he was beginning his year as a Knight Fellow in Science Journalism at MIT. Collision Detection has become one of the most well-regarded blogs on technology and culture. The blog receives approximately 3,000 to 4,000 hits a day. His piece on literacy appeared in *Wired* magazine in 2009.

■ ■ ■

A s the school year begins, be ready to hear pundits fretting once again about how kids today can't write—and technology is to blame. Facebook encourages narcissistic blabbering, video and PowerPoint have replaced carefully crafted essays, and texting has dehydrated language into "bleak, bald, sad shorthand" (as University College of London English professor John Sutherland has moaned). An age of illiteracy is at hand, right?   1

Andrea Lunsford isn't so sure. Lunsford is a professor of writing and rhetoric at Stanford University, where she has organized a mammoth project called the Stanford Study of Writing to scrutinize college students' prose. From 2001 to 2006, she collected 14,672 student writing samples—everything from in-class assignments, formal essays, and   2 journal entries to e-mails, blog posts, and chat sessions. Her conclusions are stirring.

"I think we're in the midst of a literacy revolution the likes of which we haven't seen since Greek civilization," she says. For Lunsford, technology isn't killing our ability to write. It's reviving it—and pushing our literacy in bold new directions.   3

The first thing she found is that young people today write far more than any generation before them. That's because so much socializing takes place online, and it almost always involves text. Of all the writing that the Stanford students did, a stunning 38 percent of it took place out of the classroom—life writing, as Lunsford calls it. Those Twitter updates and lists of 25 things about yourself add up.   4

It's almost hard to remember how big a paradigm shift this is. Before the Internet came along, most Americans never wrote anything, ever, that wasn't a school assignment. Unless they got a job that required producing text (like in law, advertising, or media), they'd leave school and virtually never construct a paragraph again.   5

But is this explosion of prose good, on a technical level? Yes. Lunsford's team found that the students were remarkably adept at what rhetoricians call *kairos*—assessing their audience and adapting their tone and technique to best get their point across. The modern world of online writing, particularly in chat and on discussion threads, is conversational and public, which makes it closer to the Greek tradition of argument than the asynchronous letter and essay writing of 50 years ago.   6

The fact that students today almost always write for an audience (something virtually no one in my generation did) gives them a different sense of what constitutes good writing. In interviews, they defined good prose as something that had an effect on the world. For them, writing is about persuading and organizing and debating, even if it's over something as quotidian as what movie to go see. The Stanford students were almost always less enthusiastic about their in-class writing because it had no audience but the professor: It didn't serve any purpose other than to get them a grade. As for those texting short-forms and smileys defiling *serious* academic writing? Another myth. When Lunsford examined the work of first-year students, she didn't find a single example of texting speak in an academic paper.   7

Of course, good teaching is always going to be crucial, as is the mastering of formal academic prose. But it's also becoming clear that online media are pushing literacy into cool directions. The brevity of texting and status updating teaches young people to deploy haiku-like concision. At the same time, the proliferation of new forms of online pop-cultural exegesis—from sprawling TV-show recaps to 15,000-word videogame walkthroughs—has given them a chance to write enormously long and complex pieces of prose, often while working collaboratively with others.   8

We think of writing as either good or bad. What today's young people   9
know is that knowing who you're writing for and why you're writing
might be the most crucial factor of all.

■ Describe the Key Claims of the Text

As you read through a text with the purpose of summarizing it, you want
to identify how the writer develops his or her argument. You can do this by
what we call "chunking," grouping related material together into the argument's key claims. Here are two strategies to try.

Notice how paragraphs begin and end.   Often, focusing on the first and last
sentences of paragraphs will alert you to the shape and direction of an
author's argument. It is especially helpful if the paragraphs are lengthy
and full of supporting information, as much academic writing is.

Because of his particular journalistic forum, *Wired* magazine, the
paragraphs Thompson writes are generally rather short, but it's still
worth taking a closer look at the first and last sentences of his opening
paragraphs:

> *Paragraph 1:* As the school year begins, be ready to hear pundits fretting
> once again about how kids today can't write—and technology is to blame.
> Facebook encourages narcissistic blabbering, video and PowerPoint have
> replaced carefully crafted essays, and texting has dehydrated language
> into "bleak, bald, sad shorthand" (as University College of London
> English professor John Sutherland has moaned). An age of illiteracy is at
> hand, right?

> *Paragraph 2:* Andrea Lunsford isn't so sure. Lunsford is a professor of
> writing and rhetoric at Stanford University, where she has organized a
> mammoth project called the Stanford Study of Writing to scrutinize college
> students' prose. From 2001 to 2006, she collected 14,672 student writing
> samples—everything from in-class assignments, formal essays, and jour-
> nal entries to e-mails, blog posts, and chat sessions. Her conclusions are
> stirring.

Right away you can see that Thompson has introduced a topic in each
paragraph—pundits' criticism of students' use of electronic media in the
first, and a national study designed to examine students' literacy in the
second—and has indicated a connection between them. In fact, Thompson
is explicit in doing so. He asks a question at the end of the first paragraph
and then raises doubts as to the legitimacy of critics' denunciation of young
people's reliance on blogs and posts to communicate. How will Thompson
elaborate on this connection? What major points does he develop?

Notice the author's point of view and use of transitions.   Another strategy for identifying major points is to pay attention to descriptive words and transitions. For example, Thompson uses a rhetorical question ("An age of illiteracy is at hand, right?") and then offers a tentative answer ("Andrea Lunsford isn't so sure") that places some doubt in readers' minds.

Notice, too, the words that Thompson uses to characterize the argument in the first paragraph, which he appears to challenge in the second paragraph. Specifically, he describes these critics as "pundits," a word that traditionally refers to an expert or knowledgeable individual. However, the notion of a pundit, someone who often appears on popular talk shows, has also been used negatively. Thompson's description of pundits "fretting," wringing their hands in worry that literacy levels are declining, underscores this negative association of what it means to be a pundit. Finally, Thompson indicates that he does not identify with those who describe students as engaging in "narcissistic blabbering." This is clear when he characterizes the professor as having "moaned."

Once you identify an author's point of view, you will start noticing contrasts and oppositions in the argument—instances where the words are less positive, or neutral, or even negative—which are often signaled by how the writer uses transitions.

For example, Thompson begins with his own concession to critics' arguments when he acknowledges in paragraph 8 that educators should expect students to "[master] formal academic prose." However, he follows this concession with the transition word "but" to signal his own stance in the debate he frames in the first two paragraphs: "online media are pushing literacy into cool directions." Thompson also recognizes that students who write on blogs tend to write short, abbreviated texts. Still, he qualifies his concern with another transition, "at the same time." This transition serves to introduce Thompson's strongest claim: New media have given students "a chance to write enormously long and complex pieces of prose, often while working collaboratively with others."

These strategies can help you recognize the main points of an essay and explain them in a few sentences. For example, you could describe Thompson's key claims in this way:

1. Electronic media give students opportunities to write more than in previous generations, and students have learned to adapt what they are writing in order to have some tangible effect on what people think and how they act.

2. Arguably, reliance on blogging and posting on Twitter and Facebook can foster some bad habits in writing.

3. But at least one major study demonstrates that the benefits of using the new media outweigh the disadvantages. This study indicates that students write lengthy, complex pieces that contribute to creating significant social networks and collaborations.

■ Select Examples to Illustrate the Author's Argument

A summary should be succinct, which means you should limit the number of examples or illustrations you use. As you distill the major points of the argument, try to choose one or two examples to illustrate each major point. Here are the examples (in italics) you might use to support Thompson's main points:

1. Electronic media give students opportunities to write more than in previous generations, and students have learned to adapt what they are writing in order to have some tangible effect on what people think and how they act. *Examples from the Stanford study: Students "defined good prose as something that had an effect on the world. For them, writing is about persuading and organizing and debating"* (para. 7).

2. Arguably, reliance on blogging and posting on Twitter and Facebook can foster some bad habits in writing. *Examples of these bad habits include critics' charges of "narcissistic blabbering," "bleak, bald, sad shorthand," and "dehydrated language"* (para. 1). *Thompson's description of texting's "haiku-like concision"* (para. 8) *seems to combine praise (haiku can be wonderful poetry) with criticism (it can be obscure and unintelligible).*

3. But at least one major study demonstrates that the benefits of using the new media outweigh the disadvantages. *Examples include Thompson's point that the writing in the new media constitutes a "paradigm shift"* (para. 5). *Andrea Lunsford observes that students are "remarkably adept at what rhetoricians call* kairos—*assessing their audience and adapting their tone and technique to best get their point across"* (para. 6).

A single concrete example may be sufficient to clarify the point you want to make about an author's argument. Throughout the essay, Thompson derives examples from the Stanford study to support his argument in the final two paragraphs. The most concrete, specific example of how the new media benefit students as writers appears in paragraph 6, where the primary research of the Stanford study describes students' acquisition of important rhetorical skills of developing writing that is opportune (*kairos*) and purposeful. This one example may be sufficient for the purposes of summarizing Thompson's essay.

■ Present the Gist of the Author's Argument

When you present the **gist** of an argument, you are expressing the author's central idea in a sentence or two. The gist is not quite the same thing as the author's thesis statement. Instead, it is your formulation of the author's main idea, composed for the needs of your own argument.

Thompson's observations in paragraph 8 represent his thesis: "But it's also becoming clear that online media are pushing literacy into cool directions. . . . [T]he proliferation of new forms of online pop-cultural exegesis—from sprawling TV-show recaps to 15,000-word videogame walkthroughs—has given [students] a chance to write enormously long and complex pieces of prose, often while working collaboratively with others." In this paragraph, Thompson clearly expresses his central ideas in two sentences, while also conceding some of the critics' concerns. However, in formulating the gist of his argument, you want to do more than paraphrase Thompson. You want to use his position to support your own. For example, suppose you want to qualify the disapproval that some educators have expressed in drawing their conclusions about the new media. You would want to mention Thompson's own concessions when you describe the gist of his argument:

GIST

In his essay "On the New Literacy," Clive Thompson, while acknowledging some academic criticism of new media, argues that these media give students opportunities to write more than in previous generations and that students have learned to adapt what they are writing in order to have some tangible effect on what people think and how they act.

Notice that this gist could not have been written based only on Thompson's thesis statement. It reflects knowledge of Thompson's major points, his examples, and his concessions.

■ Contextualize What You Summarize

Your summary should help readers understand the context of the conversation:

- Who is the author?
- What is the author's expertise?
- What is the title of the work?
- Where did the work appear?
- What was the occasion of the work's publication? What prompted the author to write the work?
- What are the issues?
- Who else is taking part in the conversation, and what are their perspectives on the issues?

Again, because a summary must be concise, you must make decisions about how much of the conversation your readers need to know. If your assignment is to practice summarizing, it may be sufficient to include only information about the author and the source. However, if you are using the summary to build your own argument, you may need to provide more context. Your practice summary of Thompson's essay should mention that

KEY CLAIM(S)	EXAMPLES	GIST	CONTEXT
1. Electronic media prompt more student writing than ever before, and students use their writing to make a difference.	The Stanford study: Students "defined good prose as something that had an effect on the world" (para. 7).	In his essay "On the New Literacy," Clive Thompson, while acknowledging some academic criticism of new media, argues that these media give students opportunities to write more than in previous generations and that students have learned to adapt what they are writing in order to have some tangible effect on what people think and how they act.	Thompson is a journalist who has written widely on issues in higher education. His essay "On the New Literacy" appeared in *Wired* in August 2009 (http://www.wired.com/techbiz/people/magazine/17-09/st_thompson). Under consideration is the debate that he frames in his opening paragraphs.
2. Arguably, reliance on blogging and posting can foster some bad writing habits.	Complaints of "bleak, bald, sad shorthand" and "narcissistic blabbering" (para. 1); texting can be obscure.		
3. But one major study shows the benefits of new media on student writing.	A "paradigm shift" (para. 5) to fluency in multiple formats and skill in assessing and persuading audiences.		

FIGURE 3.1   Worksheet for Writing a Summary

he is a journalist and should cite the title of and page references to his essay. You also may want to include information about Thompson's audience, publication information, and what led to the work's publication. Was it published in response to another essay or book, or to commemorate an important event?

We compiled our notes on Thompson's essay (key claims, examples, gist, context) in a worksheet (Figure 3.1). All of our notes in the worksheet constitute a type of prewriting, our preparation for writing the summary. Creating a worksheet like this can help you track your thoughts as you plan to write a summary.

Here is our summary of Thompson's essay:

The gist of Thompson's argument.

This concession helps to balance enthusiasm based on a single study.

Thompson's main point with example.

In his essay "On the New Literacy," Clive Thompson, while acknowledging some academic criticism of new media, argues that these media give students opportunities to write more than in previous generations and that students have learned to adapt what they are writing in order to have some tangible effect on what people think and how they act. Arguably, reliance on blogging and posting on Twitter and Facebook can foster some bad habits in writing. But at least one major study demonstrates that the benefits of using the new media outweigh the disadvantages. Students write lengthy, complex pieces that contribute to creating significant social networks and collaborations.

Steps to Writing a Summary

1 Describe the key claims of the text. To understand the shape and direction of the argument, study how paragraphs begin and end, and pay attention to the author's point of view and use of transitions. Then combine what you have learned into a few sentences describing the key claims.

2 Select examples to illustrate the author's argument. Find one or two examples to support each key claim. You may need only one example when you write your summary.

3 Present the gist of the author's argument. Describe the author's central idea in your own language with an eye to where you expect your argument to go.

4 Contextualize what you summarize. Cue your readers into the conversation. Who is the author? Where and when did the text appear? Why did the author write? Who else is in the conversation?

A Practice Sequence: Writing a Summary

1. Summarize a text that you have been studying for research or for one of your other classes. You may want to limit yourself to an excerpt of just a few paragraphs or a few pages. Follow the four steps we've described, using a summary worksheet for notes, and write a summary of the text. Then share the excerpt and your summary of it with two of your peers. Be prepared to justify your choices in composing the summary. Do your peers agree that your summary captures what is important in the original?

2. With a classmate, choose a brief text of about three pages. Each of you should use the method we describe above to write a summary of the text. Exchange your summaries and worksheets, and discuss the effectiveness of your summaries. Each of you should be prepared to discuss your choice of key claims and examples and your wording of the gist. Did you set forth the context effectively?

WRITING YOURSELF INTO ACADEMIC CONVERSATIONS

In her essay "The Flight from Conversation" (see p. 59), Sherry Turkle reflects upon her research on mobile technology and what she sees as the unfortunate trend toward "sacrificing conversation for mere connection."

You are probably familiar with the experience of walking into a coffee shop or the library on campus and seeing friends sitting across from one another but engaged with laptops or phones instead of with each other. "Alone together," as Turkle puts it, and she laments the "diminished chances to learn skills of self-reflection," a habit of mind that we agree is vital to academic writing and thinking. Thus, she blames technology that encourages broad and shallow connection without real face-to-face engagement. But as we also suggest, much academic conversation occurs on the page and screen, involving the exchange of ideas through writing. The philosopher Kenneth Burke uses this metaphor of an ongoing parlor conversation to capture the spirit of academic writing:

> Imagine that you enter a parlor. You come late. When you arrive, others have long preceded you, and they are engaged in a heated discussion, a discussion too heated for them to pause and tell you exactly what it is about. In fact, the discussion had already begun long before any of them got there, so that no one present is qualified to retrace for you all the steps that had gone before. You listen for a while, until you decide that you have caught the tenor of the argument; then you put in your oar. Someone answers; you answer him; another comes to your defense; another aligns himself against you, to either the embarrassment or gratification of your opponent, depending upon the quality of your ally's assistance. However, the discussion is interminable. The hour grows late, you must depart. And you do depart, with the discussion still vigorously in progress.*

Now that you have learned some important skills of rhetorical analysis and summary, then, it is important to think about ways to write yourself into academic conversations. Doing so will depend on three strategies:

- which previously stated arguments you share;
- which previously stated argument you want to refute; and
- what new opinions and supporting information you are going to bring to the conversation.

You may, for example, affirm others for raising important issues about the environment, employment opportunities, or the tendency of new technologies to limit community building and democratic deliberation. Then again, as you consider the arguments of others, you may feel that they have not given sufficient thought or emphasis to ideas that you think are important. In the end, you can write yourself into the conversation by explaining that writers have ignored a related issue entirely. So you are looking for gaps in others' arguments—something we discuss in more detail in the chapters that follow—an opening that provides an opportunity to provide a unique perspective in the conversation of ideas.

*Kenneth Burke, *The Philosophy of Literary Form* (Berkeley: University of California Press, 1941, pp. 110–11).

Steps to Writing Yourself into an Academic Conversation

- **Retrace the conversation**, including the relevance of the topic and situation, for readers by briefly discussing an author's key claims and ideas. This discussion can be as brief as a sentence or two and include a quotation for each author you cite.
- **Respond to the ideas of others** by helping readers understand the context in which another's claims make sense. "I get this if I see it this way."
- **Discuss possible implications** by putting problems aside and asking, "Do their claims make sense?"
- **Introduce conflicting points of view** and raise possible criticisms to indicate something the authors whose ideas you discuss may have overlooked.
- **Formulate your own claim** to assert what you think.
- **Ensure that your own purpose as a writer is clear to readers.**

A Practice Sequence: Writing Yourself into an Academic Conversation

1   We would like you to read an excerpt from Tom Standage's book *Writing on the Wall*, follow the steps to writing yourself into the conversation, and write a short, one-page argument. In doing so, retrace the conversation by explaining Standage's argument in ways that demonstrate your understanding of it. In turn, formulate your own position by explaining whether you believe that Standage has represented the issue well. Is there an opening in his argument that enables you to offer a perspective that he has perhaps ignored or overlooked?

2   An option for group work:
- As a group, discuss Sherry Turkle's argument in Chapter 2 that mobile technology has led to sacrificing conversation for mere connection—that we are "alone together." List the reasons why her argument makes sense and reasons why your group might take issue with her perspective. What do you feel she might have ignored or overlooked?
- Next, compare Turkle's argument with Standage's point of view in which he challenges Turkle's assertion that new technologies encourage "flight from conversation."
- Finally, each member of the group should write an argument that takes into account the conversation that Turkle and Standage have initiated with their efforts to make sense of how mobile technology has affected our lives.

TOM STANDAGE

History Retweets Itself

A writer and journalist from England with a degree from Oxford University, Tom Standage has published six books, including *The Victorian Internet* and *Writing on the Wall*, from which the excerpt that follows is taken. He has published articles on science, technology, and business in the *New York Times*, *Wired*, and the *Daily Telegraph*. He has also worked as a science and technology writer for the *Guardian* and deputy editor at *The Economist*.

■ ■ ■

1   Social media, whether in the form of the printing press or the Internet, can be a force for freedom and openness, simply because oppressive regimes often rely on manipulating their citizens' view of the world, and a more open media environment makes that harder to accomplish. But the other side of the scales is not empty; this benefit must be weighed against the fact that social media can make repression easier, too. As Morozov notes, the Internet "penetrates and reshapes all walks of political life, not just the ones conducive to democratization." Anyone who hopes that the Internet will spread Western-style liberal democracy must bear in mind that the same digital tools have also been embraced by campaigners with very different aims, such as Hezbollah in Lebanon and ultra-right-wing nationalist groups in Russia. The test case in this argument is China, which now has more Internet users than any other country—more than in North America and Europe combined. Weibo and other online forums have given Chinese Internet users unprecedented freedom to express their views. Yet the swift and ruthless censoring of blog posts and weibo messages criticizing senior officials or calling for real-world demonstrations shows that widespread Internet adoption need not necessarily threaten the regime. Indeed, the ability to monitor the Internet may make it easier for the government to keep the lid on dissent.

2   A rather more mundane but widely expressed concern about social media is that the ease with which anyone can now publish his or her views online, whether on Twitter, on blogs, or in comment threads, has led to a coarsening of public discourse. Racism, sexism, bigotry, incivility, and ignorance abound in many online discussion forums. Twitter allows anyone to send threats or abuse directly to other users. No wonder the Internet is often likened to a sewer by politicians, clergymen, and newspaper columnists.

3   Yet the history of media shows that this is just the modern incarnation of the timeless complaint of the intellectual elite, every time

technology makes publishing easier, that the wrong sort of people will use it to publish the wrong sorts of things. In the early sixteenth century, Erasmus complained that printers "fill the world with pamphlets and books that are foolish, ignorant, malignant, libelous, mad, impious and subversive; and such is the flood that even things that might have done some good lose all their goodness." Worse, these "swarms of new books" were "hurtful to scholarship" because they lured readers away from the classics, which is what Erasmus felt people ought to have been reading.

Printers had, however, quickly realized that there was a far larger audience, and more money to be made, printing pamphlets and contemporary works rather than new editions of classical works. Similarly, in England, the Worshipful Company of Stationers bemoaned the explosion of unlicensed pamphlets that appeared after the collapse of press controls in 1641, complaining that "every ignorant person that takes advantage of a loose presse may publish the fancies of every idle brain as so manyfestly appeareth by the swarmes of scandalous and irksome pamphletts that are cryed about the streetes." The Company was hoping to be granted a renewed monopoly on printing, which had previously allowed it to control what was printed, and therefore what people read. Its grumbling is not dissimilar to that of professional journalists bemoaning the rise of pajama-clad bloggers, invading their turf and challenging the status quo.

Those in authority always squawk, it seems, when access to publishing is broadened. Greater freedom of expression, as John Milton noted in *Areopagitica*, means that bad ideas will proliferate as well as good ones, but it also means that bad ideas are more likely to be challenged. Better to provide an outlet for bigotry and prejudice, so they can be argued against and addressed, than to pretend that such views, and the people who hold them, do not exist. In a world where almost anyone can publish his or her views, the alternative, which is to restrict freedom of expression, is surely worse. As Milton's contemporary Henry Robinson put it in 1644, "It were better that many false doctrines were published, especially with a good intention and out of weaknesse only, than that one sound truth should be forcibly smothered or wilfully concealed; and by the incongruities and absurdities which accompany erroneous and unsound doctrines, the truth appears still more glorious, and wins others to the love thereof." One man's coarsening of discourse is another man's democratization of publishing. The genie is out of the bottle. Let truth and falsehood grapple!

Whatever you think about the standards of online discussions, there is no doubt that people are spending a lot of time engaging in them. This raises another concern: that social media is a distracting waste of time that diverts people from more worthwhile pursuits, such as work and study. Surveys carried out in 2009 found that more than half of British and American companies had banned workers from using Twitter, Facebook, and other social sites. Many employers also block access to LinkedIn, a social-networking site for business users, because they worry that it allows employees to spend their time networking and advertising themselves to other potential employers. Simply put, companies readily equate social networking with social notworking.

This too is a familiar worry. Coffeehouses, the social-media plat- 7 forms of their day, inspired similar reactions in the seventeenth century. They were denounced in the 1670s as "a vast loss of time grown out of a pure novelty" and "great enemies to diligence and industry." But the mixing of people and ideas that occurred in coffeehouses, where patrons from many walks of life would gather to discuss the latest pamphlets, led to innovations in science, commerce, and finance. By providing an environment in which unexpected connections could be made, coffeehouses proved to be hotbeds of collaborative innovation.

Similarly, a growing number of companies have concluded that 8 social networking does have a role to play in the workplace, if done in the right way. They have set up "enterprise social networks," which create a private, Facebook-like social network to facilitate communication among employees and, in some cases, with workers at client and supplier companies, too. This sort of approach seems to have several benefits: its similarity to Facebook means little or no training is required; sharing documents and communicating via discussion threads is more efficient than using e-mail; it is easier to discover employees' hidden knowledge and talents; and it makes it easier for far-flung teams to collaborate.

A study by McKinsey and Company, a management consulting firm, 9 found that the use of social networking within companies could increase the productivity of skilled knowledge workers by 20 to 25 percent and that the adoption of the technology in four industries (consumer goods, financial services, professional services, and advanced manufacturing) could create economic benefits worth between $900 billion and $1.3 trillion a year. Such predictions should always be taken with a very large dose of salt, but McKinsey found that 70 percent of companies were already using social technologies to some extent; and more than 90 percent said they were already benefitting as a result. Far from being a waste of time, then, Facebook-like social networks may in fact be the future of business software.

Even if it has value in the office, however, is there a danger that social 10 media is harming our personal lives? Some observers worry that social media is in fact antisocial, because it encourages people to commune with people they barely know online to the detriment of real-life relationships with family and friends. "Does virtual intimacy degrade our experience of the other kind and, indeed, of all encounters, of any kind?" writes Sherry Turkle, an academic at MIT, in her book *Alone Together*. She worries that "relentless connection leads to a new solitude. We turn to new technology to fill the void, but as technology ramps up, our emotional lives ramp down." Similarly, William Powers, author of *Hamlet's BlackBerry*, laments the way that his family would rather chat with their online friends than with each other. "The digital crowd has a way of elbowing its way into everything, to the point where a family can't sit in a room together for half an hour without somebody, or everybody, peeling off," he writes. His proposed solution: an "Unplugged Sunday" when the use of computers and smartphones is banned.

It is clear that the desire to be connected to one's distant friends, using whatever technology is available, is timeless. Cicero particularly valued the way letters connected him to his friends in the months after the death of his beloved daughter Tullia in 45 B.C. And he relished the contact his daily letters with his friend Atticus provided, even when they contained little information. "Write to me . . . every day," he wrote to Atticus. "When you have nothing to say, why, say just that!" Concerns about unhealthy dependence on new media technologies also have a long history: recall Plato's objections to writing in the *Phaedrus*, and Seneca's derision of his fellow Romans as they rushed to the docks to get their mail. By the seventeenth century, satirists were lampooning news junkies and the hunger with which they sought out the latest corantos. *11*

From Roman letter-writers to manuscript poetry-sharing networks to news-sharing clergymen in the American colonies, the exchange of media has long been used to reinforce social connections. The same is true today. Zeynep Tufekci, a media theorist at Princeton University, suggests that the popularity of social media stems from its ability to reconnect people in a world of suburbanization, long working hours, and families scattered around the globe by migration. Social media, she argues, is also a welcome antidote to the lonely, one-way medium of television. People who use social media can stay in contact with people they would otherwise lose touch with and make contact with like-minded individuals they might otherwise have never met. "Social media is enhancing human connectivity as people can converse in ways that were once not possible," Tufekci argues. A study published in 2011 by researchers at the University of Pennsylvania concluded that "it is incorrect to maintain that the Internet benefits distant relationships at the expense of local ties. The Internet affords personal connections at extreme distances but also provides the opportunity for new and supplemental local interaction." Another analysis, conducted in 2009 by researchers at the University of Toronto and involving four thousand Canadians, found that 35 percent felt that technology made them feel closer and more connected to other family members, and only 7 percent *12* said that technology made them feel less connected. Tellingly, 51% of respondents said it made no difference, which suggests that many people no longer make a distinction between online and offline worlds, but regard them as an integrated whole.

New technologies are often regarded with suspicion. Turkle worries   13
about the "flight from conversation," citing teenagers who would rather send a text than make a phone call. And on Unplugged Sunday, Powers and his family engage in communal pursuits that include watching television together. It seems odd to venerate the older technologies of the telephone and the television, though, given that they were once condemned for being anti-social in the same way social media is denounced today. ("Does the telephone make men more active or more lazy? Does it break up home life and the old practice of visiting friends?" asked a survey carried out in San Francisco in 1926.) There is always an adjustment period when new technologies appear, as societies work out the appropriate etiquette for their use and technologies are modified in response. During this transitional phase, which takes years or even decades, technologies are often criticized for disrupting existing ways of doing things. But the technology that is demonized today may end up being regarded as wholesome and traditional tomorrow, by which time another apparently dangerous new invention will be causing the same concerns.

What clues can history provide about the future evolution of social   14
media? Even though Facebook, Twitter, and other social platforms provide a way for people to share information by sharing along social connections, they still resemble old-fashioned media companies such as newspapers and broadcasters in two ways: they are centralized (even though the distribution of information is carried out by the users, rather than the platform owners) and they rely on advertising for the majority of their revenue. Centralization grants enormous power to the owners of social platforms, giving them the ability to suspend or delete users' accounts and censor information if they choose to do so— or are compelled to do so by governments. Relying on advertising revenue, meanwhile, means platform owners must keep both advertisers and users happy, even though their interests do not always align. As they try to keep users within the bounds of their particular platforms, to maximize their audience for advertising, the companies that operate social networks have started to impose restrictions on what their customers can do and on how easily information can be moved from one social platform to another. In their early days, it makes sense for new social platforms to be as open as possible, to attract a large number of users. Having done so, however, such platforms often try to fence their users into "walled gardens" as they start trying to make money.

The contrast between big social platforms on the one hand, and   15
e-mail and the web on the other, is striking. Both e-mail and web

publishing work in an entirely open, decentralized way. The servers that store and deliver e-mail and the programs used to read and write messages are all expected to work seamlessly with each other, and for the most part they do. The same is true of web servers, which store and deliver pages, and the web browsers used to display pages and navigate between them. Anyone who wants to set up a new e-mail or web server can add it to the Internet's existing ecosystem of such servers. If you are setting up a new blog or website, there are also plenty of companies to choose from who will host it for you, and you can move from one to another if you are unsatisfied with their service. None of this is true for social networking, however, which takes place inside huge, proprietary silos owned by private companies. Moving your photos, your list of friends, or your archive of posts from one service to another is difficult at best, and impossible at worst. It may be that healthy competition among those companies, and a reluctance to alienate their hundreds of millions of users by becoming too closed, will enable the big social platforms to continue in this semi-open state for many years to come.

But another possibility is that today's social platforms represent a transitional stage, like AOL and CompuServe in the 1990s. They were proprietary, centralized services that introduced millions of people to the wonders of the Internet, but they were eventually swept aside by the open web. Similarly, perhaps the core features of social networking and social media—maintaining lists of friends, and exchanging information with them—will move to an open, decentralized model. Such a model is possible for e-mail and web publishing because of the existence of agreed technical standards on how e-mail messages and web pages ought to be encoded and transmitted. Several such standards have already been proposed for decentralized or distributed social networks, though none has yet gained much traction. There will be technical difficulties synchronizing friend lists, maintaining privacy and security, and delivering updates quickly across millions of users, all of which give centralized social networks a clear advantage at the moment. But every time a major social network is involved in a privacy violation, an unpopular change in the terms of service, or a spat over censorship, a few more adventurous users decide to give one of the various decentralized social networks a try. "I think it's important to design new systems that work in a distributed way," says Tim Berners-Lee. "We must make systems in which people can collaborate together, but do it in a way that's decentralized, so it's not based on one central hub."

A decentralized social platform could be based around personal silos of data over which users would have direct control. This approach would also address concerns that the new online public sphere that has been brought into being by social media is largely in the hands of private companies who are beholden to advertisers and shareholders rather than users. But there is another way for Facebook, Twitter, and other platforms to make themselves more accountable to users and less dependent on advertisers: to start charging users for some or all services. Many Internet services operate on a model in which a small percentage of paying customers subsidize a much larger number of nonpaying users. Social platforms could charge for things such as providing detailed analytics to commercial users of their platforms, more customization options for user profiles, or an advertising-free service. App.net, a subscription-funded Twitter-like service launched in September 2012, prides itself on being an "ad-free social network" that is based on "selling our product, not our users." This ensures, the company says, that its financial incentives are aligned with those of its members. Whether or not its particular model proves to have broad appeal, the future of social media is likely to see new models based on decentralized architectures and paying customers being added to the mix.

But whatever form social media takes in the future, one thing is   *18* clear: it is not going away. As this book has argued, social media is not new. It has been around for centuries. Today, blogs are the new pamphlets. Microblogs and online social networks are the new coffeehouses. Media-sharing sites are the new commonplace books. They are all shared, social platforms that enable ideas to travel from one person to another, rippling through networks of people connected by social bonds, rather than having to squeeze through the privileged bottleneck of broadcast media. The rebirth of social media in the Internet age represents a profound shift—and a return, in many respects, to the way things used to be.

From Identifying Claims to Analyzing Arguments

A claim is an assertion of fact or belief that needs to be supported with **evidence**—the information that backs up a claim. A main claim, or **thesis**, summarizes the writer's position on a situation and answers the question(s) the writer addresses. It also encompasses the minor claims, along with their supporting evidence, that the writer makes throughout the argument.

As readers, we need to identify a writer's main claim, or thesis, because it helps us organize our own understanding of the writer's argument. It acts as a signpost that tells us, "This is what the essay is about," "This is what I want you to pay attention to," and "This is how I want you to think, change, or act."

When you evaluate a claim, whether it is an argument's main claim or a minor claim, it is helpful to identify the type of claim it is: a claim of fact, a claim of value, or a claim of policy. You also need to evaluate the reasons for the claim and the evidence that supports it. Because academic argument should acknowledge multiple points of view, you should also be prepared to identify what, if any, concessions a writer offers his or her readers, and what counterarguments he or she anticipates from others in the conversation.

IDENTIFYING TYPES OF CLAIMS

To illustrate how to identify a writer's claims, let's take a look at a text written by an educator in the field of business ethics, Dana Radcliffe, that examines the relationship between social media and democracy.

The text is followed by our analysis of the types of claims (fact, value, and policy) and then, in the next section, of the nature of arguments (use of evidence, concessions, and counterarguments) the author presents.

DANA RADCLIFFE

Dashed Hopes: Why Aren't Social Media Delivering Democracy?

Dana Radcliffe has taught business ethics at the Samuel Curtis Johnson Graduate School of Management at Cornell University since 2000. As an adjunct at Syracuse University, he teaches ethics courses in the Maxwell School of Citizenship and Public Affairs and the College of Engineering and Computer Science. As a blogger for the *Huffington Post*, he has written about ethics in business, politics, and public policy. Professor Radcliffe earned a PhD from Syracuse University, an MBA from the University of California, Los Angeles, an MPhil in philosophy from Yale University, and a BA in philosophy from Fort Hays State University. This essay is a version of remarks presented to a session of the Pacific Council on International Policy, October 10, 2015. It follows up on his 2011 blog post "Can Social Media Undermine Democracy?"

■ ■ ■

Four years ago, in the months following the Arab Spring,[1] hopes ran high that the growing use of social media would bring a flowering of democracy throughout the world. Facebook and Twitter had helped dissidents drive tyrants from power in Tunisia, Egypt, and Libya. In established democracies, citizens' groups—most notably, the Tea Party in the U.S.—were influencing politics by leveraging social media. Indeed, a *Forbes* cover story on the power of social media concluded that "the world is becoming more democratic and reflective of the will of ordinary people."

Sadly, such optimism proved ill-founded. Now, in 2015, popular government seems to be receding globally. With the qualified exception of Tunisia, the Arab Spring did not transform dictatorships into democracies, and democratic governments seem unable to find consensus solutions to many pressing policy questions. What happened? Why haven't social media made the world more democratic?

In seeking an answer, we can begin with [the] nature of democracy itself. Because a country's citizens have competing interests and values, their effectively governing themselves through elections of leaders

[1] *Editor's note:* Arab Spring was a revolutionary wave of demonstrations, protests, and civil wars that began on December 17, 2010. Most insurgencies occurred in Syria, Libya, and Yemen, with uprisings in other countries, including Saudi Arabia, Iraq, Algeria, Kuwait, and Morocco.

and other democratic processes requires *deliberation*. It requires that citizens and their representatives discuss and debate what the government should or should not do, defending their views by appealing to shared principles and purposes. As one scholar, Daniel Gayo-Avello, recently observed, "Deliberation is crucial in modern democracy . . . Proper democratic deliberation assumes that citizens are equal participants, opposing viewpoints are not only accepted but encouraged, and that the main goal is to achieve 'rationally motivated consensus.'" Political philosophers Amy Gutmann and Dennis Thompson, in their influential *Democracy and Disagreement* (Belknap, 1996), point out that "the demand for deliberation has been a familiar theme in the American constitutional tradition. It is integral to the ideal of republican government as the founders understood it. James Madison judged the design of political institutions in part by how well they furthered deliberation."

To be sure, "deliberative democracy" is an ideal to which existing democratic systems only roughly approximate. Nevertheless, the concept provides a plausible standard for evaluating democracies. Moreover, it reminds us that the health of a democracy depends in large part on its fostering deliberation that leads to policies whose legitimacy most citizens accept. Hence, the impact of social media on democratic deliberation may help explain why they have not brought about a new global era of democracy.   *4*

The issue here is the political power of social media, and it entails three key questions: What power do they confer? Who possesses that power? How do those who have the power use it?   *5*

First, the power of social media is evident. Functionally, it is the ability to communicate, instantaneously, with a large number of people. Politically, it is the power to inform or misinform, to engage or manipulate, to mobilize or control. In general, it is the power to affect, directly and on a vast scale, the political beliefs and actions of citizens.   *6*

Second, when the government controls social media, this power is in its hands. When the government does not control social media, its political power belongs to citizens who can access them and is exercised by groups of like-minded individuals who use them to organize and coordinate political activities.   *7*

Third, as for how the political power of social media is wielded by those who possess them, recent history gives us some salient examples: *8*

- Protesters using them in organizing mass demonstrations against oppressive governments during the Arab Spring;
- the Chinese government's allowing critics of public officials and policies to "vent" online but tightly censoring calls for collective action;

- the Russian government's employing its immense digital propaganda machine to convince many Europeans that the CIA shot down the Malaysian airliner over Ukraine;
- the Islamic State's utilizing social media to recruit disaffected Muslim youths from around the world;
- in 2008, the Obama campaign's innovative application of social media to raise record amounts of money from small donors and customize its messages to different demographics;
- the use of social media by an impassioned minority of Americans angry at "big government" to form and advance the Tea Party movement.

In all these cases, social media were—or are—used as *political weapons*. Of course, I am not implying moral equivalence in these examples. My point is that the political power of social media has been used most effectively in *adversarial* contexts—in circumstances of *struggle* or *competition*. In those cases, the regime, organization, or group holding the power uses it against individuals, groups, or institutions whose interests or goals conflict with theirs. Consequently, whether they are revolutionaries, totalitarian governments, candidates for office, or special interests, political partisans using social media as tactical weapons are not concerned about *deliberation*.   *9*

Who, then, cares about promoting democratic deliberation? It is citizens and leaders who understand that democratic processes necessitate deliberative disagreement and, in the legislative process, negotiation and compromise. However, when these advocates of democracy look to social media to establish and strengthen democratic processes, they encounter a basic problem: social media appear unsuited to serve as forums of political deliberation. Research into online behavior suggests several reasons: *10*

- Users tend not to seek opportunities to engage in serious political dialogue with people whose views differ from their own. Rather, as social media expert Curtis Hougland notes, "people choose to reinforce their existing political opinions through their actions online."
- A recent Pew Research Center report offers evidence that people are much less willing to post their political views on social media when they believe their followers would disagree with them.
- Daniel Gayo-Avello has found that "when political discussions occur they are not rational and democratic deliberations . . . [because] political information in social media generally lacks quality and strong arguments, is usually incoherent and highly opinionated."

To these I would add some intuitions of mine:

- When people who have strong political opinions avoid engaging opponents in reasoned debate but have them bolstered by social media followers, they tend to become more rigid in those views—and so, are even less interested in democratic deliberation.

- As a result, political partisans connected through social media tend to oppose legislative compromises on their pet issues, demanding that elected representatives they support "stand on principle," regardless of political realities or the common good.

- Finally, perhaps because using social media is, physically, a solitary activity, it tends not to cultivate civic virtues—such as respect for opponents—that Gutmann and Thompson argue are critical to democratic deliberation.

In short, with regard to political discussion, current use of social media favors affinity over engagement, expression over debate, silence over disagreement, dogmatism over compromise, and—toward opponents—disdain over respect. This, I believe, is largely why we have so far been unable to move beyond the use of social media as political weapons to make them instruments of deliberative democracy.

■ Identify Claims of Fact

Claims of fact are assertions (or arguments) that seek to define or classify something or establish *that a problem or condition has existed, exists, or will exist*. Claims of fact are made by individuals who believe that something is true; but claims are never simply facts, and some claims are more objective, and so easier to verify, than others.

For example, "It's raining in Portland today" is a "factual" claim of fact; it's easily verified. But consider the argument some make that the steel and automotive industries in the United States have depleted our natural resources and left us at a crisis point. This is an assertion that a condition exists. A careful reader must examine the basis for this kind of claim: Are we truly facing a crisis? And if so, are the steel and automotive industries truly responsible? A number of politicians counter this claim of fact by insisting that if the government were to harness the vast natural resources in Alaska, there would be no "crisis." This is also a claim of fact, in this case an assertion that a condition will exist in the future. Again, it is based on evidence, evidence gathered from various sources that indicates sufficient resources in Alaska to keep up with our increasing demands for resources and to allay a potential crisis.

Our point is that most claims of fact are debatable and challenge us to provide evidence to verify our arguments. They may be based on factual information, but they are not necessarily true. Most claims of fact present **interpretations** of evidence derived from **inferences**. That is, a writer will examine evidence (for example, about the quantity of natural resources in Alaska and the rate that industries harness those resources and process them into goods), draw a conclusion based on reasoning (an inference), and offer an explanation based on that conclusion (an interpretation).

So, for example, an academic writer will study the evidence on the quantity of natural resources in Alaska and the rate that industries harness those resources and process them into goods; only after the writer makes an informed decision on whether Alaska's resources are sufficient to keep pace with the demand for them will he or she take a position on the issue.

Claims that seek to define or classify are also claims of fact. For example, researchers have sought to define a range of behaviors such as autism that actually resist simple definition. After all, autism exists along a behavioral spectrum attributed variably to genetics and environment. Psychologists have indeed tried to define autism using a diagnostic tool to characterize behaviors associated with communication and social interaction. However, definitions of autism have changed over time, reflecting changing criteria for assessing human behavior and the perspective one takes. So do we in fact have a "crisis" in the over diagnosis of autistic behaviors as some have claimed? For that matter, who gets to decide what counts as a crisis?

Let's now come to Radcliffe's claim of fact that social media services have not fulfilled the promise of fostering a more democratic world, nor have they promoted (as the *Forbes* article asserts) "the will of ordinary people." Despite a few exceptions in which social media services have empowered democratic change, Radcliffe's review of the global political climate forces readers to reconsider claims that connect social media and the growth of democracy. Do social media services actually have a causal relationship with the Arab Spring—the wave of insurrections across the Middle East that triggered subsequent shifts to democracy? Radcliffe takes issue with this apparently factual **causal claim**. But the careful reader will want to see how Radcliffe goes about challenging others' claims to support his own claim of fact that "such optimism proved ill-founded." Note how he asks questions to propel his argument ("What happened? Why haven't social media made the world more democratic?") and provides a claim of definition. Radcliffe's **definitional claim** serves as an important rhetorical strategy for making an argument about what democracy is and the conditions that exist to support democratic principles. After all, how can others maintain that social media services such as Twitter and Facebook foster the spread of democracy if they have not defined a key term like "democracy"? This is especially true if a primary component of democracy is what Radcliffe describes as a "deliberative process."

We invite you to examine Radcliffe's primary claim and the evidence he uses to challenge a prevailing argument in the media and to support his own view that a true democracy "requires that citizens and their representatives discuss and debate what the government should or should not do, defending their views by appealing to shared principles and purposes." Does he convincingly present his argument that others overstate the effect of social media because, at least implicitly, they fail to adequately define democracy and the democratic process? That is, do you accept his definition as the standard—or at least a plausible standard rooted in a **factual claim**—upon which to measure others' arguments? Do social media services confer power? If so, who uses such power, and how do they use it? Finally, to what extent do social media services act as adequate forums for deliberation?

■ Identify Claims of Value

A claim of fact is different from a **claim of value**, which *expresses an evaluation of a problem or condition that has existed, exists, or will exist*. Is a condition good or bad? Is it important or inconsequential?

For example, an argument that developing the wilderness in Alaska would irreversibly mar the beauty of the land indicates that the writer values the beauty of the land over the possible benefits of development. A claim of value presents a judgment, which is sometimes signaled by a value-laden word like *ugly*, *beautiful*, or *immoral*, but may also be conveyed more subtly by the writer's tone and attitude.

Radcliffe makes a claim of value when he concludes by stating "with regard to political discussion, current use of social media favors affinity over engagement, expression over debate, silence over disagreement, dogmatism over compromise, and—toward opponents—disdain over respect." This statement follows from Radcliffe's initial observation that use of social media does not support the "reflective . . . will of ordinary people," and from the evidence presents that social media services can be detrimental to the will of people when controlled by oppressive leaders. He writes, "When people who have strong political opinions avoid engaging opponents in reasoned debate but have them bolstered by social media followers, they tend to become more rigid in those views. . . . As a result, political partisans connected through social media tend to oppose legislative compromises on their pet issues . . . regardless of political realities or the common good." Radcliffe underscores these observations in the final paragraph: "This, I believe, is largely why we have so far been unable to move beyond the use of social media as political weapons to make them instruments of deliberative democracy." This may seem like a claim of fact, but Radcliffe's claim is based on interpretation of the evidence he presents and the definition he establishes as the standard on which to judge whether a country is democratic. Whether you are persuaded by Radcliffe's claim depends on the evidence and reasons he uses for support. We discuss the nature of evidence and what constitutes "good" reasons later in this chapter.

■ Identify Claims of Policy

A **claim of policy** is an argument for what should be the case, *that a condition should exist*. It is a call for change or a solution to a problem.

Two recent controversies on college campuses center on claims of policy. One has activists arguing that universities and colleges should have a policy that all workers on campus earn a living wage. The other has activists arguing that universities and colleges should have a policy that prevents them from investing in countries where the government ignores human rights. Claims of policy are often signaled by words like *should* and *must*: "For public universities to live up to their democratic mission, they *must* provide all their workers with a living wage."

In "Ten Ways Social Media Can Improve Campaign Engagement and Reinvigorate American Democracy," political scientist Darrell West describes how social media can "reinvigorate American democracy." West develops an argument that echoes Dana Radcliffe's claim that social media services do not foster or promote democratic practices, much less the kind of civic engagement that others (such as the author of the *Forbes* article Radcliffe cites) suggest. Although West makes a **claim of fact** when he observes that "Despite social networking's track record for generating democratic engagement . . . it has proven difficult to sustain political interest and activism online over time and move electronic engagement from campaigns to governance," he is most concerned with fostering policies that increase interest in the political process.

West describes a meeting of experts at the Brookings Institute, where participants share ways to encourage grassroots efforts to create change and govern at local, state, and national levels. One participant, political consultant Mindy Finn, argues that political advocacy "should take advantage of [social] networks to set the agenda and drive civic discussions," explaining that advocacy should "involve everything from the questions that get asked during debates to the manner in which journalists cover the election." Finn appears less interested in the deliberative process that preoccupies Radcliffe and embraces the role that social media can play in motivating citizenship and engagement. Another participant, professor of government Diana Owens, suggests that universities "[should] take on the responsibility as a matter of policy to increase civic education for political action." A policy claim points readers to a set of actions they can take in the future, and West's participants all declare policies they would like to see pursued.

Not all writers make their claims as explicitly as these authors do, and it is possible that claims of fact may seem like interpretive claims, as they are based on the inferences we draw from evidence. Thus, it is the writer's task to make a distinction between a claim of fact and interpretation with sufficient evidence. But you should be able to identify the different types of claims. Moreover, you should keep in mind what the situation is and what kind of argument can best address what you see as a problem. Ask yourself: Does the situation involve a question of fact? Does the situation involve a question of value? Does the situation require a change in policy? Or is some combination at work?

Steps to Identifying Claims

1 **Ask:** Does the argument assert that a problem or condition has existed, exists, or will exist? Does the argument seek to establish that a definition is true and can serve as a standard for making relevant judgments? Does the argument ask you to accept the premise that one thing has caused another? If so, it's claim of fact.

2 **Ask:** Does the argument express an evaluation of a problem or condition that has existed, exists, or will exist? If so, it's a claim of value.

3 **Ask:** Does the argument call for change, and is it directed at some future action? If so, it's a claim of policy.

A Practice Sequence: Identifying Claims

What follows is a series of claims. Identify each one as a claim of fact, value, or policy. Be prepared to justify your categorizations.

1. Taxing the use of fossil fuels will end the energy crisis.

2. We should reform the welfare system to ensure that people who receive support from the government also work.

3. Images of violence in the media create a culture of violence in schools.

4. The increase in homelessness is a deplorable situation that contradicts the whole idea of democracy.

5. Distributing property taxes more equitably is the one sure way to end poverty and illiteracy.

6. Individual votes don't really count.

7. Despite the 20 percent increase in the number of females in the workforce over the past forty years, women are still not treated equitably.

8. Affirmative action is a policy that has outlived its usefulness.

9. There are a disproportionate number of black males in American prisons.

10. The media are biased, which means we cannot count on newspapers or television news for the truth.

ANALYZING ARGUMENTS

Analyzing an argument involves identifying the writer's main and minor claims and then examining (1) the reasons and evidence given in support of each claim, (2) the writer's concessions, and (3) the writer's attempts to handle counterarguments.

■ Analyze the Reasons Used to Support a Claim

Stating a claim is one thing; supporting that claim is another. As a critical reader, you need to evaluate whether a writer has provided *good reasons* to support his or her position. Specifically, you will need to decide whether the support for a claim is recent, relevant, reliable, and accurate. As a writer, you will need to use the same criteria when you support your claims.

Is the source recent?   Knowledgeable readers of your written arguments not only will be aware of classic studies that you should cite as "intellectual touchstones"; they will also expect you to cite recent evidence, evidence published within five years of when you are writing.

Of course, older research can be valuable. For example, in a paper about molecular biology, you might very well cite James Watson and Francis Crick's groundbreaking 1953 study in which they describe the structure of DNA. That study is an intellectual touchstone that changed the life sciences in a fundamental way.

Or if you were writing about educational reform, you might very well mention E. D. Hirsch's 1987 book *Cultural Literacy*. Hirsch's book did not change the way people think about curricular reform as profoundly as Watson and Crick's study changed the way scientists think about biology, but his term *cultural literacy* continues to serve as useful shorthand for a particular way of thinking about curricular reform that remains influential to this day.

Although citing Hirsch is an effective way to suggest you have studied the history of an educational problem, it will not convince your readers that there is a crisis in education today. To establish that, you would need to use as evidence studies published over the past few years to show, for example, that there has been a steady decline in test scores since Hirsch wrote his book. And you would need to support your claim that curricular reform is the one sure way to bring an end to illiteracy and poverty with data that are much more current than those available to Hirsch in the 1980s. No one would accept the judgment that our schools are in crisis if your most recent citation is decades old.

Is the source relevant?   Evidence that is relevant must have real bearing on your issue. It also depends greatly on what your readers expect. For example, suppose two of your friends complain that they were unable to sell their condominiums for the price they asked. You can claim there is a crisis in the housing market, but your argument won't convince most readers if your only evidence is personal anecdote.

Such *anecdotal evidence* may alert you to a possible topic and help you connect with your readers, but you will need to test the **relevance** of your friends' experience—Is it pertinent? Is it typical of a larger situation or condition?—if you want your readers to take your argument seriously. For example, you might scan real estate listings to see what the asking prices are for properties comparable to your friends' properties. By comparing listings, you are defining the grounds for your argument. If your friends are disappointed that their one-bedroom condominiums sold for less than a three-bedroom condominium with deeded parking in the same neighborhood, it may well be that their expectations were too high.

In other words, if you aren't comparing like things, your argument is going to be seriously flawed. If your friends' definition of what constitutes a "reasonable price" differs dramatically from everyone else's, their experience is probably irrelevant to the larger question of whether the local housing market is depressed.

Is the source reliable?   You also need to evaluate whether the data you use to support your argument are reliable. After all, some researchers present findings based on a very small sample of people that can also be rather selective.

For example, a researcher might argue that 67 percent of the people he cited believe that school and residential integration are important concerns. But how many people did this person interview? More important, who responded to the researcher's questions? A reliable claim cannot be based on a few of the researcher's friends.

Let's return to the real estate example. You have confirmed that your friends listed their condominiums at prices that were not out of line with the market. Now what? You need to seek out reliable sources to continue testing your argument. For example, you might search the real estate or business section of your local newspaper to see if there are any recent stories about a softening of the market; and you might talk with several local real estate agents to get their opinions on the subject.

In consulting local newspapers and local agents, you are looking for **authoritative sources** against which to test your anecdotal evidence—the confirmation of experts who report on, study, evaluate, and have an informed opinion on local real estate. Local real estate agents are a source of **expert testimony**, firsthand confirmation of the information you have discovered. You would probably not want to rely on the testimony of a single real estate agent, who may have a bias; instead, talk with several agents to see if a consensus emerges.

Is the source accurate?   To determine the accuracy of a study that you want to use to support your argument, you have to do a little digging to find out who else has made a similar claim. For instance, if you want to cite authoritative research that compares the dropout rate for white students with the rate for students of color, you could look at research conducted by the Civil Rights Project. Of course, you don't need to stop your search there. You could also check the resources available through the National Center for Education Statistics. You want to show your readers that you have done a relatively thorough search to make your argument as persuasive as possible.

The accuracy of **statistics**—factual information presented numerically or graphically (for example, in a pie or bar chart)—is difficult to verify. To a certain extent, then, their veracity has to be taken on faith. Often the best you can do is assure yourself that the source of your statistical information is authoritative and reliable—government and major research universities generally are "safe" sources—and that whoever is interpreting the statistical information is not distorting it.

Returning again to our real estate example, let's say you've read a newspaper article that cites statistical information about the condition of the local real estate market (for example, the average price of property and volume of sales this year in comparison to last year). Presumably the author of the article is an expert, but he or she may be interpreting rather than simply reporting on the statistics.

To reassure yourself one way or the other, you may want to check the sources of the author's statistics—go right to your source's sources—which a responsible author will cite. That will allow you to look over the raw data and come to your own conclusions. A further step you could take would be to discuss the article with other experts—local real estate agents—to find out what they think of the article and the information it presents.

Now, let's go back to Dana Radcliffe's essay. How does he develop his assertion that social media services do not foster democratic principles of deliberation or help participants engage in serious dialogue about views different from their own? For that matter, how does Radcliffe arrive at the conclusion—or claim—that "social media appear unsuited to serve as forums of political deliberation?" Radcliffe first establishes what he sees as a plausible standard for defining deliberation as a key principle underlying a democratic society. He bolsters his argument by citing two well-known political philosophers, Amy Gutmann and Dennis Thompson, whose influential *Democracy and Disagreement* (Belknap, 1996) he quotes: "They point out that the demand for deliberation has been a familiar theme in the American constitutional tradition. It is integral to the ideal of republican government as the founders understood it. James Madison judged the design of political institutions in part by how well they furthered deliberation." Importantly, Gutmann and Thompson cite former president and founding father James Madison to identify deliberation as a significant component of democracy and a standard with which to measure the extent to which a society promotes democratic principles.

Radcliffe then makes a series of observations about events that have occurred across the world since the Arab Spring. He points out that the Chinese government seems to allow "critics of public officials and policies to 'vent' online but tightly censors calls for collective action." He also suggests that the Islamic State uses "social media to recruit disaffected Muslim youths from around the world," and as you will note, he uses additional examples to illustrate the extent to which social media services have been "used as *political weapons*." As readers, we may take for granted that Radcliffe's observations are based in "fact," but Radcliffe does not actually cite sources of his "data" to show that "the regime, organization, or group holding the power uses it against individuals, groups, or institutions whose interests or goals conflict with theirs." You would be right to question the basis of such a claim.

In advancing his claim that social media does not support democratic engagement, Radcliffe relies on authoritative sources to explain the behavior of those who use social media. He cites a recent Pew Research Center report, which "offers evidence that people are much less willing to post their political views on social media when they believe their followers would disagree with them." The Pew Research Center describes itself as a "nonpartisan, non-advocacy group" whose aim is to stimulate citizen involvement in community issues and conduct research on public opinion on social and political issues. Radcliffe also cites Daniel Gayo-Avello, who concludes that "when political discussions occur they are not rational and democratic deliberations . . . [because] political information in social media generally lacks quality and strong arguments [and] is usually incoherent and highly opinionated." A professor of computer science at the University of Oviedo in Spain who conducts social media research, Gayo-Avello serves as a credible source of data to support Radcliffe's claim. However, as critical readers, we should inquire into the nature of authors' claims, the source of evidence, and the accuracy of the information authors rely on to advance their claims.

■ Identify Concessions

Part of the strategy of developing a main claim supported with good reasons is to offer a **concession**, an acknowledgment that readers may not agree with every point the writer is making. A concession is a writer's way of saying, "Okay, I can see that there may be another way of looking at the issue or another way to interpret the evidence used to support the argument I am making."

For instance, you may not want your energy costs to go up, but after examining the reasons why it may be necessary to increase taxes on gasoline—to lower usage and conserve fossil fuels—you might concede that a tax increase on gasoline could be useful. The willingness to make concessions is valued in academic writing because it acknowledges both complexity and the importance of multiple perspectives. It also acknowledges the fact that information can always be interpreted in different ways.

Dana Radcliffe makes a concession when he acknowledges that not every reader will define democracy as he does, with an emphasis on deliberation. "Who, then, cares about promoting democratic deliberation?" He maintains that much is at stake for readers who identify with the value he attaches to deliberation as a core principle of democracy: "It is citizens and leaders who understand that democratic processes necessitate deliberative disagreement and, in the legislative process, negotiation and compromise."

Often a writer will signal concessions with phrases like the following:

- "It is true that . . ."
- "I agree with X that Y is an important factor to consider."
- "Some studies have convincingly shown that . . ."

Generally, the writer will then go on to address the concession, explaining how it needs to be modified or abandoned in the light of new evidence or the writer's perspective on the issue.

■ Identify Counterarguments

As the term suggests, a **counterargument** is an argument raised in response to another argument. You want to be aware of and acknowledge what your readers may object to in your argument. Anticipating readers' objections is an important part of developing a conversational argument.

For example, if you were arguing in support of universal health care, you would have to acknowledge that the approach departs dramatically from the traditional role the federal government has played in providing health insurance. That is, most people's access to health insurance has depended on their individual ability to afford and purchase this kind of insurance. You would have to anticipate how readers would respond to your proposal, especially readers who do not feel that the federal government should ever play a role in what has typically been an individual responsibility.

Anticipating readers' objections demonstrates that you understand the complexity of the issue and are willing at least to entertain different and conflicting opinions.

In Dana Radcliffe's essay on social media and democracy, he implicitly concedes that not all readers will care about promoting deliberative democracy; he acknowledges a possible counterargument by citing a *Forbes* article, the author of which contends that "the world is becoming more democratic and reflective of the will of ordinary people." Of course, this is the point that Radcliffe takes issue with, one that clearly resonates for others. Radcliffe remains mindful of critical readers when he reiterates the counterargument that challenges his very definition of whether a nation promotes democracy. "To be sure, 'deliberative democracy' is an ideal to which existing democratic systems only roughly approximate. Nevertheless, the concept provides a plausible standard for evaluating democracies." That is, he recognizes that his definition is the "ideal" and that few governments in practice actually reflect this ideal. But he is invested in such an idea and returns to his original premise: "Nevertheless, the concept provides a plausible standard for evaluating democracies. Moreover, it reminds us that the health of a democracy depends in large part on its fostering deliberation that leads to policies whose legitimacy most citizens accept."

In an argument that is more conversational than confrontational, writers establish areas of common ground, both to convey different views that are understood and to acknowledge the conditions under which those different views are valid. Writers do this by making concessions and anticipating and responding to counterarguments.

This conversational approach is what many people call a **Rogerian approach to argument**, based on psychologist Carl Rogers's approach to psychotherapy. The objective of a Rogerian strategy is to reduce listeners' sense of threat so that they are open to alternatives. For academic writers, it involves four steps:

1. Conveying to readers that their different views are understood.
2. Acknowledging conditions under which readers' views are valid.
3. Helping readers see that the writer shares common ground with them.
4. Creating mutually acceptable solutions to agreed-on problems.

The structure of an argument, according to the Rogerian approach, grows out of the give-and-take of conversation between two people and the topic under discussion. In a written conversation, the give-and-take of face-to-face conversation takes the form of anticipating readers' counterarguments and uses language that is both empathetic and respectful, to put the readers at ease.

AN ANNOTATED STUDENT ARGUMENT

We have annotated the following essay to show the variety of claims the student writer uses, as well as some of the other argumentative moves he performs. The assignment was to write an argument out of personal experience and observation about the cultural impact of a technological innovation. Marques Camp chose to write about the Kindle, an electronic reading device developed by the online retailer Amazon that allows users to download books for a fee. The user cannot share the download electronically with other users. Camp touches on a number of issues reflected in his claims.

As you read the essay, imagine how you would respond to his various claims. Which do you agree with, which do you disagree with, and why? What evidence would you present to support or counter his claims? Do you detect a main claim? Do you think his overall essay develops and supports it?

Camp 1

Marques Camp
Professor Fells
English 1020
January 28, 20—
The End of the World May Be Nigh, and It's the Kindle's Fault

"Libraries will in the end become cities."
— Gottfried Wilhelm Leibniz, German polymath

The student presents a claim of fact that others have made.

The future of written human history will come, as they will have us believe, in the form of the Amazon Kindle and its millions of titles, ready to change the way people read, ready to revolutionize the way people see the world.

He lays the basis for a counterargument by questioning whether this is a real threat at all, citing some technological precedents.

The Kindle is a signpost for our times, a major checkpoint in our long and adventurous journey from the world of printed paper to the twenty-first-century world of digitalization. We first saw this paradigm shift with newspapers, where weekly columns were taken over by daily blog posts, where 48-point sans-serif headlines transformed into 12-point Web links. We then moved on into television, where Must-See TV was replaced with On-Demand TV, where consumers no longer sat around in the living room with their families during prime time but rather watched the latest episode of their favorite show commercial-free from the comfortable and convenient confines of their laptop, able to fast-forward, rewind, and pause with a delightful and devilish sense of programming omnipotence. We are now seeing it, slowly but surely, slay the giant that we never thought could be slain: the world of books.

In this paragraph, he makes a claim of fact about unequal access to technological innovation and offers a concession to what many see as the value of the Kindle.

Contrary to popular belief, easier access to a wider quantity of literature is not a universal revolution. The Kindle speaks to the world that measures quantity by the number of cable television channels it has, speed by the connectivity of its wireless networks, and distance by the number of miles a family travels for vacation. Yes, the Kindle is the new paradigm for universal access and literary connectivity. But it is much like a college degree in the sense that it is merely a gateway to a wealth of opportunity. The problem, however, is gaining access to this gateway in the first place.

1

2

3

Camp 2

He supports his claim of fact with evidence based on experience: that sharing books provides something technology cannot offer.

Books often pass from hand to hand, from friend to friend, from generation to generation, many times with the mutual understanding that remuneration is not necessary — merely the promise of hope that the new reader is as touched and enlightened by the book as the previous one. This transfer serves more than a utilitarian function; symbolically, it represents the passage of hope, of knowledge, of responsibility.

Evidence from observation: not everyone has access to new technologies, but people will always have access to books.

The book, in many cases, represents the only sort of hope for the poorest among us, the great equalizer in a world full of financial and intellectual capital and highly concentrated access to this capital. The wonderful quality of the book is that its intellectual value is very rarely proportional to its financial value; people often consider their most valuable book to be one they happened to pick up one day for free.

An evaluative claim — that the widening gap between rich and poor is dangerous — adds another layer to the argument.

The proliferation of the Kindle technology, however, will result in a wider disconnect between the elite and the non-elite — as the old saying goes, the rich will get richer and the poor will get poorer. Unfortunately for the poor, this is no financial disconnect — this is a widening of the gap in the world of ideas. And this is, perhaps, the most dangerous gap of all.

A further evaluative claim — that new technological devices offer little hope to "victims" of illiteracy — is followed by a claim of fact that books inspire people to create change in the world.

The Kindle Revolution, ironically, may end up contributing to the very disease that is antithetical to its implied function: illiteracy. Make no mistake, the Kindle was not designed with the poor in mind. For those in most need of the printed word, for those who are the most vulnerable victims of the illiteracy threat, the pricey Kindle offers little in the way of hope. One book for a poor person is all he or she needs to be inspired and change the world; with the Kindle, that one book is consolidated and digitized, transformed from a tangible piece of hope and the future into a mere collection of words in the theoretically infinite dimension of cyberspace. A "book" on the Kindle is a book wedged among many other books, separated by nothing more than title, devoid of essence, devoid of uniqueness, devoid of personality, devoid of its unique position in space — precisely what makes a book a "book," as opposed to a mere collection of words. It is no longer singular, no longer serendipitous, no longer distinguishable.

The e-book cannot, like a bound book, pass through multiple hands and eventually settle itself on the right person, ready

4

5

6

7

8

Camp 3

An evaluative claim in which the author observes that technology can make reading passive. Then a claim of fact: that the experience of reading can be transformative.

to be unleashed as a tool to change the world. Due to the restrictions on sharing and reselling e-books with the Kindle, the very nature of reading books transforms from highly communal to individualistic, from highly active to somewhat passive. The Kindle will lead to the mystification of books, wherein they become less unique capsules of thoughts and ideas and experiences and more utility-oriented modes of information-giving. What many Kindle advocates fail to realize is that oftentimes, the transformative quality of books resides less in the actual words comprising the book and more in the actual experience of reading.

There is also something to be said for the utter corporeality of books that lies at the heart of Leibniz's metaphor. Libraries are physical testaments to all that we have learned and recorded during human history. The sheer size of libraries and the sheer number of volumes residing in them tell us, in a spatial sense, of all the theoretical knowledge we have accumulated in the course of our existence, and all the power we have to further shape and define the world we live in.

The student offers a final evaluative claim, observing that the Kindle threatens to mask the relationship between ideas and the world.

The Kindle and other digital literary technologies are threatening the very connection between the world of ideas and the material world, threatening to take our literal measures of progress and hide them away in the vast database of words and ideas, available only to those with money to spare and a credit card for further purchases.

His concluding claim falls just short of making a proposal — but he does suggest that those in positions of power must ensure the proliferation of books.

If libraries will indeed become cities, then we need to carefully begin to lay the foundations, book on top of book on top of book, and we are going to have to ensure that we have enough manpower to do it.

9

10

Steps to Analyzing an Argument

1 **Identify the type of claim.** Is it a claim of fact? Value? Policy?

2 **Analyze the reasons used to support the claim.** Are they recent? Relevant? Reliable? Accurate?

3 **Identify concessions.** Is there another argument that even the author acknowledges is legitimate?

4 **Identify counterarguments.** What arguments contradict or challenge the author's position?

> ## A Practice Sequence: Analyzing an Argument
>
> Use the criteria in the "Steps to Analyzing an Argument" box to analyze the following blog post by Susan D. Blum. What types of claim does she advance? What seems to be her main claim? Do you find her reasons recent, relevant, reliable, and accurate? What sort of concessions does she make? What counterarguments would you raise?

SUSAN D. BLUM

The United States of (Non)Reading: The End of Civilization or a New Era?

Susan D. Blum is a professor of anthropology at the University of Notre Dame whose wide areas of professional interest and expertise include Asian studies and education. She has written or edited many publications, including *Portraits of "Primitives": Ordering Human Kinds in the Chinese Nation* (2001), *My Word! Plagiarism and College Culture* (2009), and *Making Sense of Language: Readings in Culture and Communication* (2009; 2013). She also writes the Learning versus Schooling blog for the *Huffington Post*, where this essay was posted on October 8, 2013.

■ ■ ■

1 Just the other day one of my undergraduate assistants reported a friend's boast that he had not read anything for school since fifth grade. A student at an excellent university, successful, "clever," "smart," he can write papers, take exams, participate in class or online discussions. Why would he have to read?

2 Students sometimes don't buy the class books. Professors are shocked.

3 Several years ago a student told me that she regarded all assigned reading as "recommended," even if the professors labeled it "required." Were professors so dumb that they didn't know that?

4 The idea of assigned reading, as the core activity of college students, is old. Students don't see it as central; faculty do.

5 And though I used to, and sometimes still do, spend a lot of energy lamenting this, by taking a broader view of the nature of reading and writing, I have come to understand it and even to some extent accept it.

6 Student avoidance of reading is not an entirely new problem. When I was in graduate school, in the 1980s, one of my most indelible memories was of a new classmate, straight out of a first-rate college,

complaining in our anthropology theory class that we had to keep finding out what other people thought. When was it time for us to convey
our viewpoints? Why all that reading?

Some college course evaluations ask students what percentage of the 7
reading they did. Some report they did as much as 90 percent. Some as
little as 25 percent.

In a systematic study of college students' reading, Kylie Baier and 8
four colleagues reported that students mostly (40 percent) read for
exams. Almost 19 percent don't read for class. In terms of time, 94 percent of students spend less than two hours on any given reading for
class; 62 percent spend less than an hour. Thirty-two percent believe
they could get an A without reading; 89 percent believe they could get
at least a C.

Among many other educational crises, there is a perceived crisis 9
given that "students are increasingly reading less and less."

When faculty enter new institutions, they often ask colleagues: 10
How much reading should I assign? Some departments offer guidelines about the number of pages: Assign twenty-five pages for each
meeting of first-year classes, but no more than one hundred pages a
week for any course. This has always struck me as strange, given that
a page of a novel and a page of a double-column textbook have completely different amounts of text, and take different kinds of attention
and time. In response to this faculty challenge, Steve Volk—named
the Carnegie Professor of the Year in 2011, so he knows something
about teaching—wrote on the Web site of Oberlin College's Center for
Teaching Innovation and Excellence that there is no magic formula for
numbers of pages. He suggests instead that faculty consider "What do
you want the reading to do?"

But it is not only college teachers who worry about how much 11
people are reading. There is a widespread belief that Americans in
general read less and less. This perception builds on public conversations about the lack of reading. In 2007 a National Endowment for the
Arts study concluded that adults' reading habits were in severe decline.
Only 57 percent of adults read a book voluntarily in 2002, down from
61 percent in 1992.

This was supposed to have all sorts of terrible consequences: educa- 12
tional, of course, but also economic, social, moral, you name it.

Reversing the cup-half-empty conclusion, a 2013 study showed that 13
more than half read books for pleasure—just not what the NEA defines
(or would if the Government were functioning) as "literature."

And the Pew interpretation was that if reading for work and school is 14
added to "voluntary reading," then almost all people read "books" at some
point during the year: 79 percent of 18 to 24 year-olds, and 90 percent of
16 to 17 year-olds.

It is undeniable that people are reading (looking at) writing all   *15*
the time. It may not be in physical books, however. And just this week,
USA Today argued that digital devices increase book reading (on the
devices).

David Carr wrote in 2008 about the decline in attention—not only   *16*
in our students. Attention spans, focus, mindfulness . . . all these are
shrinking. Technology plays a role in this, as many of us spend much
of our lives looking at short items. *The Onion*, the humor website,
puts most of its efforts into its headlines. Blogs should be at most one
thousand words, but three hundred is better. (This one is too long.)

So if students are sipping text constantly on their devices, and   *17*
suddenly they are asked to consume what sounds like an insurmountable mountain of pages in some other form—and for what!?—they are
likely to avoid it entirely.

"Flipping the classroom" has attempted to seek some kind of   *18*
accountability from students for their reading, so that they have to
engage in one way or another with their material prior to assembling
for the precious moment of face-to-face interaction. This requires
reading—but reading with a goal. Students often like to do that, as a
kind of scavenger hunt for what is useful and important. Just having
them read for background ideas seems to be fading.

Actually, I have stopped worrying constantly about this. Students   *19*
are reading. The public is reading. They may not sit for hours, still and
attentive, and focus on one item. They may confuse their facts. They
may miss a complex argument.

Don't misunderstand. I worship reading. When I travel for three   *20*
days, in addition to all my devices I bring six books and five (print)
magazines. Yet I cannot concentrate the way I used to. So those less
devoted. . . . Should we cut them off from the world, isolate them in
soundproof rooms with no WiFi, and force them to read a book?

Writing has evolved, and will evolve. And with it reading changes.   *21*
From clay tablets designed to record debts to bronze proclamations of
kings and emperors, from bamboo strips recording rituals to complex
philosophical arguments on paper, from paintings for the royal afterlife
to paperback novels, from stone tablets proclaiming a new moral code
to infinitesimal elements on a shiny handheld device—from its origins,
writing has transformed, and will continue to change. It is not entirely
that the medium is the message, but the medium affects the message.
Since humans are the ones doing the writing, we get the writing that
suits our purposes.

We are all getting a front-row seat to a sudden change in medium,   *22*
and therefore in writing and reading. What a quick and shocking ride
this is!

Read all about it!

23

ANALYZING AND COMPARING ARGUMENTS

As an academic writer, you will often need to compare disparate claims and evidence from multiple arguments addressing the same topic. Rarely, however, will those arguments be simplistic pro/con pairs meant to represent two opposing sides to an issue. Certainly the news media thrive on such black-and-white conflict, but academic writers seek greater complexity and do not expect to find simple answers. Analyzing and comparing essays on the same topic or issue will often reveal the ways writers work with similar evidence to come up with different, and not necessarily opposed, arguments.

The next two selections are arguments about grade inflation. Both are brief, and we recommend you read through them as a prelude to the activity in analyzing and comparing arguments that follows them. As you read, try to note their claims, the reasons used to support them, concessions, and counterarguments.

STUART ROJSTACZER

Grade Inflation Gone Wild

A former professor of geophysics at Duke University with a PhD in applied earth sciences, Stuart Rojstaczer has written or coauthored many geological studies in his career as a scientist. He has also published a book, *Gone for Good: Tales of University Life after the Golden Age* (1999), and numerous articles on higher education and grading. He is the creator of gradeinflation.com, where he posts a variety of charts and graphs chronicling his data about grade inflation. This op-ed piece appeared in the *Christian Science Monitor* on March 24, 2009.

About six years ago, I was sitting in the student union of a small   *1*
liberal arts college when I saw a graph on the cover of the student newspaper that showed the history of grades given at that institution in the past 30 years.

Grades were up. Way up.   *2*

I'm a scientist by training and I love numbers. So when I looked at   *3*
that graph, I wondered, "How many colleges and universities have data like this that I can find?" The answer is that a lot of schools have data like this hidden somewhere. Back then, I found more than 80 colleges and universities with data on grades, mostly by poking around the Web. Then I created a website (gradeinflation.com) so that others could find this data. I learned that grades started to shoot up nationwide in the 1960s, leveled off in the 1970s, and then started rising again in

the 1980s. Private schools had much higher grades than public schools, but virtually everyone was experiencing grade inflation.

What about today? 4

Grades continue to go up regardless of the quality of education. 5 At a time when many are raising questions about the quality of U.S. higher education, the average GPA at public schools is 3.0, with many flagship state schools having average GPAs higher than 3.2. At a private college, the average is now 3.3. At some schools, it tops 3.5 and even 3.6. "A" is average at those schools! At elite Brown University, two-thirds of all letter grades given are now A's.

These changes in grading have had a profound influence on college 6 life and learning. When students walk into a classroom knowing that they can go through the motions and get a B+ or better, that's what they tend to do, give minimal effort. Our college classrooms are filled with students who do not prepare for class. Many study less than 10 hours a week—that's less than half the hours they spent studying 40 years ago. Paradoxically, students are spending more and more money for an education that seems to deliver less and less content.

With so few hours filled with learning, boredom sets in and students have to find something to pass the time. Instead of learning, they drink. A recent survey of more than 30,000 first-year students across the country showed that nearly half were spending more hours drinking than they were studying. If we continue along this path, we'll end up with a generation of poorly educated college graduates who have used their four years principally to develop an addiction to alcohol.

There are many who say that grade inflation is a complicated issue 8 with no easy fix. But there are solutions. At about the same time that I started to collect data on rising grades, Princeton University began to actually do something about its grade-inflation problem. Its guidelines have the effect of now limiting A's on average to 35 percent of students in a class. Those guidelines have worked. Grades are going back down at Princeton and academic rigor is making a comeback. A similar successful effort has taken place at Wellesley College in Massachusetts. And through a concerted effort on the part of faculty and leadership, grades at Reed College in Oregon have stayed essentially constant for 20 years.

Princeton, Wellesley, and Reed provide evidence that the effort to 9 keep grade inflation in check is not impossible. This effort takes two major steps. First, school officials must admit that there is a problem. Then they must implement policies or guidelines that truly restore excellence.

I asked Dean Nancy Malkiel at Princeton why so few schools seem to 10 be following Princeton's lead. "Because it's hard work," she answered.

"Because you have to persuade the faculty that it's important to do the work."

Making a switch will take hard work, but the effort is worthwhile. The alternative is a student body that barely studies and drinks out of boredom. That's not acceptable. Colleges and universities must roll up their sleeves, bring down inflated grades, and encourage real learning. It's not an impossible task. There are successful examples that can be followed. I'm looking forward to the day when we can return to being proud of the education that our nation's colleges and universities provide.

11

PHIL PRIMACK

Doesn't Anybody Get a C Anymore?

Phil Primack is a journalist, editor, and policy analyst who teaches journalism at Tufts University, where he is a senior fellow at the Jonathan M. Tisch College of Citizenship and Public Service. His articles have appeared in many regional and national publications, including the *New York Times*, the *Boston Globe*, and *Columbia Journalism Review*. The following piece appeared in the *Boston Globe* on October 5, 2008.

■ ■ ■

The student deserved a B-minus. Maybe even a C-plus, I had decided. One paper was especially weak; another was late. But then I began to rationalize. The student had been generally prepared and contributed to class discussion, so I relented and gave what I thought was a very generous B. At least I wouldn't get a complaint about this grade, I figured. Then came the e-mail.

1

Why such a "low grade," the indignant student wrote.

2

"Low grade"? Back when I attended Tufts in the late 1960s, a B in certain courses was something I could only dream about. But grade inflation, the steady rise in grade point averages that began in the 1960s, now leaves many students regarding even the once-acceptable B—which has always stood for "good"—as a transcript wrecker, and a C—that is, "average"—as unmitigated disaster. More and more academic leaders may lament grade inflation, but precious few have been willing to act against it, leaving their professors all alone in the minefield between giving marks that reflect true merit and facing the wrath of students for whom entitlement begins with the letter A.

3

Grade inflation "is a huge problem," says former U.S. senator Hank Brown, who tried to make it a priority issue as president of the

4

University of Colorado in 2006. "Under the current system at a lot of schools, there is no way to recognize the difference between an outstanding job and a good job. Grade inflation hides laziness on the part of the students, and as long as it exists, even faculty who want to do a good job [in grading] don't feel they can."

That's because many professors fear that "tough grading" will trigger poor student evaluations or worse, which in turn can jeopardize the academic career track. "In my early years, students would say they liked my class, but the grades were low and the work level high," says retired Duke University professor Stuart Rojstaczer. "I had to get with the program and reduce my own expectations of workload and increase grades in order to have students leave my class with a positive impression to give to other students so they would attend [next year]. I was teaching worse, but the student response was much more positive." 5

Harvard University is the poster campus for academic prestige—and for grade inflation, even though some of its top officials have warned about grade creep. About 15 percent of Harvard students got a B-plus or better in 1950, according to one study. In 2007, more than half of all Harvard grades were in the A range. Harvard declined to release more current data or officially comment for this article. At the University of Massachusetts at Amherst, the average GPA in 2007 was 3.19 (on a four-point scale), up from 3.02 a decade earlier. That "modest increase" simply reflects better students, UMass spokesman Ed Blaguszewski says in an e-mail. "Since our students have been increasingly well-prepared . . . it makes sense that their UMass grades have crept up. Essentially, the profile of the population has changed over time, so we don't consider this to be grade inflation." 6

That's certainly the most common argument to explain away grade inflation—smarter students naturally get higher grades. But is it that simple? Privately, many faculty members and administrators say colleges are unwilling to challenge and possibly offend students and their hovering, tuition-paying parents with some tough grade love. And without institutional backing, individual faculty members simply yield to whining students. 7

But not everywhere. The most cited—and extreme—case of taking on grade inflation is at Princeton University, which in 2004 directed that A's account for less than 35 percent of undergraduate course grades. From 2004 to 2007, A's (A-plus, A, A-minus) accounted for 40.6 percent of undergraduate course grades, down from 47 percent in the period 2001 to 2004. 8

Closer to home, Wellesley College calls for the average grade in basic undergraduate courses to be no higher than a B-plus (3.33 GPA). "It's not that we're trying to get grades down, but we're trying to get grades to mean something," says associate dean of the college Adele Wolfson, who teaches chemistry. Wellesley's GPA, which stood at 3.47 in 2002 9 and was 3.4 when the policy was implemented two years later, fell to 3.3 this year, mainly because of more B grades and fewer A's. "The A has really become the mark of excellence," she says, "which is what it should be."

The problem, says Rojstaczer, is that such policies are the excep-   *10* tions, and that grade inflation will be reduced only through consistent prodding and action by top officials. "In truth, some university leaders are embarrassed that grading is so lax, but they are loath to make any changes," he says in an e-mail. "Grade inflation in academia is like the alcoholic brother you pretend is doing just fine. When someone calls your brother a drunk, you get angry and defend him, although privately you worry. That's where we are with grade inflation: public denial and private concern."

A Practice Sequence: Analyzing and Comparing Arguments

1   To practice these strategies, first break up into small groups to discuss four different concerns surrounding grade inflation:

> *Group 1:* Define what you think grade inflation is.
>
> *Group 2:* Discuss whether you think grade inflation is a problem at the university or college you attend. What evidence can you provide to suggest that it is or is not a problem?
>
> *Group 3:* Why should students or faculty be concerned with grade inflation? What's at stake?
>
> *Group 4:* How would you respond if the administration at your university or college decided to limit the number of A's that faculty could give students?

Reassemble as a class and briefly report on the discussions.

2   Analyze Stuart Rojstaczer's argument in "Grade Inflation Gone Wild," addressing the following questions:

- What evidence does Rojstaczer use to indicate that there is a problem?

- How would you characterize this evidence (for example, scientific, anecdotal), and to what extent are you persuaded by the evidence he provides to suggest that grade inflation has a profound effect on "life and learning"?

- To what extent does he persuade you that a change in policy is necessary or that such a change would make a difference?

3 Now compare Phil Primack's and Stuart Rojstaczer's strategies for developing an argument.

- How does Primack establish that there is a problem? To what extent is his approach as persuasive as Rojstaczer's?

- What strategies would you identify in either argument as strategies that you might employ to develop your own argument?

- To what extent are you persuaded by the counterargument that Primack introduces?

- What do you think Primack wants you to do or think about in his analysis?

- In the end, does Primack add anything to your understanding of the problem of whether your college or university should introduce a policy to limit grade inflation?

4 As an alternative assignment, write a three-page essay in which you compare the arguments student Marques Camp and Professor Susan D. Blum make about the state of reading today. Consider their main claims and how they support them. Explain which argument you find more persuasive, and why. Feel free to draw on your own experience and make use of personal anecdotes to make your case.

5

From Identifying Issues to Forming Questions

Remember that inquiry is central to the process of composing. As you move from reading texts to writing them, you will discover that writing grows out of answering these questions:

- What are the concerns of the authors I've been reading?
- What situations motivate them to write?
- What frames or contexts do these writers use to construct their arguments?
- What is my argument in response to their writing?
- What is at stake in my argument?
- Who will be interested in reading what I have to say?
- How can I connect with both sympathetic and antagonistic readers?
- What kinds of evidence will persuade my readers?
- What objections are they likely to raise?

To answer these questions, you must read in the role of writer, with an eye toward

- *identifying an issue* (an idea or a statement that is open to dispute) that compels you to respond in writing,
- *understanding the situation* (the factors that give rise to the issue and shape your response), and
- *formulating a question* (what you intend to answer in response to the issue).

TABLE 5.1   A Series of Situations with Related Issues and Questions

SITUATION	ISSUE	QUESTION
Different state legislatures are passing legislation to prevent Spanish-speaking students from using their own language in schools.	Most research on learning contradicts the idea that students should be prevented from using their own language in the process of learning a new language.	Under what conditions should students be allowed to use their own language while they learn English?
A manufacturing company has plans to move to your city with the promise of creating new jobs in a period of high unemployment.	You feel that this company will compromise the quality of life for the surrounding community because the manufacturing process will pollute the air.	What would persuade the city to prevent this company from moving in, even though the company will provide much-needed jobs?
Your school has made an agreement with a local company to supply vending machines that sell drinks and food. The school plans to use its share of the profits to improve the library and purchase a new scoreboard for the football field.	You see that the school has much to gain from this arrangement, but you also know that obesity is a growing problem at the school.	Is there another way for the school to generate needed revenue without putting students' health at risk?
An increasing number of homeless people are seeking shelter on your college campus.	Campus security has stepped up its efforts to remove the homeless, even though the shelters off campus are over-crowded.	How can you persuade the school to shelter the homeless and to provide funds to support the needs of the homeless in your city?

In Table 5.1, we identify a series of situations and one of the issues and questions that derive from each of them. Notice that the question you ask defines the area of inquiry as you read; it also can help you formulate your working thesis, the statement that answers your question. (We say more about developing a thesis in Chapter 6.) In this chapter, in addition to further discussing the importance of situation, we look at how you can identify issues and formulate questions to guide your reading and writing.

IDENTIFYING ISSUES

In this section we present several steps to identifying an issue. You don't have to follow them in this particular order, and you may find yourself going back and forth among them as you try to bring an issue into focus.

Keep in mind that issues do not simply exist in the world well formed. Instead, writers construct what they see as issues from the situations they observe. For example, consider legislation to limit downloads from the Internet. If such legislation conflicts with your own practices and sense of freedom, you may have begun to identify an issue: the clash of values over what constitutes fair use and what does not. Be aware that others may not understand your issue and that in your writing you will have to explain carefully what is at stake.

■ Draw on Your Personal Experience

You may have been taught that formal writing is objective, that you must keep a dispassionate distance from your subject, and that you should not use *I* in a college-level paper. The fact is, however, that our personal experiences influence how we read, what we pay attention to, and what inferences we draw. It makes sense, then, to begin with you—where you are and what you think and believe.

We all use personal experience to make arguments in our everyday lives. In an academic context, the challenge is to use personal experience to argue a point, to illustrate something, or to illuminate a connection between theories and the sense we make of our daily experience. You don't want simply to tell your story. You want your story to strengthen your argument.

For example, in *Cultural Literacy*, E. D. Hirsch personalizes his interest in reversing the cycle of illiteracy in America's cities. To establish the nature of the problem in the situation he describes, he cites research showing that student performance on standardized tests in the United States is falling. But he also reflects on his own teaching in the 1970s, when he first perceived "the widening knowledge gap [that] caused me to recognize the connection between specific background knowledge and mature literacy." And he injects anecdotal evidence from conversations with his son, a teacher. Those stories heighten readers' awareness that school-aged children do not know much about literature, history, or government. (For example, his son mentions a student who challenged his claim that Latin is a "dead language" by demanding, "What do they speak in Latin America?")

Hirsch's use of his son's testimony makes him vulnerable to criticism, as readers might question whether Hirsch can legitimately use his son's experience to make generalizations about education. But in fact, Hirsch is using personal testimony—his own and his son's—to augment and put a human face on the research he cites. He presents his issue, that schools must teach cultural literacy, both as something personal and as something with which we should all be concerned. The personal note helps readers see Hirsch as someone who has long been concerned with education and who has even raised a son who is an educator.

■ Identify What Is Open to Dispute

An issue is something that is open to dispute. Sometimes the way to clarify an issue is to think of it as a *fundamental tension* between two or more conflicting points of view. If you can identify conflicting points of view, an issue may become clear.

Consider E. D. Hirsch, who believes that the best approach to educational reform is to change the curriculum in schools. His position: A curriculum based on cultural literacy is the one sure way to reverse the cycle of poverty and illiteracy in urban areas.

What is the issue? Hirsch's issue emerges in the presence of an alternative position. Jonathan Kozol, a social activist who has written extensively about educational reform, believes that policymakers need to address reform by providing the necessary resources that all students need to learn. Kozol points out that students in many inner-city schools are reading outdated textbooks and that the dilapidated conditions in these schools — windows that won't close, for example — make it impossible for students to learn.

In tension are two different views of the reform that can reverse illiteracy: Hirsch's view that educational reform should occur through curricular changes, and Kozol's view that educational reform demands socioeconomic resources.

▪ Resist Binary Thinking

As you begin to define what is at issue, try to tease out complexities that may not be immediately apparent. That is, try to resist the either/or mindset that signals binary thinking.

If you considered only what Hirsch and Kozol have to say, it would be easy to characterize the problems facing our schools as either curricular or socioeconomic. But it may be that the real issue combines these arguments with a third or even a fourth, that neither curricular nor socioeconomic changes by themselves can resolve the problems with American schools.

After reading essays by both Hirsch and Kozol, one of our students pointed out that both Hirsch's focus on curriculum and Kozol's socioeconomic focus ignore another concern. She went on to describe her school experience in racial terms. In the excerpt below, notice how this writer uses personal experience (in a new school, she is not treated as she had expected to be treated) to formulate an issue.

> Moving from Colorado Springs to Tallahassee, I was immediately struck by the differences apparent in local home life, school life, and community unity, or lack thereof. Ripped from my sheltered world at a small Catholic school characterized by racial harmony, I was thrown into a large public school where outward prejudice from classmates and teachers and "race wars" were common and tolerated. . . .
>
> In a school where students and teachers had free rein to abuse anyone different from them, I was constantly abused. As the only black student in English honors, I was commonly belittled in front of my "peers" by my teacher. If I developed courage enough to ask a question, I was always answered with the use of improper grammar and such words as "ain't" as my teacher attempted to simplify the material to "my level" and to give me what he called "a little learning." After discussing several

subjects, he often turned to me, singling me out of a sea of white faces, and asked, "Do *you* understand, Mila?" When asking my opinion of a subject, he frequently questioned, "What do *your* people think about this?" Although he insisted on including such readings as Martin Luther King's "I Have a Dream" speech in the curriculum, the speech's themes of tolerance and equity did not accompany his lesson.

Through her reading, this student discovered that few prominent scholars have confronted the issue of racism in schools directly. Although she grants that curricular reform and increased funding may be necessary to improve education, she argues that scholars also need to address race in their studies of teaching and learning.

Our point is that issues may be more complex than you first think they are. For this student, the issue wasn't one of two positions—reform the curriculum or provide more funding. Instead, it combined a number of different positions, including race ("prejudice" and "race wars") and the relationship between student and teacher ("Do *you* understand, Mila?") in a classroom.

In this passage, the writer uses her experience to challenge binary thinking. Like the student writer, you should examine issues from different perspectives, avoiding either/or propositions that oversimplify the world.

■ Build on and Extend the Ideas of Others

Academic writing builds on and extends the ideas of others. As an academic writer, you will find that by extending other people's ideas, you will extend your own. You may begin in a familiar place, but as you read more and pursue connections to other readings, you may well end up at an unexpected destination.

For example, one of our students was troubled when he read Melissa Stormont-Spurgin's description of homeless children. The student uses details from her work (giving credit, of course) in his own:

The children . . . went to school after less than three hours of sleep. They wore the same wrinkled clothes that they had worn the day before. What will their teachers think when they fall asleep in class? How will they get food for lunch? What will their peers think? What could these homeless children talk about with their peers? They have had to grow up too fast. Their worries are not the same as other children's worries. They are worried about their next meal and where they will seek shelter. Their needs, however, are the same. They need a home and all of the securities that come with it. They also need an education (Stormont-Spurgin 156).

Initially the student was troubled by his own access to quality schools, and the contrast between his life and the lives of the children Stormont-Spurgin describes. Initially, then, his issue was the fundamental tension between his own privileged status, something he had taken for granted, and the struggle that homeless children face every day.

However, as he read further and grew to understand homelessness as a concern in a number of studies, he connected his personal response to a larger conversation about democracy, fairness, and education:

> Melissa Stormont-Spurgin, an author of several articles on educational studies, addresses a very real and important, yet avoided issue in education today. Statistics show that a very high percentage of children who are born into homeless families will remain homeless, or in poverty, for the rest of their lives. How can this be, if everyone actually does have the same educational opportunities? There must be significant educational disadvantages for children without homes. In a democratic society, I feel that we must pay close attention to these disadvantages and do everything in our power to replace them with equality.

Ultimately, the student refined his sense of what was at issue: *Although all people should have access to public education in a democratic society, not everyone has the opportunity to attend quality schools in order to achieve personal success.* In turn, his definition of the issue began to shape his argument:

> Parents, teachers, homeless shelters, and the citizens of the United States who fund [homeless] shelters must address the educational needs of homeless children, while steering them away from any more financial or psychological struggles. Without this emphasis on education, the current trend upward in the number of homeless families will inevitably continue in the future of American society.

The student shifted away from a personal issue—the difference between his status and that of homeless children—to an issue of clashing values: the principle of egalitarian democracy on the one hand and the reality of citizens in a democracy living in abject poverty on the other. When he started to read about homeless children, he could not have made the claim he ends up making, that policymakers must make education a basic human right.

This student offers us an important lesson about the role of inquiry and the value of resisting easy answers. He has built on and extended his own ideas—and the ideas of others—after repeating the process of reading, raising questions, writing, and seeing problems a number of times.

■ Read to Discover a Writer's Frame

A more specialized strategy of building on and extending the ideas of others involves reading to discover a writer's **frame**, the perspective through which a writer presents his or her arguments. Writers want us to see the world a certain way, so they frame their arguments much the same way photographers and artists frame their pictures.

For example, if you were to take a picture of friends in front of the football stadium on campus, you would focus on what you would most like to remember—your friends' faces—blurring the images of the people walking behind your friends. Setting up the picture, or framing it, might require using light and shade to make some details stand out more than others. Writers do the same with language.

E. D. Hirsch uses the concept of *cultural literacy* to frame his argument for curricular reform. For Hirsch, the term is a benchmark, a standard: People who are culturally literate are familiar with the body of information that every educated citizen should know. Hirsch's implication, of course, is that people who are not culturally literate are not well educated. But that is not necessarily true. In fact, a number of educators insist that literacy is simply a means to an end—reading to complete an assignment, for example, or to understand the ramifications of a decision—not an end in itself. By defining and using *cultural literacy* as the goal of education, Hirsch is framing his argument; he is bringing his ideas into focus.

When writers use framing strategies, they also call attention to the specific conversations that set up the situation for their arguments. Framing often entails quoting specific theories and ideas from other authors and then using those quotations as a perspective, or lens, through which to examine other material. In his memoir *Hunger of Memory: The Education of Richard Rodriguez* (1982), Richard Rodriguez uses this method to examine his situation as a nonnative speaker of English desperate to enter the mainstream culture, even if it means sacrificing his identity as the son of Mexican immigrants. Reflecting on his life as a student, Rodriguez comes across Richard Hoggart's book *The Uses of Literacy* (1957). Hoggart's description of "the scholarship boy" presents a lens through which Rodriguez can see his own experience. Hoggart writes:

> With his family, the boy has the intense pleasure of intimacy, the family's consolation in feeling public alienation. Lavish emotions texture home life. *Then*, at school, the instruction bids him to trust lonely reason primarily. Immediate needs set the pace of his parents' lives. From his mother and father the boy learns to trust spontaneity and nonrational ways of knowing. *Then*, at school, there is mental calm. Teachers emphasize the value of a reflectiveness that opens a space between thinking and immediate action.
>
> Years of schooling must pass before the boy will be able to sketch the cultural differences in his day as abstractly as this. But he senses those differences early. Perhaps as early as the night he brings home an assignment from school and finds the house too noisy for study. He has to be more and more alone, if he is going to "get on." He will have, probably unconsciously, to oppose the ethos of the hearth, the intense gregariousness of the working-class family group. . . . The boy has to cut himself off mentally, so as to do his homework, as well as he can.

Here is Rodriguez's response to Hoggart's description of the scholarship boy:

> For weeks I read, speed-read, books by modern educational theorists, only to find infrequent and slight mention of students like me. . . . Then one day, leafing through Richard Hoggart's *The Uses of Literacy*, I found, in his description of the scholarship boy, myself. For the first time I realized that

there were other students like me, and so I was able to frame the meaning of my academic success, its consequent price—the loss.

Notice how Rodriguez introduces ideas from Hoggart "to frame" his own ideas: "I found, in his description of the scholarship boy, myself. For the first time I realized that there were other students like me, and so I was able to frame the meaning of my academic success, its consequent price—the loss." Hoggart's scholarship boy enables Rodriguez to revisit his own experience with a new perspective. Hoggart's words and idea advance Rodriguez's understanding of the problem he identifies in his life: his inability to find solace at home and within his working-class roots. Hoggart's description of the scholarship boy's moving between cultural extremes—spontaneity at home and reflection at school—helps Rodriguez bring his own youthful discontent into focus.

Rodriguez's response to Hoggart's text shows how another writer's lens can help frame an issue. If you were using Hoggart's term *scholarship boy* as a lens through which to clarify an issue in education, you might ask how the term illuminates new aspects of another writer's examples or your own. And then you might ask, "To what extent does Hirsch's cultural literacy throw a more positive light on what Rodriguez and Hoggart describe?" or "How do my experiences challenge, extend, or complicate the scholarship-boy concept?"

■ Consider the Constraints of the Situation

In identifying an issue, you have to understand the situation that gives rise to the issue, including the contexts in which it is raised and debated. One of the contexts is the *audience*. In thinking about your issue, you must consider the extent to which your potential readers are involved in the dialogue you want to enter, and what they know and need to know. In a sense, audience functions as both context and **constraint**, a factor that narrows the choices you can make in responding to an issue. An understanding of your potential readers will help you choose the depth of your discussion; it will also determine the kind of evidence you can present and the language you can use.

Another constraint on your response to an issue is the form that response takes. For example, if you decide to make an issue of government-imposed limits on what you can download from the Internet, your response in writing might take the form of an editorial or a letter to a legislator. In this situation, length is an obvious constraint: Newspapers limit the word count of editorials, and the best letters to legislators tend to be brief and very selective about the evidence they cite. A few personal examples and a few statistics may be all you can include to support your claim about the issue. By contrast, if you were making your case in an academic journal, a very different set of constraints would apply. You would have more space for illustrations and support, for example.

Finally, the situation itself can function as a major constraint. For instance, suppose your topic is the decline of educational standards. It's difficult to imagine any writer making the case for accelerating that decline, or any audience being receptive to the idea that a decline in standards is a good thing.

Steps to Identifying Issues

1 **Draw on your personal experience.** Start with your own sense of what's important, what puzzles you, or what you are curious about. Then build your argument by moving on to other sources to support your point of view.

2 **Identify what is open to dispute.** Identify a phenomenon or some idea in a written argument that challenges what you think or believe.

3 **Resist binary thinking.** Think about the issue from multiple perspectives.

4 **Build on and extend the ideas of others.** As you read, be open to new ways of looking at the issue. The issue you finally write about may be very different from what you set out to write about.

5 **Read to discover a writer's frame.** What theories or ideas shape the writer's focus? How can these theories or ideas help you frame your argument?

6 **Consider the constraints of the situation.** Craft your argument to meet the needs of and constraints imposed by your audience and form.

IDENTIFYING ISSUES IN AN ESSAY

In the following editorial, published in 2002 in *Newsweek*, writer Anna Quindlen addresses her concern that middle-class parents overschedule their children's lives. She calls attention to the ways leisure time helped her develop as a writer and urges parents to consider the extent to which children's creativity depends on having some downtime. They don't always have to have their time scheduled. As you read Quindlen's "Doing Nothing Is Something," note what words and phrases Quindlen uses to identify the situation and to indicate who her audience is. Identify her main claim as one of fact, value, or policy. Finally, answer the questions that follow the selection to see if you can discern how she locates, defines, and advances her issue.

ANNA QUINDLEN

Doing Nothing Is Something

Anna Quindlen is a best-selling author of novels and children's books, but she is perhaps most widely known for her nonfiction and commentary on current events and contemporary life. She won a Pulitzer Prize in 1992 for her "Public and Private" column in the *New York Times,* and for ten years wrote a biweekly column for *Newsweek.* Some of her novels are *Object Lessons* (1991), *Blessings* (2002), and *Every Last One* (2010). Her nonfiction works and collections include *Living Out Loud* (1988), *Thinking Out Loud* (1994), *Loud and Clear* (2004), and *Good Dog. Stay.* (2007).

S ummer is coming soon. I can feel it in the softening of the air, but I can see it, too, in the textbooks on my children's desks. The number of uncut pages at the back grows smaller and smaller. The loose-leaf is ragged at the edges, the binder plastic ripped at the corners. An old remembered glee rises inside me. Summer is coming. Uniform skirts in mothballs. Pencils with their points left broken. Open windows. Day trips to the beach. Pickup games.

Hanging out. How boring it was.

Of course, it was the making of me, as a human being and a writer. Downtime is where we become ourselves, looking into the middle distance, kicking at the curb, lying on the grass, or sitting on the stoop and staring at the tedious blue of the summer sky. I don't believe you can write poetry, or compose music, or become an actor without downtime, and plenty of it, a hiatus that passes for boredom but is really the quiet moving of the wheels inside that fuel creativity.

And that, to me, is one of the saddest things about the lives of American children today. Soccer leagues, acting classes, tutors—the calendar of the average middle-class kid is so over the top that soon Palm handhelds will be sold in Toys "R" Us. Our children are as overscheduled as we are, and that is saying something.

This has become so bad that parents have arranged to schedule times for unscheduled time. Earlier this year the privileged suburb of Ridgewood, New Jersey, announced a Family Night, when there would be no homework, no athletic practices, and no after-school events. This was terribly exciting until I realized that this was not one night a week, but one single night. There is even a free-time movement, and Web site: familylife1st.org. Among the frequently asked questions provided online: "What would families do with family time if they took it back?"

Let me make a suggestion for the kids involved: How about nothing? It is not simply that it is pathetic to consider the lives of children who don't have a moment between piano and dance and homework to talk about their day or just search for split ends, an enormously satisfying leisure-time activity of my youth. There is also ample psychological research suggesting that what we might call "doing nothing" is when human beings actually do their best thinking, and when creativity comes to call. Perhaps we are creating an entire generation of people whose ability to think outside the box, as the current parlance of business has it, is being systematically stunted by scheduling.

A study by the University of Michigan quantified the downtime deficit; in the last twenty years American kids have lost about four unstructured hours a week. There has even arisen a global Right to Play movement: in the Third World it is often about child labor, but in the United States it is about the sheer labor of being a perpetually busy child. In Omaha, Nebraska, a group of parents recently lobbied for additional recess. Hooray, and yikes.

How did this happen? Adults did it. There is a culture of adult distrust that suggests that a kid who is not playing softball or attending science-enrichment programs—or both—is huffing or boosting cars: If kids are left alone, they will not stare into the middle distance and consider the meaning of life and how come your nose in pictures never looks the way you think it should, but instead will get into trouble. There is also the culture of cutthroat and unquestioning competition that leads even the parents of preschoolers to gab about prestigious colleges without a trace of irony: This suggests that any class in which you do not enroll your first grader will put him at a disadvantage in, say, law school.

Finally, there is a culture of workplace presence (as opposed to productivity). Try as we might to suggest that all these enrichment activities are for the good of the kid, there is ample evidence that they are really for the convenience of parents with way too little leisure time of their own. Stories about the resignation of presidential aide Karen Hughes unfailingly reported her dedication to family time by noting that she arranged to get home at 5:30 one night a week to have dinner with her son. If one weekday dinner out of five is considered laudable, what does that say about what's become commonplace?

Summer is coming. It used to be a time apart for kids, a respite from the clock and the copybook, the organized day. Every once in a while, either guilty or overwhelmed or tired of listening to me keen about my monumental boredom, my mother would send me to some rinky-dink park program that consisted almost entirely of three-legged races and making things out of Popsicle sticks. Now, instead, there are music camps, sports camps, fat camps, probably thin camps. I mourn hanging out in the backyard. I mourn playing Wiffle ball in the street without a sponsor and matching shirts. I mourn drawing in the dirt with a stick.

Maybe that kind of summer is gone for good. Maybe this is the leading edge of a new way of living that not only has no room for contemplation but is contemptuous of it. But if downtime cannot be squeezed during the school year into the life of frantic and often joyless activity with which our children are saddled while their parents pursue frantic and often joyless activity of their own, what about summer? Do most adults really want to stand in line for Space Mountain or sit in traffic to get to a shore house that doesn't have enough saucepans? Might it be even more enriching for their children to stay at home and do nothing? For those who say they will only watch TV or play on the computer, a piece of technical advice: The cable box can be unhooked, the modem removed. Perhaps it is not too late for American kids to be given the gift of enforced boredom for at least a week or two, staring into space, bored out of their gourds, exploring the inside of their own heads. "To contemplate is to toil, to think is to do," said Victor Hugo. "Go outside and play," said Prudence Quindlen. Both of them were right.

Reading as a Writer

1. What evidence of Quindlen's personal responses and experiences can you identify?
2. What phenomenon has prompted her to reflect on what she thinks and believes? How has she made it into an issue?
3. Where does she indicate that she has considered the issue from multiple perspectives and is placing her ideas in conversation with those of others?
4. What sort of lens does she seem to be using to frame her argument?
5. What constraints (such as the format of an editorial) seem to be in play in the essay?

A Practice Sequence: Identifying Issues

This sequence of activities will give you practice in identifying and clarifying issues based on your own choice of reading and collaboration with your classmates.

1   Draw on your personal experience. Reflect on your own responses to what you have been reading in this class or in other classes, or issues that writers have posed in the media. What concerns you most? Choose a story that supports or challenges the claims people are making in what you have read or listened to. What questions do you have? Make some notes in response to these questions, explaining your personal stake in the issues and questions you formulate.

2   Identify what is open to dispute. Take what you have written and formulate your ideas as an issue, using the structure we used in our example of Hirsch's and Kozol's competing arguments:

- Part 1: Your view of a given topic
- Part 2: At least one view that is in tension with your own

If you need to, read further to understand what others have to say about this issue.

3   Resist binary thinking. Share your statement of the issue with one or more peers and ask them if they see other ways to formulate the issue that you may not have thought about. What objections, if any, do they make to your statement in part 1? Write these objections down in part 2 so that you begin to look at the issue from multiple perspectives.

4   Build on and extend the ideas of others. Now that you have formulated an issue from different perspectives, explaining your personal stake in the issue, connect what you think to a broader conversation in what you are reading. Then try making a claim using this structure: "Although some people would argue _____, I think that _____."

5   Read to discover a writer's frame. As an experiment in trying out multiple perspectives, revise the claim you make in exercise 4 by introducing the frame, or lens, through which you want readers to understand your argument. You can employ the same sentence structure. For example, here is a claim framed in terms of race: "Although people should have access to public education, recent policies have worsened racial inequalities in public schools." In contrast, here is a claim that focuses on economics: "Although people should have access to public education, the unequal distribution of tax money has created what some would call an 'economy of education.'" The lens may come from reading you have done in other courses or from conversations with your classmates, and you may want to attribute the lens to a particular author or classmate: "Although some people would argue_____, I use E. D. Hirsch's notion of cultural literacy to show_____."

6   Consider the constraints of the situation. Building on these exercises, develop an argument in the form of an editorial for your local newspaper. This means that you will need to limit your argument to about 250 words. You also will need to consider the extent to which your potential readers are involved in the conversation. What do they know? What do they need to know? What kind of evidence do you need to use to persuade readers?

FORMULATING ISSUE-BASED QUESTIONS

As we have said, when you identify an issue, you need to understand it in the context of its situation. Ideally, the situation and the issue will be both relevant and recent, making the task of connecting to your audience that much easier when you write about the issue. For example, the student writer who was concerned about long-standing issues of homelessness and lack of educational opportunity connected to his readers by citing recent statistics and giving the problem of homelessness a face: "The children . . . went to school after less than three hours of sleep. They wore the same wrinkled clothes that they had worn the day before." If your issue does not immediately fulfill the criteria of relevance and timeliness, you need to take that into consideration as you continue your reading and research on the issue. Ask yourself, "What is on people's minds these days?" "What do they need to know about?" Think about why the issue matters to you, and imagine why it might matter to others. By the time you write, you should be prepared to make the issue relevant for your readers.

In addition to understanding the situation and defining the issue that you feel is most relevant and timely, you can formulate an issue-based question that can help you think through what you might be interested in writing about. This question should be specific enough to guide inquiry into what others have written. An issue-based question can also help you accomplish the following:

- clarify what you know about the issue and what you still need to know;
- guide your inquiry with a clear focus;
- organize your inquiry around a specific issue;
- develop an argument (rather than simply collecting information) by asking *How?*, *Why?*, *Should?*, or *To what extent is this true (or not true)?*;
- consider who your audience is;
- determine what resources you have, so that you can ask a question that you will be able to answer with the resources available to you.

A good question develops out of an issue, some fundamental tension that you identify within a conversation. In "Doing Nothing Is Something," Anna Quindlen identifies a problem that middle-class parents need to know about: that overscheduling their children's lives may limit their children's potential for developing their creativity. As she explores the reasons why children do not have sufficient downtime, she raises a question that encourages parents to consider what would happen if they gave their children time to do nothing: "Might it be even more enriching for their children to stay at home and do nothing?" (para. 11). Through identifying what is at issue, you should begin to understand for whom it is an issue — for whom you are answering the question. In turn, the answer to your question will help you craft your thesis.

In the following section, we trace the steps one of our students took to formulate an issue-based question on the broad topic of language diversity. Although we present the steps in sequence, be aware that they are guidelines only: The steps often overlap, and there is a good deal of room for rethinking and refining along the way.

■ Refine Your Topic

Generally speaking, a **topic** is the subject you want to write about. For example, homelessness, tests, and violence are all topics. So are urban homelessness, standardized tests, and video game violence. And so are homelessness in New York City, aptitude tests versus achievement tests, and mayhem in the video game *Grand Theft Auto*. As our list suggests, even a specific topic needs refining into an issue before it can be explored effectively in writing.

The topic our student wanted to focus on was language diversity, a subject her linguistics class had been discussing. She was fascinated by the extraordinary range of languages spoken in the United States, not just by immigrant groups but by native speakers whose dialects and varieties of English are considered nonstandard. She herself had relatives for whom English was not a first language. She began refining her topic by putting her thoughts into words:

> I want to describe the experience of being raised in a home where non–Standard English is spoken.

> I'd like to know the benefits and liabilities of growing up bilingual.

> I am curious to know what it's like to live in a community of nonnative speakers of English while trying to make a living in a country where the dominant language is English.

Although she had yet to identify an issue, her attempts to articulate what interested her about the topic were moving her toward the situation of people in the United States who don't speak Standard English or don't have English as their first language.

■ Explain Your Interest in the Topic

At this point, the student encountered E. D. Hirsch's *Cultural Literacy* in her reading, which had both a provocative and a clarifying effect on her thinking. She began to build on and extend Hirsch's ideas. Reacting to Hirsch's assumption that students should acquire the same base of knowledge and write in Standard Written English, her first, somewhat mischievous thought was, "I wonder what Hirsch would think about cultural literacy being taught in a bilingual classroom?" But then her thinking took another turn, and she began to contemplate the effect of Hirsch's cultural-literacy agenda on speakers whose English is not standard or for whom English is not a first language. She used a demographic fact that she had learned in her linguistics class in her explanation of her interest in the topic: "I'm curious about the consequences of limiting language diversity when the presence of ethnic minorities in our educational system is growing."

■ Identify an Issue

The more she thought about Hirsch's ideas, and the more she read about language diversity, the more concerned our student grew. It seemed to her that Hirsch's interest in producing students who all share the same base of knowledge and all write in Standard Written English was in tension with her sense that this kind of approach places a burden on people whose first language is not English. That tension clarified the issue for her. In identifying the issue, she wrote:

> Hirsch's book actually sets some priorities, most notably through his list of words and phrases that form the foundations of what it means to be "American." However, this list certainly overlooks several crucial influences in American culture. Most oversights generally come at the expense of the minority populations.

These two concerns — with inclusion and with exclusion — helped focus the student's inquiry.

■ Formulate Your Topic as a Question

To further define her inquiry, the student formulated her topic as a question that pointed toward an argument: "To what extent can E. D. Hirsch's notion of 'cultural literacy' coexist with our country's principles of democracy and inclusion?" Notice that her choice of the phrase *To what extent* implies that both goals do not go hand in hand. If she had asked, "Can common culture coexist with pluralism?" her phrasing would imply that a yes or no answer would suffice, possibly foreclosing avenues of inquiry and certainly ignoring the complexity of the issue.

Instead, despite her misgivings about the implications of Hirsch's agenda, the student suspended judgment, opening the way to genuine inquiry. She acknowledged the usefulness and value of sharing a common language and conceded that Hirsch's points were well taken. She wrote:

> Some sort of unification is necessary. Language, . . . on the most fundamental level of human interaction, demands some compromise and chosen guidelines. . . . How can we learn from one another if we cannot even say hello to each other?

Suspending judgment led her to recognize the complexity of the issue, and her willingness to examine the issue from different perspectives indicated the empathy that is a central component of developing a conversational argument.

■ Acknowledge Your Audience

This student's question ("To what extent can E. D. Hirsch's notion of 'cultural literacy' coexist with our country's principles of democracy and inclusion?") also acknowledged an audience. By invoking cultural literacy, she assumed an audience of readers who are familiar with Hirsch's ideas, probably including policymakers and educational administrators. In gesturing toward democracy, she cast her net very wide: Most Americans probably admire the "principles of democracy." But in specifying inclusion as a democratic principle, she wisely linked all Americans who believe in democratic principles, including the parents of schoolchildren, with all people who have reason to feel excluded by Hirsch's ideas, especially non-native speakers of English, among them immigrants from Mexico and speakers of African American Vernacular English. Thus, this student was acknowledging an audience of policymakers, administrators, parents (both mainstream and marginalized), and those who knew about and perhaps supported cultural literacy.

Steps to Formulating an Issue-Based Question

1 **Refine your topic.** Examine your topic from different perspectives. For example, what are the causes of homelessness? What are its consequences?

2 **Explain your interest in the topic.** Explore the source of your interest in this topic and what you want to learn.

3 **Identify an issue.** Determine what is open to dispute.

4 **Formulate your topic as a question.** Use your question to focus your inquiry.

5 **Acknowledge your audience.** Reflect on what readers may know about the issue, why they may be interested, and what you would like to teach them.

A Practice Sequence: Formulating an Issue-Based Question

As you start developing your own issue-based question, it might be useful to practice a five-step process that begins with a topic, a word or phrase that describes the focus of your interests. Here, apply the process to the one-word topic *homelessness*.

1 Expand your topic into a phrase. "I am interested in the *consequences* of homelessness," "I want to *describe* what it means to be homeless," or "I am interested in discussing the *cause* of homelessness."

2 Explain your interest in this topic. "I am interested in the consequences of homelessness because homelessness challenges democratic principles of fairness."

3 Identify an issue. "The persistence of homelessness contradicts my belief in social justice."

4 Formulate your topic as a question. "To what extent can we allow homelessness to persist in a democratic nation that prides itself on providing equal opportunity to all?"

5 Acknowledge your audience. "I am interested in the consequences of homelessness because I want people who believe in democracy to understand that we need to work harder to make sure that everyone has access to food, shelter, and employment."

The answer to the question you formulate in step 4 should lead to an assertion, your main claim, or *thesis*. For example, you could state your main claim this way: "Although homelessness persists as a widespread problem in our nation, we must develop policies that eliminate homelessness, ensuring that everyone has access to food, shelter, and employment. This is especially important in a democracy that embraces social justice and equality."

The thesis introduces a problem and makes an assertion that you will need to support: "We must develop policies that eliminate homelessness, ensuring that everyone has access to food, shelter, and employment." What is at issue? Not everyone would agree that policies must be implemented to solve the problem. In fact, many would argue that homelessness is an individual problem, that individuals must take responsibility for lifting themselves out of poverty, homelessness, and unemployment. Of course, you would need to read quite a bit to reach this final stage of formulating your thesis.

Try using the five-step process we describe above to formulate your own topic as a question, or try formulating the following topics as questions:

- violence in video games
- recycling
- the popularity of a cultural phenomenon (a book, a film, a performer, an icon)
- standardized tests
- professional sports injuries
- town-gown relationships
- media representation and gender
- government and religion
- vegetarianism

AN ACADEMIC ESSAY FOR ANALYSIS

The following essay by William Deresiewicz provides an intriguing academic extension of the topic that Anna Quindlen writes about (p. 123): the need for the young to have solitary, unscheduled time. His essay illustrates many of the strategies we have discussed thus far: raising questions, stating a thesis by placing an argument in the stream of a broader conversation, using evidence to support his claims. As you read Deresiewicz's essay, you might use the following questions as a guide:

- What is Deresiewicz's thesis? Would you characterize his claim as one of fact? Value?
- What types of evidence does he use to support his claim?
- What do Deresiewicz's vocabulary and citations indicate about his target audience?
- What does Deresiewicz want his readers to do or think about?

WILLIAM DERESIEWICZ

The End of Solitude

William Deresiewicz taught English at Yale University from 1998 to 2008. He is now a contributing writer at *The Nation* and was nominated for a 2009 National Magazine Award for his reviews and criticism. His essay "The End of Solitude" appeared in *The Chronicle of Higher Education* in January 2009 and represents one of many debates about literacy that scholars have waged concerning the benefits and limits of new technologies. Deresiewicz observes that technology fulfills a human impulse to be known, to be connected with others. Posting on social media enables us to be visible and helps validate who we are as individuals. However, he worries that this instinct to be connected also has an adverse effect: We lose a sense of solitude and the space he believes we all need to have in order to understand who we are, what we believe, and what we value. He worries, too, that a new generation does not see the point of solitude because so many young people equate solitude with loneliness.

■ ■ ■

What does the contemporary self want? The camera has created a culture of celebrity; the computer is creating a culture of connectivity. As the two technologies converge—broadband tipping the Web from text to image, social-networking sites spreading the mesh of interconnection ever wider—the two cultures betray a common impulse. Celebrity and connectivity are both ways of becoming known. This is what the contemporary self wants. It wants to be recognized, wants to be connected: It wants to be visible. If not to the *1* millions, on *Survivor* or *Oprah*, then to the hundreds, on Twitter or Facebook. This is the quality that validates us, this is how we become real to ourselves—by being seen by others. The great contemporary terror is anonymity. If Lionel Trilling was right, if the property that grounded the self, in Romanticism, was sincerity, and in modernism it was authenticity, then in postmodernism it is visibility.

So we live exclusively in relation to others, and what disappears from our lives is solitude. Technology is taking away our privacy and our concentration, but it is also taking away our ability to be alone. Though I shouldn't say taking away. We are doing this to ourselves; we are discarding these riches as fast as we can. I was told by one of her older relatives that a teenager I know had sent 3,000 text messages one recent month. That's 100 a day, or about one every 10 waking minutes, morning, noon, and night, weekdays and weekends, class time, lunch time, homework time, and toothbrushing time. So on average, she's never alone for more than 10 minutes at once. Which means, she's never alone. 2

I once asked my students about the place that solitude has in their lives. One of them admitted that she finds the prospect of being alone so unsettling that she'll sit with a friend even when she has a paper to write. Another said, why would anyone want to be alone? 3

To that remarkable question, history offers a number of answers. Man may be a social animal, but solitude has traditionally been a societal value. In particular, the act of being alone has been understood as an essential dimension of religious experience, albeit one restricted to a self-selected few. Through the solitude of rare spirits, the collective renews its relationship with divinity. The prophet and the hermit, the sadhu and the yogi, pursue their vision quests, invite their trances, in desert or forest or cave. For the still, small voice speaks only in silence. Social life is a bustle of petty concerns, a jostle of quotidian interests, and religious institutions are no exception. You cannot hear God when people are chattering at you, and the divine word, their pretensions notwithstanding, demurs at descending on the monarch and the priest. Communal experience is the human norm, but the solitary encounter with God is the egregious act that refreshes that norm. (Egregious, for no man is a prophet in his own land. Tiresias was reviled before he was vindicated, Teresa interrogated before she was canonized.) Religious solitude is a kind of self-correcting social mechanism, a way of burning out the underbrush of moral habit and spiritual custom. The seer returns with new tablets or new dances, his face bright with the old truth. 4

Like other religious values, solitude was democratized by the Reformation and secularized by Romanticism. In Marilynne Robinson's interpretation, Calvinism created the modern self by focusing the soul inward, leaving it to encounter God, like a prophet of old, in "profound isolation." To her enumeration of Calvin, Marguerite de Navarre, and 5

Milton as pioneering early-modern selves we can add Montaigne, Hamlet, and even Don Quixote. The last figure alerts us to reading's essential role in this transformation, the printing press serving an analogous function in the sixteenth and subsequent centuries to that of television and the Internet in our own. Reading, as Robinson puts it, "is an act of great inwardness and subjectivity." "The soul encountered itself in response to a text, first Genesis or Matthew and then *Paradise Lost* or *Leaves of Grass*." With Protestantism and printing, the quest for the divine voice became available to, even incumbent upon, everyone.

But it is with Romanticism that solitude achieved its greatest   6
cultural salience, becoming both literal and literary. Protestant solitude is still only figurative. Rousseau and Wordsworth made it physical. The self was now encountered not in God but in Nature, and to encounter Nature one had to go to it. And go to it with a special sensibility: The poet displaced the saint as social seer and cultural model. But because Romanticism also inherited the eighteenth-century idea of social sympathy, Romantic solitude existed in a dialectical relationship with sociability—if less for Rousseau and still less for Thoreau, the most famous solitary of all, then certainly for Wordsworth, Melville, Whitman, and many others. For Emerson, "the soul environs itself with friends, that it may enter into a grander self-acquaintance or solitude; and it goes alone, for a season, that it may exalt its conversation or society." The Romantic practice of solitude is neatly captured by Trilling's "sincerity": the belief that the self is validated by a congruity of public appearance and private essence, one that stabilizes its relationship with both itself and others. Especially, as Emerson suggests, one beloved other. Hence the famous Romantic friendship pairs: Goethe and Schiller, Wordsworth and Coleridge, Hawthorne and Melville.

Modernism decoupled this dialectic. Its notion of solitude was   7
harsher, more adversarial, more isolating. As a model of the self and its interactions, Hume's social sympathy gave way to Pater's thick wall of personality and Freud's narcissism—the sense that the soul, self-enclosed and inaccessible to others, can't choose but be alone. With exceptions, like Woolf, the modernists fought shy of friendship. Joyce and Proust disparaged it; D. H. Lawrence was wary of it; the modernist friendship pairs— Conrad and Ford, Eliot and Pound, Hemingway and Fitzgerald—were altogether cooler than their Romantic counterparts. The world was now understood as an assault on the self, and with good reason.

The Romantic ideal of solitude developed in part as a reaction   8
to the emergence of the modern city. In modernism, the city is not only more menacing than ever, it has become inescapable, a labyrinth: Eliot's London, Joyce's Dublin. The mob, the human mass, presses in. Hell is other people. The soul is forced back into itself—hence

the development of a more austere, more embattled form of self-validation, Trilling's "authenticity," where the essential relationship is only with oneself. (Just as there are few good friendships in modernism, so are there few good marriages.) Solitude becomes, more than ever, the arena of heroic self-discovery, a voyage through interior realms made vast and terrifying by Nietzschean and Freudian insights. To achieve authenticity is to look upon these visions without flinching; Trilling's exemplar here is Kurtz. Protestant self-examination becomes Freudian analysis, and the culture hero, once a prophet of God and then a poet of Nature, is now a novelist of self—a Dostoyevsky, a Joyce, a Proust.

But we no longer live in the modernist city, and our great fear is not submersion by the mass but isolation from the herd. Urbanization gave way to suburbanization, and with it the universal threat of loneliness. What technologies of transportation exacerbated—we could live farther and farther apart—technologies of communication redressed—we could bring ourselves closer and closer together. Or at least, so we have imagined. The first of these technologies, the first simulacrum of proximity, was the telephone. "Reach out and touch someone." But through the 1970s and 1980s, our isolation grew. Suburbs, sprawling ever farther, became exurbs. Families grew smaller or splintered apart, mothers left the home to work. The electronic hearth became the television in every room. Even in childhood, certainly in adolescence, we were each trapped inside our own cocoon. Soaring crime rates, and even more sharply escalating rates of moral panic, pulled children off the streets. The idea that you could go outside and run around the neighborhood with your friends, once unquestionable, has now become unthinkable. The child who grew up between the world wars as part of an extended family within a tight-knit urban community became the grandparent of a kid who sat alone in front of a big television, in a big house, on a big lot. We were lost in space.

Under those circumstances, the Internet arrived as an incalculable blessing. We should never forget that. It has allowed isolated people to communicate with one another and marginalized people to find one another. The busy parent can stay in touch with far-flung friends. The gay teenager no longer has to feel like a freak. But as the Internet's dimensionality has grown, it has quickly become too much of a good thing. Ten years ago we were writing e-mail messages on desktop computers and transmitting them over dial-up connections. Now we are sending text messages on our cell phones, posting pictures on our Facebook pages, and following complete strangers on Twitter. A constant stream of mediated contact, virtual, notional, or simulated, keeps us wired in to the electronic hive—though contact, or at least two-way contact, seems increasingly beside the point. The goal now, it seems, is simply to become known, to turn oneself into a sort of miniature celebrity. How many friends do I have on Facebook? How many people are reading my blog? How many Google hits does my name generate? Visibility secures our self-esteem, becoming a substitute, twice removed, for genuine connection. Not long ago, it was easy to feel lonely. Now, it is impossible to be alone.

As a result, we are losing both sides of the Romantic dialectic.   *11*
What does friendship mean when you have 532 "friends"? How does it enhance my sense of closeness when my Facebook News Feed tells me that Sally Smith (whom I haven't seen since high school, and wasn't all that friendly with even then) "is making coffee and staring off into space"? My students told me they have little time for intimacy. And of course, they have no time at all for solitude.

But at least friendship, if not intimacy, is still something they want.   *12*
As jarring as the new dispensation may be for people in their 30s and 40s, the real problem is that it has become completely natural for people in their teens and 20s. Young people today seem to have no desire for solitude, have never heard of it, can't imagine why it would be worth having. In fact, their use of technology—or to be fair, our use of technology—seems to involve a constant effort to stave off the possibility of solitude, a continuous attempt, as we sit alone at our computers, to maintain the imaginative presence of others. As long ago as 1952, Trilling wrote about "the modern fear of being cut off from the social group even for a moment." Now we have equipped ourselves with the means to prevent that fear from ever being realized. Which does not mean that we have put it to rest. Quite the contrary. Remember my student, who couldn't even write a paper by herself. The more we keep aloneness at bay, the less are we able to deal with it and the more terrifying it gets.

There is an analogy, it seems to me, with the previous generation's   *13*
experience of boredom. The two emotions, loneliness and boredom, are closely allied. They are also both characteristically modern. The *Oxford English Dictionary*'s earliest citations of either word, at least in the contemporary sense, date from the nineteenth century. Suburbanization, by eliminating the stimulation as well as the sociability of urban or traditional village life, exacerbated the tendency to both. But the great age of boredom, I believe, came in with television, precisely because television was designed to palliate that feeling. Boredom is not a necessary consequence of having nothing to do, it is only the negative experience of that state. Television, by obviating the need to learn how to make use of one's lack of occupation, precludes one from ever discovering how to enjoy it. In fact, it renders that condition fearsome, its prospect intolerable. You are terrified of being bored—so you turn on the television.

I speak from experience. I grew up in the 1960s and 1970s, the *14* age of television. I was trained to be bored; boredom was cultivated within me like a precious crop. (It has been said that consumer society wants to condition us to feel bored, since boredom creates a market for stimulation.) It took me years to discover—and my nervous system will never fully adjust to this idea; I still have to fight against boredom, am permanently damaged in this respect—that having nothing to do doesn't have to be a bad thing. The alternative to boredom is what Whitman called idleness: a passive receptivity to the world.

So it is with the current generation's experience of being alone. *15* That is precisely the recognition implicit in the idea of solitude, which is to loneliness what idleness is to boredom. Loneliness is not the absence of company, it is grief over that absence. The lost sheep is lonely; the shepherd is not lonely. But the Internet is as powerful a machine for the production of loneliness as television is for the manufacture of boredom. If six hours of television a day creates the aptitude for boredom, the inability to sit still, a hundred text messages a day creates the aptitude for loneliness, the inability to be by yourself. Some degree of boredom and loneliness is to be expected, especially among young people, given the way our human environment has been attenuated. But technology amplifies those tendencies. You could call your schoolmates when I was a teenager, but you couldn't call them 100 times a day. You could get together with your friends when I was in college, but you couldn't always get together with them when you wanted to, for the simple reason that you couldn't always find them. If boredom is the great emotion of the TV generation, loneliness is the great emotion of the Web generation. We lost the ability to be still, our capacity for idleness. They have lost the ability to be alone, their capacity for solitude.

And losing solitude, what have they lost? First, the propensity for *16* introspection, that examination of the self that the Puritans, and the Romantics, and the modernists (and Socrates, for that matter) placed at the center of spiritual life—of wisdom, of conduct. Thoreau called it fishing "in the Walden Pond of [our] own natures," "bait[ing our] hooks with darkness." Lost, too, is the related propensity for sustained reading. The Internet brought text back into a televisual world, but it brought it back on terms dictated by that world—that is, by its remapping of our attention spans. Reading now means skipping and skimming; five minutes on the same Web page is considered an eternity. This is not reading as Marilynne Robinson described it: the encounter with a second self in the silence of mental solitude.

But we no longer believe in the solitary mind. If the Romantics had *17* Hume and the modernists had Freud, the current psychological model—

and this should come as no surprise—is that of the networked or social mind. Evolutionary psychology tells us that our brains developed to interpret complex social signals. According to David Brooks, that reliable index of the social-scientific zeitgeist, cognitive scientists tell us that "our decision-making is powerfully influenced by social context"; neuroscientists, that we have "permeable minds" that function in part through a process of "deep imitation"; psychologists, that "we are organized by our attachments"; sociologists, that our behavior is affected by "the power of social networks." The ultimate implication is that there is no mental space that is not social (contemporary social science dovetailing here with postmodern critical theory). One of the most striking things about the way young people relate to one another today is that they no longer seem to believe in the existence of Thoreau's "darkness."

The MySpace page, with its shrieking typography and clamorous   *18*
imagery, has replaced the journal and the letter as a way of creating and communicating one's sense of self. The suggestion is not only that such communication is to be made to the world at large rather than to oneself or one's intimates, or graphically rather than verbally, or performatively rather than narratively or analytically, but also that it can be made completely. Today's young people seem to feel that they can make themselves fully known to one another. They seem to lack a sense of their own depths, and of the value of keeping them hidden.

If they didn't, they would understand that solitude enables us to   *19*
secure the integrity of the self as well as to explore it. Few have shown this more beautifully than Woolf. In the middle of *Mrs. Dalloway*, between her navigation of the streets and her orchestration of the party, between the urban jostle and the social bustle, Clarissa goes up, "like a nun withdrawing," to her attic room. Like a nun: She returns to a state that she herself thinks of as a kind of virginity. This does not mean she's a prude. Virginity is classically the outward sign of spiritual inviolability, of a self untouched by the world, a soul that has preserved its integrity by refusing to descend into the chaos and self-division of sexual and social relations. It is the mark of the saint and the monk, of Hippolytus and Antigone and Joan of Arc. Solitude is both the social image of that state and the means by which we can approximate it. And the supreme image in *Mrs. Dalloway* of the dignity of solitude itself is the old woman whom Clarissa catches sight of through her window. "Here was one room," she thinks, "there another." We are not merely social beings. We are each also separate, each solitary, each alone in our own room, each miraculously our unique selves and mysteriously enclosed in that selfhood.

To remember this, to hold oneself apart from society, is to begin   *20*
to think one's way beyond it. Solitude, Emerson said, "is to genius

the stern friend." "He who should inspire and lead his race must be defended from traveling with the souls of other men, from living, breathing, reading, and writing in the daily, time-worn yoke of their opinions." One must protect oneself from the momentum of intellectual and moral consensus—especially, Emerson added, during youth. "God is alone," Thoreau said, "but the Devil, he is far from being alone; he sees a great deal of company; he is legion." The university was to be praised, Emerson believed, if only because it provided its charges with "a separate chamber and fire"—the physical space of solitude. Today, of course, universities do everything they can to keep their students from being alone, lest they perpetrate self-destructive acts, and also, perhaps, unfashionable thoughts. But no real excellence, personal or social, artistic, philosophical, scientific, or moral, can arise without solitude. "The saint and poet seek privacy," Emerson said, "to ends the most public and universal." We are back to the seer, seeking signposts for the future in splendid isolation.

21 Solitude isn't easy, and isn't for everyone. It has undoubtedly never been the province of more than a few. "I believe," Thoreau said, "that men are generally still a little afraid of the dark." Teresa and Tiresias will always be the exceptions, or to speak in more relevant terms, the young people—and they still exist—who prefer to loaf and invite their soul, who step to the beat of a different drummer. But if solitude disappears as a social value and social idea, will even the exceptions remain possible? Still, one is powerless to reverse the drift of the culture. One can only save oneself—and whatever else happens, one can still always do that. But it takes a willingness to be unpopular.

22 The last thing to say about solitude is that it isn't very polite. Thoreau knew that the "doubleness" that solitude cultivates, the ability to stand back and observe life dispassionately, is apt to make us a little unpleasant to our fellows, to say nothing of the offense implicit in avoiding their company. But then, he didn't worry overmuch about being genial. He didn't even like having to talk to people three times a day, at meals; one can only imagine what he would have made of text-messaging. We, however, have made of geniality—the weak smile, the polite interest, the fake invitation—a cardinal virtue. Friendship may be slipping from our grasp, but our friendliness is universal. Not for nothing does "gregarious" mean "part of the herd." But Thoreau understood that securing one's self-possession was worth a few wounded feelings. He may have put his neighbors off, but at least he was sure of himself. Those who would find solitude must not be afraid to stand alone.

Writing as a Reader

1. Recast Deresiewicz's essay as Anna Quindlen might in her *Newsweek* column. Obviously, her *Newsweek* column is much shorter (an important constraint). She also writes for a more general audience than Deresiewicz, and her tone is quite different. To strengthen your sense of her approach, you may want to browse some of Quindlen's other essays in editions of *Newsweek* or in some of her essay collections listed in the headnote on page 123.

2. Recast Deresiewicz's essay in terms of a writer you read regularly—for example, a columnist in your local newspaper or a blogger in some online venue. Use your imagination. What is the audience, and how will you have to present the issue to engage and persuade them?

From Formulating to Developing a Thesis

A cademic writing explores complex issues that grow out of relevant, timely conversations in which something is at stake. An academic writer reads as a writer to understand the issues, situations, and questions that lead other writers to make claims. Readers expect academic writers to take a clear, specific, logical stand on an issue, and they evaluate how writers support their claims and anticipate counterarguments. The logical stand is the **thesis**, an assertion that academic writers make at the beginning of what they write and then support with evidence throughout their essay. The illustrations and examples that a writer includes must relate to and support the thesis. Thus, a thesis encompasses all of the information writers use to further their arguments; it is not simply a single assertion at the beginning of an essay.

One of our students aptly described the thesis using the metaphor of a shish kebab: The thesis runs through every paragraph, holding the paragraphs together, just as a skewer runs through and holds the ingredients of a shish kebab together. Moreover, the thesis serves as a signpost throughout an essay, reminding readers what the argument is and why the writer has included evidence—examples, illustrations, quotations—relevant to that argument.

An academic thesis

- makes an assertion that is clearly defined, focused, and supported.
- reflects an awareness of the conversation from which the writer has taken up the issue.
- is placed at the beginning of the essay.

- runs through every paragraph like the skewer in a shish kebab.
- acknowledges points of view that differ from the writer's own, reflecting the complexity of the issue.
- demonstrates an awareness of the readers' assumptions and anticipates possible counterarguments.
- conveys a significant fresh perspective.

It is a myth that writers first come up with a thesis and then write their essays. The reality is that writers use issue-based questions to read, learn, and develop a thesis throughout the process of writing. Through revising and discussing their ideas, writers hone their thesis, making sure that it threads through every paragraph of the final draft. The position writers ultimately take in writing—their thesis—comes at the end of the writing process, after not one draft but many.

WORKING VERSUS DEFINITIVE THESES

Writers are continually challenged by the need to establish their purpose and to make a clear and specific assertion of it. To reach that assertion, you must first engage in a prolonged process of inquiry, aided by a well-formulated question. The question serves as a tool for inquiry that will help you formulate your **working thesis**, your first attempt at an assertion of your position. A working thesis is valuable in the early stages of writing because it helps you read selectively, in the same way that your issue-based question guides your inquiry. Reading raises questions, helping you see what you know and need to know, and challenging you to read on.

Never accept your working thesis as your final position. Instead, continue testing your assertion as you read and write, and modify your working thesis as necessary. A more definitive thesis will come once you are satisfied that you have examined the issue from multiple perspectives.

For example, one of our students wanted to study representations of femininity in the media. In particular, she focused on why the Barbie doll has become an icon of femininity despite what many cultural critics consider Barbie's "outrageous and ultimately unattainable physical characteristics." Our student's working thesis suggested she would develop an argument about the need for change:

> The harmful implications of ongoing exposure to these unattainable ideals, such as low self-esteem, eating disorders, unhealthy body image, and acceptance of violence, make urgent the need for change.

The student assumed that her research would lead her to argue that Barbie's unattainable proportions have a damaging effect on women's self-image and that something needs to be done about it. However, as she read scholarly research to support her tentative thesis, she realized that a more compelling project would be less Barbie-centric. Instead, she chose to examine the broader phenomenon of how the idea of femininity is created and reinforced by society. That is, her personal interest in Barbie was supplanted by her discoveries about cultural norms of beauty and the power they have to influence self-perception and behavior. In her final draft, this was her definitive thesis:

> Although evidence may be provided to argue that gender is an innate characteristic, I will show that it is actually the result of one's actions, which are then labeled *masculine* or *feminine* according to society's definitions of ideal gender. Furthermore, I will discuss the communication of such definitions through the media, specifically in music videos, on TV, and in magazines, and the harmful implications of being exposed to these ideals.

Instead of arguing for change, the student chose to show her readers how they were being manipulated, leaving it to them to decide what actions they might want to take.

DEVELOPING A WORKING THESIS: FOUR MODELS

What are some ways to develop a working thesis? We suggest four models that may help you organize the information you gather in response to the question guiding your inquiry.

■ The Correcting-Misinterpretations Model

This model is used to correct writers whose arguments you believe have misconstrued one or more important aspects of an issue. The thesis typically takes the form of a factual claim. Consider this example and the words we have underlined:

> <u>Although scholars have addressed curriculum</u> to explain low achievement in schools, <u>they have failed to fully appreciate the impact of limited resources</u> to fund up-to-date textbooks, quality teachers, and computers. Therefore, reform in schools must focus on economic need as well as curriculum.

The clause beginning with "Although" lays out the assumption that many scholars make, that curriculum explains low educational achievement; the clause beginning with "they have failed" identifies the error those scholars have made by ignoring the economic reasons for low achievement in schools. Notice that the structure of the sentence reinforces the author's position. He explains what he sees as the faulty assumption in a subordinate clause and reserves the main clause for his own position. The two clauses indicate that different authors hold conflicting opinions. Note that the writer could have used a phrase such as "they [scholars] have *understated* the impact of limited resources" as a way to reframe the problem in his thesis. In crafting your thesis, choose words that signal to readers that you are correcting others' ideas, or even misinterpretations, without being dismissive. One more thing: Although it is a common myth that a thesis can be phrased in a single sentence (a legacy of the five-paragraph theme, we suspect), this example shows that a thesis can be written in two (or more) sentences.

■ The Filling-the-Gap Model

The gap model points to what other writers may have overlooked or ignored in discussing a given issue. The gap model typically makes a claim of value. Consider this student's argument that discussions of cultural diversity in the United States are often framed in terms of black and white. Our underlining indicates the gap the writer has identified:

> If America is truly a "melting pot" of cultures, as it is often called, then why is it that stories and events seem only to be in black and white? Why is it that when history courses are taught about the period of the civil rights movement, only the memoirs of African Americans are read, like those of Melba Pattillo Beals and Ida Mae Holland? Where are the works of Maxine Hong Kingston, who tells the story of alienation and segregation in schools through the eyes of a Chinese child? African Americans were denied the right to vote, and many other citizenship rights; but Chinese Americans were denied even the opportunity to become citizens. I am not diminishing the issue of discrimination against African Americans, or belittling the struggles they went through. I simply want to call attention to discrimination against other minority groups and their often-overlooked struggles to achieve equality.

In the student's thesis, the gap in people's knowledge stems from their limited understanding of history. They need to understand that many minority groups were denied their rights.

A variation on the gap model also occurs when a writer suggests that although something might appear to be the case, a closer look reveals something different. For example: "Although it would *appear* that women have achieved equality in the workplace, their paychecks suggest that this is not true."

One of our students examined two poems by the same author that appeared to contradict each other. She noticed a gap others had not seen:

> In both "The Albatross" and "Beauty," Charles Baudelaire chooses to explore the plight of the poet. Interestingly, despite their common author, the two poems' portrayals of the poet's struggles appear contradictory. "The Albatross" seems to give a somewhat sympathetic glimpse into the exile of the poet — the "winged voyager" so awkward in the ordinary world. "Beauty" takes what appears to be a less forgiving stance: The poet here is docile, simply a mirror. Although both pieces depict the poet's struggles, a closer examination demonstrates how the portrayals differ.

In stating her thesis, the student indicates that although readers might expect Baudelaire's images of poets to be similar, a closer examination of his words would prove them wrong.

■ The Modifying-What-Others-Have-Said Model

The modification model of thesis writing assumes that mutual understanding is possible. For example, in proposing a change in policy, one student asserts:

> Although scholars have claimed that the only sure way to reverse the cycle of homelessness in America is to provide an adequate education, we need to build on this work, providing school-to-work programs that ensure graduates have access to employment.

Here the writer seeks to modify other writers' claims, suggesting that education alone does not solve the problem of homelessness. The challenge he sets for himself is to understand the complexity of the problem by building on and extending the ideas of others. In effect, he is in a constructive conversation with those whose work he wants to build on, helping readers see that he shares common ground with the other writers and that he hopes to find a mutually acceptable solution to the agreed-on problem.

■ The Hypothesis-Testing Model

The hypothesis-testing model begins with the assumption that writers may have good reasons for supporting their arguments, but that there are also a number of legitimate reasons that explain why something is, or is not, the case. The questions motivating your research will often lead you to a number of possible answers, but none are necessarily more correct than others. That is, the evidence is based on a hypothesis that researchers will continue to test by examining individual cases through an inductive method until the evidence refutes that hypothesis.

For example, over the last decade, researchers have generated a number of hypotheses to explain the causes of climate change. Some have argued that climate change, or global warming, can be explained by natural causes, that change is a cyclical process. Those who adopt such a view might use evidence to demonstrate that oceans produce heat and that change can be attributed to a steady increase in heat production over time. Others have persuasively shown that humans have caused global warming by burning fossil fuels that increase the amount of carbon in the air, which creates what scientists call the "greenhouse effect." Each assertion is based on a set of inferences from observation and the data available to test each hypothesis. Moreover, the truth value of any assertion is based on the probability that global warming can be attributed to any one cause or explanation.

The hypothesis-testing model assumes that the questions you raise will likely lead you to multiple answers that compete for your attention. The following is one way to formulate such an argument in which you examine rival hypotheses before coming to a conclusion.

> Some people explain *this* by suggesting *that*, but a close analysis of the problem reveals several compelling, but competing explanations.

You may not find a definitive explanation, so you will need to sort through the evidence you find, develop an argument, and acknowledge the reasonable counterarguments that critical readers will raise. In the end, you are not really proving that something is the case, such as the causes of global warming, but you are helping readers understand what you see as the best case given the available evidence.

Steps to Formulating a Working Thesis: Four Models

1 **Misinterpretations model:** "Although many scholars have argued about A and B, a careful examination suggests C."

2 **Gap model:** "Although scholars have noted A and B, they have missed the importance of C."

3 **Modification model:** "Although I agree with the A and B ideas of other writers, it is important to extend/refine/limit their ideas with C."

4 **Hypothesis-testing model:** "Some people explain A by suggesting B, but a close analysis of the problem reveals the possibility of several competing/complementary explanations such as C, D, and E."

A Practice Sequence: Identifying Types of Theses

Below is a series of working theses. Read each one and then identify the model—misinterpretations, gap, modification, or hypothesis-testing—that it represents.

1   A number of studies indicate that violence on television has a detrimental effect on adolescent behavior. However, few researchers have examined key environmental factors like peer

pressure, music, and home life. In fact, I would argue that many researchers have oversimplified the problem.

2   Although research indicates that an increasing number of African American and Hispanic students are dropping out of high school, researchers have failed to fully grasp the reasons why this has occurred.

3   I want to argue that studies supporting single-sex education are relatively sound. However, we don't really know the long-term effects of single-sex education, particularly on young women's career paths.

4   Although recent studies of voting patterns in the United States indicate that young people between the ages of 18 and 24 are apathetic, I want to suggest that not all of the reasons these studies provide are valid.

5   Indeed, it's not surprising that students are majoring in fields that will enable them to get a job after graduation. But students may not be as pragmatic as we think. Many students choose majors because they feel that learning is an important end in itself.

6   Some reformers have assumed that increasing competition will force public schools to improve the quality of education, but it seems that a number of recent initiatives can be used to explain why students have begun to flourish in math and reading, particularly in the primary grades.

7   It is clear that cities need to clean up the dilapidated housing projects that were built over half a century ago; but few, if any, studies have examined the effects of doing so on the life chances of those people who are being displaced.

8   In addition to its efforts to advance the cause of social justice in the new global economy, the university must make a commitment to ending poverty on the edge of campus.

9   Although the writer offers evidence to explain the sources of illiteracy in America, he overstates his case when he ignores other factors, among them history, culture, and economic well-being. Therefore, I will argue that we place the discussion in a broader context.

10   More and more policymakers argue that English should be the national language in the United States. Although I agree that English is important, we should not limit people's right to maintain their own linguistic and cultural identity.

ESTABLISHING A CONTEXT FOR A THESIS

In addition to defining the purpose and focus of an essay, a thesis must set up a **context** for the writer's claim. The process of establishing a background for understanding an issue typically involves four steps:

1. Establish that the topic of conversation, the issue, is current and relevant—that it is on people's minds or should be.

2. Briefly summarize what others have said to show that you are familiar with the topic or issue.

3. Explain what you see as the problem—a misinterpretation, a gap, or a modification that needs to be made in how others have addressed the topic or issue—perhaps by raising the questions you believe need to be answered.

4. State your thesis, suggesting that your view on the issue may present readers with something new to think about as it builds on and extends what others have argued.

You need not follow these steps in this order as long as your readers come away from the first part of your essay knowing why you are discussing a given issue and what your argument is.

AN ANNOTATED STUDENT INTRODUCTION: PROVIDING A CONTEXT FOR A THESIS

We trace these four steps below in our analysis of the opening paragraphs of a student's essay. Motivating his argument is his sense that contemporary writers and educators may not fully grasp the issues that limit the opportunities for low-income youth to attend college. His own family struggled financially, and he argues that a fuller appreciation of the problem can help educators partner with families to advise youth in more informed ways.

O'Neill 1

Colin O'Neill

Money Matters:
Framing the College Access Debate

The student establishes the timeliness and relevance of an issue that challenges widely held assumptions about the value of attending college.

College is expensive. And with prices continuing to rise each year, there are those who are beginning to question whether or not college is a worthy investment. In a recent *Newsweek* article, journalist Megan McArdle (2012) asserts that the process of obtaining a college degree has morphed into a "national neurosis"

O'Neill 2

and calls upon Americans to question whether college is necessary for lifelong success. McArdle joins a chorus of voices calling upon a reevaluation of the current educational pipeline at a time when the number of American students who are ill-prepared to face the rigors of a college curriculum has increased. Some writers suggest that a renaissance of vocational education may, in fact, begin to compensate for the disparate nature of American education. Based on research conducted by Bozick and DeLuca (2011), it is clear that these opinions are grounded in reality.

He begins to summarize what others have said to demonstrate his familiarity with the conversation in popular media and scholarship.

Of nearly 3,000 surveyed "college non-enrollees," roughly 50 percent attributed their withdrawal from the education system to either the high cost of college education or the desire to look for work and embark along their chosen career path. However, for those like me, who believe strongly that higher education is a right that ought to be available to all students, McArdle's and others' assertions add to the list of physical and social barriers that keep students of poorer backgrounds from pursuing their educational aspirations. The ability to pay for college may not be the only consideration keeping students from exploring higher education. Instead, researchers have overlooked the extent to which knowledge (or the lack of it) of college costs and awareness of different financing options (such as grants, scholarships, and loans) may preemptively alter the way in which children envision themselves within the college experience.

The student identifies what he sees as a problem signaled by words like "however," "overlooked," and "instead" and begins to formulate his own argument.

He points out a misconception that he wants to correct.

In many cities where the median household income often hovers slightly above $30,000, college is, according to some educators, a pipedream to which nearly every family aspires, but most are not convinced this goal will ever become a reality (United States Census Bureau). Indeed, with the average cost of a college education rising to upwards of $20,000, it is unclear whether this dream will, in fact, come true. Although parents have a strong desire to send their kids to college, the financial numbers do not seem to add up. While educators have tended to leave parents responsible for educating their children on the financial realities of higher education, researchers such as Elliot, Sherraden, Johnson, and Guo (2010) make the case that awareness of college costs makes its way into the worldview of students as young as second grade. In light of this work, it becomes important to note that the large price tag of a college

The student cites research to further define the problem and show that he is aware of the very real barriers that affect college access for low-income youth.

O'Neill 3

degree may have implications that spread far beyond a particular family's capacity to fund their children's education. As the recent research of Bozick and DeLuca (2011) suggests, the cost of college is changing and challenging the way students begin to examine the purpose and necessity of college education. College costs are diminishing one's access to college in more ways than restricting their ability to foot the bill. For low-income students and their families, for whom every day is filled with financial burdens of all sorts, high college costs are changing the way they perceive college as an institution.

He uses research to understand further a problem that others may have overlooked or ignored.

The correlation between the college choice process and students' perceptions of the cost of higher education is not an unexamined phenomenon. Many researchers have looked at the ways in which the cost of a college education affects the ways low-income students begin to foster a relationship with the college system. The existing body of research, however, has tended to focus solely on high school students, students who are mere months away from beginning the college search process. According to Cabrera and La Nasa (2000), the college choice process actually begins much earlier, commencing between the time a child enters middle school and embarks upon his or her high school journey. It is this process that ultimately dictates the level of college access a particular student does or does not have. Therefore, my study will focus primarily on what Cabrera and La Nasa (2000) termed the "predisposition" stage. Between grades seven and nine, predisposition draws upon parental encouragement, socioeconomic status, and "information about college." Along the trajectory set in place by Cabrera and La Nasa (2000), these factors have a profound influence on the search and choice stages of the college-access process. Recognizing the interrelational nature of these different stages, that is, both how they are different and how each one builds upon the other, is key to navigating the ill-defined nature of the pre-collegiate experience.

Citing a key study, the student underscores a gap in the research, again signaled by "however."

He adopts a frame through which to think about the issue and narrow his focus.

Given the findings of prior research, it is important to push back the discussion about college affordability and college access to examine how the notion of cost impacts the fragile, emerging relationship that middle school students are just beginning to develop. To recognize how students begin to understand college

He begins to offer a solution to a problem researchers have not fully appreciated.

4

5

O'Neill 4

The student explains that the purpose of his research is to fill the gap he identifies above and correct a misunderstanding.

and develop college aspirations, then, I conducted interviews with middle school children to assess how early awareness of college costs plays a role in shaping families' decisions about the need, desire for, and accessibility of higher education. By doing so, I have tried to fill a gap left behind by previous research and add to the wider discussion of college affordability and its overall impact on college access amongst students of all ages. Although educators may argue that American education ought to revert to an old, draconian system of vocational education, preparing low-income students to enter technical fields, I argue that it is important to create programs that encourage parents, teachers, and students to think early about the costs of college and the possibilities that exist to help children pursue a college degree.

Here he makes a policy-related claim that challenges a conflicting point of view.

▪ Establish That the Issue Is Current and Relevant

Ideally, you should convey to readers that the issue you are discussing is both current (what's on people's minds) and relevant (of sufficient importance to have generated some discussion and written conversation). In the first two sentences of the first paragraph, O'Neill explains that the increase in college costs has not only become a focus of national attention, evidenced in the *Newsweek* article he cites, but has motivated writers to question whether the cost to low-income families is a worthwhile investment. In the next sentence, he explains that the author of this article, Megan McArdle, is not alone in challenging some widely held assumptions about the value of attending college. In fact, O'Neill indicates that McArdle "joins a chorus of voices calling upon a reevaluation of the current educational pipeline at a time when the number of American students who are ill-prepared to face the rigors of a college curriculum has increased." Thus, O'Neill demonstrates that the issue he focuses on is part of a lively conversation and debate that has captured the imagination of many writers at the time he was writing about college access.

▪ Briefly Present What Others Have Said

It is important to introduce who has said what in the conversation you are entering. After all, you are joining that conversation to make your contribution, and those who are in that conversation expect you to have done your homework and acknowledge those who have already made important contributions.

In the first few sentences of his introduction, O'Neill sets the stage for his review of research by citing McArdle's *Newsweek* article. Although he takes issue with McArdle, he is careful to explain her argument. In addition, he refers to research in the final sentence of the first paragraph to suggest the extent to which her argument may be "grounded in reality." Indeed, in the second paragraph, he cites a study that reports on the significant number of students surveyed who dropped out of college, nearly half attributing their decision to the high costs of pursuing a college degree. However, O'Neill, who makes clear that he believes everyone has a "right" to an education, uses his review to reframe the issue, calling attention to the way McArdle and others have "overlooked the extent to which knowledge (or the lack of it) of college costs and awareness of different financing options (such as grants, scholarships, and loans) may preemptively alter the way in which children envision themselves within the college experience." In turn, O'Neill highlights research that focuses on parents' and children's perceptions of college access as a way to challenge those writers who call for a "reevaluation of the current educational pipeline."

By pointing out what journalists and researchers may have overlooked in discussing the college-going prospects of low-income youth, O'Neill is doing more than listing the sources he has read. He is establishing that a problem, or issue, exists. Moreover, his review gives readers intellectual touchstones, the scholars (e.g., Cabrera and La Nasa [2000]) who need to be cited in any academic conversation about college access. A review is not a catchall for anyone writing on a topic. Instead it should represent a writer's choice of the most relevant participants in the conversation. O'Neill's choice of sources and his presentation of them convey that he is knowledgeable about his subject. (Of course, it is his readers' responsibility to read further to determine whether he has reviewed the most relevant work and has presented the ideas of others accurately. If he has, readers will trust him, whether or not they end up agreeing with him on the issue.)

■ Explain What You See as the Problem

If a review indicates a problem, as O'Neill's review does, the problem can often be couched in terms of the models we discussed earlier: misinterpretations, gaps, modification, or hypothesis testing. In paragraph 4, O'Neill identifies what he sees as a gap in how journalists and researchers approach the cost of attending college and the question of "whether college is necessary to lifelong success." He suggests that such a view is the consequence of a gap in knowledge (notice our underlining):

> The existing body of research, however, has tended to focus solely on high school students, students who are mere months away from beginning the college search process. According to Cabrera and La Nasa (2000), the college choice process actually begins much earlier, commencing between the time a child enters middle school and embarks upon his or her high school journey.

While O'Neill acknowledges the value of others' writing, his review of research culminates with his assertion that it is important to understand the problem of college costs with greater depth and precision. After all, researchers and journalists have overlooked or ignored important sources of information. At stake for O'Neill is that limiting low-income youth's access to higher education challenges a more equitable view that all children deserve a chance to have a successful life. Moreover, at the end of paragraph 3, he shifts the burden from parents, alone, to educators who clearly influence the "way students begin to examine the purpose and necessity of college education."

■ State Your Thesis

An effective thesis statement helps readers see the reasoning behind a writer's claim; it also signals what readers should look for in the remainder of the essay. O'Neill closes paragraph 5 with a statement that speaks to both the purpose and the substance of what he writes:

> Although educators may argue that American education ought to revert to an old, draconian system of vocational education, preparing low-income students to enter technical fields, I argue that it is important to create programs that encourage parents, teachers, and students to think early about the costs of college and the possibilities that exist to help children pursue a college degree.

In your own writing, you can make use of the strategies that O'Neill uses in his essay. Words like *although, however, but, instead,* and *yet* can set up the problem you identify. Here is a variation on what O'Neill writes: "One might argue that vocational programs may provide a reasonable alternative to meeting the needs of low-income students for whom college seems unaffordable and out of reach; however [but, yet], such an approach ignores the range of possibilities that exist for changing policies to ensure that all children have access to a college education."

Steps to Establishing a Context for a Thesis

1 **Establish that the issue is current and relevant.** Point out the extent to which others have recognized the problem, issue, or question that you are writing about.

2 **Briefly present what others have said.** Explain how others have addressed the problem, issue, or question you are focusing on.

3 **Explain what you see as the problem.** Identify what is open to dispute.

4 **State your thesis.** Help readers see your purpose and how you intend to achieve it — by correcting a misconception, filling a gap, modifying a claim others have accepted, or stating an hypothesis.

■ Analyze the Context of a Thesis

In "Teaching Toward Possibility," educator Kris Gutiérrez argues that teaching should focus on student learning and provide students with multiple tools from different disciplines to ensure that students engage in what she describes as "deep learning." She also explains that culture plays a key role in learning, particularly for students from nondominant groups. However, she reframes the notion of culture as a set of practices, as a verb, which she distinguishes from inert conceptions of culture based on individuals' membership in a particular ethnic community. Her essay, published in 2011, is addressed to educators, teachers, and policy makers. As you read the following excerpt, you may feel puzzled by some of Gutiérrez's vocabulary and perhaps even excluded from the conversation at times. Our purpose in reprinting this excerpt is to show through our annotations how Gutiérrez has applied the strategies we have been discussing in this chapter. As you read, make your own annotations, and then try to answer the questions—which may involve careful rereading—that we pose after the selection. In particular, watch for signpost words or phrases that signal the ideas the writer is challenging.

KRIS GUTIÉRREZ

From Teaching Toward Possibility: Building Cultural Supports for Robust Learning

The author establishes the relevance and timeliness of the issue.

Consider the potential learning power of a unit on environmental inequities or environment racism for middle or high school students in which students are provided the opportunity to examine the issue deeply and broadly. We did just this over a number of years in rigorous summer programs for high school students from migrant farm worker backgrounds. Students learned environmental science, learned traditional information about the environment, learned about the history of the area of study, as well as the history of environmental issues in their local and immediate communities. This way of learning required interdisciplinary reading, including reading across genres, points of view, and across historical time and space. These learning practices enticed students to want to learn more, to research, and to make connections across relevant ideas and their varied meanings within and across academic

This is particularly relevant for an audience of teachers who want to know how to motivate students whose backgrounds they may be unfamiliar with.

1

and home communities. In short, instruction was coherent, historicized, textured, layered, and deeply supported in ways that allowed students to access and engage with rigorous texts and high status knowledge, as well as work in and through the contradictions and tensions inherent in knowledge production and authentic science/learning issues.

Gutiérrez further establishes the relevance of teaching non-dominant students and seeks to correct a misconception about the nature of teaching, learning, and culture.

In the following section, I draw on the case of teaching science to migrant students mentioned above to elaborate a challenge to reductive approaches to teaching and learning that offer the "quick-fix" and provide "off the shelf" solutions to education; that is, those relying on silver bullet solutions to solve complex educational problems or using theory and research uncritically or without sufficient understanding because it is fashionable to do so. One such quick-fix approach is found in learning styles approaches to learning, particularly cultural learning styles conceptions in which regularities in cultural communities are characterized as static and unchanging and general traits of individuals are attributable categorically to ethnic group membership.

She cites her own work to support her argument and then reviews relevant studies to challenge approaches to teaching and learning that fail to conceptualize the notion of culture adequately.

In my work (Gutiérrez, 2002; Gutiérrez & Rogoff, 2003), I have argued the importance of moving beyond such narrow assumptions of cultural communities by focusing both on regularity and variance in a community's practices (as well as those of individuals). Employing a cultural-historical-activity theoretical approach to learning and development (Cole & Engeström, 2003; Engeström, 1987; Leontiev, 1981) is one productive means toward challenging static and ahistorical understandings of cultural communities and their practices, as this view focuses attention on variations in individual and group histories of engagement in cultural practices. Variations, then, are best understood as proclivities of people who have particular histories of engagement with specific cultural activities, not as traits of individuals or collections of individuals. In other words, individual and group experience in activities—not their traits—become the focus.

Gutiérrez reframes the way educators should view culture, and this new frame is the lens through which she develops her argument.

2

3

Through this new conception of culture, Gutiérrez defines what she sees as a gap in what educators know and need to know. She attributes this gap to what educators have ignored and cites additional research to make her point.

Within this view, it becomes easier to understand the limitations of learning styles approaches in which individuals from one group might be characterized as "holistic learners"—where individuals from another group may be characterized as learning analytically or individuals may be divided into cooperative versus individualist learners on the basis of membership in a particular cultural group. Such methods ignore or minimize variation and focus on perceived or over-generalized regularities. Further, learning styles pedagogical practices have been used to distinguish the learning styles of "minority" group members and to explain "minority" student failure (see Foley, 1997; Kavale & Forness, 1987; Irvine & York, 1995 for reviews). Of consequence, addressing learning styles as traits linked to membership in cultural communities also seems to be a common way to prepare teachers about diversity (Guild, 1994; Matthews, 1991). Understandably, teaching to a difference that can be labeled (e.g., learning modalities) may be appealing to teachers who have limited resources, support, or training to meet the challenges of new student populations. However, attribution of learning style or difference based on group membership can serve to buttress persistent deficit model orientations to teaching students from nondominant communities; without acknowledging both the regularity and variance makes it harder to understand the relation of individual learning and the practices of cultural communities, which in turn can hinder effective assistance to student learning (Gutiérrez & Rogoff, 2003).

Her use of "however" distinguishes what she sees as a prevailing school of thought and what she believes should be the case. Educators' misconceptions about culture are the source of the problem she identifies.

Gutiérrez reaffirms the issue between two competing ideas.

The key issue here is that learning styles approaches are grounded in reductive notions of culture that conflate race/ethnicity with culture—a practice that often leads to one-size-fits-all approaches and understandings of the learning process of students from non-dominant communities. Consider familiar statements such as "My Latino students learn this way" or "I need to teach to the cultural background of my African American students" and even, "Asian students are good at math." Such generalizations are based on the assumption that people hold uniform cultural practices based on their membership in a particular community. Culture from this perspective is something you can observe from people's phenotype, physical characteristics, national origin, or language. Culture, then, is best considered a verb or said differently, culture is better understood as people's practices or how people live culturally (Moll, 1998). This more dynamic and instrumental role of culture should help us avoid the tendency to conflate culture with race and ethnicity and assumptions about people's cultural practices.

The lens of culture that she has adopted helps us understand the nature of the misconception that she identifies and solve a problem in educating students from non-dominant groups. This last sentence is her main claim.

To avoid conflating race/ethnicity with culture, I often remind researchers and educators to invoke the "100-percent Piñata rule"—that is, 100-percent of Mexicans do not hit piñatas 100-percent of the time. While piñatas may in fact be a prevalent cultural artifact in many Mexican and Mexican-descent communities (and now across many household and communities in the Southwest), we would not make generalizations about their use and would expect variation in piñata practices, their meaning, value, and use. Thus, while cultural artifacts mediate human activity, they have varying functions in use and in practice, just as there is regularity and variance in any cultural community and its practices.

She restates her claim about culture.

6

Reading as a Writer

1. What specific places can you point to in the selection that illustrate what is at issue for Gutiérrez?

2. How does she use her review to set up her argument?

3. What specific words and phrases does she use to establish what she sees as the problem? Is she correcting misinterpretations, filling a gap, or modifying what others have said?

4. What would you say is Gutiérrez's thesis? What specifics can you point to in the text to support your answer?

5. What would you say are the arguments Gutiérrez wants you to avoid? Again, what specific details can you point to in the text to support your answer?

A Practice Sequence: Building a Thesis

We would like you to practice some of the strategies we have covered in this chapter. If you have already started working on an essay, exercises 1 through 4 present an opportunity to take stock of your progress, a chance to sort through what you've discovered, identify what you still need to discover, and move toward refining your thesis. Jot down your answer to each of the questions below and make lists of what you know and what you need to learn.

1   Have you established that your issue is current and relevant, that it is or should be on people's minds? What information would you need to do so?

2   Can you summarize briefly what others have said in the past to show that you are familiar with how others have addressed the issue? List some of the key texts you have read and the key points they make.

3   Have you identified any misunderstandings or gaps in how others have addressed the issue? Describe them. Do you have any ideas or information that would address these misunderstandings or help fill these gaps? Where might you find the information you need? Can you think of any sources you should reread to learn more? (For example, have you looked at the works cited or bibliographies in the texts you've already read?)

4   At this point, what is your take on the issue? Try drafting a working thesis statement that will present readers with something new to think about, building on and extending what others have argued. In drafting your thesis statement, try out the models discussed in this chapter and see if one is an especially good fit:

- *Misinterpretations model:* "Although many scholars have argued about A and B, a careful examination suggests C."

- *Gap model:* "Although scholars have noted A and B, they have missed the importance of C."

- *Modification model:* "Although I agree with A and B ideas of other writers, it is important to extend/refine/limit their ideas with C."

- *Hypothesis-testing model:* "Some people explain A by suggesting B, but a close analysis of the problem reveals the possibility of several competing/complementary explanations such as C, D, and E."

5 If you haven't chosen a topic yet, try a group exercise. Sit down with a few of your classmates and choose one of the following topics to brainstorm about as a group. Choose a topic that everyone in the group finds interesting, and work through exercises 1 through 4 in this practice sequence. Here are some suggestions:

- the moral obligation to vote
- the causes or consequences of poverty
- the limits of academic freedom
- equity in education
- the popularity of _____
- gender stereotypes in the media
- linguistic diversity
- the uses of a liberal education
- journalism and truth
- government access to personal information

AN ANNOTATED STUDENT ESSAY: STATING AND SUPPORTING A THESIS

We have annotated the following student essay to illustrate the strategies we have discussed in this chapter for stating a thesis that responds to a relevant, timely problem in a given context. The assignment was to write an argument focusing on literacy, based on research. Veronica Stafford chose to write about her peers' habit of texting and the ways in which this type of social interaction affects their intellectual development. Stafford develops a thesis that provides a corrective to a misconception that she sees in the ongoing conversations about texting. Her approach is a variation on the strategy in which writers correct a misinterpretation. In turn, you will see that she makes claims of fact and evaluation in making an argument for changing her peers' penchant for texting.

As you read the essay, reflect on your own experiences: Do you think the issue she raises is both timely and relevant? How well do you think she places her ideas in conversation with others? How would you respond to her various claims? Which do you agree with and disagree with, and why? What evidence would you present to support or counter her claims? Do you think she offers a reasonable corrective to what she believes is a misconception about texting?

Stafford 1

Veronica Stafford
Professor Wilson
English 1102
April 20 —

Texting and Literacy

As students walk to class each day, most do not notice the other people around them. Rather than talking with others, they are texting their friends in the next building, in their dorm, or back home. Although social networking is the most common use for text messages, they are not used solely for socializing. While texting is a quick and easy way to keep up with friends, it threatens other aspects of our lives. When students spend time texting rather than focusing on those other important aspects, texting becomes detrimental. Students' enjoyment of reading, their schoolwork, and their relationships with others are all negatively affected by text messaging.

Due to the mass appeal of text messaging, students pass their free time chatting through their cell phones rather than enjoying a great book. Texting is so widespread because 25 percent of students under age eight, 89 percent of students ages eleven to thirteen, and over 95 percent of students over age fifteen have a cell phone ("Mobile Phones"). On average, 75.6 million text messages are sent in a day, with 54 percent of the population texting more than five times per day ("Mobile Phones"). In contrast to the time they spend texting, fifteen- to twenty-four-year-olds read a mere seven minutes per day for fun and only 1.25 hours a week (NEA 10), which is less than half the time that seventh-grade students spend texting: 2.82 hours a week (Bryant et al.). While more than half of the population texts every day, almost as many (43 percent) have not read a single book in the past year (NEA 7). It seems there is a direct correlation between reading and texting because, as text messaging increases in popularity, reading decreases. The National Endowment for the Arts surveyed eighteen- to twenty-four-year-olds and discovered that the enjoyment of reading in this age group is declining the fastest. Inversely, it is the group that sends the most text messages: 142 billion a year (NEA 10). From 1992 to 2002, 2.1 million potential readers, aged eighteen to twenty-four years old, were lost (NEA 27). As proved by the direct correlation, reading does not have

The student identifies an issue, or problem, and states her thesis as an evaluative claim that attempts to correct a misconception.

She summarizes research, placing the conversation in a larger context. Her citations also indicate that the problem she identifies is relevant and timely.

She uses evidence to support her thesis — that we take for granted a mode of communication that actually threatens the development of literacy.

1

2

Stafford 2

the same appeal because of texting. Students prefer to spend time in the technological world rather than sitting with a book.

She refines her thesis, first stating what people assume is true and then offering a corrective in the second part of her thesis.

However, reading well is essential to being successful academically. Although some argue that text messages force students to think quickly and allow them to formulate brief responses to questions, their habit is actually stifling creativity. When a group of twenty students was given a chance to write responses to open-ended questions, the students who owned cell phones with text messaging wrote much less. They also had more grammatical errors, such as leaving apostrophes out of contractions and substituting the letter "r" for the word "are"

She also makes a secondary claim related to her thesis.

(Ward). Because of text messages, students perceive writing as a fun way to communicate with friends and not as a way to strongly voice an opinion. Students no longer think of writing as academic, but rather they consider it social. For instance, in Scotland, a thirteen-year-old student wrote this in a school essay about her summer vacation: "My smmr hols wr CWOT. B4 we used 2 go to NY 2C my bro, & 3 kids FTF ILNY, its gr8 . . ." (Ward). She used writing that would appear in a text message for

And she elaborates on this claim to point out one of the detrimental effects of texting.

a friend rather than in a report for school. Furthermore, students who text become so accustomed to reading this type of shorthand lingo that they often overlook it in their own writing (O'Connor). This means that teachers have to spend even longer correcting these bad habits. Regardless, Lily Huang, a writer for *Newsweek*, believes that text messages increase literacy because a student must first know how to spell a word to abbreviate it in texting.

The student presents a possible counter-argument from a published writer and then restates her thesis in an effort to correct a misconception.

However, texting affects not only the way that students write, but also the way in which they think about language. As a critic of Huang's article writes, "Habitual use of shorthand isn't just about choppy English, but choppy thinking" (Muffie). Writers who text will have trouble thinking creatively, and will especially have trouble composing intricate works like poetry because of the abridged way of thinking to which they are accustomed.

Outside of school, students' interactions with one another are similarly altered. Three in five teens would argue with a friend and one in three would break up with someone through a text message ("Technology Has Tremendous Impact"). Text messaging is now the most popular way for students to arrange to meet with friends, have a quick conversation, contact

Stafford 3

a friend when bored, or invite friends to a party ("Technology Has Tremendous Impact"). Eight out of ten teens would rather text than call ("Mobile Phones"). Although it is true that text messaging has made conversations much simpler and faster, it has not improved communication. Texting may make it more convenient to stay in contact with friends, but it does not ensure that the contact is as beneficial as talking in person. Text messages do not incorporate all of the body language and vocal inflections that a face-to-face conversation does. These nonverbal cues are essential to fully comprehending what is being communicated. Only 7 percent of a message is verbal. When the message is not communicated face-to-face, 93 percent of that message is lost ("Importance of Nonverbal"), and this nonverbal message is crucial to maintaining close relationships. According to Don McKay, a contributor to healthinfosource.com, the most important aspect of lasting friendships is effective communication. Friends must be able to convey emotions and empathize with others (McKay). However, friends who communicate solely through text messages will miss out on any truly personal interaction because they can never see the other person's posture, body language, or gestures.

All of the negative effects of text messaging additionally deteriorate literacy. The enjoyment of reading leads to avid readers who eagerly absorb written words. A devotion to schoolwork encourages students to read so that they may be informed about important topics. Through book clubs and conversations about great literature, even relationships can foster a love for reading. However, text messaging is detracting from all three. In today's society, literacy is important. Schools focus on teaching English at an early age because of the active role that it forces students to take (Le Guin). While students can passively text message their friends, they need to focus on reading to enjoy it. In order to really immerse themselves in the story, they need to use a higher level of thinking than that of texting. This learning is what causes avid readers to become so successful. Those who read for fun when they are young score better on standardized tests, are admitted to more selective universities, and are able to secure the most competitive jobs (NEA 69). The decline in literacy caused by text messaging

She restates an evaluative claim that runs through the essay like the skewer we discussed earlier.

She provides current research to support her thesis.

She concludes by restating her premise about the value of reading and her evaluation of texting as a form of communication that erodes what she considers the very definition of literacy.

She also concludes with a claim in which she proposes that students need to elevate the way they read and write.

5

could inevitably cost a student a selective job. If students spent less time texting and more time reading, it could give them an advantage over their peers. Imagine a scenario between classes without any students' eyes to the ground. Imagine that Notre Dame students are not texting acquaintances hours away. Perhaps instead they are all carrying a pen and notebook and writing a letter to their friends. Maybe they are conversing with those around them. Instead of spending time every week text messaging, they are reading. When those other students text "lol," it no longer is an abbreviation for "laugh out loud," but for "loss of literacy."

Works Cited

Bryant, J. Alison, et al. "IMing, Text Messaging, and Adolescent Social Networks." *Journal of Computer-Mediated Communication*, vol. 11, no. 2, Jan. 2006, pp. 577–92.

Huang, Lily. "Technology: Textese May be the Death of English." *Newsweek*, 1 Aug. 2008, www.newsweek.com/ technology-textese-may-be-death-english-87727.

"The Importance of Nonverbal Communication." *EruptingMind Self Improvement Tips*, 2008, www.eruptingmind.com/ the-importance-of-nonverbal-communication/.

Le Guin, Ursula K. "Staying Awake: Notes on the Alleged Decline of Reading." *Harper's Magazine*, Feb. 2008, harpers.org/ archive/2008/02/staying-awake/.

McKay, Don. "Communication and Friendship." *EzineArticles*, 22 Feb. 2006, ezinearticles.com/?Communication-And -Friendship&id=150491.

"Mobile Phones, Texting, and Literacy." *National Literacy Trust*, 2008, www.literacytrust.org.uk/news/mobile_phones _texting_and_literacy.

Muffie. Comment on "Technology: Textese May be the Death of English," by Lily Huang. *Newsweek*, 18 Aug. 2008, www.newsweek.com/technology-textese-may-be-death -english-87727.

Stafford 5

O'Connor, Amanda. "Instant Messaging: Friend or Foe of
    Student Writing?" *New Horizons for Learning*, Johns Hopkins
    School of Education, Mar. 2005, education.jhu.edu/PD/
    newhorizons/strategies/topics/literacy/articles/
    instant-messaging/.
"Technology Has Tremendous Impact on How Teens
    Communicate." *Cellular-news*, 19 Feb. 2007,
    www.cellular-news.com/story/22146.php.
To Read or Not To Read: A Question of National Consequence.
    National Endowment for the Arts, Nov. 2007, www.arts.gov/
    publications/read-or-not-read-question-national
    -consequence-0.
Ward, Lucy. "Texting 'Is No Bar to Literacy.'" *The Guardian*,
    23 Dec. 2004, www.theguardian.com/technology/2004/
    dec/23/schools.mobilephones.

7

From Finding to Evaluating Sources

In this chapter, we look at strategies for expanding the base of sources you work with to support your argument. The habits and skills of close reading and analysis that we have discussed and that you have practiced are essential for evaluating the sources you find. Once you find sources, you will need to assess the claims the writers make, the extent to which they provide evidence in support of those claims, and the recency, relevance, accuracy, and reliability of the evidence. The specific strategies we discuss here are those you will use to find and evaluate the sources you locate in your library's electronic catalog or on the Internet. These strategies are core skills for developing a researched academic argument.

Finding sources is not difficult; finding and identifying reliable, relevant sources is challenging. You know how simple it is to look up a subject in an encyclopedia or to use a search engine like Google to discover basic information on a subject or topic. Unfortunately, this kind of research will take you only so far. What if the information you find doesn't really address your question? True, we have emphasized the importance of thinking about an issue from multiple perspectives—and finding multiple perspectives is easy when you search the Internet. But how do you know whether a perspective is authoritative or trustworthy or even legitimate? Without knowing how to find and identify good sources, you can waste a lot of time reading material that will not contribute to your essay. Our goal is to help you use your time wisely to collect the sources you need to support your argument.

IDENTIFYING SOURCES

We assume that by the time you visit the library or search the Internet to find sources, you are not flying blind. At the very least you will have chosen a topic you want to explore (something in general you want to write about), possibly will have identified an issue (a question or problem about the topic that is arguable), and perhaps will even have a working thesis (a main claim that you want to test against other sources).

Let's say, for example, that you are interested in the topic of nutrition and obesity. Perhaps you have begun to formulate an issue: Trends show that obesity is increasing at a time when published reports are also showing that the food industry may have been complicit by engineering processed foods with high fat, sugar, and salt content. In fact, these reports point to the lack of nutritional value of processed foods. The issue might be between what you see as an unfortunate trend that affects the health of a growing population of children and adults in the United States and the extent to which food manufacturers contribute to the problem. You may have begun to formulate a question about who is responsible for addressing this problem. Should individuals be more responsible for making good choices? Should food manufacturers monitor themselves and be more responsible to consumers? Should the government intervene to ensure that processed foods provide adequate nutrients and less fat, sugar, and salt? The closer you are to identifying an issue or question, the more purposeful your research will be and the more you will be able to home in on the materials that will be most useful. As you read, your research will help you refine your idea, formulate a question, and develop a working thesis.

However, a working thesis is just a place to begin. As you digest all of the perspectives that your research yields, your interest in the topic or issue may shift significantly. Maybe you'll end up writing about the extent to which the government should have a role, any role, in regulating the food industry rather than about obesity. Perhaps you become interested in trends in food distribution and end up writing about what some call the "locavore" movement. Be open to revising your ideas and confronting the complexities inherent in any topic. Pursue what interests you and what is timely and relevant to your readers. The question, then, is what are you trying to learn and demonstrate?

If you are unsure about where to start, we provide a list of standard resources for conducting research in Table 7.1. For example, you could begin by looking up abstracts, a tool researchers use to get a brief snapshot of the field and summaries of potentially relevant articles. You can simply do a Google search, type in "abstracts," and add the topic that interests you ("abstracts in health sciences"). You can also look up book reviews to see how others might have responded to a book from which you first learned about the problems of obesity, nutrition, food production, and the like. More specialized searches will take you to databases available on a given library's Web site.

TABLE 7.1   Standard Resources for Conducting Research

SOURCE	TYPE OF INFORMATION	PURPOSE	LIMITATIONS	EXAMPLES
Abstract	Brief summary of a text and the bibliographic information needed to locate the complete text	To help researchers decide whether they want to read the entire source	May be too brief to fully assess the value of a source	*Biological Abstracts* *Historical Abstracts* *New Testament Abstracts* *Reference Sources in History: An Introductory Guide*
Bibliography	List of works, usually by subject and author, with full publication information	For an overview of what has been published in a field and who the principal researchers in the field are	Difficult to distinguish the best sources and the most prominent researchers	Bibliography of the History of Art *MLA International Bibliography*
Biography	Story of an individual's life and the historical, cultural, or social context in which he or she lived	For background on a person of importance	Lengthy and reflects the author's bias	Biography and Genealogy Master Index Biography Resource Center Biography.com Literature Resource Center *Oxford Dictionary of National Biography*
Book review	Description and usually an evaluation of a recently published book	To help readers stay current with research and thought in their field and to evaluate scholarship	Reflects the reviewer's bias	ALA *Booklist* *Book Review Digest* Book Review Index *Bowker Books in Print*
Database	Large collection of citations and abstracts from books, journals, and digests, often updated daily	To give researchers access to a wide range of current sources	Lacks evaluative information	EBSCOhost Education Resources Information Center (ERIC) Humanities International Index Index to Scientific & Technical Proceedings United Nations Bibliographic Information System
Data, statistics	Measurements derived from studies or surveys	To help researchers identify important trends (e.g., in voting, housing, residential segregation)	Requires a great deal of scrutiny and interpretation	American FactFinder American National Election Studies Current Index to Statistics Current Population Survey *U.S. Census Bureau National Data Book*

(continued on next page)

TABLE 7.1 *(continued)*

Source	Type of Information	Purpose	Limitations	Examples
Dictionary	Alphabetical list of words and their definitions	To explain key terms and how they are used		*Merriam-Webster's Collegiate Dictionary* *Oxford English Dictionary* *The Oxford Dictionary of Current English*
Encyclopedia	Concise articles about people, places, concepts, and things	A starting point for very basic information	Lack of in-depth information	*The CQ Researcher* Encyclopedia Brittanica Online *McGraw-Hill Encyclopedia of Science & Technology*
Internet search engine	Web site that locates online information by keyword or search term	For quickly locating a broad array of current resources	Reliability of information open to question	Google Google Scholar
Newspaper, other news sources	Up-to-date information	To locate timely information	May reflect reporter's or medium's bias	America's Historical Newspapers LexisNexis Academic Newspaper Source ProQuest Historical Newspapers World News Connection
Thesaurus	Alphabetical list of words and their synonyms	For alternative search terms		*Roget's II: The New Thesaurus* *Pro Quest Thesaurus*

■ Consult Experts Who Can Guide Your Research

Before you embark on a systematic hunt for sources, you may want to consult with experts who can help guide your research. The following experts are nearer to hand and more approachable than you may think.

Your writing instructor.　Your first and best expert is likely to be your writing instructor, who can help you define the limits of your research and the kinds of sources that would prove most helpful. Your writing instructor can probably advise you on whether your topic is too broad or too narrow, help you identify your issue, and perhaps even point you to specific reference works or readings you should consult. He or she can also help you figure out whether you should concentrate mainly on popular or scholarly sources (for more about popular and scholarly sources, see pp. 170–73).

Librarians at your campus or local library.   In all likelihood, there is no better repository of research material than your campus or local library, and no better guide to those resources than the librarians who work there. Their job is to help you find what you need (although it's up to you to make the most of what you find). Librarians can give you a map or tour of the library and provide you with booklets or other handouts that instruct you in the specific resources available and their uses. They can explain the catalog system and reference system. And, time allowing, most librarians are willing to give you personal help in finding and using specific sources, from books and journals to indexes and databases.

Experts in other fields.   Perhaps the idea for your paper originated outside your writing course, in response to a reading assigned in, say, your psychology or economics course. If so, you may want to discuss your topic or issue with the instructor in that course, who can probably point you to other readings or journals you should consult. If your topic originated outside the classroom, you can still seek out an expert in the appropriate field. If so, you may want to read the advice on interviewing we present in Chapter 13.

Manuals, handbooks, and dedicated Web sites.   These resources exist in abundance, for general research as well as for discipline-specific research. They are especially helpful in identifying a wide range of authoritative search tools and resources, although they also offer practical advice on how to use and cite them. Indeed, your writing instructor may assign one of these manuals or handbooks, or recommend a Web site, at the beginning of the course. If not, he or she can probably point you to the one that is best suited to your research.

▪ Develop a Working Knowledge of Standard Sources

As you start your hunt for sources, it helps to know broadly what kinds of sources are available and what they can help you accomplish. Table 7.1 lists a number of the resources you are likely to rely on when you are looking for material, the purpose and limitations of each type of resource, and some well-known examples. Although it may not help you pinpoint specific resources that are most appropriate for your research, the table does provide a basis for finding sources in any discipline. And familiarizing yourself with the types of resources here should make your conversations with the experts more productive.

▪ Distinguish between Primary and Secondary Sources

As you define the research task before you, you will need to understand the difference between primary and secondary sources and figure out which you will need to answer your question. Your instructor may specify which he or she prefers, but chances are you will have to make the decision yourself. A **primary source** is a firsthand, or eyewitness, account, the kind of account you find in letters or newspapers or research reports in which the researcher explains his or her impressions of a particular phenomenon. A **secondary source** is an analysis of information reported in a primary source.

If you were exploring issues of language diversity and the English-only movement, you would draw on both primary and secondary sources. You would be interested in researchers' firsthand (primary) accounts of language learning and use by diverse learners for examples of the challenges nonnative speakers face in learning a standard language. And you would also want to know from secondary sources what others think about whether national unity and individuality can and should coexist in communities and homes as well as in schools. You will find that you are often expected to use both primary and secondary sources in your research.

■ Distinguish between Popular and Scholarly Sources

To determine the type of information to use, you also need to decide whether you should look for popular or scholarly books and articles. **Popular sources** of information—newspapers like *USA Today* and *The Chronicle of Higher Education*, and large-circulation magazines like *Time Magazine* and *Field & Stream*—are written for a general audience. This is not to say that popular sources cannot be specialized: *The Chronicle of Higher Education* is read mostly by academics; *Field & Stream*, by people who love the outdoors. But they are written so that any educated reader can understand them. **Scholarly sources**, by contrast, are written for experts in a particular field. *The New England Journal of Medicine* may be read by people who are not physicians, but they are not the journal's primary audience. In a manner of speaking, these readers are eavesdropping on the journal's conversation of ideas; they are not expected to contribute to it (and in fact would be hard pressed to do so). The articles in scholarly journals undergo **peer review**. That is, they do not get published until they have been carefully evaluated by the author's peers, other experts in the academic conversation being conducted in the journal. Reviewers may comment at length about an article's level of research and writing, and an author may have to revise an article several times before it sees print. And if the reviewers cannot reach a consensus that the research makes an important contribution to the academic conversation, the article will not be published.

When you begin your research, you may find that popular sources provide helpful information about a topic or an issue—the results of a national poll, for example. Later, however, you will want to use scholarly sources to advance your argument. You can see from Table 7.2 that popular magazines and scholarly journals can be distinguished by a number of characteristics. Does the source contain advertisements? If so, what kinds of advertisements? For commercial products? Or for academic events and resources? How do the advertisements appear? If you find ads and glossy pictures and illustrations, you are probably looking at a popular magazine. This is in contrast to the tables, charts, and diagrams you are likely to find in an education, psychology, or microbiology journal. Given your experience with rhetorical analyses, you should also be able to determine the makeup of your audience—specialists or nonspecialists—and the level of language you need to use in your writing.

Again, as you define your task for yourself, it is important to consider why you would use one source or another. Do you want facts? Opinions? News reports? Research studies? Analyses? Personal reflections? The extent to which the information can help you make your argument will serve as your basis for determining whether a source of information is of value.

TABLE 7.2   Popular Magazines versus Scholarly Journals

Criteria	Popular Magazines	Scholarly Journals
Advertisements	Numerous full-page color ads	Few if any ads
Appearance	Eye-catching; glossy; pictures and illustrations	Plain; black-and-white graphics, tables, charts, and diagrams
Audience	General	Professors, researchers, and college students
Author	Journalists	Professionals in an academic field or discipline
Bibliography	Brief acknowledgment of sources in text, usually without complete citation information	Extensive bibliography at the end of each article; footnotes and other documentation
Content	General articles to inform, update, or introduce a contemporary issue	Research projects, methodology, and theory
Examples	*Newsweek, National Review, PC World, Psychology Today*	*International Journal of Applied Engineering Research, New England Journal of Medicine*
Language	Nontechnical, simple vocabulary	Specialized vocabulary
Publisher	Commercial publisher	Professional organization, university, research institute, or scholarly press

Information from materials at the Hesburgh Library, University of Notre Dame.

Steps to Identifying Sources

1 **Consult experts who can guide your research.** Talk to people who can help you formulate issues and questions.

2 **Develop a working knowledge of standard sources.** Identify the different kinds of information that different types of sources provide.

3 **Distinguish between primary and secondary sources.** Decide what type of information can best help you answer your research question.

4 **Distinguish between popular and scholarly sources.** Determine what kind of information will persuade your readers.

A Practice Sequence: Identifying Sources

We would now like you to practice using some of the strategies we have discussed so far: talking with experts, deciding what sources of information you should use, and determining what types of information can best help you develop your paper and persuade your readers. We assume you have chosen a topic for your paper, identified an issue, and perhaps formulated a working thesis. If not, think back to some of the topics mentioned in earlier chapters. Have any of them piqued your interest? If not, here are five very broad topics you might work with:

- higher education student loans
- the media and gender
- global health
- science and religion
- immigration

Once you've decided on a topic, talk to experts and decide which types of sources you should use: primary or secondary, popular or scholarly. Consult with your classmates to evaluate the strengths and weaknesses of different sources of information and the appropriateness of using different types of information. Here are the steps to follow:

1   Talk to a librarian about the sources you might use to get information about your topic (for example, databases, abstracts, or bibliographies). Be sure to take notes.

2   Talk to an expert who can provide you with some ideas about current issues in the field of interest. Be sure to take detailed notes.

3   Decide whether you should use primary or secondary sources or some combination of the two. What type of information would help you develop your argument?

4   Decide whether you should use popular or scholarly sources or whether some of each would be appropriate. What type of information would your readers find compelling?

SEARCHING FOR SOURCES

Once you've decided on the types of sources you want to use—primary or secondary, popular or scholarly—you can take steps to locate the information you need. You might begin with a tour of your university or local library, so that you know where the library keeps newspapers, government documents, books, journals, and other sources of information. Notice where the reference desk is: This is where you should head to ask a librarian for help if you get stuck. You also want to find a computer where you can log on to your library's catalog to start your search. Once you have located your sources in the library, you can begin to look through them for the information you need.

You may be tempted to rely on the Internet and a search engine like Google. But keep in mind that the information you retrieve from the Internet may not be trustworthy: Anyone can post his or her thoughts on a Web site. Of course, you can also find excellent scholarly sources on the Internet. (For example, Johns Hopkins University Press manages Project MUSE, a collection of 300-plus academic journals that can be accessed online through institutional subscription.) School libraries also offer efficient access to government records and other sources essential to scholarly writing.

Let's say you are about to start researching a paper on language diversity and the English-only movement. When you log on to the library's site, you find a menu of choices: Catalog, Electronic Resources, Virtual Reference Desk, and Services & Collections. (The wording may vary slightly from library to library, but the means of locating information will be the same.) When you click on Catalog, another menu of search choices appears: Keyword, Title, Author, and Subject (Figure 7.1). The hunt is on.

■ Perform a Keyword Search

A **keyword** is essentially your topic: It defines the topic of your search. To run a keyword search, you can look up information by

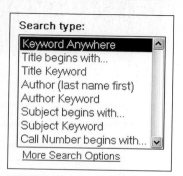

FIGURE 7.1   Menu of Basic Search Strategies

author, title, or subject. You would search by author to locate all the works a particular author has written on a subject. So, for example, if you know that Paul Lang is an expert on the consequences of the English-only movement, you might begin with an author search. You can use the title search to locate all works with a key term or phrase in the title. The search results are likely to include a number of irrelevant titles, but you should end up with a list of authors, titles, and subject headings to guide another search.

A search by subject is particularly helpful as you begin your research, while you are still formulating your thesis. You want to start by thinking of as many words as possible that relate to your topic. (A thesaurus can help you come up with different words you can use in a keyword search.) Suppose you type in the phrase "English only." A number of different sources appear on the screen, but the most promising is Paul Lang's book *The English Language Debate: One Nation, One Language?* You click on this record, and another screen appears with some valuable pieces of information, including the call number (which tells you where in the library you can find the book) and an indication that the book has a bibliography, something you can make use of once you find the book (Figure 7.2). Notice that the subject listings—*Language policy, English language–Political aspects, English-only movement, Bilingual education*—also give you additional keywords to use in finding relevant information. The lesson here is that it is important to generate keywords to get initial information and then to look at that information carefully for

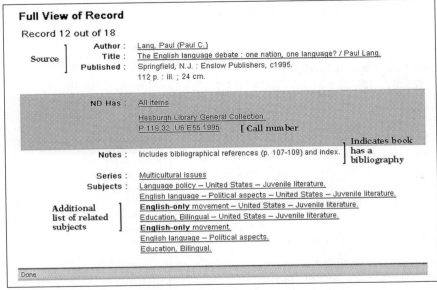

FIGURE 7.2 Full-View Bibliographic Entry

more keywords and to determine if the source has a bibliography. Even if this particular source isn't relevant, it may lead you to other sources that are.

■ Try Browsing

Browse is a headings search; it appears in the menu of choices in Figure 7.1 as "Subject begins with..." This type of search allows you to scroll through an alphabetical index. Some of the indexes available are the Author Index, the Title Index, and the Library of Congress Subject Headings, a subject index. Browse

- displays an alphabetical list of entries;
- shows the number of records for each entry;
- indicates whether there are cross-references for each entry.

What appears in the window is "Browse List: Choose a field, enter a phrase and click the 'go' button." Figure 7.3 shows the results of a preliminary browse when the words "English-only" are entered. Notice that a list of headings or titles appears on the screen. This is not a list of books, and not all of the entries are relevant. But you can use the list to determine which headings are relevant to your topic, issue, or question.

For your paper on the English-only movement, the first two headings seem relevant: *English-only debate and English-only movement.* A further click would reveal the title of a relevant book and a new list of subject headings (Figure 7.4) that differs from those of your initial search. This list gives you a new bibliography from which you can gather new leads and a list of subject headings to investigate.

Browse List: Subjects

No. of Recs	Entry
	English one-act plays - [LC Authority Record] See: One-act plays, English
	English-only debate - [LC Authority Record] See: English-only movement
4	English-only movement - [LC Authority Record]
1	English-only movement — California — Case studies
1	English-only movement — Colorado
4	English-only movement — United States
1	English-only movement — United States — Juvenile literature
	English-only question - [LC Authority Record] See: English-only movement
1	English — Ontario — Correspondence
1	English oration

FIGURE 7.3   Preliminary Browse of "English-only" Subject Heading

#	Year	Author	Title
1 ☐	2006	United States.	English as the official language : hearing before the Subcommittee on Education Reform of the Co <Book>
			Click for ONLINE ACCESS (Text version:)
			Documents Center Owned: 1 Checked Out: 0
			Display full record
2 ☐	1996	United States.	S. 356—Language of Government Act of 1995 : hearings before the Committee on Governmental Affai <Book>
			Documents Center
			Display full record
3 ☐	1996	United States.	Hearing on English as the common language : hearing before the Subcommittee on Early Childhood, <Book>
			Documents Center
			Display full record
4 ☐	1995	United States.	Hearing on English as a common language : hearing before the Subcommittee on Early Childhood, Yo <Book>
			Documents Center
			Display full record

Done

FIGURE 7.4   Results of Browsing Deeper: A New List of Sources

We suggest that you do a keyword search first and then a browse search to home in on a subject. Especially when you don't know the exact subject, you can do a quick keyword search, retrieve many sets of results, and then begin looking at the subjects that correspond to each title. Once you find a subject that fits your needs, you can click on the direct subject (found in each bibliographic record) and execute a new search that will yield more relevant results.

■ Perform a Journal or Newspaper Title Search

Finally, you can search by journal or newspaper title. For this kind of search, you will need exact information. You can take the name of a journal, magazine, or newspaper cited in your keyword or browse search. The journal or newspaper title search will tell you if your library subscribes to the publication and in what format—print, microform or microfilm, or electronic.

Suppose you want to continue your search for information on the English-only movement by looking for articles in the *New York Times*. You would run a basic search under the category "Periodicals": "Periodical Title begins with . . ." That would give you access to a limited number of articles that focused on the debate surrounding the English-only movement. To find more recent articles, you could go to the *New York Times* Web site (nytimes.com), where you could find many potentially useful listings. Newspaper articles will lack the depth and complexity of more scholarly studies, but they are undeniably useful in helping you establish the timeliness and relevance of your research. You can usually preview the articles because the Web site will include a few sentences describing the content of each article. If a site requires that you subscribe or pay a nominal fee before viewing the full text of an article, check to see if you already have free access through your school's library.

Steps to Searching for Sources

1 **Perform a keyword search.** Choose a word or phrase that best describes your topic.

2 **Try browsing.** Search an alphabetical list by subject.

3 **Perform a journal or newspaper title search.** Find relevant citations by limiting your search with the exact title of a journal or newspaper.

A Practice Sequence: Searching for Sources

If you tried the practice sequence on identifying sources (pp. 172–73), explore your topic further by practicing the types of searches discussed in this section: a keyword search; a browse; and a journal or newspaper title search (or a subject search).

EVALUATING LIBRARY SOURCES

The information you encounter will vary in terms of its relevance and overall quality. You will want to evaluate this information as systematically as possible to be sure that you are using the most appropriate sources to develop your argument. Once you have obtained at least some of the sources you located by searching your library's catalog, you should evaluate the material as you read it. In particular, you want to evaluate the following information for each article or book:

- the author's background and credentials (What is the author's educational background? What has he or she written about in the past? Is this person an expert in the field?)
- the author's purpose
- the topic of discussion
- the audience the author invokes and whether you are a member of that audience
- the nature of the conversation (How have others addressed the problem?)
- what the author identifies as a misinterpretation or a gap in knowledge, an argument that needs modifying, or a hypothesis
- what the author's own view is

- how the author supports his or her argument (that is, with primary or secondary sources, with popular or scholarly articles, with facts or opinions)

- the accuracy of the author's evidence (Can you find similar information elsewhere?)

If your topic is current, chances are your searches are going to turn up a large number of possible sources. How do you go about choosing which sources to rely on in your writing? Of course, if time were not an issue, you could read them all from start to finish. But in the real world, assignments come with due dates. To decide whether a library source merits a close reading and evaluation, begin by skimming each book or article. **Skimming**—briefly examining the material to get a sense of the information it offers—involves four steps:

1. Read the introductory sections.
2. Examine the table of contents and index.
3. Check the notes and bibliographic references.
4. Skim for the argument.

■ Read the Introductory Sections

Turn to the introductory sections of the text first. Many authors use a preface or an introduction to explain the themes they focus on in a book. An **abstract** serves a similar purpose, but article abstracts are usually only 250 words long. In the introductory sections, writers typically describe the issue that motivated them to write and indicate whether they believe the work corrects a misconception, fills a gap, or builds on and extends the research of others. For example, in the preface to her book *Learning and Not Learning English: Latino Students in American Schools* (2001), Guadalupe Valdés explains that even after two years of language instruction, many students remain at a low level of language competence. In this passage, Valdés makes clear the purpose of her work:

> This book examines the learning of English in American schools by immigrant children. It focuses on the realities that such youngsters face in trying to acquire English in settings in which they interact exclusively with other non-English-speaking youngsters the entire school day. It is designed to fill a gap in the existing literature on non-English-background youngsters by offering a glimpse of the challenges and difficulties faced by four middle-school students enrolled in the United States for the first time when they were 12 or 13 years old. It is my purpose here to use these youngsters' lives and experiences as a lens through which to examine the policy and instructional dilemmas that now surround the education of immigrant children in this country. (p. 2)

If you were looking for sources for a paper on the English-only movement, in particular the consequences of that movement for young students, you might very well find Valdés's words compelling and decide the book is worth a closer reading.

▪ Examine the Table of Contents and Index

After reading the introductory sections, you will find it useful to analyze the **table of contents** to see how much emphasis the writer gives to topics that are relevant to your own research. For example, the table of contents to *Learning and Not Learning English* includes several headings that may relate to your interest: "Educating English-Language Learners," "Challenges and Realities," "Implications for Policy and Practice," and the "Politics of Teaching English." You also should turn to the back of the book to examine the **index**, an alphabetical list of the important and recurring concepts in a book, and the page numbers on which they appear. An index also would include the names of authors cited in the book. In the index to Valdés's book, you would find references to "English-language abilities and instruction" with specific page numbers where you can read what the author has to say on this subject. You would also find references to "English-only instruction," "equal educational opportunities," and "sheltered instruction."

▪ Check the Notes and Bibliographic References

Especially in the initial stages of your writing, you should look closely at writers' notes and bibliographies to discern who they feel are the important voices in the field. Frequent citation of a particular researcher's work may indicate that the individual is considered to be an expert in the field you are studying. Notes usually provide brief references to people, concepts, or context; the bibliography includes a long list of related works. Mining Valdés's bibliography, you would find such titles as "Perspectives on Official English," "Language Policy in Schools," "Not Only English," "Language and Power," and "The Cultural Politics of English."

▪ Skim for the Argument

Skimming a book or an article entails briefly looking over the elements we have discussed so far: the preface or abstract, the table of contents and the index, and the notes and bibliography. Skimming also can mean reading chapter titles, headings, and the first sentence of each paragraph to determine the relevance of a book or an article.

Skimming the first chapter of *Learning and Not Learning English*, you would find several topic sentences that reveal the writer's purpose:

"In this book, then, I examine and describe different expressions that both learning and not-learning English took among four youngsters."

"In the chapters that follow . . ."

"What I hope to suggest . . ."

These are the types of phrases you should look for to get a sense of what the author is trying to accomplish and whether the author's work will be of use to you.

If, after you've taken these steps, a source still seems promising, you should reflect on whether it might help you answer your research question. Keep in mind the critical reading skills you've learned and see if you can discern the author's overall situation, purpose, claims, and audience. Assess the evidence used to support the claims—is it recent, relevant, accurate, reliable? What kinds of evidence does the author use? Primary or secondary? Popular or scholarly? What kind of data, facts, or statistical evidence? Note whether facts or opinions seem to predominate. Ultimately you have to determine whether to set the source aside or commit yourself to a thorough understanding of its argument and all the note taking and critical thinking that will entail.

Steps to Evaluating Library Sources

1 **Read the introductory sections.** Get an overview of the author's argument.

2 **Examine the table of contents and index.** Consider the most relevant chapters to your topic and the list of relevant subjects.

3 **Check the notes and bibliographic references.** Identify other writers an author refers to and the titles of both books and articles (are the names and titles cited in many other works?).

4 **Skim for the argument.** Read chapter titles, headings, and topic sentences to determine the source's relevance to your research. Go deeper to assess the type and quality of evidence the author uses. Note whether the author uses credible evidence to support the argument.

A Practice Sequence: Evaluating Library Sources

For this exercise, we would like you to choose a specific book or article to examine to practice these strategies. If you are far along on your own research, use a book or an article you have identified as potentially useful.

1   Read the introductory sections. What issue is the author responding to? What is the author's purpose? To correct a misconception? To fill a gap? To build on or extend the work of others? To address a hypothesis?

2   Examine the table of contents and index. What key words or phrases are related to your own research? Which topics does the author focus on? Are you intending to give these topics similar emphasis? (Will you give more or less emphasis?)

3   Check the notes and bibliographic references. Make a list of the sources you think you want to look up for your own research. Do certain sources seem more important than others?

4   Skim for the argument. What is the author's focus? Is it relevant to your own topic, issue, question, working thesis? What kinds of evidence does the author use? Does the author use primary or secondary sources? Popular or scholarly articles? Statistics? Facts or opinions? Do you want to commit yourself to grappling with the author's argument?

EVALUATING INTERNET SOURCES

Without question, the Internet has revolutionized how research is conducted. It has been a particular boon to experienced researchers who have a clear sense of what they are looking for, giving them access to more information more quickly than ever before. But the Internet is rife with pitfalls for inexperienced researchers. That is, sites that appear accurate and reliable may prove not to be. The sources you find on the Internet outside your school library's catalog pose problems because anyone can post anything he or she wants. Although Internet sources can be useful, particularly because they are often current, you must take steps to evaluate them before using information from them.

■ Evaluate the Author of the Site

If an author's name appears on a Web site, ask the following: Who is this person? What credentials and professional affiliations qualify this person to make a legitimate argument in the field being investigated?

One of our students googled "English only" and clicked on the first result, "Language Policy—English Only Movement," which eventually led her to James Crawford's Language Policy Web Site & Emporium. On the site, Crawford explains that he is "a writer and lecturer—formerly the Washington editor of *Education Week*—who specializes in the politics of language."* He notes that "since 1985, I have been reporting on the English Only movement, English Plus, bilingual education, Native American

---

Education Week has been published since 1981 by Editorial Projects in Education, a nonprofit organization that was founded with the help of a Carnegie grant. The publication covers issues related to primary and secondary education. If you are not familiar with a publication and are uncertain about its legitimacy, you can always ask your instructor, a librarian, or another expert to vouch for its reliability.

language revitalization, and language rights in the U.S.A." Between 2004 and 2006, he also served as executive director of the National Association for Bilingual Education. Perhaps most important, Crawford has authored four books and a number of articles and has testified before Congress on "Official English Legislation." From this biographical sketch, the student inferred that Crawford is credentialed to write about the English-only movement.

Less certain, however, are the credentials of the writer who penned an article titled "Should the National Anthem Be Sung in English Only?" which appeared on another Web site our student visited. Why? Because the writer's name never appears on the site. An anonymous posting is the first clue that you want to move on to a more legitimate source of information.

■ Evaluate the Organization That Supports the Site

You have probably noticed that Internet addresses usually end with a domain name extension: .edu, .gov, .org, or .com. The .edu extension means the site is associated with a university or college, which gives it credibility. The same holds true for .gov, which indicates a government agency. Both types of sites have a regulatory body that oversees their content. The extension .org indicates a nonprofit organization; .com, a commercial organization. You will need to approach these Web sites with a degree of skepticism because you cannot be sure that they are as carefully monitored by a credentialed regulatory body. (In fact, even .edu sites may turn out to be postings by a student at a college or university.)

Our student was intrigued by James Crawford's site because he appears to be a credible source on the English-only movement. She was less sure about the reference to the Institute for Language and Education Policy. Is the institute a regulatory body that oversees what appears on the site? How long has the institute existed? Who belongs to the institute? Who sits on its board of directors? As a critical thinker, the student had to ask these questions.

■ Evaluate the Purpose of the Site

Information is never objective, so whenever you evaluate a book, an article, or a Web site, you should consider the point of view the writer or sponsor is taking. It's especially important to ask if there is a particular bias among members of the group that sponsors the site. Can you tell what the sponsors of the site advocate? Are they hoping to sell or promote a product, or to influence opinion?

Not all Web sites provide easy answers to these questions. However, James Crawford's Language Policy Web Site & Emporium is quite explicit. In fact, Crawford writes that "the site is designed to encourage discussion of language policy issues, expose misguided school 'reforms,'" and, among other goals, "promote [his] own publications." (Notice "Emporium" in the name of the site.) He is candid about his self-interest, which does raise a question about his degree of objectivity.

What about a site like Wikipedia ("The Free Encyclopedia")? The site appears to exist to convey basic information. Although the popularity of Wikipedia recommends it as a basic resource, you should approach the site with caution because it is not clear whether and how the information posted on the site is regulated. It is prudent to confirm information from Wikipedia by checking on sites that are regulated more transparently rather than take Wikipedia as an authoritative source.

■ Evaluate the Information on the Site

In addition to assessing the purpose of a Web site like Wikipedia, you need to evaluate the extent to which the information is recent, accurate, and consistent with information you find in print sources and clearly regulated Web sites. For example, clicking on "The modern English-only movement" on Wikipedia takes you to a timeline of sorts with a number of links to other sites. But again, what is the source of this information? What is included? What is left out? You should check further into some of these links, reading the sources cited and keeping in mind the four criteria for evaluating a claim — recency, relevance, reliability, and accuracy. In general, it is wise to treat Wikipedia as only a potential starting point. Most instructors don't allow students to cite Wikipedia entries as sources, but looking at relevant entries may lead you to trustworthy sources. Because you cannot be certain that Internet sources are reviewed or monitored, you need to be scrupulous about examining the claims they make: How much and what kind of evidence supports the author's (or site's) argument? Can you offer counterarguments?

In the last analysis, it comes down to whether the information you find stands up to the criteria you've learned to apply as a critical reader and writer. If not, move on to other sources. In a Web-based world of information, there is no shortage of material, but you have to train yourself not to settle for the information that is most readily available if you cannot determine that it is credible.

Steps to Evaluating Internet Sources

1 **Evaluate the author of the site.** Determine whether the author is an expert.

2 **Evaluate the organization that supports the site.** Find out what the organization stands for and the extent of its credibility.

3 **Evaluate the purpose of the site.** What interests are represented on the site? What is the site trying to do? Provide access to legitimate statistics and information? Advance an argument? Spread propaganda?

4 **Evaluate the information on the site.** Identify the type of information on the site and the extent to which the information is recent, relevant, reliable, and accurate.

A Practice Sequence: Evaluating Internet Sources

For this exercise, we would like you to work in groups on a common topic. The class can choose its own topic or use one of the topics we suggest on page 172. Then google the topic and agree on a Web site to analyze:

> *Group 1:* Evaluate the author of the site.
>
> *Group 2:* Evaluate the organization that supports the site.
>
> *Group 3:* Evaluate the purpose of the site.
>
> *Group 4:* Evaluate the information on the site.

Next, each group should share its evaluation. The goal is to determine the extent to which you believe you could use the information on this site in writing an academic essay.

WRITING AN ANNOTATED BIBLIOGRAPHY

In this chapter, we have suggested some strategies that you can use to locate information to help you learn more about a topic, issue, or question and to assess the extent to which this information can help you develop a legitimate, credible, and well-supported argument. As you read, it is important to write down the citation, or bibliographic information, of each source, including the author's name, date of publication, the title of an article or book, the journal title where an article appears, page numbers, and publishing information for a book.

Collecting the basic information about each source is useful, but we also suggest that you write an annotated bibliography to record your preliminary evaluation of the information you find. In writing an annotation, you should include the key ideas and claims from each source. You can also identify where you see gaps, misconceptions, and areas that you can build upon in developing your own argument. That is, in addition to stating what a given source is about, you can address the following questions: What is the issue the author responds to? What is the author's purpose? To what extent is the argument persuasive? Does it overlook any issues that are important? Finally, you can explain the relevance of this work to your own research, given your own purpose for writing and what you want to demonstrate.

You can limit each annotation to a few sentences in which you present the author's key claims and ideas, briefly analyze the author's argument, and then explain how you will use that information in your own researched argument. The annotation below provides one such example, using APA format for the citation.

> Loftstrom, M., & Tyler, J. H. (2009). Finishing high school: Alternative pathways and dropout recovery. *The Future of Children, 19*(1), 77–103. Retrieved from http://www.jstor.org /stable/27795036

> This article provides a good history and analysis of the present dropout problem facing our nation. Researchers examine the discrepancy in statewide high school completion requirements that have led to debates about reality of dropout rates. The authors also examine social and economic consequences of failure to complete high school and the inadequacy of a GED certificate as a replacement for a high school diploma. The researchers conclude by examining some dropout prevention programs and by calling for more research in this area. In doing so, they identify a gap that my research at an alternative high school can help to fill, especially my interviews with students currently enrolled in the program and those who have dropped out.

Steps to Writing an Annotated Bibliography

1 **Present key ideas.** Describe in just a few sentences what this research is about and what you have learned.

2 **Analyze.** Explain the situation the author responds to, the purpose of the research, possible gaps in reasoning or misconceptions, and adequacy of evidence.

3 **Determine relevance.** Discuss how you might use this research in developing your own argument. As background for your own work? To explain how you fill a gap or correct a misconception? Will you build upon and extend this work?

A Practice Sequence: Writing an Annotated Bibliography

Write an annotation of a book, book chapter, or article that you have read for your research. Follow the steps in the previous box by first discussing the content of what you have read and analyzing the author's argument. Then determine the relevance of this research to your own work. If you have not chosen a topic yet, we invite you to write an annotation of a book, book chapter, or article related to any of the following broad topics:

- higher education student loans
- the media and gender
- global health
- science and religion
- immigration

From Synthesis to Researched Argument

A **synthesis** is a discussion that forges connections between the arguments of two or more authors. Like a summary (discussed in Chapter 3), a synthesis requires you to understand the key claims of each author's argument, including his or her use of supporting examples and evidence. Also like a summary, a synthesis requires you to present a central idea, a *gist*, to your readers. But in contrast to a summary, which explains the context of a source, a synthesis creates a context for your own argument. That is, when you write a synthesis comparing two or more sources, you demonstrate that you are aware of the larger conversation about the issue and begin to claim your own place in that conversation.

Comparing different points of view prompts you to ask why they differ. It also makes you more aware of *counterarguments*—passages where claims conflict ("writer X says this, but writer Y asserts just the opposite") or at least differ ("writer X interprets this information this way, while writer Y sees it differently"). And it starts you formulating your own counterarguments: "Neither X nor Y has taken this into account. What if they had?"

Keep in mind that the purpose of a synthesis is not merely to list the similarities and differences you find in different sources or to assert your agreement with one source as opposed to others. Instead, it sets up your argument. Once you discover connections among texts, you have to decide what those connections mean to you and your readers. What bearing do they have on your own thinking? How can you make use of them in your argument?

WRITING A SYNTHESIS

To compose an effective synthesis, you must (1) make connections among ideas in different texts, (2) decide what those connections mean, and (3) formulate the gist of what you've read, much like you did when you wrote a summary. The difference is that in a synthesis, your gist should be a succinct statement that brings into focus not the central idea of one text but the relationship among different ideas in multiple texts.

To help you grasp strategies of writing a synthesis, read the following essays from activist Paul Rogat Loeb, who writes about building community through grassroots activism; educators Anne Colby and Thomas Ehrlich, whose work with the Carnegie Foundation for Teaching and Learning focuses on the reasons why young people, especially undergraduates, need to be more civically engaged in their communities; and Laurie Ouellette, a professor of communication studies who writes about media and the recent trend toward the media's efforts to do good works in local communities at a time when the federal government in the United States has cut social programs and continues to rely on private entities to support families in need. We have annotated these readings not only to comment on the ideas that these authors have put forth, but also to model some of the ways that you might annotate texts as a useful first step in writing a synthesis.

PAUL ROGAT LOEB

Making Our Lives Count
(from *Soul of a Citizen*)

Paul Rogat Loeb is an American social and political activist. A graduate of Stanford University, he has published widely in both newspapers and journals. *Hope in Hard Times* is one of several books that he has written and depicts ordinary Americans involved in grassroots peace activism, while *Soul of a Citizen* seeks to inspire civic engagement activism. His book *The Impossible Will Take a Little While*, an anthology of the achievements of activists in history who faced enormous obstacles, was named the #4 political book of 2004 by the History Channel and the American Book Association and won the Nautilus Book Award for the best social change book that year.

Souls are like athletes that need opponents worthy of them if they are to be tried and extended and pushed to the full use of their powers.

—THOMAS MERTON

***

Heart," "spark," "spirit"—whatever word we use for the mysterious force that animates us, its full potential cannot be realized in isolation. Indeed, according to developmental psychologists, individual growth is possible only through interaction with the human and natural world, and through experiences that challenge us. "Souls are like athletes," wrote the Trappist monk Thomas Merton, "that need opponents worthy of them if they are to be tried and extended and pushed to the full use of their powers."

Many of us may already know the value of stretching our souls in personal life. We know the virtue of learning to voice our needs, fight for our choices, and recover from psychological intimidation. This process may require acknowledging painful truths, withstanding conflict, standing firm on what seems like shaky ground. We may need to question familiar habits, overcome self-doubt, and begin to separate who we really are from the roles we've been taught. Jungian analysts like James Hillman would say that by taking these steps we reconnect with what the Greeks called the *daimon,* the "acorn" of character at the core of our being. Psychiatrist M. Scott Peck described spiritual healing as "an ongoing process of becoming increasingly conscious."

We are slower to attempt such transformations in the public sphere. Self-assertion there requires us not only to modify our outlook and behavior but also to confront a bewildering and often disorienting maze of institutions and individuals, powers and principalities. So we stay silent in the face of common choices that we know are unwise or morally troubling. We keep our opinions to ourselves, because we doubt our voices will be heard, mistrust our right to speak,

1

2

3

Cites research to emphasize the value of human interaction.

Acknowledges that many of us are aware of the value of voicing our own needs and taking care of ourselves, and sets up the argument about community building.

Expresses concern that we may be less likely to think about our well-being as connected to others in the public sphere. Also identifies with those who may be reluctant to be assertive in the public sphere because they fear their voices won't be heard.

or fear the consequences if we do speak out. We feel we lack essential political skills. Like … Rosa Parks before her first NAACP meeting, we simply do not know we have it in us.

Yet coming out of one's cocoon in the public sphere is just as necessary to self-realization as it is in the private. I once told a young Puerto Rican activist about the notion, common among many of his fellow students, that they'd lose their identity by getting involved—find themselves "swallowed up" by the movements they joined. He laughed and said the reverse was true. "You learn things you never knew about yourself. You get pushed to your limits. You meet people who make you think and push you further. You don't lose your identity. You begin to find out who you really are. I feel sad for people who will never have this experience."

You begin to find out who you really are. The implication is clear enough: We become human only in the company of other human beings. And this involves both opening our hearts and giving voice to our deepest convictions. The biblical vision of *shalom* describes this process with its concept of "right relationships" with our fellow humans, and with all of God's creation. The turning point for the Buddha, writes James Hillman, came only "when he left his protected palace gardens to enter the street. There the sick, the dead, the poor, and the old drew his soul down into the question of how to live life in the world." As Hillman stresses, the Buddha became who he was precisely by leaving the cloistered life. A doctor I know works in a low-income clinic because, she says, "seeing the struggles of others helps me be true to myself. It helps me find out how people in very different circumstances live out their humanity." Community involvement, in other words, is the mirror that best reflects our individual choices, our strengths and weaknesses, our accomplishments and failures. It allows our lives to count for something.

Marginal notes:

Elaborates on his point that human connection is necessary. Uses an anecdote to show how getting involved with others helps us better understand who we are as individuals.

Reiterates his point that interacting with others teaches us about who we are and what we value. Cites the work of a scholar who studies Buddhism and a doctor who believes her work in low-income communities has helped her be a better version of herself.

Community involvement helps us see that we matter.

Paragraph numbers: 4   5

The Cost of Silence

Offers an illustration to support the value of activism but also shows that speaking out for what we value can have its costs.

Twenty years after Harvard Law School hired him as its first fulltime African American professor, Derrick Bell took an unpaid protest leave, refusing to teach until the school hired a minority woman to its faculty. It was not a decision made in haste. Bell had long campaigned for this. But each time a new position opened, the Law School somehow could find not a single minority female candidate in the world who was worthy enough to hire. The school's resistance continued despite Bell's stand. After three years, the school forced him to resign. His conscience had cost him a tenured job at the most prestigious law school in America.

6

What might seem like failure can actually be a factor that bolsters our commitment to make a difference.

Yet Bell didn't feel defeated. Quite the opposite. His public stance had preserved his core identity and integrity. "It is the determination to protect our sense of who we are," he writes, "that leads us to risk criticism, alienation, and serious loss while most others, similarly harmed, remain silent."

7

Helps readers understand that remaining silent about issues that matter can be more costly than failed action.

What Bell means is that silence is more costly than speaking out, because it requires the ultimate sacrifice—the erosion of our spirit. The toll we pay for stifling our emotions in personal life is fairly obvious. Swallowed words act like caustic acids, eating at our gut. If the condition persists and the sentiments are sufficiently intense, we grow numb, detached, dead to the world around us. When, however, we take steps to redress our private losses and sorrows, we often feel a renewed sense of strength and joy, of reconnecting with life.

8

One cost to remaining silent is that we are no longer true to ourselves and we lose our ability to be whole human beings.

A similar process occurs when we want to address public issues but stay silent. It takes energy to mute our voices while the environment is ravaged, greed runs rampant, and families sleep in the streets. It takes energy to distort our words and actions because we fear the consequences of speaking out. It takes energy, in other words, to sustain what the psychiatrist Robert Jay Lifton calls "the broken connection," splitting our

9

lives from our values. Like autistic children, we can blank out the voices of our fellow human beings. But if we do, we risk the decay of our humanity. When we shrink from the world, our souls shrink, too.

Social involvement reverses this process, releasing our choked-off energy, overcoming the psychic paralysis that so many of us feel, reintegrating mind and heart, body and soul, so that we can speak in one voice—our own—and mean what we say. There's even a physical corollary to this integration. In *The Healing Power of Doing Good*, Allan Luks describes various studies that confirm what he calls the "helper's high." People who volunteer in their communities experience significantly greater physical pleasure and well-being in the process of their work, a general sense of increased energy, and in some cases an easing of chronic pain. A Harvard School of Public Health study found that African Americans who challenged repeated discrimination had lower blood pressure than those who did not. So taking stands for what we believe may help us save more than our souls.

Sociologist Parker Palmer describes the resulting unleashing of truth, vision, and strength in the lives of people like Rosa Parks, Vaclav Havel, Nelson Mandela, and Dorothy Day, who've acted on their deepest beliefs. "These people," he wrote, "have understood that no punishment could be worse than the one we inflict on ourselves by living a divided life." And nothing could be more powerful than the decision to heal that rift, "to stop acting differently on the outside from what they knew to be true inside."

Learned Helplessness

America's predominant culture insists that little we do can matter. It teaches us not to get involved in shaping the world we'll pass on to our children. It encourages us to leave such important decisions to others—whether they be corporate and government leaders, or social activists whose lifestyles seem impossibly selfless or foreign. Sadly, and ironically, in

Cites additional research to explain how serving our communities with others can have an effect on us physically, not just psychologically, and contribute to our health and well-being.

Cites further evidence to explain the importance of acting on our convictions.

Laments the extent to which American culture seems to work against the idea of activism, community work, and human agency — the ability to envision change and the capacity to act on our convictions in meaningful ways.

10

11

12

a country born of a democratic political revolution, to be American in recent years is too often to be apolitical. For many, civic withdrawal has become the norm. The 2008 presidential campaign challenged this trend by inspiring vast numbers of previously disengaged citizens to volunteer in ways that shifted not only the presidential race, but also close races for the Senate, the House, and state governorships. But even then over a third of potentially eligible Americans ended up staying home. And despite all the passionate volunteers, far more citizens did little beyond casting their vote. Absent a highly contested election, it's easier still to sit on the sidelines and simply hope our leaders will take care of things.

Argues that we need to adopt a view of democratic engagement that our Founding Fathers offered.

Overcoming our instinctive civic withdrawal requires courage. It requires learning the skills and developing the confidence to participate.... It also requires creating a renewed definition of ourselves as citizens—something closer to the nation of active stakeholders that leaders like Thomas Jefferson had in mind. *13*

The importance of citizens' direct participation in a democracy was expressed thousands of years ago, by the ancient Greeks. In fact, they used the word "idiot" for people incapable of involving themselves in civic life. Now, the very word "political" has become so debased in our culture that we use it to describe either trivial office power plays or leaders who serve largely personal ambitions. We've lost sight of its original roots in the Greek notion of the *polis*: the democratic sphere in which citizens, acting in concert, determine the character and direction of their society. "All persons alike," wrote Aristotle, should share "in the government to the utmost." *14*

Uses a play to illustrate the extent to which it is not enough to focus on problems without taking action.

Reclaiming this political voice requires more than just identifying problems, which itself can feed our sense of overload. I think of an Arthur Miller play, *Broken Glass,* whose heroine obsesses while Hitler steadily consolidates his power. From her safe home in Brooklyn, she reads newspaper articles about *Kristallnacht:* synagogues smashed and looted; old *15* men forced to scrub streets with toothbrushes while storm troopers laugh at them; and finally, children shipped off to the camps in cattle cars. Her concern contrasts with the approach of her family and friends, who insist, despite the mounting evidence, that such horrors are exaggerated. Yet she does nothing to address the situation publicly, except to grow more anxious. Eventually she becomes psychosomatically paralyzed.

The approach Miller's protagonist takes toward the horrors of Nazism echoes that of far too many people who spend hours following every twist and turn of the twenty-four-hour news cycle, yet never take action that might address them. It also resembles the condition of learned helplessness. People who suffer from severe depression, psychologist Martin Seligman found, do so less as a result of particular unpleasant experiences than because of their "explanatory style"—the story they tell themselves about how the world works. Depressed people have become convinced that the causes of their difficulties are permanent and pervasive, inextricably linked to their personal failings. There's nothing to be done because nothing can be done. This master narrative of their lives excuses inaction; it provides a rationale for remaining helpless. In contrast, individuals who function with high effectiveness tend to believe that the problems they face result from factors that are specific, temporary, and therefore changeable. The story they live by empowers them.

The story we tell ourselves about the world can either lead us to a feeling of helplessness or a sense of empowerment — that there are things we can do to create change.

16

This is not to say that change is easy, nor that everyone is in an equal position to bring it about. Some individuals and groups in America possess far more material and organizational resources than others. This reflects our deep social and economic inequities. But as *Tikkun* magazine founder Rabbi Michael Lerner has observed, we often fail to use the resources we do have, which may be of a different kind. "Most of us," Lerner says, "have been subjected to a set of experiences in our childhood and adult lives that makes us feel that we do not deserve to have power." Consequently, we can't imagine changing the direction of

17

our society. We decide that things are worse than they actually are—a condition Lerner refers to as "surplus powerlessness."...

The illusion of powerlessness can just as easily afflict the fortunate among us. I know many people who are confident and successful in their work and have loving personal relationships, yet can hardly conceive of trying to work toward a more humane society. Materially comfortable and professionally accomplished, they could make important social contributions. Instead they restrict their search for meaning and integrity to their private lives. Their sense of shared fate extends only to their immediate families and friends. Despite their many advantages, they, too, have been taught an "explanatory style" that precludes participation in public life, except to promote the most narrow self-interest.

Points out that some of the most well-off people are driven by self-interest when they might use their wealth to make important "social contributions."

18

Whatever our situations, we all face a choice. We can ignore the problems that lie just beyond our front doors; we can allow decisions to be made in our names that lead to a meaner and more desperate world. We can yell at the TV newscasters and complain about how bad things are, using our bitterness as a hedge against involvement. Or we can work, as well as we can, to shape a more generous common future.

Leaves us with a clear decision about whether or not we allow others to make choices for us or to take on the responsibility of working for the common good.

19

ANNE COLBY AND THOMAS EHRLICH, WITH ELIZABETH BEAUMONT AND JASON STEPHENS
Undergraduate Education and the Development of Moral and Civic Responsibility

At the time that the two primary authors published this essay, they worked at the Carnegie Foundation for the Advancement of Teaching, a U.S.-based education policy and research center founded by Andrew Carnegie in 1905. The foundation embraces a commitment to developing networks of ideas, individuals, and institutions to advance teaching and learning. Anne Colby holds a PhD in psychology from Columbia and currently serves as a consulting professor at Stanford University. Prior to that, she was director of the Henry Murray Research Center at Harvard University. With Thomas Ehrlich, she published *Educating for Democracy: Preparing Undergraduates for Responsible Political Engagement* and won the 2013 Frederic W. Ness Book Award for their book *Rethinking Undergraduate Business Education: Liberal Learning for the Profession.* Thomas Ehrlich is a consulting professor at the Stanford Graduate School of Education. He is a graduate of Harvard College and Harvard Law School and holds five honorary degrees. Professor Ehrlich has previously served as president of Indiana University, provost of the University of Pennsylvania, and dean of Stanford Law School. His most recent book (2013) is *Civic Work, Civic Lessons: Two Generations Reflect on Public Service.*

Shares a concern that Loeb expresses about trends toward increased individualism and lack of civic engagement. Especially interested in reaching out to undergraduates, whereas Loeb addresses a more general audience.

W̲e are among those increasingly concerned about two related trends in contemporary American culture—excessive individualism and moral relativism on the one hand and popular disdain for civic engagement, particularly political involvement, on the other. In our view, undergraduate years are an important time for developing in students moral and civic responsibility that can help reverse these trends. This essay describes our work-in-progress, under the auspices of the Carnegie Foundation for the Advancement of Teaching, to analyze the American undergraduate scene in terms of efforts to promote students' moral and civic responsibility and to encourage our colleges and universities to strengthen those efforts.

Stresses the responsibility that universities and colleges have to encourage students to be involved.

As concerned with morality as with civic engagement, which is a departure from Loeb. Maintains that moral and civic responsibility are inextricably linked.

Some people who have written about these issues have focused exclusively on civic responsibility, avoiding the more controversial area of morality (e.g., Barber, 1998). We include moral as well as civic responsibility in the scope of our project, because we believe the two are inseparable. Our democratic principles, including tolerance and respect for others, procedural impartiality, and concern for both the rights of the individual and the welfare of the group, are all grounded in moral principles. Likewise, the problems that the civically engaged citizen must confront always include strong moral themes—for example, fair access to resources such as housing, the moral obligation to consider future generations in making environmental policy, and the conflicting claims of multiple stakeholders in community decision-making. None of these issues can be adequately resolved

Elaborates on how moral principles are tied to democratic principles. Contends that decision making relies on having a "strong moral compass."

1

2

Educators must commit themselves to teaching civic responsibility and morality.

without a consideration of moral questions. A person can become civically and politically active without good judgment and a strong moral compass, but it is hardly wise to promote that kind of involvement. Because civic responsibility is inescapably threaded with moral values, we believe that higher education must aspire to foster both moral and civic maturity and must confront educationally the many links between them.

Defines moral engagement in broad terms to promote thoughtful reflection and call upon institutions of higher education to foster moral engagement.

What do we mean by "moral" and by "civic"? We consider "moral," in its broadest sense, to include matters of values both personal and public. As we use the term, "morality" is not confined to a specific sphere of life or action, nor is it necessarily tied to religion. In advocating moral engagement, we are not promoting any particular moral or meta-ethical viewpoint. Rather, we are interested in fostering more thoughtful moral reflection generally and the adoption of viewpoints and commitments that emerge from reasoned consideration. We believe that higher education should encourage and facilitate the development of students' capacities to examine complex situations in which competing values are often at stake, to employ both substantive knowledge and moral reasoning to evaluate the problems and values involved, to develop their own judgments about those issues, and then to act on their judgments.

3

Defines civic engagement as a necessary means for sustaining a democracy that encompasses both thoughtful reflection and subsequent action.

We consider "civic" to range over all social spheres beyond the family, from neighborhoods and local communities to state, national, and cross-national arenas. Political engagement is a particular subset of civic engagement that is required for sustaining American democracy. We are not promoting a single type of civic or political engagement, but instead urging that the effective operation of social systems and the successful achievement of collective goals demand the time, attention, understanding, and action of all citizens. Institutions of higher education have both the opportunity and obligation to cultivate in their graduates an appreciation for the responsibilities and rewards of civic engagement, as well as to

4

foster the capacities necessary for thoughtful participation in public discourse and effective participation
in social enterprises.

In general terms, we believe that a morally and   5
civically responsible individual recognizes himself
or herself as a member of a larger social fabric and
therefore considers social problems to be at least
partly his or her own; such an individual is willing to
see the moral and civic dimensions of issues, to make
and justify informed moral and civic judgments, and
to take action when appropriate.

We believe that moral and civic development is   6
enhanced by mutually interdependent sets of knowledge, virtues, and skills. Because they are interdependent, no simple listing of attributes is adequate.
Such a listing may imply that the elements involved
have precise definitions and parameters that might be
gained through a single course or even from reading

The teaching of civic
and moral engage-
ment should occur
in different fields of
study and programs
supported by a
national organization
such as the Carnegie
Foundation for the
Advancement of
Teaching.

a few books. We have come to understand through
studying various colleges and universities that this is
not the case. Instead, enriching the moral and civic
responsibility of all members of the campus community is best achieved through the cumulative, interactive effect of numerous curricular and extracurricular
programs, within an environment of sustained institutional commitment to these overarching goals. . . .

Included in the core knowledge we consider inte-   7
gral to moral and civic learning is knowledge of basic

Avoids defining values
that can inform judg-
ment, but offers a
description of core
knowledge and con-
cepts that educators
should impart to their
students.

ethical concepts and principles, such as justice and
equity, and how they have been interpreted by various
seminal thinkers. Also included is a comprehension
of the diversity of American society and global cultures, and an understanding of both the institutions
and processes of American and international civic,
political, and economic affairs. Finally, deep substantive knowledge of the particular issues in which one is
engaged is critical.

This core of knowledge cannot be separated from   8
the virtues and skills that a morally and civically
responsible individual should strive to attain. The

Core knowledge of
key issues and an
understanding of
civic, political, and
economic concerns
should go hand in hand
with moral and civic
learning.

virtues and skills we have in mind are not distinct to
moral and civic learning but are necessary for active

engagement in many personal and professional realms. Among the core virtues is the willingness to engage in critical self-examination and to form reasoned commitments, balanced by open-mindedness and a willingness to listen to and take seriously the ideas of others. Moral and civic responsibility also requires honesty in dealings with others, and in holding oneself accountable for one's action and inactions. Without a basis of trust, and habits of cooperation, no community can operate effectively. Empathy and compassion are also needed, not only for relating to those in one's immediate social sphere, but for relating to those in the larger society as well. Willingness to form moral and civic commitments and to act on those is a core virtue that puts the others into practice.

Elaborates upon the idea of community building that Loeb introduces, particularly empathy, trust, and compassion.

Finally, the core skills of moral and civic responsibility are essential for applying core knowledge and virtues, transforming informed judgments into action. They include the abilities to recognize the moral and civic dimensions of issues and to take a stand on those issues. But they also include skills that apply to much broader arenas of thought and behavior, such as abilities to communicate clearly orally and in writing, to collect, organize, and analyze information, to think critically and to justify positions with reasoned arguments, to see issues from the perspectives of others and to collaborate with others. They also include the ability and willingness to lead, to build a consensus, and to move a group forward under conditions of mutual respect.

Maintains that to act requires applying core knowledge and values, in contrast to Loeb, who uses evidence from sociology, health, and psychology to inspire people to become civically and politically engaged.

LAURIE OUELLETTE

Citizen Brand: ABC and the Do Good Turn in US Television

Laurie Ouellette is a professor of communication studies at the University of Minnesota. The author of *Lifestyle TV* and coauthor of *Better Living through Reality TV: Television and Post-Welfare Citizenship*, she has published extensively about public broadcasting, TV history, fashion and style, self-help culture, and social media.

The greatest moments in life are not concerned with self-ish achievement, but rather with the things we do for other people.

—WALT DISNEY

***

Better Communities and Corporate Citizens

Introduces the idea of corporate sponsorship of community involvement and raises the question of what has motivated this kind of initiative to involve viewers, actors, and the like.

In 2002, ABC launched its long-running Better Community public outreach campaign, with a mission of advancing the television network's standing as a corporate citizen through "community outreach efforts that serve the public interest, inform and inspire." ... Encompassing announcements urging TV viewers to perform community service, as well as an online guide to volunteering and a slate of popular entertainment programs showcasing corporate and personal humanitarianism, the campaign positioned ABC as a socially responsible corporate citizen. More than this, it constituted ABC as a gateway to a Better Community comprising network stars, nonprofit partners, commercial sponsors, and socially conscious TV viewers who—much more than other television consumers—contribute resources (time and money) to the well-being of the communities in which they live. Why would ABC pursue what it claimed to be the "comprehensive and recognizable public service initiative" on US television in the wake of deregulatory policies? To make sense of the Better Community initiative—and the television industry's investment in civic empowerment more broadly—it is useful to trace the burgeoning and deeply intertwined currency of communitarian discourse and corporate social responsibility.

Uses the term "civic empowerment," which is different from Loeb, as well as Colby and her colleagues. Also introduces the word "communitarian" to the conversation.

Offers some historical perspective and describes some of the economic reforms in government that have placed more responsibility on private citizens, among others, to support children and families living in poverty.

The Better Community campaign appeared in the midst of the reinvention of government in the US, an assemblage of reforms encompassing public sector downsizing, the encouragement of public–private partnerships, the outsourcing of many government services to commercial firms, and the dismantling of welfare programs.... ABC translated a bipartisan call for private initiative and personal responsibility as empowering alternatives to big government into

1

2

TV stations like ABC interpreted the call for more private and personal responsibility as a way to promote volunteerism and their own interests. Community activism would replace social welfare programs, while the government fostered a free, unregulated economic market.

fifteen-second public service announcements that doubled as station promotions, and advertising stuffed entertainment revolving around corporate giving and volunteerism. The campaign embraced the entrepreneurial zeal guiding political reform, but it also inserted the ABC television network and its viewers into communitarian solutions to the underside of unfettered capitalism. Like other examples of do good television, the Better Community campaign exemplifies an enterprising turn in governing and at the same time seeks to help overcome the consequences of a pure market logic in the civic realm.

Corporate social responsibility seems separate from political interests while still supporting democracy, but corporate involvement has its roots in efforts by both former presidents Bush and Clinton to find alternatives to welfare programs.

Community is an especially popular corporate civic objective due to its positive currency and safe distance from unruly political activism or controversy. The turn to community, which is also a dominant theme in do good television, is also closely intertwined with communitarian political discourses and strategies of governing. Communitarianism is an applied political philosophy that endorses market capitalism and limited public powers but calls for additional changes to ensure the civic functionality of democratic societies. It advocates the nourishing of voluntary associations as a buffer between the downsized welfare state and the competitive self-interest found in the commercial marketplace.... Both the Clinton and Bush administrations adopted communitarian models of "governing through community," from the designation of community empowerment zones as an alternative to public housing programs (Clinton) to the creation of

Observes that an ethic of communitarianism derives from policy, in contrast to the moral argument that Colby and her colleagues describe or the humanitarian principles that Loeb explains. Communitarianism has become necessary in the absence of government-supported programs.

the Office of Faith-Based and Community Initiatives to "nourish dispersed religious and civil alternatives to public welfare programs" and a USA Freedom Corps Volunteer Network to mobilize citizens into "armies of compassion" (Bush). Bush also entrusted the new President's Council on National and Community Service, composed of leaders from business, entertainment, sports, the nonprofit sector, education, and media, to help the White House cultivate a stronger ethic of service and responsibility in the US. While there were crucial differences between Clinton

3

and Bush, the point to be made here is that community has become an objective of governing across political regimes. This matters for our purposes for two reasons: First, good communities (like good citizens) are not born but made—constituted through policies, political discourses, and cultural technologies such as television. Second, as Nikolas Rose persuasively contends, community has become "another word for citizenship" that stresses civic duties rather than collective entitlements. Rose sees the uptake of communitarianism as a substitute for a diminishing social contract—an intervention that softens the "harshest dimensions of neo-capitalist restructuring" by encouraging citizens to serve associations (neighborhoods, localities, social networks, families) that are "decidedly private and which more or less absolve the state of responsibility for society." . . .

In the US, communitarianism is closely associated with prominent scholar and political consultant Amitai Etzioni. . . . In his many books, speeches, and ongoing work with the Institute for Communitarian Studies at George Washington University, Etzioni promotes an understanding of community as a counterbalance to a model of society created in the image of the "marketplace, in which self-serving individuals compete with one another." . . . Communities, he contends, also offset the need for public oversight by reinforcing a voluntary moral order rooted in "traditional values" of respectability, responsibility, and independence. Conceived as dispersed, self-managed ethical zones, community poses an alternative not only to the welfare state but also to the model of democracy associated with broadcast regulation and earlier interpretations of the public interest in television. As Rose points out, community as conceived by Etzioni and other influential thinkers offers a way to "regenerate society" that comes not from "law, information, reason, or deliberative democracy" but from moral "dialogue and action" within voluntary associations. . . .

Traces the term "communitarianism" to one scholar who developed a model of communitarian values that seems to mirror those of Colby and her colleagues, given their similar emphasis on "moral dialogue and action."

4

While Etzioni naturalizes the space of community, he concedes that citizens *must be trained* to "participate in communitarian society." Even those who have "acquired virtue" will require ongoing guidance, "for if left to their own devices… [they] gradually lose much of their commitment to values."… What Rose calls technologies of community have proliferated since the 1990s, offering tutelage and instruction. This is partly a response to widely circulating reports of declining volunteerism, everyday philanthropy, and civic engagement in the US. Robert Putnam's influential study *Bowling Alone* lamented the collapse of voluntary associations, indicating that few contemporary Americans demonstrate the civic propensities that Alexis de Tocqueville credited with the "capacity to make democracy work."… By the mid-1990s, barely one American in three reported any charitable giving in the previous month, and fewer than two in five claimed even "occasional religious giving," according to Putnam's study.… These trends paralleled an equally sharp reduction in participation in community institutions, from lodges to parent-teacher associations.… As Rose points out, the "decline of community" ascribed to these trends was also held responsible for a slew of civic problems, from "drugs, crime and alienation, to family breakdown and the loss of good neighborliness."… For Putnam (who penned Bush's 2001 inaugural speech), any attempt to reinvent government also needed to "revitalize" community and its subjects.

While communitarianism gained currency, corporate social responsibility was also actively encouraged as a dimension of governmental reform. Both Clinton and Bush called on the corporate sector to partner in social programs and fill gaps left by the divested welfare state. As Andrew Barry argues, the market's willingness to take on responsibility for ethical problems is not surprising. In an era when "direct state control has declined," he explains, corporations are increasingly expected to "perform the job of government at

5

6

Cites Putnam's study reported in Bowling Alone and reiterates concerns of others about the decline of volunteerism and civic engagement. This decline seems connected, according to another scholar, Rose, to a number of social problems.

Introduces the term "cause marketing," which combines the ideas of corporate social responsibility and profit. This concept highlights the role that businesses have taken on in the context of economic reform and the responsibility of businesses to make money. It seems that corporate social responsibility is a key to financial success.

a distance."... Yet, the rise of cause marketing, corporate philanthropy, and other manifestations of what Barry calls ethical capitalism are only viable to the extent that they are also profitable. The age of paternalistic philanthropy, exemplified by Andrew Carnegie's view of wealth as a "sacred trust, which its possessor was bound to administer for the good of the community," passed some time ago.... In 1970, Milton Friedman, a leading figure of the Chicago school of neoliberalism, unapologetically declared in the *New York Times,* "The social responsibility of business is to increase profits."... Nonetheless, corporations have increasingly embraced objectives (fundraising for cures, promoting recycling, citizenship training) that blur boundaries between public and private, governing and profiteering. According to business historian David Vogel, this development is not only the outcome of public sector downsizing and government at a distance. As the entrepreneurial spirit was reforming the welfare state, many corporations were discovering a lucrative "market for virtue." Today, says Vogel, corporate social responsibility is approached not as an unprofitable duty but as the key to successful profit maximization....

Cites one scholar who reiterates a concern the author shares: corporate social responsibility has become a means for creating wealth rather than a virtuous act of being involved in "ethical issues" and "civic affairs."

In his genealogy of corporate social responsibility, Vogel argues that contemporary advocates of ethical capitalism have basically accepted "Friedman's position that the primary responsibility of companies is to create wealth for their shareholders"—with an important twist: in order for companies to maximize profit, he explains, the prevailing assumption is that "they must now act virtuously." In other words, social responsibility is enacted less as a paternalistic duty than as a competitive business strategy. "Never before has the claim that corporate virtue can and should be profitable enjoyed so much currency or influence," Vogel writes.... The new tendency to approach social responsibility as an instrument of profitability is the outcome of the neoliberal reforms, including deregulation and expanded entrepreneurialism, that Friedman and his colleagues promoted, and that spawned a

7

perceived need for greater corporate involvement in ethical issues and civic affairs....

Points out that the trend toward "citizen branding" represents this shift in emphasis away from civic engagement for its own sake toward profitability. Doing so has entailed masking the profit motive to project an image of a company committed to doing good work in the community.

The concept of the citizen brand, which has revolutionized marketing in recent years, takes this a step further by placing corporations and consumer culture at the center of governing and citizenship. In his book *Citizen Brand: 10 Commandments Transforming Brand Culture in a Consumer Democracy* (2002), Mark Gobé argues that corporations that wish to increase profits will have to distance themselves from the greed and exploitation associated with deregulated global capitalism. One way of doing so, he suggests, is to integrate do good activities into business plans and branding strategies so that an image of trust and ethics can be built on a "real dedication to being part of human solutions around the world." ... In his manual *Citizen Brands: Putting Society at the Heart of Your Business* (2003), Michael Willmott agrees that citizenship must "be a part of branding" and explains how the public interest can be harnessed as a form of market intelligence.... As one example, he suggests that public support for community (bolstered by the policies and discourses discussed earlier) can be appropriated as an objective of corporate citizenship and channeled into "economic success." ...

The Better Community campaign exemplifies the ethical turn in capitalism, presented not as an obligation (which might imply public oversight) but as ABC's *choice* to advance an empowering civic agenda. ABC is positioned at the center of communitarian strategies for activating citizens and buffering the consequences of privatization and welfare reform. Public outreach entails channeling the demands being placed on individuals and communities into the ethical value of the ABC network. It is not coincidental that the Better Community project is overseen entirely by ABC Corporate Initiatives, for its approach to doing good is much more compatible with new directions in marketing and branding than were earlier (unrealized) public service ideals emphasizing rational debate and an informed citizenry.

Citizen Disney and the Rebranding of ABC

Disney, overseeing the rebranding of ABC, represents the trend the author has described — taking on the role of responsible corporate citizen and promoting the role of the good citizen.

The Disney Corporation, the parent corporation of ABC, is a prime example of the multilayered use of community as a technology of governing, a strategic business practice, and a branding strategy. The Disney Corporation, the largest media conglomerate in the world, characterizes itself as a good neighbor visibly committed to social responsibility (exemplified by employee volunteer programs and corporate giving) and humanitarian causes—particularly community and the environment. Disney has diffused these commitments across its corporate holdings, including film studios, theme parks, television networks, and cable channels.... The Disney-owned ESPN channel incorporates volunteerism and community service into its operations, enticing employees and "sports enthusiasts" at home to make a difference by volunteering on behalf of nonprofit organizations. The (now defunct) SOAPNet partnered with volunteer events in Hollywood and sponsored community outreach programs in public schools, using soap opera clips to promote family, responsibility, and communication skills. The Disney-ABC Television Group, which oversees the Disney Channel and ABC, is also dedicated to "serving and inspiring individuals and communities through a variety of public service initiatives and outreach programs." Disney-ABC claims that it "proudly supports non-profit organizations in their endeavors to make the world a better place," while its television channels—with their capacity to reach millions of people—provide "ideal platforms to inspire viewers to drive positive change in their communities."...

10

Attributes Disney's investment in humanitarian endeavors to changes in federal policies. While writers such as Putnam and Etzioni might lament the fragmentation of community, media is also now responsible for increased civic engagement and community building.

Disney's investment in community and volunteerism is related to the reinvention of government. Disney was a corporate partner in the Bush White House's efforts to encourage volunteerism as a solution to postwelfare needs and problems. Disney also sponsored the National Conference on Volunteering and Service organized by the Corporation for National Community Service, the Points of Light

11

Foundation, and the USA Freedom Corps. At the 2005 meeting, leaders from government and the corporate sector met to devise strategies for developing volunteer service (a term used to describe everything from corporate giving to bake sales) to meet America's "pressing social needs." The responsibilities bestowed upon corporations and individual citizens were evident by the keynote speeches: US Department of Health and Human Services secretary Mike Leavitt lectured on the importance of "economic goodness" and the closing remarks were delivered by Mark Victor Hansen, best-selling author of the Christian self-help book *Chicken Soup for the Soul....* It is telling, but not surprising, that culture industries and popular media figured heavily in the brainstorming session. Although communitarians (including Etzioni and Putnam) condemn mass media as a factor in the decline of community, television and the web are also recognized as useful instruments for retraining citizens and rebuilding voluntary associations independently of big government. ABC's Better Community campaign is one such technology, operating at a distance from the state to constitute responsibility for post-welfare society as a corporate and community affair.

Despite the benefits of citizen branding, the author again reminds us that we cannot ignore the profit motive of companies that have fulfilled a role once played by the federal government in what is now a postwelfare state. To what extent are these roles in conflict with one another?

ABC has inserted itself into the communitarian space between the uncaring market and so-called welfare dependency. The question remains: If corporate social responsibility is now practiced as a profit-making endeavor, as Vogel suggests, how does the Better Community campaign fuel ABC's and Disney's coffers? To understand how valuable commitments to ethical business and community building have become for the cultural industries, it is worth juxtaposing the current approach to public service with the "all-business" mentality unleashed by broadcast deregulation. While Disney has always billed itself as an all-American company committed to traditional values, the media mergers and takeovers of the 1980s led all conglomerates to an intensified focus on the bottom line. Within an increasingly competitive

12

industrial climate, former Disney CEO Michael Eisner confessed in a 1981 memo, "We have no obligation to make history; we have no obligation to make art; we have no obligation to make a statement; to make money is our only objective." ... Sounding a lot like Milton Friedman a decade earlier, Eisner acknowledged that the company's primary, indeed sole, purpose was to maximize profits for shareholders. As late as 1997, the ABC television network (recently purchased by Disney) owned up to a similar sentiment with its TV is Good branding campaign. Mocking any notion that television should serve a purpose higher than producing wealth, the spots proudly positioned ABC as a venue for the hedonistic consumption of trivial entertainment. Pitting TV viewers seeking pleasure and escape against the concerns of do good reformers, the advertisements offered tongue-in-cheek advice such as "Life is short. Watch TV" and "Don't worry, you've got billions of brain cells."

ABC's attempt to brand the right to consume television with no redeeming attributes was short-lived. In 2002, the network switched gears dramatically with what it called the most visible public service campaign on television. Branded as ABC—A Better Community, the campaign generated more than 100 public service announcements to date, in which ABC stars urge TV viewers to "make a difference" in their communities. Early in the campaign, the talent read quotations by famous historical figures in order to situate ABC within a recognizable genealogy of ethical activity and public service. Interspersed with pitches for automobiles, mouthwash, and diet soda were reminders that: *"You make a living by what you get, but you make a life by what you give"* (Winston Churchill); *"Everyone has the power for greatness ... because greatness is determined by service"* (Dr. Martin Luther King Jr.); *"No man can sincerely help another without helping himself"* (Ralph Waldo Emerson); *"The best way to find yourself ... is to lose yourself in the service of others"* (Mahatma Gandhi); and *"The greatest moments in life are not concerned with selfish*

13

Describes how ABC and Disney rebranded themselves with public service announcements and connecting their work in media with public service.

achievement, but rather with the things we do for other people" (Walt Disney).

Visually framed by the ABC Better Community logo, accompanied by inspirational music and ending with a call to action (including a visit to the ABC website), the spots linked ABC to an iconic pantheon of civic leadership. Within the logic of the campaign, the political differences between entrepreneurs like Disney and activists like King were insignificant; what mattered was their shared commitment to doing good—a moral disposition to which the ABC audience should aspire. Once ABC had established its ethical credibility, the inspirational passages were dropped and well-known ABC stars such as George Lopez (*The George Lopez Show*), Nicollette Sheridan (*Desperate Housewives*), and Evangeline Lilly (*Lost*) urged TV viewers to take specific actions, like becoming a mentor or cleaning up a neighborhood park. The stars took over as civic tutors in the new promotions, guiding the conduct of individuals while also constituting ABC as a Better Community on the basis of values presumably shared by executives, talent, and audiences. While the initial spots had selectively linked civic progress to the legacy of political figures like King, the announcements that followed disassociated good citizenship from any reminder of grassroots activism or critique. What was radical about the campaign, however, was its aggressive attempt to move TV viewers away from their sets, into civic life. Breaking commercial television's associations with leisure, domesticity, and passive consumption, it recast the ABC audience as an active community of unselfish, civically responsible people. The imagined viewer was addressed as an ethical subject who, with gentle reminders and practical advice, could make a difference in the world outside commercial television. In this way the public service campaign provides what Etzioni calls the training required to "restrain impulses," "delay gratification," and balance "pleasure and living up to one's moral commitments."...

14

Takes a critical stance toward ABC's rebranding that associated their calls for public service with Martin Luther King's leadership during the civil rights movement. Ignoring differences enabled ABC to project an image that is problematic but clearly served ABC's goals.

Acknowledges the extent to which this strategy was able to position ABC as an ethical corporation and viewers as responsible citizens.

In 2006, ABC re-launched the Better Community *15* initiative with much fanfare. The renewed commitment to community service provided the occasion for a new round of publicity kicked off by a special announcement from actress Geena Davis. Davis, who portrayed the first female president of the US on ABC's (now-canceled) drama *Commander-in-Chief,* addressed the audience during a special network showing of *The Ten Commandments.* Drawing civic credibility from her television character and a moral compass from the biblical film, she reiterated the ABC network's unique contributions to community service and volunteerism. Davis also reminded viewers of their crucial role in realizing the network's mission by making a difference in the communities in which they live. Here as before, the Better Community was doubly constituted as an imagined community whose membership involved consuming ABC, and as the outcome of suggested civic actions. Carried out across multiple sites, these actions supported the communitarian turn in government while also providing coveted ethical value to the ABC brand.

Illustrates the way media corporations can use celebrities to add credibility to their message, even when the reference is a fictional character on TV.

The profitability of corporate social responsibility and community is realized in the generation of *16* brand identity and value. The stakes are high for a mass television network in the age of cultural fragmentation and niche marketing. As one handbook on the television business explains, "In a world with dozens and eventually hundreds of television channels, those with the most clearly differentiated brands would be the ones most likely to succeed."… ABC combines the concept of the citizen brand with the brand community to differentiate the network's compassion and civic relevance. "Brand community" is a relatively new term used by market researchers to describe a "specialized, non-geographically bound community, based on a structured set of social relationships among admirers of a brand."… Like other communities, brand communities are believed to possess "a shared consciousness, rituals and traditions, and a sense of moral responsibility."… The Better

Adds one more term, "brand community," to describe corporations' efforts to distinguish their product from others in an increasingly competitive market and foster the development of a community that shares their values — in this case, the shared sense of ethical responsibility.

Community campaign envisions the mass audience as a brand community composed of ABC viewers, each of whom exercises ethical dispositions and capacities within existing institutions (schools, hospitals, charities) and spaces (neighborhoods, parks, municipalities). Although this ethical activity takes place outside television culture, it can only be realized through the ABC brand, which activates and rewards action with affirmation and belonging. ABC operates as what Celia Lury calls a branded interface—not only to the consumption of television but to the duties and practices of contemporary citizenship.... TV is no longer good in the self-interested sense evoked by the earlier ABC campaign. ABC is the gateway for civic obligations in the double service of the "community" and the Better Community brand.

■ Make Connections among Different Texts

The texts by Loeb, Colby and her colleagues, and Ouellette all deal with some aspect of civic engagement, activism, and community building. The authors write about efforts to motivate people to work with one another to foster the health of communities based on moral or humanistic principles or to take up the call to compensate for changing economic policies. The texts are very much in conversation with one another, as the authors focus on relevant experiences and research to convey what they see as the value of civic and political engagement. However, each author offers a slightly different perspective that forces readers to ask if morality has a place in the ways we conceptualize civic engagement, the role that colleges and universities should play in promoting civic engagement in the undergraduate curriculum, or the extent to which corporations' commitment to community building is in conflict with their profit motives.

- Loeb urges readers to value the human connection that results from working together for the common good of a community and uses research to convey the psychological and physiological benefits of doing so. He also brings into focus the consequences of silence and the disconnect that can occur when we see injustice and fail to act.

- Colby and her colleagues share Loeb's perceptions about the value of community engagement but argue that teaching moral principles and core knowledge can have the positive effect of serving as a compass or guide for action. Though the authors are reluctant to identify specific values that they believe students should learn, they are particularly interested in the education of undergraduates and see the importance of helping students develop the ability to make informed judgments.

- Ouellette takes a different approach when she uses ABC as a case example to document the ways corporations have taken on the responsibility of serving families in need with changes in economic policy. In telling this story, she affirms the value of building community and shows that media can foster community; however, she also seems to question the profit-making motive that underlies the branding of corporations as civically engaged.

■ Decide What Those Connections Mean

Having annotated the selections, we filled out the worksheet in Figure 8.1, making notes in the grid to help us see the three texts in relation to one another. Our worksheet included columns for

- author and source information,
- the gist of each author's argument,
- supporting examples and illustrations,
- counterarguments, and
- our own thoughts.

A worksheet like this one can help you concentrate on similarities and differences in the texts to determine what the connections among texts mean. Of course, you can design your own worksheet as well, tailoring it to your needs and preferences. If you want to take very detailed notes about your authors and sources, for example, you may want to have separate columns for each.

Once you start making connections, including points of agreement and disagreement, you can start identifying counterarguments in the reading—that perhaps educators should not be inclined to teach morality in their classes and that the human connection that Loeb describes will serve as a sufficient motive for acting on behalf of the common good in a given community. Perhaps we need to look more critically at a corporation's interest in communities where their executives do not live, work, go to school, and shop. Identifying questions and even counterarguments can give you a sense of what is at issue for each author and what is at stake. And how can we test the claims that experts make about how policies have affected the health and well-being of communities where many children and families may be feeling the consequences of policies designed to shift the responsibility from the federal government to private corporations and private agencies? What causes the fragmentation that concerns some of the authors cited in these essays? What are the best ways to build community? For that matter, how effective have media corporations been in fostering the health of communities and a shared sense of responsibility?

▪ Formulate the Gist of What You've Read

Remember that your gist should bring into focus the relationship among different ideas in multiple texts. Looking at the information juxtaposed on the worksheet (Figure 8.1), you can begin to construct the gist of your synthesis:

- Paul Loeb cites studies and uses his own experiences to motivate readers to be more civically engaged in their communities, to resist focusing on their own interests, and to enter into relationships with others to fulfill what it means to be human. He addresses those readers who may be discouraged by others who would silence or ignore their voices and commit themselves to speaking out about the issues that concern them. He points out the consequences of remaining silent and explains that we should not be discouraged by our "failed" attempts to create change.

- Anne Colby and her colleagues share a common concern that Loeb expresses about trends toward increased individualism and lack of civic engagement. The authors are especially interested in reaching out to undergraduates and speak to the need to equip young people with the kinds of tools that would enable them to translate what they are learning into actions they can take as civic-minded, politically engaged citizens. One of those tools is judgment, and the best way to teach judgment is by imparting values and core knowledge that can serve as a moral compass and guide action.

- Ouellette broadens the discussion of civic engagement and political action by looking at the branding of corporations as socially responsible "citizens." Her analysis explains the extent to which presidents Clinton and then Bush reached out to businesses to provide initiatives to support children and families in need given changes in federal economic policies.

How do you formulate this information into a gist? You can use a transition word such as *although* or *however* to connect ideas that different authors bring together while conveying their differences. Thus, a gist of these essays might read:

GIST OF A SYNTHESIS

As a response to increased fragmentation of American society, Paul Loeb and Anne Colby and her colleagues underscore the reasons individuals need to be more involved in both civic and political engagement. They help highlight the ways human interaction makes us more fully human and the extent to which community engagement fulfills the Founding Fathers' vision of democracy. However, Laurie Ouellette broadens readers' understanding of why it is necessary to be more involved. She focuses on changes in economic policy in the United States that have shifted funding for families and children with the greatest needs to private entities and corporations.

AUTHOR AND SOURCE	GIST OF ARGUMENT	EXAMPLES/ILLUSTRATIONS	COUNTERARGUMENTS/CHALLENGING ASSUMPTIONS	WHAT I THINK
Paul Rogat Loeb "Making Our Lives Count" from *Soul of a Citizen*	Argues that connecting to others through civic participation and working for the common good is what makes us more fully human.	Uses research from psychology, public health, and sociology, as well as personal stories to explain the value of community involvement. He also describes a number of negative effects of failing to be engaged and living with the disconnect between our convictions and our decision not to act on those convictions.	If there is a counterargument, it is implied when Loeb anticipates readers who have been silenced and feel their points of view do not matter. These readers are skeptical of the benefits of engagement.	The examples serve as compelling reasons to be involved, but I also understand why others feel that their voices might not be heard or taken seriously. This is often the case, but remaining silent can also be difficult. I also appreciate his point about failure. What might seem like failure can actually be a factor that bolsters our commitment to make a difference.
Anne Colby and Thomas Ehrlich with Elizabeth Beaumont and Jason Stephens "Undergraduate Education and the Development of Moral and Civic Responsibility"	Shares the concern Loeb raises—that there is a growing trend away from being civically and politically engaged. The authors add that moral principles are inextricably tied to democratic principles of rights, respect, tolerance, and community.	Limits the argument to the authors' own conceptions of civic and moral engagement, as well as the kind of core knowledge that is necessary to translate judgments into actions that people can take in a participant democracy.	Recognizes the extent to which the focus on moral engagement sets the authors' ideas apart from others like Loeb who try to motivate people to be civically engaged. It is implicit that others may feel uncomfortable with an argument that includes moral engagement, and the authors are careful to explain that they do not have a specific set of values in mind. Still, the counterargument may very well be that educators should not blur the line between the subject they teach and values.	I agree that universities should take more responsibility for the communities they are a part of. Classes in political science might address both theories of government and action—not just voting but community involvement. I am not sure I agree that professors should teach values.

Author and Source	Gist of Argument	Examples/Illustrations	Counterarguments/Challenging Assumptions	What I Think
Laurie Ouellette "Citizen Brand: ABC and the Do Good Turn in US Television"	Examines the reasons corporate social responsibility has emerged in recent years, emphasizing shifts in government policies that placed greater responsibility on the private sector for supporting children and families living in poverty. Argues that initiatives like "The Better Community" campaign are not altogether altruistic and serve corporate interests in creating wealth for their stakeholders.	Uses case examples of ABC's Better Community public outreach campaign and ABC's parent company to illustrate roles that corporations have taken on. On the one hand, they have taken on the mantle of social responsibility, and on the other hand, they use social responsibility as a marketing tool to create profits.	Acknowledges the value of ABC's strategy of positioning itself as a socially conscious corporation. However, looks critically at efforts that associate the leadership of figures such as Martin Luther King and the grassroots movement of the Civil Rights struggle with civic-minded projects that ABC has promoted. Also questions whose interests are served when corporations promote civic engagement as a profit-making venture.	I hadn't really thought about the economic factors that have prompted corporations to be more invested in community development. I am a little skeptical of the role that corporations can or should play in communities and worry that their motives blur, serving a community as a good in itself and doing so to make money.

FIGURE 8.1   Worksheet for Writing a Synthesis

Having drafted the gist, we returned to our notes on the worksheet to complete the synthesis, presenting examples and using transitions to signal the relationships among the texts and their ideas. Here is our brief synthesis of the three texts:

The gist of our synthesis.

As a response to increased fragmentation of society, Paul Loeb and Anne Colby and her colleagues underscore the reasons why individuals need to be more involved in both political and civic engagement. They help highlight the ways human interaction makes us more fully human and the extent to which community engagement fulfills the Founding Fathers' vision of democracy. Loeb's research in psychology, public health, and sociology also demonstrates the ways that community engagement contributes to our own sense of well-being. Colby and her colleagues share Loeb's outlook, but they add that moral principles are inextricably tied to democratic principles of rights, respect, tolerance, and community. They also argue that individuals need tools to make decisions, especially a core knowledge of key issues and a moral compass to serve as a guide to action that is aimed at the common good. Still, they recognize the extent to which their focus on moral engagement sets their ideas apart from others like Loeb who try to motivate people to be civically engaged. It is implicit that others may feel uncomfortable with an argument that includes moral engagement, and the authors are careful to explain that they do not have a specific set of values in mind.

Transition: There is an alternative reason individuals should be civically and politically engaged.

However, Laurie Ouellette broadens readers' understanding of why it is necessary to be more involved. This is especially true when she focuses her analysis on changes in economic policy in the United States that have shifted funding for families and children with the greatest needs to private entities and corporations. In pointing to this shift in policy, she shows how corporations such as Disney have rebranded themselves as socially responsible, marketing themselves in a way that appeals to viewers who share a view of themselves as altruistic. Thus, Ouellette helps show that there are reasons beyond the humanizing principles that Loeb advances and the kinds of values that Colby and her colleagues believe are inextricably tied to teaching and learning in institutions of higher education. That is, communities may appear to be more fragmented than ever before, but the urgency created by government social welfare programs serves as a pragmatic call to service that we cannot ignore.

Evidence demonstrates that the urgency of a changing economy is a strong factor in motivating individuals to get involved, especially when sponsored by corporations that have been given the responsibility to fulfill what was an obligation of the federal government.

1

2

One formulation of an argument that emerges from the three texts. The transition "yet" and the questions posed set up the direction of what is to follow.

While some may argue that corporations act out of self-interest in branding themselves as socially responsible, evidence indicates that the media may be more successful at motivating individuals to be involved than other means. Yet in considering the reasons why it is important to be an engaged citizen, whether as individuals or as a corporation, Ouellette, among others, forces us to ask whose interests are served when any of us becomes invested in communities where we do not live, work, shop, or go to school. Despite the benefits of citizen branding, Ouellette reminds us that we cannot ignore the profit motive of companies that have fulfilled a role once played by the federal government in what is now a postwelfare state. To what extent, if at all, are these roles in conflict with one another? For that matter, what values should guide investments and personal responsibility in reaching out to communities with the greatest needs?

3

Writing a synthesis, like writing a summary, is principally a strategy for framing your own argument. It's one thing to synthesize what you read and convey to your readers how various points in a conversation intersect and diverge. It's quite another to write yourself into the conversation. This entails thinking critically about what you are reading, raising questions, conducting further research, and taking a stance based on your own understanding of what you have read, what you believe and value, and the available evidence.

Steps to Writing a Synthesis

1 **Make connections between and among different texts.** Annotate the texts you are working with, with an eye to comparing them. As you would for a summary, note major points in the texts, choose relevant examples, and formulate the gist of each text.

2 **Decide what those connections mean.** Fill out a worksheet to compare your notes on the different texts, track counterarguments, and record your thoughts. Decide what the similarities and differences mean to you and what they might mean to your readers.

3 **Formulate the gist of what you've read.** Identify an overarching idea that brings together the ideas you've noted, and write a synthesis that forges connections and makes use of the examples you've noted. Use transitions to signal the direction of your synthesis.

A Practice Sequence: Writing a Synthesis

1 To practice the strategies for synthesizing that we describe in this chapter, read the following three essays, which focus on the role that online media play in conveying information to diverse groups of readers or viewers. As you discuss the strategies the authors use to develop their arguments, consider these questions:

- How would you explain the popularity of blogs, Twitter, and YouTube?
- What themes have the writers focused on as they have sought to enter the conversation surrounding the use of electronic media?
- To what extent do you think the criticisms of media presented by the authors are legitimate?
- Do blogs, Twitter, and YouTube pose a threat to traditional journalism?
- Do you think that blogs, Twitter, and YouTube add anything to print journalism? If so, what?

2 To stimulate a conversation, or a debate, we suggest that you break up into four different groups:

> *Group 1:* Print journalism
>
> *Group 2:* Blogs
>
> *Group 3:* Twitter
>
> *Group 4:* YouTube

Students in each group should prepare an argument indicating the strengths and limitations of the particular mode of communication that they represent. In preparing the argument, be sure to acknowledge what other modes of communication might add to the ways we learn about news and opinions. One student from each group will present this argument to the other groups.

3 Based on the discussion you have had in exercise 1 and/or exercise 2, write a synthesis of the three essays using the steps we have outlined in this chapter.

- Summarize each essay.
- Explain the ways in which the authors' arguments are similar or different, using examples and illustrations to demonstrate the similarities and differences.
- Formulate an overall gist that synthesizes the points each author makes.

DAN KENNEDY

Political Blogs: Teaching Us Lessons about Community

Dan Kennedy, an assistant professor of journalism at Northeastern University, writes on media issues for *The Guardian* and for *CommonWealth* magazine. His blog, Media Nation, is online at dankennedy.net.

■ ■ ■

The rise of blogging as both a supplement and a challenge to traditional journalism has coincided with an explosion of opinion mongering. Blogs—and the role they play in how Americans consume and respond to information—are increasingly visible during our political season, when our ideological divide is most apparent. From nakedly partisan sites such as Daily Kos on the left and Little Green Footballs on the right, to more nuanced but nevertheless ideological enterprises such as Talking Points Memo, it sometimes seems there is no room in blogworld for straight, neutral journalism.

The usual reasons given for this are that reporting is difficult and expensive and that few bloggers know how to research a story, develop and interview sources, and assemble the pieces into a coherent, factual narrative. Far easier, so this line of thinking goes, for bloggers to sit in their pajamas and blast their semi-informed opinions out to the world.

There is some truth to this, although embracing this view wholeheartedly requires us to overlook the many journalists who are now writing blogs, as well as the many bloggers who are producing journalism to a greater or lesser degree. But we make a mistake when we look at the opinion-oriented nature of blogs and ask whether bloggers are capable of being "objective," to use a hoary and now all but meaningless word. The better question to ask is why opinion-oriented blogs are so popular—and what lessons the traditional media can learn from them without giving up their journalistic souls.

Perhaps what's happening is that the best and more popular blogs provide a sense of community that used to be the lifeblood of traditional news organizations and, especially, of newspapers. Recently I reread part of Jay Rosen's book, *What Are Journalists For?*, his 1999 postmortem on the public journalism movement. What struck me was Rosen's description of public journalism's origins, which were grounded in an attempt to recreate a sense of community so that people might discover a reason to read newspapers. "Eventually I came to the conclusion … that journalism's purpose was to see the public into fuller existence," Rosen writes. "Informing people followed that."

Rosen's thesis—that journalism could only be revived by reawak- 5
ening the civic impulse—is paralleled by Robert Putnam's 2000 book,
Bowling Alone, in which he found that people who sign petitions, attend
public meetings, and participate in religious and social organizations are more likely to be newspaper readers than those who do not.
"Newspaper readers are older, more educated, and more rooted in their
communities than is the average American," Putnam writes.

Unfortunately for the newspaper business, the traditional idea of 6
community, based mainly on geography, remains as moribund today
as it was when Rosen and Putnam were analyzing its pathologies. But
if old-fashioned communities are on the decline, the human impulse to
form communities is not. And the Internet, as it turns out, is an ideal
medium for fostering a new type of community in which people have
never met, and may not even know each other's real names, but share
certain views and opinions about the way the world works. It's interesting that Rosen has become a leading exponent of journalism tied
to these communities, both through his PressThink blog and through
NewAssignment.net, which fosters collaborations between professional
and citizen journalists.

Attitude First, Facts Second

This trend toward online community-building has given us a mediascape 7
in which many people—especially those most interested in politics and
public affairs—want the news delivered to them in the context of their
attitudes and beliefs. That doesn't mean they want to be fed a diet of
self-reinforcing agit-prop (although some do). It does mean they see
their news consumption as something that takes place within their
community, to be fit into a preexisting framework of ideas that may be
challenged but that must be acknowledged.

Earlier this year John Lloyd, a contributing editor for the *Financial* 8
Times, talked about the decline of just-the-facts journalism on *Open*
Source, a Web-based radio program hosted by the veteran journalist
Christopher Lydon. It has become increasingly difficult, Lloyd said, to
report facts that are not tied to an ideological point of view. The emerging paradigm, he explained, may be "that you can only get facts through
by attaching them to a very strong left-wing, right-wing, Christian, athe-
ist position. Only then, only if you establish your bona fides within this
particular community, will they be open to facts."

No less a blogging enthusiast than Markos Moulitsas, founder of 9
Daily Kos, has observed that political blogs are a nonentity in Britain,
where the newspapers themselves cater to a wide range of different
opinions. "You look at the media in Britain, it's vibrant and it's exciting

and it's fun, because they're all ideologically tinged," Moulitsas said at an appearance in Boston last fall. "And that's a good thing, because people buy them and understand that their viewpoints are going to be represented."

The notion that journalism must be tied to an ideological community   *10*
may seem disheartening to traditionalists. In practice, though, journalism based on communities of shared interests and beliefs can be every bit as valuable as the old model of objectivity, if approached with rigor and respect for the truth.

Last year, for instance, Talking Points Memo (TPM) and its related   *11*
blogs helped break the story of how the U.S. Department of Justice had fired eight U.S. attorneys for what appeared to be politically motivated reasons, a scandal that led to the resignation of Attorney General Alberto Gonzales. TPM's reporting was based in part on information dug up and passed along by its liberal readership. The founder and editor, Joshua Micah Marshall, received a George Polk Award, but it belonged as much to the community he had assembled as it did to him personally.

Of course, we still need neutral, non-opinionated journalism to help   *12*
us make sense of the world around us. TPM's coverage of the U.S. attorneys scandal was outstanding, but it was also dismissive of arguments that it was much ado about nothing, or that previous administrations had done the same or worse. Liberals or conservatives who get all of their news from ideologically friendly sources don't have much incentive to change their minds.

Connecting to Communities of Shared Interests

Even news outlets that excel at traditional, "objective" journalism do so   *13*
within the context of a community. Some might not find liberal bias in the news pages of the *New York Times*, as the paper's conservative critics would contend, but there's little doubt that the *Times* serves a community of well-educated, affluent, culturally liberal readers whose preferences and tastes must be taken into account. Not to be a journalistic relativist, but all news needs to be evaluated within the context in which it was produced, even an old-fashioned, inverted-pyramid-style dispatch from the wires. Who was interviewed? Who wasn't? Why? These are questions that must be asked regardless of the source.

We might now be coming full circle as placeblogs—chatty, conver-   *14*
sational blogs that serve a particular geographic community—become more prevalent. Lisa Williams, founder of H2Otown, a blog that serves her community of Watertown, Massachusetts, believes that such forums could help foster the sense of community that is a necessary

precondition to newspaper readership. Williams also runs a project called Placeblogger.com, which tracks local blogs around the world.

"The news creates a shared pool of stories that gives us a way to talk   15
to people who aren't family or close friends or people who we will never meet—in short, our fellow citizens," Williams says by e-mail. "The truth is, people still want those neighbor-to-neighbor contacts, but the traditional ways of doing it don't fit into the lives that people are actually living today. Your core audience is tired, sitting on the couch with their laptop, and watching *Lost* with one eye. Give them someone to sit with."

Critics of blogs have been looking at the wrong thing. While tradi-   16
tionalists disparage bloggers for their indulgence of opinion and hyperbole, they overlook the sense of community and conversation that blogs have fostered around the news. What bloggers do well, and what news organizations do poorly or not at all, is give their readers someone to sit with. News consumers—the public, citizens, us—still want the truth. But we also want to share it and talk about it with our like-minded neighbors and friends. The challenge for journalism is not that we'll lose our objectivity; it's that we won't find a way to rebuild a sense of community.

JOHN DICKERSON

Don't Fear Twitter

John Dickerson is a political columnist for *Slate* magazine and chief Washington correspondent for CBS News. Before joining *Slate*, Dickerson covered politics for *Time* magazine, including four years as the magazine's White House correspondent. Dickerson has also written for the *New York Times* and *Washington Post* and is a regular panelist on *Washington Week in Review*. This essay first appeared in the Summer 2008 issue of *Nieman Reports*.

■ ■ ■

If I were cleverer, this piece on Twitter and journalism would fit in   1
Twitter's 140-character limitation. The beauty of Twitter when properly used—by both the reader and the writer—is that everyone knows what it is. No reader expects more from Twitter than it offers, and no one writing tries to shove more than necessary into a Twitter entry, which is sometimes called a Tweet, but not by me, thank you.

Not many people know what Twitter is, though, so I'm going to go on   2
for a few hundred words. Twitter is a Web site that allows you to share your thoughts instantly and on any topic with other people in the Twitter network as long as you do so in tight little entries of 140 characters

or less. If you're wondering how much you can write with that space limitation, this sentence that you're reading right now hits that mark perfectly.

For some, journalism is already getting smaller. Newspapers are shrinking. Serious news is being pushed aside in favor of entertainment and fluff stories. To many journalists and guardians of the trade, the idea that any journalist would willingly embrace a smaller space is horrifying and dumb. One journalism professor drew himself up to his full height and denounced Twitter journalism—or microjournalism, as someone unfortunately called it—as the ultimate absurd reduction of journalism. (I think he may have dislodged his monocle, he was waving his quill pen so violently.) Venerable CBS newsman Roger Mudd had a far lighter touch when he joked to me that he could barely say the word "texting" when he and I were talking about the idea of delivering a couple of sentences and calling it journalism.

We can all agree that journalism shouldn't get any smaller, but Twitter doesn't threaten the traditions of our craft. It adds, rather than subtracts, from what we do.

As I spend nearly all of my time on the road these days reporting on the presidential campaigns, Twitter is the perfect place for all of those asides I've scribbled in the hundreds of notebooks I have in my garage from the campaigns and stories I've covered over the years. Inside each of those notebooks are little pieces of color I've picked up along the way. Sometimes these snippets are too off-topic or too inconsequential to work into a story. Sometimes they are the little notions or sideways thoughts that become the lead of a piece or the kicker. All of them now have found a home on Twitter.

As journalists we take people places they can't go. Twitter offers a little snapshot way to do this. It's informal and approachable and great for conveying a little moment from an event. Here's an entry from a McCain rally during the Republican primaries: "Weare, NH: Audience man to McCain: 'I heard that Hershey is moving plants to Mexico and I'll be damned if I'm going to eat Mexican chocolate.'" In Scranton covering Barack Obama I sent this: "Obama: 'What's John McCain's problem?' Audience member: 'He's too old.' Obama: 'No, no that's not the problem. There are a lot of wise people....'" With so many Democrats making an issue of McCain's age, here was the candidate in the moment seeming to suggest that critique was unfair.

Occasionally, just occasionally, reporters can convey a piece of news that fits into 140 characters without context. If Twitter had been around when the planes hit the World Trade Center, it would have been a perfect way for anyone who witnessed it to convey at that moment what they'd seen or heard. With Twitter, we can also pull back the curtain on our lives

3

4

5

6

7

a little and show readers what it's like to cover a campaign. ("Wanna be a reporter? On long bus rides learn to sleep in your own hand.")

The risk for journalism, of course, is that people spend all day Twittering and reading other people's Twitter entries and don't engage with the news in any other way. This seems a pretty small worry. If written the right way, Twitter entries build a community of readers who find their way to longer articles because they are lured by these moment-by-moment observations. As a reader, I've found that I'm exposed to a wider variety of news because I read articles suggested to me by the wide variety of people I follow on Twitter. I'm also exposed to some keen political observers and sharp writers who have never practiced journalism.   8

Twitter is not the next great thing in journalism. No one should try to make Twitter do more than it can and no reader should expect too much from a 140-character entry. As for the critics, their worries about Twitter and journalism seem like the kind of obtuse behavior that would make a perfect observational Twitter entry: "A man at the front of the restaurant is screaming at a waiter and gesticulating wildly. The snacks on the bar aren't a four-course meal!"   9

STEVE GROVE

YouTube: The Flattening of Politics

Steve Grove is director of Google News Lab, and formerly directed all news, political programming, and citizen journalism for YouTube. He has been quoted as saying that he regards himself less as an editor than as a curator of the Web site's "chaotic sea of content." A native of Northfield, Minnesota, he worked as a journalist at the *Boston Globe* and ABC News before moving to YouTube.

▪ ▪ ▪

For a little over a year, I've served as YouTube's news and political director—perhaps a perplexing title in the eyes of many journalists. Such wonderment might be expected since YouTube gained its early notoriety as a place with videos of dogs on skateboards or kids falling off of trampolines. But these days, in the ten hours of video uploaded to YouTube every minute of every day (yes—every minute of every day), an increasing amount of the content is news and political video. And with YouTube's global reach and ease of use, it's changing the way that politics—and its coverage—is happening.   1

Each of the sixteen one-time presidential candidates had YouTube channels; seven announced their candidacies on YouTube. Their staffs   2 uploaded thousands of videos that were viewed tens of millions of times. By early March of this year, the Obama campaign was uploading two to three videos to YouTube every day. And thousands of advocacy groups and nonprofit organizations use YouTube to get their election messages into the conversation. For us, the most exciting aspect is that ordinary people continue to use YouTube to distribute their own political content; these range from "gotcha" videos they've taken at campaign rallies to questions for the candidates, from homemade political commercials to video mash-ups of mainstream media coverage.

What this means is that average citizens are able to fuel a new meritocracy for political coverage, one unburdened by the gatekeeping "middleman." Another way of putting it is that YouTube is now the world's largest town hall for political discussion, where voters connect with candidates—and the news media—in ways that were never before possible. *3*

In this new media environment, politics is no longer bound by traditional barriers of time and space. It doesn't matter what time it is, or where someone is located—as long as they have the means to connect through the Web, they can engage in the discussion. This was highlighted in a pair of presidential debates we produced with CNN during this election cycle during which voters asked questions of the candidates via YouTube videos they'd submitted online. In many ways, those events simply brought to the attention of a wider audience the sort of exchanges that take place on YouTube all the time.... *4*

News Organizations and YouTube

Just because candidates and voters find all sorts of ways to connect directly on YouTube does not mean there isn't room for the mainstream media, too. In fact, many news organizations have launched YouTube channels, including the Associated Press, the *New York Times*, the BBC, CBS, and the *Wall Street Journal*. *5*

Why would a mainstream media company upload their news content to YouTube? *6*

Simply put, it's where eyeballs are going. Research from the Pew Internet & American Life project found that 37 percent of adult Internet users have watched online video news, and well over half of online adults have used the Internet to watch video of any kind. Each day on YouTube hundreds of millions of videos are viewed at the same time that television viewership is decreasing in many markets. If a mainstream news organization wants its political reporting seen, YouTube offers visibility without a cost. The ones that have been doing this for a while rely on a strategy of building audiences on YouTube and then *7* trying to drive viewers back to their Web sites for a deeper dive into the content. And these organizations can earn revenue as well by running ads against their video content on YouTube.

In many ways, YouTube's news ecosystem has the potential to offer much more to a traditional media outlet. Here are some examples: 8

1. **Interactivity:** YouTube provides an automatic focus group for news content. How? YouTube wasn't built as merely a "series of tubes" to distribute online video. It is also an interactive platform. Users comment on, reply to, rank, and share videos with one another and form communities around content that they like. If news organizations want to see how a particular piece of content will resonate with audiences, they have an automatic focus group waiting on YouTube. And that focus group isn't just young people: 20 percent of YouTube users are over age 55 — which is the same percentage that is under 18. This means the YouTube audience roughly mirrors the national population.

2. **Partner with audiences:** YouTube provides news media organizations new ways to engage with audiences and involve them in the programming. Modeled on the presidential debates we cohosted last year, YouTube has created similar partnerships, such as one with the BBC around the mayoral election in London and with a large public broadcaster in Spain for their recent presidential election. Also on the campaign trail, we worked along with Hearst affiliate WMUR-TV in New Hampshire to solicit videos from voters during that primary. Hundreds of videos flooded in from across the state. The best were broadcast on that TV station, which highlighted this symbiotic relationship: On the Web, online video bubbles the more interesting content to the top and then TV amplifies it on a new scale. We did similar arrangements with news organizations in Iowa, Pennsylvania, and on Super Tuesday, as news organizations leveraged the power of voter-generated content. What the news organizations discover is that they gain audience share by offering a level of audience engagement — with opportunities for active as well as passive experiences.

For news media organizations, audience engagement is much 9 easier to achieve by using platforms like YouTube than it is to do on their own. And we just made it easier: Our open API (application programming interface), nicknamed "YouTube Everywhere" — just launched a few months ago — allows other companies to integrate our upload functionality into their online platforms. It's like having a mini YouTube on your Web site and, once it's there, news organizations can encourage—and publish—video responses and comments on the reporting they do.

Finally, reporters use YouTube as source material for their stories. *10* With hundreds of thousands of video cameras in use today, there is a much greater chance than ever before that events will be captured—by someone—as they unfold. No need for driving the satellite truck to the scene if someone is already there and sending in video of the event via their cell phone. It's at such intersections of new and old media that YouTube demonstrates its value. It could be argued, in fact, that the YouTube platform is the new frontier in newsgathering. On the election trail, virtually every appearance by every candidate is captured on video—by someone—and that means the issues being talked about are covered more robustly by more people who can steer the public discussion in new ways. The phenomenon is, of course, global, as we witnessed last fall in Burma (Myanmar) after the government shut down news media outlets during waves of civic protests. In time, YouTube was the only way to track the violence being exercised by the government on monks who'd taken to the streets. Videos of this were seen worldwide on YouTube, creating global awareness of this situation—even in the absence of journalists on the scene.

Citizen journalism on YouTube—and other Internet sources—is *11* often criticized because it is produced by amateurs and therefore lacks a degree of trustworthiness. Critics add that because platforms like YouTube are fragmenting today's media environment, traditional newsrooms are being depleted of journalists, and thus the denominator for quality news coverage is getting lower and lower. I share this concern about what is happening in the news media today, but I think there are a couple of things worth remembering when it comes to news content on YouTube.

Trusting What We See

When it comes to determining the trustworthiness of news content on *12* YouTube, it's important to have some context. People tend to know what they're getting on YouTube, since content is clearly labeled by username as to where it originated. A viewer knows if the video they're watching is coming from "jellybean109" or "thenewyorktimes." Users also know that YouTube is an open platform and that no one verifies the truth of content better than the consumer. The wisdom of the crowd on YouTube is far more likely to pick apart a shoddy piece of "journalism" than it is to elevate something that is simply untrue. In fact, because video is ubiquitous and so much more revealing and compelling than text, YouTube can provide a critical fact-checking platform in today's media environment. And in some ways, it offers a backstop for accuracy since a journalist can't afford to get the story wrong; if they do, it's likely that someone else who was there got it right—and posted it to YouTube.

Scrutiny cuts both ways. Journalists are needed today for the work   *13*
they do as much as they ever have been. While the wisdom of crowds might provide a new form of fact checking, and the ubiquity of technology might provide a more robust view of the news, citizens desperately need the Fourth Estate to provide depth, context, and analysis that only comes with experience and the sharpening of the craft. Without the work of journalists, the citizens—the electorate—lose a critical voice in the process of civic decision making.

This is the media ecosystem in which we live in this election cycle.   *14*
Candidates and voters speak directly to one another, unfiltered. News organizations use the Internet to connect with and leverage audiences in new ways. Activists, issue groups, campaigns, and voters all advocate for, learn about, and discuss issues on the same level platform. YouTube has become a major force in this new media environment by offering new opportunities and new challenges. For those who have embraced them—and their numbers grow rapidly every day—the opportunity to influence the discussion is great. For those who haven't, they ignore the opportunity at their own peril.

AVOIDING PLAGIARISM

Whether you paraphrase, summarize, or synthesize, it is essential that you acknowledge your sources. Academic writing requires you to use and document sources appropriately, making clear to readers the boundaries between your words and ideas and those of other writers. Setting boundaries can be a challenge because so much of academic writing involves interweaving the ideas of others into your own argument. Still, you must acknowledge your sources. It's only fair. Imagine how you would feel if you were reading a text and discovered that the writer had incorporated a passage from one of your papers, something you had slaved over, without giving you credit. You would see yourself as a victim of plagiarism, and you would be justified in feeling very angry indeed.

In fact, **plagiarism**—the unacknowledged use of another's work, passed off as one's own—is a serious breach of academic integrity, and colleges and universities deal with it severely. If you are caught plagiarizing in your work for a class, you can expect to fail that class and you may even be expelled from your college or university. Furthermore, although a failing grade on a paper or in a course, honestly come by, is unlikely to deter an employer from hiring you, the stigma of plagiarism can come back to haunt you when you apply for a job. Any violation of the principles set forth in Table 8.1 could have serious consequences for your academic and professional career.

TABLE 8.1   Principles Governing Plagiarism

1. All written work submitted for any purpose is accepted as your own work. This means it must not have been written, even in part, by another person.

2. The wording of any written work you submit is assumed to be your own. This means you must not submit work that has been copied, wholly or partially, from a book, an article, an essay, a newspaper, another student's paper or notebook, or any other source. Another writer's phrases, sentences, or paragraphs can be included only if they are presented as quotations and the source acknowledged.

3. The ideas expressed in a paper or report are assumed to originate with you, the writer. Written work that paraphrases a source without acknowledgment must not be submitted for credit. Ideas from the work of others can be incorporated in your work as starting points, governing issues, illustrations, and the like, but in every instance the source must be cited.

4. Remember that any online materials you use to gather information for a paper are also governed by the rules for avoiding plagiarism. You need to cite electronic sources as well as printed and other sources.

5. You may correct and revise your writing with the aid of reference books. You also may discuss your writing with your peers in a writing group or with peer tutors at your campus writing center. However, you may not submit writing that has been revised substantially by another person.

Even if you know what plagiarism is and wouldn't intentionally plagiarize, watch out for unintentional plagiarism. Again, paraphrasing can be especially tricky: Attempting to restate a passage without using the original words and sentence structure is, to a certain extent, an invitation to plagiarism. If you remember that your paper is *your* argument, and understand that any paraphrasing, summarizing, or synthesizing should reflect *your* voice and style, you will be less likely to have problems with plagiarism. Your paper should sound like you. And, again, the surest way to protect yourself is to cite your sources and carefully check your work.

Steps to Avoiding Plagiarism

1 **Always cite the source.** Signal that you are paraphrasing, summarizing, or synthesizing by identifying your source at the outset—"According to Laurie Ouellette," "Paul Loeb argues," "Anne Colby and her colleagues … point out." And if possible, indicate the end of the paraphrase, summary, or synthesis with relevant page references to the source. If you cite a source several times in your paper, don't assume that your first citation has you covered; acknowledge the source as often as you use it.

2 **Provide a full citation in your bibliography.** It's not enough to cite a source in your paper; you must also provide a full citation for every source you use in the list of sources at the end of your paper.

INTEGRATING QUOTATIONS INTO YOUR WRITING

When you integrate quotations into your writing, bear in mind a piece of advice we've given you about writing the rest of your paper: Take your readers by the hand and lead them step by step. When you quote other authors to develop your argument—using their words to support your thinking or to address a counterargument—discuss and analyze the words you quote, showing readers how the specific language of each quotation contributes to the larger point you are making in your essay. When you integrate quotations, then, there are three basic things you want to do: (1) Take an active stance, (2) explain the quotations, and (3) attach short quotations to your own sentences.

■ Take an Active Stance

Critical reading requires that you adopt an active stance toward what you read—that you raise questions in response to a text. You should be no less active when you are using other authors' texts to develop your own argument.

Taking an active stance when you are quoting means knowing when to quote. Don't quote when a paraphrase or summary will convey the information from a source more effectively. More important, you have to make fair and wise decisions about what and how much you should quote to make your argument.

- You want to show that you understand the writer's argument, and you want to make evenhanded use of it in your own argument. It's not fair (or wise) to quote selectively—choosing only passages that support your argument—when you know you are distorting the argument of the writer you are quoting.

- Remember that your ideas and argument—your thesis—are what is most important to the readers and what justifies a quotation's being included at all. It's not wise (or fair to yourself) to flesh out your paper with an overwhelming number of quotations that could make readers think that you do not know your topic well or do not have your own ideas. Don't allow quotations to take over your paragraphs.

Above all, taking an active stance when you quote means taking control of your writing. You want to establish your own argument and guide your readers through it, allowing sources to contribute to but not dictate its direction. You are responsible for plotting and pacing your essay. Always keep in mind that your thesis is the skewer that runs through every paragraph, holding all of the ideas together. When you use quotations, then, you must organize them to enrich, substantiate, illustrate, and help support your central claim or thesis.

■ Explain the Quotations

When you quote an author to support or advance your argument, make sure that readers know exactly what they should learn from the quotation.

Read the excerpt below from one student's early draft of an argument that focuses on the value of service learning in high schools. The student reviews several relevant studies—but then simply drops in a quotation, expecting readers to know what they should pay attention to in it.

> Other research emphasizes community service as an integral and integrated part of moral identity. In this understanding, community service activities are not isolated events but are woven into the context of students' everyday lives (Yates, 1995); the personal, the moral, and the civic become "inseparable" (Colby, Ehrlich, Beaumont, & Stephens, 2003, p. 15). In their study of minority high schoolers at an urban Catholic school who volunteered at a soup kitchen for the homeless as part of a class assignment, Youniss and Yates (1999) found that the students underwent significant identity changes, coming to perceive themselves as lifelong activists. The researchers' findings are worth quoting at length here because they depict the dramatic nature of the students' changed viewpoints. Youniss and Yates wrote,
>
>> Many students abandoned an initially negative view of homeless people and a disinterest in homelessness by gaining appreciation of the humanity of homeless people and by showing concern for homelessness in relation to poverty, job training, low-cost housing, prison reform, drug and alcohol rehabilitation, care for the mentally ill, quality urban education, and welfare policy. Several students also altered perceptions of themselves from politically impotent teenagers to involved citizens who now and in the future could use their talent and power to correct social problems. They projected articulated pictures of themselves as adult citizens who could affect housing policies, education for minorities, and government programs within a clear framework of social justice. (p. 362)

The student's introduction to the quoted passage provided a rationale for quoting Youniss and Yates at length, but it did not help her readers see how the research related to her argument. The student needed to frame the quotation for her readers. Instead of introducing the quotation by saying "Youniss and Yates wrote," she should have made clear that the study supports the argument that community service can create change. A more appropriate frame for the quotation might have been a summary like this one:

Frames the quoted material, explaining it in the context of the student's argument.

One particular study underscores my argument that service can motivate change, particularly when that change begins within the students who are involved in service. Youniss and Yates (1999) wrote that over the course of their research, the students developed both an "appreciation of the humanity of homeless people" and a sense that they would someday be able to "use their talent and power to correct social problems" (p. 362).

In the following example, notice that the student writer uses Derrick Bell's text to say something about how the effects of desegregation have been muted by political manipulation.* The writer shapes what he wants readers to focus on, leaving nothing to chance.

> The effectiveness with which the meaning of *Brown v. Board of Education* has been manipulated, Derrick Bell argued, is also evidenced by the way in which such thinking has actually been embraced by minority groups. Bell claimed that a black school board member's asking "But of what value is it to teach black children to read in all-black schools?" indicates this unthinking acceptance that whiteness is an essential ingredient to effective schooling for blacks. Bell continued:
>
>> The assumption that even the attaining of academic skills is worthless unless those skills are acquired in the presence of white students illustrates dramatically how a legal precedent, namely the Supreme Court's decision in Brown v. Board of Education, has been so constricted even by advocates that its goal — equal educational opportunity — is rendered inaccessible, even unwanted, unless it can be obtained through racial balancing of the school population. (p. 255)
>
> Bell's argument is extremely compelling, particularly when one considers the extent to which "racial balancing" has come to be defined in terms of large white majority populations and small nonwhite minority populations.

Notice that the student's last sentence helps readers understand what the quoted material suggests and why it's important by embedding and extending Bell's notion of racial balancing into his explanation.

In sum, you should always explain the information that you quote so that your readers can see how the quotation relates to your own argument. ("Take your readers by the hand ...") As you read other people's writing, keep an eye open to the ways writers introduce and explain the sources they use to build their arguments.

■ Attach Short Quotations to Your Sentences

The quotations we discussed above are **block quotations,** lengthy quotations of more than five lines that are set off from the text of a paper with indention. Make shorter quotations part of your own sentences so that your readers can easily follow along and understand how the quotations connect to your argument. How do you make a quotation part of your own sentences? There are two main methods:

---

*This quotation is from Derrick Bell's *Silent Covenants: Brown v. Board of Education and the Unfulfilled Hopes for Racial Reform* (New York: Oxford UP, 2005).

- Integrate quotations within the grammar of your writing.
- Attach quotations with punctuation.

If possible, use both to make your integration of quotations more interesting and varied.

Integrate quotations within the grammar of a sentence.   When you integrate a quotation into a sentence, the quotation must make grammatical sense and read as if it is part of the sentence:

> Fine, Weiss, and Powell (1998) expanded upon what others call "equal status contact theory" by using a "framework that draws on three traditionally independent literatures — those on community, difference, and democracy" (p. 37).

If you add words to the quotation, use square brackets around them to let readers know that the words are not original to the quotation:

> Smith and Wellner (2002) asserted that they "are not alone [in believing] that the facts have been incorrectly interpreted by Mancini" (p. 24).

If you omit any words in the middle of a quotation, use an **ellipsis,** three periods with spaces between them, to indicate the omission:

> Riquelme argues that "Eliot tries ... to provide a definition by negations, which he also turns into positive terms that are meant to correct misconceptions" (p. 156).

If you omit a sentence or more, make sure to put a period before the ellipsis points:

> Eagleton writes, "What Eliot was in fact assaulting was the whole ideology of middle-class liberalism.... Eliot's own solution is an extreme right-wing authoritarianism: men and women must sacrifice their petty 'personalities' and opinions to an impersonal order" (p. 39).

Whatever you add (using square brackets) or omit (using ellipses), the sentence must read grammatically. And, of course, your additions and omissions must not distort the author's meaning.

> Leah is also that little girl who "stares at her old street and look[s] at the abandoned houses and cracked up sidewalks."

Attach quotations with punctuation.   You also can attach a quotation to a sentence by using punctuation. For example, this passage attaches the run-in quotation with a colon:

> For these researchers, there needs to be recognition of differences in a way that will include and accept all students. Specifically, they raised this key question: "Within multiracial settings, when are young people invited to discuss, voice, critique, and re-view the very notions of race that feel so fixed, so hierarchical, so damaging, and so accepted in the broader culture?" (p. 132).

In conclusion, if you don't connect quotations to your argument, your readers may not understand why you've included them. You need to explain a significant point that each quotation reveals as you introduce or end it. This strategy helps readers know what to pay attention to in a quotation, particularly if the quotation is lengthy.

Steps to Integrating Quotations into Your Writing

1 **Take an active stance.** Your sources should contribute to your argument, not dictate its direction.

2 **Explain the quotations.** Explain what you quote so your readers understand how each quotation relates to your argument.

3 **Attach short quotations to your sentences.** Integrate short quotations within the grammar of your own sentences, or attach them with appropriate punctuation.

A Practice Sequence: Integrating Quotations

1   Using several of the sources you are working with in developing your paper, try integrating quotations into your essay. Be sure you are controlling your sources. Carefully read the paragraphs where you've used quotations. Will your readers clearly understand why the quotations are there—the points the quotations support? Do the sentences with quotations read smoothly? Are they grammatically correct?

2   Working in a small group, agree on a substantial paragraph or passage (from this book or some other source) to write about. Each member should read the passage and take a position on the ideas, and then draft a page that quotes the passage using both strategies for integrating these quotations. Compare what you've written, examining similarities and differences in the use of quotations.

AN ANNOTATED STUDENT RESEARCHED ARGUMENT: SYNTHESIZING SOURCES

The student who wrote the essay "A Greener Approach to Groceries: Community-Based Agriculture in LaSalle Square" did so in a first-year writing class that gave students the opportunity to volunteer in the local community. For this assignment, students were asked to explore debates about community and citizenship in contemporary America and to focus their research and writing on a social justice–related issue of their choice. The context of the course guided their inquiry as all the students in the course explored community service as a way to engage meaningfully and to develop relationships in the community.

We have annotated her essay to show the ways that she summarized and paraphrased research to show the urgency of the problem of food insecurity that exists around the world and to offer possible solutions. Notice how she synthesizes her sources, taking an active stance in using what she has read to advance her own argument.

Paul 1

Nancy Paul

Professor McLaughlin

English 2102

May 11, 20—

A Greener Approach to Groceries:

Community-Based Agriculture in LaSalle Square

In our post–9/11 society, there is incessant concern for the security of our future. Billions of dollars are spent tightening borders, installing nuclear detectors, and adjudicating safety measures so that the citizens of the United States can grow and prosper without fear. Unfortunately, for some urban poor, the threat from terrorism is minuscule compared to the cruelty of their immediate environment. Far from the sands of the Afghan plains and encapsulated in the midst of inner-city deterioration, many find themselves in gray-lot deserts devoid of vegetation and reliable food sources. Abandoned by corporate supermarkets, millions of Americans are maimed by a "food insecurity" — the nutritional poverty that cripples them developmentally, physically, and psychologically.

The student's thesis

The midwestern city that surrounds our university has a food-desert sitting just west of the famously lush campus. Known as LaSalle Square, it was once home to the lucrative Bendix plant and has featured both a Target and a Kroger supermarket in recent years. But previous economic development decisions have driven both stores to the outskirts of town, and without a local supplier, the only food available in the neighborhood is prepackaged and sold at the few small convenience stores. This available food is virtually devoid

She calls attention to both the immediacy and urgency of the problem

1

2

Paul 2

of nutrition and inhibits the ability of the poor to prosper and thrive.
Thus, an aging strip mall, industrial site, and approximately three
acres of an empty grass lot between the buildings anchor — and
unfortunately define — the neighborhood.

She proposes a possible solution.

While there are multiple ways of providing food to the
destitute, I am proposing a co-op of community gardens built
on the grassy space in LaSalle Square and on smaller sites within
the neighborhood, supplemented by extra crops from Michiana
farmers, which would supply fresh fruit and vegetables to be sold
or distributed to the poor. Together the co-op could meet the
nutritional needs of the people, provide plenty of nutritious food,
not cost South Bend any additional money, and contribute to
neighborhood revitalization, yielding concrete increases in property

She places her solution in a larger context to indicate its viability.

values. Far from being a pipe dream, LaSalle Square already hosted
an Urban Garden Market this fall, so a co-op would simply build
upon the already recognized need and desire for healthy food in the
area. Similar coalitions around the world are harnessing the power
of community to remedy food insecurity without the aid of corporate
enterprise, and South Bend is perfectly situated to reproduce and
possibly exceed their successes.

Many, myself previously included, believe that the large-volume,
cheap industrialization of food and the welfare system have obliterated
hunger in the United States. Supermarkets like Wal-Mart and Kroger seem
ubiquitous in our communities, and it is difficult to imagine anyone
being beyond their influence. However, profit-driven corporate business
plans do not mix well with low-income, high-crime populations, and
the gap between the two is growing wider. This polarization, combined
with the vitamin deficiency of our high-fructose corn syrup society,
has created food deserts in already struggling communities where
malnutrition is the enemy *inconnu* of the urban poor.

More context

LaSalle Square's food insecurity is typical of many urban
areas. The grocery stores that used to serve the neighborhood have
relocated to more attractive real estate on the outskirts of the city,
and only local convenience stores, stocking basic necessary items and
tobacco products, remain profitable. Linda Wolfson, a member of the
steering committee for the LaSalle Square Redevelopment Plan, notes
that if the community was fiscally healthy, it would be reasonable

3

4

5

Paul 3

to expect the inhabitants to simply drive the six miles to the strip mall district, but unfortunately many are marginally employed and do not have access to cars. For them, it is economically irresponsible to spend the extra money to get to the supermarket, and so they feed their families on the cheap soda, chips, and processed food

Synthesizing helps illustrate the extent of the problem and bolster her view that the poor suffer the most from the problem she identifies (Garnett; Smith; Brown and Carter).

that are readily available at the convenience store. Especially since high-calorie, low-nutrient, packaged food tends to be denser, urban mothers find that it helps their children feel full (Garnett). Sadly, a health investigation released in 2006 concluded that by the age of three, more than one-third of urban children are obese, due in large part to the consumption of low-quality food obtained from corner stores (Smith). A recent analysis of urban stores in Detroit found that only 19 percent offer the healthy food array suggested by the FDA food pyramid (Brown and Carter 5). The food that is offered contains 25 percent less nutrient density, and consequently, underprivileged socioeconomic populations consume significantly lower levels of the micronutrients that form the foundation for proper protein and brain

Here she paraphrases findings.

development. In a recent study of poor households, it was found that two-thirds of children were nutritionally poor and that more than 25 percent of women were deficient in iron, vitamin A, vitamin C, vitamin B6, thiamin, and riboflavin (Garnett). Of course, some may challenge the relevance of these vitamins and nutrients since they are not something the average person consciously incorporates into his or her diet on a daily basis. Yet modern research, examining the severely homogenous diets of the poor, has found severe developmental consequences associated with the lack of nutritional substance. For those afflicted, these deficiencies are not simply inconvenient, but actually exacerbate their plight and hinder their progress toward a sustainable lifestyle.

The human body is a complex system that cannot be sustained merely on the simple sugars and processed carbohydrates that comprise most cheap and filling foodstuffs, and research shows a relationship between nutritional deficiencies and a host of cognitive and developmental impairments that are prevalent in the undernourished families from urban America. Standardized tests of impoverished siblings, one of whom received nutritional supplements and the other who did not, showed cognitive gains in the well-

6

Paul 4

Again she both summarizes and cites a relevant study to advance her argument.

nourished child as well as increased motor skills and greater interest in social interactions when compared to the other child. In the highly formative toddler years, undernutrition can inhibit the myelination of nerve fibers, which is responsible for neurotransmitting and proper brain function. Collaborators Emily Tanner from the University of Oxford and Matia Finn-Stevenson from Yale University published a comprehensive analysis of the link between nutrition and brain development in 2002. Their analysis, which they linked to social policy, indicated that a shortage of legumes and leafy green vegetables, which are nearly impossible to find in corner stores, is the leading cause of the iron-deficiency anemia afflicting 25 percent of urban children. This extreme form of anemia is characterized by impaired neurotransmission, weaker memory, and reduced attention span (Tanner and Finn-Stevenson 186). For those who do not have access to the vitamins, minerals, and micronutrients found in fruits and vegetables, these maladies are not distant risks, but constant, inescapable threats.

In light of these severe consequences of undernutrition, the term "food insecurity" encapsulates the condition wherein the economically disadvantaged are vulnerable simply because their bodies are unable to receive adequate fuel for optimal functioning. Just as one cannot expect a dry, parched plant to bloom and pollinate a garden, by constraining the development of individuals, food insecurity also constrains the development of the neighborhoods in which the individuals contribute. For the health of a city and its communities, all roadblocks to progress must be removed, and food insecurity must be cut out at its roots so that individuals have the resources for advancement.

As socially conscious citizens and local governments have recognized the prevalence and danger of food insecurity in inner cities, there have been attempts at a remedy. Obviously, the easiest solution is simply to introduce a grocery store that would provide a variety of quality, healthful foods. However, for big-box supermarkets driven by the bottom line, urban areas are less than desirable business locales from a standpoint of both profitability and maintenance. It is simply irrational for a supermarket to invest in an urban area with less revenue potential, size constraints, an

Paul 5

unattractive locale, and an increased threat of theft and defacement when it is so easy to turn a profit in spacious and peaceful suburbia (Eisenhauer 131). Supermarkets must have significant incentive, beyond humanitarian ends, if they are to take the financial risk of entering a poor, urban marketplace.

She takes an active stance in citing initiatives that could be applied more effectively to alleviate the problem of food insecurity.

Certain cities are using the power of Tax Increment Financing (TIF) districts to encourage supermarkets to invest in urban centers. Under these redevelopment laws, tax revenues from retail development or other commercial enterprises are devoted, for a specified number of years, to infrastructural improvement of the district ("TIF Reform"). This approach has been effective in enticing new businesses; in fact, the exterior growth around South Bend is the result of a TIF district established in the late 1980s. LaSalle Square is currently part of a TIF district, but there is discussion as to how the TIF monies should best be applied (Wolfson). It may be possible to use the power of the TIF to encourage another large retailer such as Kroger to establish a presence in the square, but a smaller enterprise may be a better option. Experts indicate that for the destitute and

9

She paraphrases a researcher's findings.

food-insecure, reliance on a corporate entity is not optimal. Elizabeth Eisenhauer, a researcher from the State University of New York, investigated the interplay between supermarkets and the urban poor; she concluded that large big-box stores lack a commitment to the communities they serve and can be relied on only when it is clear they will make a profit, which may or may not happen when TIF benefits expire (131). Even when a portion of proceeds is used in the community, the majority of the cash flow from a supermarket is going to a corporate headquarters elsewhere, not directly supporting the surrounding neighborhood. Likewise, while some employees may be local, the highest-salary management positions are generally given to outsiders, making the stores and their employees set apart, rather than integrated into the neighborhood (Eisenhauer 130). Certainly a supermarket in an urban area will greatly contribute to the reduction of food insecurity, but it is not the only available option, and the city of South Bend is ripe for alternative solutions. The city is primed for a cooperative effort that could shift the paradigm for urban renewal from a quick, corporate solution, to a long-term enterprise built on community contributions and under local control.

Paul 6

She cites a number of examples as evidence to demonstrate the viability of the solution she offers.

Around the globe, many destitute urban areas have found the means to reverse nutritional poverty through a literal and figurative grassroots effort. In an effort to avoid packaged, convenience store food, neighbors in the Bronx, San Francisco, Los Angeles, London, and most successfully in Philadelphia, have been planting their own crops right in the heart of the city (Brown and Carter 3-4). Truly farming the food desert, coalitions that link community gardens, local farmers, and urban markets are providing healthy, sustainable food sources without a supermarket. Interestingly, in the process, such coalitions are generating jobs, increasing property value, and, in some cases, actually reversing the effects of poverty. The city of South Bend, uniquely situated in the breadbasket of the United States, is in the perfect position to launch a "greening" effort, modeled after the successes in other parts of the world, which would both solve the problem of food insecurity of LaSalle Square and invigorate the local economy.

11

While modern Americans have the tendency to think that food production should be, and always has been, industrialized, countries around the world, especially economically disadvantaged nations, are

The use of multiple sources would make her case even stronger than using just one source of information, in this case Brown and Carter.

exemplifying the possibilities of local gardening efforts. Far removed from industrial farms, Cubans grow half their vegetables within the city; vacant land in Russian cities produces 80 percent of the nation's vegetables, and specifically in Moscow, 65 percent of families contribute to food production. Singapore has 10,000 urban farmers, and nearly half of the residents of Vancouver grow food in their gardens (Brown and Carter 10). These habits are not simply a novelty; rather, populations that garden tend to be healthier, eating six out of the fourteen vegetable categories more regularly than nongardeners and also consuming fewer sweet and sugary foods per capita (Brown and Carter 13). These data, compiled by the North American Urban Agriculture Committee, were synthesized from the *Journal of Public Health Policy* and the *Journal of Nutrition Education* and show the interrelatedness of nutritional access and availability to healthy personal choices. While these trends toward healthful lifestyles and gardening have been gaining ground slowly in the United States, when food insecurity and poverty take their toll, cities are finding that urban agriculture is an increasingly attractive and profitable alternative.

Paul 7

American communities have shown that creativity and
collaboration can be quite effective at reversing food insecurity. The
Garden Project of the Greater Lansing Food Bank has successfully
combined gardening and Midwest access to local farms to bring
food security to urban residents and senior citizens. Their eighteen
community gardens and volunteers provide fresh fruits and
vegetables year-round to low-income families, food pantries, the

*She synthe-
sizes different
sources to make
her point.*

elderly, and social service organizations. Completely bypassing the
commercial market, the Garden Project has trained 500 families
to grow their own food in backyard plots so that they can always
have healthy food in the midst of the city (Brown and Carter 1).
The gardens are supplemented by a process known as "gleaning," in
which volunteers harvest extra crops from local farmers that would
otherwise go to waste, and deliver it to residents of subsidized
housing ("Gleaning"). In 2008 alone, the Garden Project actively
involved 2,500 individual gardeners and was able to provide over
250,000 pounds of produce from gleaning alone, plus the yields
of the community plots that were used directly by the gardeners
("GLFB Facts"). This Lansing coalition serves over 5,000 individuals
per month, yet only 4,400 reside under the poverty line in the
LaSalle Square area (*City-Data.com*). If half of the inhabitants of
LaSalle Square became engaged in the gardening effort, a similar
collaboration could meet the needs of the region, and greater
participation could yield an excess.

Similar efforts have demonstrated not only that inner-city
food production is achievable but also that it can be cost-effective
and self-sufficient, unlike a food bank. Frustrated by the inner-city
downturn she describes as "an overgrown dog toilet," industrious
London entrepreneur Julie Brown created a community gardening
company aimed at providing unmechanized, local, sustainable food.

*In this paragraph,
she summarizes
research to
address the
possible counter-
argument.*

The company, Growing Communities, uses organic box gardens and
small farms to supply more than 400 homes with weekly deliveries of
organic fruits and vegetables. After a ten-year investment in local
farmers and mini-gardens within the city, Growing Communities is
now financially independent and generates over $400,000 per year
(Willis 53). Compelled by both capitalism and social concern, Brown's
efforts have shown that community-supported agriculture not

12

13

Paul 8

only is possible but can be profitable as well! Our own community agriculture program should not be an entrepreneurial endeavor, but Brown's work in London indicates that it need not be a financial burden to the city either. Rather, the co-op would be financially self-sufficient, with the potential to generate revenues and fiscal growth in the city.

14

There are environmental factors that make South Bend an even better place to launch a profitable community agriculture program than London. Chiefly, South Bend has many more farms in the immediate vicinity than Ms. Brown could ever have dreamed of in the U.K. While Brown was limited to twenty-five local farms within 100 miles of the city, South Bend has over fifty farms within 25 miles of LaSalle Square (*Local Harvest*). Offering a broader production base creates more potential for profits by decreasing transportation time and increasing product, thereby making it easier for a coalition to become financially self-sufficient in a shorter time frame than Ms. Brown's ten-year plan.

She again cites research to address the counter-argument.

15

Urban Philadelphia has led the way in demonstrating the profitability of community solutions to food insecurity through an offshoot of the Pennsylvania Horticultural Society (PHS) known as Philadelphia Greens. Since the 1970s, this coalition has reclaimed parks, planted trees, and created community gardens, both to revitalize the neighborhood and to serve the nutritionally and economically poor. Through a process that plants trees, builds wooden fences, and gardens the more than 1,000 vacant lots of Philadelphia, PHS combines housing projects and reclaimed space to "green" and reinvigorate the neighborhood ("The Effects"). Since LaSalle Square is essentially a large empty grassy area at the moment, a community agricultural co-op should turn this vacant lot and others in the neighborhood into community gardens, which would work in tandem with the gleaning from local farms. Similar to the Philadelphia project, these gardens would simultaneously yield produce and improve the appearance of the neighborhood.

16

One PHS project, in the New Kensington neighborhood of north Philadelphia, was the subject of a recent socioeconomic study conducted by the University of Pennsylvania's renowned Wharton School of Business. In the New Kensington area, PHS recently planted

Paul 9

480 new trees, cleaned 145 side yards, developed 217 vacant lots, and established 15 new community gardens. The effort was a model of the collaborative strategy between PHS and the local community development corporation, making it the ideal subject of the Wharton study. The findings, published in 2004, showed significant increases in property values around the PHS greening projects and were the first step in quantifying the fiscal returns of neighborhood greening beyond the qualitative benefits of remedying food insecurity. After analyzing the sales records of thousands of New Kensington homes between 1980 and 2003, the study reported that PHS greening had led to a $4 million gain in property value from tree plantings alone and a $12 million gain from vacant lot improvements. Simply greening a vacant lot increased nearby property values by as much as 30 percent ("Seeing Green"). While a supermarket might modestly improve property values for those immediately near the store, community greening involves multiple plots across an area, benefiting many more people and properties. The Wharton study showed that community greening would provide increases in the value of any property near a green space, up to multiple millions of dollars. The New Kensington neighborhood covers 1.4 square miles, which is approximately the size of LaSalle Square, so while the overall property values are lower simply because South Bend is a smaller city, the gains might be proportional (*City-Data.com*). It is reasonable to believe that cleaning up LaSalle Square and planting gardens would quantitatively benefit the fiscal situation of the city and increase assets of the homeowners while subsequently improving the quality of life over many acres.

She summarizes a study and then paraphrases.

Certainly there are challenges to the sort of dynamical, community-based solution that I am proposing. Such an agricultural co-op hinges on the participation of the people it serves and cannot be successful without the dedicated support of the neighborhood. It could be noted that lower-income economic groups are less socially involved than their higher-income counterparts, and some might believe that they are unlikely to contribute to, or care about, a greening effort. Yet I believe that there is a distinction between political involvement and neighborhood interaction. Middle-class Americans are conscious of gas prices and the fluctuations of the

17

Paul 10

stock market that affect their job security and ability to provide for their families; yet the unemployed poor without cars must rely on their neighborhoods to eke out a living. Their sustenance comes not from a salary, but from odd jobs, welfare, and the munificence of fate. The battle to put food on the table is more familiar to the poor than foreign conflict and is one that they fight every day. Therefore, while the poor are less inclined to vote or worry about governmental affairs because of the difficulties associated simply with daily living, they are acutely aware of their immediate surroundings and how those surroundings challenge or contribute to their success. This position makes them uniquely inclined to invest in the betterment of their surroundings since it can have a dramatic effect on their personal lives. The real success of the sustainable food movement may come from harnessing the power of urban communities that can derive great, immediate, and lasting benefit from neighborhood revitalization.

In this paragraph, she takes an active stance in using research to alleviate fears that the local community would have to start from scratch with limited expertise.

It has been argued that urban growers, especially from lower socioeconomic classes, do not have the expertise or knowledge base to generate successful yields that will ensure food security. Fortunately, agriculture is Indiana's fourth-largest industry, and the state boasts over 63,000 farms ("A Look"). In addition to the many inhabitants of LaSalle Square who have a background in agriculture, there is a wealth of knowledge about proper planting methods available from the farmers around the local area. Many of these farmers have already shown a willingness to help by selling or donating their produce to the local Urban Market. Additionally, national urban agriculture nonprofit groups, such as Master Gardening and Cooperative Extension, offer free public education to cities beginning community agriculture programs, and some will even perform on-site training (Brown and Carter 16). By harnessing the assets of local, gratuitous knowledge and supplementing that knowledge with national support groups, South Bend has multiple resources available to train and encourage its burgeoning urban farmers.

18

The economic and nutritional gains of the people would only be heightened by the personal well-being that is born of interpersonal collaboration that crosses racial and social

19

Paul 11

boundaries. Such an effort is ambitious; it will indeed require the time and talents of many people who care about the health of their community. But the local community is rich with the necessary seeds for such a project, which may, in time, blossom and grow to feed its people.

Paul 12

Works Cited

Brown, Katherine H., and Anne Carter. *Urban Agriculture and Community Food Security in the United States: Farming from the City Center to the Urban Fringe.* Community Food Security Coalition, Oct. 2003.

City-Data.com. Advameg, 16 Apr. 2008, www.city-data.com/city/ South-Bend-Indiana.html.

"The Effects of Neighborhood Greening." *Pennsylvania Horticultural Society,* Jan. 2001, phsonline.org/programs/effects-of -neighborhood-greening.

Eisenhauer, Elizabeth. "In Poor Health: Supermarket Redlining and Urban Nutrition." *GeoJournal,* vol. 53, no. 2, Feb. 2001, pp. 125–33.

Garnett, Tara. "Farming the City." *The Ecologist,* vol. 26, no. 6, Nov./ Dec. 1996, p. 299.

"Gleaning." *Greater Lansing Food Bank,* greaterlansingfoodbank .org/programs/programs-home/the-garden-project/gleaning/. Accessed 15 Apr. 20—.

"GLFB Facts." *Greater Lansing Food Bank,* greaterlansingfoodbank .org/our-impact/fact-sheet/. Accessed 15 Apr. 20—.

LocalHarvest. Local Harvest, 2008, www.localharvest.org/south -bend-in.

"A Look at Indiana Agriculture." *National Agriculture in the Classroom,* www.agclassroom.org/kids/ag_facts.htm. Accessed 18 Apr. 20—.

Paul 13

"Seeing Green: Study Finds Greening Is a Good Investment."
     Pennsylvania Horticultural Society, 2005, phsonline.org/
     programs/seeing-green.
Smith, Stephen. "Obesity Battle Starts Young for Urban Poor." *The
     Boston Globe*, 29 Dec. 2006, archive.boston.com/news/nation/
     articles/2006/12/29/obesity_battle_starts_young_for_urban
     _poor/.
Tanner, Emily M., and Matia Finn-Stevenson. "Nutrition and Brain
     Development: Social Policy Implications." *American Journal of
     Orthopsychiatry*, vol. 72, no. 2, Apr. 2002, pp. 182–93.
"TIF Reform." *New Rules Project*, Institute for Local Self-Reliance,
     2008, ilsr.org/rule/tif-reform/.
Willis, Ben. "Julie Brown of Growing Communities." *The Ecologist*,
     vol. 38, no. 5, June 2008, pp. 58–61.
Wolfson, Linda. Personal interview, 20 Apr. 20—.

A Practice Sequence: Thinking about Copyright

1   Now that you have read about steps to avoiding plagiarism
(pp. 228–29) and Nancy Paul's essay on community gardens
(p. 235) we would like you to examine the idea of copyright. That
is, who owns the rights to images that the organizers of a community garden use to market their idea? What if you wanted to use
that image in a paper? Or what if you wanted to use a published
ad in your own paper? Under what circumstances would you be
able to use that ad for your own purposes?

2   After conducting your own inquiry into copyright, what would
you conclude about the need to document the use of images,
ideas, and text? Are the guidelines clear or are there some ambig-
uous areas for what to cite and how? What advice would you give
your peers?

From Ethos to Logos
Appealing to Your Readers

Your understanding of your readers influences how you see a particular situation, define an issue, explain the ongoing conversation surrounding that issue, and formulate a question. You may need to read widely to understand how different writers have dealt with the issue you address. And you will need to anticipate how others might respond to your argument—whether they will be sympathetic or antagonistic—and to compose your essay so that readers will "listen" whether or not they agree with you.

To achieve these goals, you will no doubt use reason in the form of evidence to sway readers. But you can also use other means of persuasion. That is, you can use your own character, by presenting yourself as someone who is knowledgeable, fair, and just, and you can appeal to your readers' emotions. Although you may believe that reason alone should provide the means for changing people's minds, people's emotions also color the way they see the world.

Your audience is more than your immediate reader—your instructor or a peer. Your audience encompasses those you cite in writing about an issue and those you anticipate responding to your argument. This is true no matter what you write about, whether it be an interpretation of the novels of a particular author, an analysis of the cultural work of horror films, the ethics of treating boys and girls differently in schools, or the moral issues surrounding homelessness in America.

In this chapter we discuss different ways of engaging your readers, centering on three kinds of appeals: **ethos,** appeals from character; **pathos,** appeals to emotion; and **logos,** appeals to reason. *Ethos, pathos,* and *logos* are terms derived from ancient Greek writers, but they are still of great value today when considering how to persuade your audience. Readers

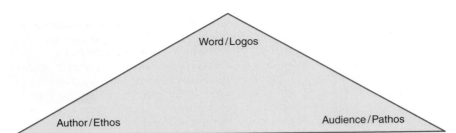

FIGURE 9.1   The Rhetorical Triangle

will judge your writing on whether or not you present an argument that is fair and just, one that creates a sense of goodwill. All three appeals rely on these qualities.

Figure 9.1, the **rhetorical triangle**, visually represents the interrelationship among ethos, pathos, and logos. Who we think our readers are (pathos: which of their emotions do we appeal to?) influences decisions about the ways we should represent ourselves to them (ethos: how can we come across as fair, credible, and just?). In turn, we use certain patterns of argument (logos: how do we arrange our words to make our case?) that reflect our interpretation of the situation to which we respond and that we believe will persuade readers to accept our point of view. Effective communication touches on each of the three points of the triangle. Your task as a writer is to determine the proper balance of these different appeals in your argument, based on your thesis, the circumstances, and your audience.

CONNECTING WITH READERS: A SAMPLE ARGUMENT

To see how an author connects with his audience, read the following excerpt from James W. Loewen's book *Lies My Teacher Told Me: Everything Your American History Textbook Got Wrong*. As you read the excerpt, note Loewen's main points and select key examples that illustrate his argument. As a class, test the claims he makes: To what extent do you believe that what Loewen argues is true? This may entail recalling your own experiences in high school history classes or locating one or more of the books that Loewen mentions.

JAMES W. LOEWEN

The Land of Opportunity

In addition to *Lies My Teacher Told Me* (1995, 2007), James Loewen, who holds a PhD in sociology, has written several other books, including *Lies across America: What Our Historic Sites Get Wrong* (1999) and *Sundown Towns: A Hidden Dimension of American Racism* (2005). As the titles of these books suggest, Loewen is a writer who questions the assumptions about history that many people take for granted. This is especially true of the following excerpt, from a chapter in which Loewen challenges a common American belief—that everyone has an equal chance in what he calls the "land of opportunity"—by arguing that we live in a class system that privileges some people and raises barriers for others. History textbook writers, he points out, are guilty of complicity in this class system because they leave a great deal of history out of their textbooks.

■ ■ ■

H igh school students have eyes, ears, and television sets (all too many have their own TV sets), so they know a lot about relative privilege in America. They measure their family's social position against that of other families, and their community's position against other communities. Middle-class students, especially, know little about how the American class structure works, however, and nothing at all about how it has changed over time. These students do not leave high school merely ignorant of the workings of the class structure; they come out as terrible sociologists. "Why are people poor?" I have asked first-year college students. Or, if their own class position is one of relative privilege, "Why is your family well-off?" The answers I've received, to characterize them charitably, are half-formed and naïve. The students blame the poor for not being successful. They have no understanding of the ways that opportunity is not equal in America and no notion that social structure pushes people around, influencing the ideas they hold and the lives they fashion.

High school history textbooks can take some of the credit for this state of affairs. Some textbooks do cover certain high points of labor history, such as the 1894 Pullman strike near Chicago that President Cleveland broke with federal troops, or the 1911 Triangle Shirtwaist fire that killed 146 women in New York City, but the most recent event mentioned in most books is the Taft-Hartley Act of sixty years ago. No book mentions any of the major strikes that labor lost in the late twentieth century, such as the 1985 Hormel meatpackers' strike in Austin, Minnesota, or the 1991 Caterpillar strike in Decatur, Illinois—defeats that signify labor's diminished power today. Nor do most textbooks describe any continuing issues facing labor, such as the growth of multinational corporations and their exporting of jobs overseas. With such omissions, textbook authors can construe labor history as something that happened long ago, like slavery, and that, like slavery, was corrected long ago. It logically follows that unions now appear anachronistic. The idea that they might be necessary for workers to have a voice in the workplace goes unstated.

These books' poor treatment of labor history is magnificent compared to their treatment of social class. *Nothing* that textbooks discuss—not even strikes—is ever anchored in any analysis of social class.[1] This amounts to delivering the footnotes instead of the lecture! Half of the eighteen high school American history textbooks I examined contain no index listing at all for *social class, social stratification, class structure, income distribution, inequality*, or any conceivably related topic. Not one book lists *upper class* or *lower class*. Three list *middle class*, but only to assure students that America is a middle-class country. "Except for slaves, most of the colonists were members of the 'middling ranks,'" says *Land of Promise*, and nails home the point that we are a middle-class country by asking students to "describe three 'middle-class' values that united free Americans of all classes." Several of the textbooks note the explosion of middle-class suburbs after World War II. Talking about the middle class is hardly equivalent to discussing social stratification, however. On the contrary, as Gregory Mantsios has pointed out, "such references appear to be acceptable precisely because they mute class differences."[2]

Stressing how middle-class we all are is increasingly problematic today, because the proportion of households earning between 75 percent and 125 percent of the median income has fallen steadily since 1967. The Reagan-Bush administrations accelerated this shrinkage of the middle class, and most families who left its ranks fell rather than rose.[3] As late as 1970, family incomes in the United States were only slightly less equal than in Canada. By 2000, inequality here was much greater than Canada's; the United States was becoming more like Mexico, a very stratified society.[4] The Bush II administration, with its tax cuts aimed openly at the wealthy, continued to increase the gap between the haves and have-nots. This is the kind of historical trend one would think history books would take as appropriate subject matter, but only five of the eighteen books in my sample provide any analysis of social stratification in the United States. Even these fragmentary analyses are set mostly in colonial America. Boorstin and Kelley, unusual in actually including *social class* in its index, lists only *social classes in 1790* and *social classes in early America*. These turn out to be two references to the same paragraph, which tells us that England "was a land of rigid social classes," while here in America "social classes were much more fluid." "One great difference between colonial and European society was that the colonists had more social mobility," echoes *The American Tradition*. Never mind that the most violent class conflicts in American history—Bacon's Rebellion and Shays's Rebellion—took place in and just after colonial times. Textbooks still say that colonial society was relatively classless and marked by upward mobility.

And things have only gotten rosier since. "By 1815," *The Challenge of Freedom* assures us, two classes had withered away and "America was a country of middle class people and of middle class goals." This book

4

5

returns repeatedly, every fifty years or so, to the theme of how open opportunity is in America. The stress on upward mobility is striking. There is almost nothing in any of these textbooks about class inequalities or barriers of any kind to social mobility. "What conditions made it possible for poor white immigrants to become richer in the colonies?" *Land of Promise* asks. "What conditions made/make it difficult?" goes unasked. Boorstin and Kelley close their sole discussion of social class (in 1790, described above) with the happy sentence, "As the careers of American Presidents would soon show, here a person might rise by hard work, intelligence, skill, and perhaps a little luck, from the lowest positions to the highest."

If only that were so! Social class is probably the single most important variable in society. From womb to tomb, it correlates with almost all other social characteristics of people that we can measure. Affluent expectant mothers are more likely to get prenatal care, receive current medical advice, and enjoy general health, fitness, and nutrition. Many poor and working-class mothers-to-be first contact the medical profession in the last month, sometimes the last hours, of their pregnancies. Rich babies come out healthier and weighing more than poor babies. The infants go home to very different situations. Poor babies are more likely to have high levels of poisonous lead in their environments and their bodies. Rich babies get more time and verbal interaction with their parents and higher quality day care when not with their parents. When they enter kindergarten, and through the twelve years that follow, rich children benefit from suburban schools that spend two to three times as much money per student as schools in inner cities or impoverished rural areas. Poor children are taught in classes that are often 50 percent larger than the classes of affluent children. Differences such as these help account for the higher school-dropout rate among poor children.

Even when poor children are fortunate enough to attend the same school as rich children, they encounter teachers who expect only children of affluent families to know the right answers. Social science research shows that teachers are often surprised and even distressed when poor children excel. Teachers and counselors believe they can predict who is "college material." Since many working-class children give off the wrong signals, even in first grade, they end up in the "general education" track in high school. "If you are the child of low-income parents, the chances are good that you will receive limited and often careless attention from adults in your high school," in the words of Theodore Sizer's bestselling study of American high schools, *Horace's Compromise*. "If you are the child of upper-middle-income parents, the chances are good that you will receive substantial and careful attention."[5] Researcher Reba Page has provided vivid accounts of how high school American history courses use rote learning to turn off lower-class

students.[6] Thus schools have put into practice Woodrow Wilson's rec-
ommendation: "We want one class of persons to have a liberal education, and we want another class of persons, a very much larger class of
necessity in every society, to forgo the privilege of a liberal education
and fit themselves to perform specific difficult manual tasks."[7]

As if this unequal home and school life were not enough, rich teenag-   8
ers then enroll in the Princeton Review or other coaching sessions for
the Scholastic Aptitude Test. Even without coaching, affluent children
are advantaged because their background is similar to that of the test
makers, so they are comfortable with the vocabulary and subtle sub-
cultural assumptions of the test. To no one's surprise, social class correlates strongly with SAT scores.

All these are among the reasons that social class predicts the rate   9
of college attendance and the type of college chosen more effectively
than does any other factor, including intellectual ability, however
measured. After college, most affluent children get white-collar jobs,
most working-class children get blue-collar jobs, and the class differences continue. As adults, rich people are more likely to have hired
an attorney and to be a member of formal organizations that increase
their civic power. Poor people are more likely to watch TV. Because
affluent families can save some money while poor families must spend
what they make, wealth differences are ten times larger than income
differences. Therefore most poor and working-class families cannot
accumulate the down payment required to buy a house, which in turn
shuts them out from our most important tax shelter, the write-off of
home mortgage interest. Working-class parents cannot afford to live
in elite subdivisions or hire high-quality day care, so the process of
educational inequality replicates itself in the next generation. Finally,
affluent Americans also have longer life expectancies than lower- and
working-class people, the largest single cause of which is better access
to health care. Echoing the results of Helen Keller's study of blindness,
research has determined that poor health is not distributed randomly
about the social structure but is concentrated in the lower class. Social
Security then become a huge transfer system, using monies contributed by all Americans to pay benefits disproportionately to longer-lived
affluent Americans.

Ultimately social class determines how people think about social   10
class. When asked if poverty in America is the fault of the poor or the
fault of the system, 57 percent of business leaders blamed the poor; just
9 percent blamed the system. Labor leaders showed sharply reversed
choices: only 15 percent said the poor were at fault while 56 percent
blamed the system. (Some people replied "don't know" or chose a
middle position.) The largest single difference between our two main

political parties lies in how their members think about social class: 55 percent of Republicans blamed the poor for their poverty, while only 13 percent blamed the system for it; 68 percent of Democrats, on the other hand, blamed the system, while only 5 percent blamed the poor.[8]

Few of these statements are news, I know, which is why I have not bothered to document most of them, but the majority of high school students do not know or understand these ideas. Moreover, the processes have changed over time, for the class structure in America today is not the same as it was in 1890, let alone in colonial America. Yet in the most recent *American Pageant*, for example, social class goes unmentioned in the twentieth century. Many teachers compound the problem by avoiding talking about social class in the twenty-first. A study of history and social studies teachers "revealed that they had a much broader knowledge of the economy, both academically and experientially, than they admitted in class." Teachers "expressed fear that students might find out about the injustices and inadequacies of their economic and political institutions."[9] By never blaming the system, American history courses thus present Republican history.

11

Notes

1. Jean Anyon, "Ideology and United States History Textbooks," *Harvard Educational Review* 49, no. 3 (8/1979): 373.

2. Gregory Mantsios, "Class in America: Myths and Realities," in Paula S. Rothernberg, ed., *Racism and Sexism: An Integrated Study* (New York: St. Martin's, 1988), 56.

3. Ibid., 60; Kevin Phillips, *The Politics of Rich and Poor* (New York: Random House, 1990); Robert Heilbroner, "Lifting the Silent Depression," *New York Review of Books*, 10/24/1991, 6; and Sylvia Nasar, "The Rich Get Richer," *New York Times*, 8/16/1992. Stephen J. Rose, *Social Stratification in the United States* (New York: New Press, 2007), is a posterbook that shows graphically the shrinkage of the middle class between 1979 and 2004.

4. "Income Disparity Since World War II—The Gini Index," in "Gini co-efficient," en.wikipedia.org/wiki/Gini_coefficient, 9/2006.

5. Sizer quoted in Walter Karp, "Why Johnny Can't Think," *Harper's*, 6/1985, 73.

6. Reba Page, "The Lower-Track Students' View of Curriculum," (Washington, D.C.: American Education Research Association, 1987).

7. Woodrow Wilson quoted in Lewis H. Lapham, "Notebook," *Harper's*, 7/1991, 10.

8. Survey data from about 1979 reported in Sidney Verba and Gary Orren, *Equality in America* (Cambridge: Harvard University Press, 1985), 72–75.

9. Linda McNeil, "Defensive Teaching and Classroom Control," in Michael W. Apple and Lois Weis, eds., *Ideology and Practice in Schooling* (Philadelphia: Temple University Press, 1983), 116.

Reading as a Writer

1. List what you think are Loewen's main points. What appeals does he seem to draw on most when he makes those points: appeals based on his own character (ethos), on the emotions of his reader (pathos), or on the reasonableness of his evidence (logos)? Are the appeals obvious or difficult to tease out? Does he combine them? Discuss your answers with your classmates.

2. Identify what you think is the main claim of Loewen's argument, and choose key examples to support your answer. Compare your chosen claim and examples to those chosen by your classmates. Do they differ significantly? Can you agree on Loewen's gist and his key examples?

3. As a class, test the claims Loewen makes by thinking about your own experiences in high school history classes. Do you remember finding out that something you were taught from an American history textbook was not true? Did you discover on your own what you considered to be misrepresentations in or important omissions from your textbook? If so, did these misrepresentations or omissions tend to support or contradict the claims about history textbooks that Loewen makes?

APPEALING TO ETHOS

Although we like to believe that our decisions and beliefs are based on reason and logic, in fact they are often based on what amounts to character judgments. That is, if a person you trust makes a reasonable argument for one choice, and a person you distrust makes a reasonable argument for another choice, you are more likely to be swayed by the argument of the person you trust. Similarly, the audience for your argument will be more disposed to agree with you if its members believe you are a fair, just person who is knowledgeable and has good judgment. Even the most well-developed argument will fall short if you do not leave this kind of impression on your readers. Thus, it is not surprising that ethos may be the most important component of your argument.

There are three strategies for evoking a sense of ethos:

1. Establish that you have good judgment.
2. Convey to readers that you are knowledgeable.
3. Show that you understand the complexity of the issue.

These strategies are interrelated: A writer who demonstrates good judgment is more often than not someone who is both knowledgeable about an issue and who acknowledges the complexity of it by weighing the strengths *and* weaknesses of different arguments. However, keep in mind that these characteristics do not exist apart from what readers think and believe.

■ Establish That You Have Good Judgment

Most readers of academic writing expect writers to demonstrate good judgment by identifying a problem that readers agree is worth addressing. In turn, good judgment gives writers credibility.

Loewen crafts his introduction to capture the attention of educators as well as concerned citizens when he claims that students leave high school unaware of class structure and as a consequence "have no understanding of the ways that opportunity is not equal in America and no notion that social structure pushes people around, influencing the ideas they hold and the lives they fashion" (para. 1). Loewen does not blame students, or even instructors, for this lack of awareness. Instead, he writes, "textbooks can take some of the credit for this state of affairs" (para. 2) because, among other shortcomings, they leave out important events in "labor history" and relegate issues facing labor to the past.

Whether an educator—or a general reader for that matter—will ultimately agree with Loewen's case is, at this point, up for grabs, but certainly the possibility that high schools in general, and history textbooks in particular, are failing students by leaving them vulnerable to class-based manipulation would be recognized as a problem by readers who believe America should be a society that offers equal opportunity for all. At this point, Loewen's readers are likely to agree that the problem of omission he identifies may be significant if its consequences are as serious as he believes them to be.

Writers also establish good judgment by conveying to readers that they are fair-minded and just and have the best interests of readers in mind. Loewen is particularly concerned that students understand the persistence of poverty and inequality in the United States and the historical circumstances of the poor, which they cannot do unless textbook writers take a more inclusive approach to addressing labor history, especially "the growth of multinational corporations and their exporting of jobs overseas" (para. 2). It's not fair to deny this important information to students, and it's not fair to the poor to leave them out of official histories of the United

States. Loewen further demonstrates that he is fair and just when he calls attention in paragraph 6 to the inequality between rich and poor children in schools, a problem that persists despite our forebears' belief that class would not determine the fate of citizens of the United States.

■ Convey to Readers That You Are Knowledgeable

Being thoughtful about a subject goes hand in hand with being knowledgeable about the subject. Loewen demonstrates his knowledge of class issues and their absence from textbooks in a number of ways (not the least of which is his awareness that a problem exists—many people, including educators, may not be aware of this problem).

In paragraph 3, Loewen makes a bold claim: "*Nothing* that textbooks discuss—not even strikes—is ever anchored in any analysis of social class." As readers, we cannot help wondering: How does the author know this? How will he support this claim? Loewen anticipates these questions by demonstrating that he has studied the subject through a systematic examination of American history textbooks. He observes that half of the eighteen textbooks he examined "contain no index listing at all for *social class, social stratification, class structure, income distribution, inequality,* or any conceivably related topic" and that "not one book lists *upper class* or *lower class.*" Loewen also demonstrates his grasp of class issues in American history, from the "violent class conflicts" that "took place in and just after colonial times" (para. 4), which contradict textbook writers' assertions that class conflicts did not exist during this period, to the more recent conflicts in the 1980s and early 1990s (paras. 2 and 4).

Moreover, Loewen backs up his own study of textbooks with references to a number of studies from the social sciences to illustrate that "social class is probably the single most important variable in society" (para. 6). Witness the statistics and findings he cites in paragraphs 6 through 10. The breadth of Loewen's historical knowledge and the range of his reading should convince readers that he is knowledgeable, and his trenchant analysis contributes to the authority he brings to the issue and to his credibility.

■ Show That You Understand the Complexity of a Given Issue

Recognizing the complexity of an issue helps readers see the extent to which authors know that any issue can be understood in a number of different ways. Loewen acknowledges that most of the history he recounts is not "news" (para. 11) to his educated readers, who by implication "know" and "understand" his references to historical events and trends. What may be news to his readers, he explains, is the extent to which class structure in the United States has changed over time. With the steady erosion of middle-class households since 1967, "class inequalities" and "barriers . . . to social mobility" (para. 5) are limiting more and more Americans' access to even the most fundamental of opportunities in a democratic society—health care and education.

Still, even though Loewen has introduced new thinking about the nature of class in the United States and has demonstrated a provocative play of mind by examining an overlooked body of data (high school history textbooks) that may influence the way class is perceived in America, there are still levels of complexity he hasn't addressed explicitly. Most important, perhaps, is the question of why history textbooks continue to ignore issues of class when there is so much research that indicates its importance in shaping the events history textbooks purport to explain.

Steps to Appealing to Ethos

1 **Establish that you have good judgment.** Identify an issue your readers will agree is worth addressing, and demonstrate that you are fair-minded and have the best interests of your readers in mind when you address it.

2 **Convey to readers that you are knowledgeable.** Support your claims with credible evidence that shows you have read widely on, thought about, and understand the issue.

3 **Show that you understand the complexity of the issue.** Demonstrate that you understand the variety of viewpoints your readers may bring—or may not be able to bring—to the issue.

APPEALING TO PATHOS

An appeal to pathos recognizes that people are moved to action by their emotions as well as by reasonable arguments. In fact, pathos is a vital part of argument that can predispose readers one way or another. Do you want to arouse readers' sympathy? Anger? Passion? You can do that by knowing what readers value.

Appeals to pathos are typically indirect. You can appeal to pathos by using examples or illustrations that you believe will arouse the appropriate emotions and by presenting them using an appropriate tone.

To acknowledge that writers play on readers' emotions is not to endorse manipulative writing. Rather, it is to acknowledge that effective writers use all available means of persuasion to move readers to agree with them. After all, if your thoughtful reading and careful research have led you to believe that you must weigh in with a useful insight on an important issue, it stands to reason that you would want your argument to convince your readers to believe as strongly in what you assert as you do.

For example, if you genuinely believe that the conditions some families are living in are abysmal and unfair, you want your readers to believe it too. And an effective way to persuade them to believe as you do, in addition to convincing them of the reasonableness of your argument and of your own good character and judgment, is to establish a kind of emotional common ground in your writing—the common ground of pathos.

■ Show That You Know What Your Readers Value

Let's consider some of the ways James Loewen signals that he knows what his readers value.

In the first place, Loewen assumes that readers feel the same way he does: Educated people should know that the United States has a class structure despite the democratic principles that the nation was founded on. He also expects readers to identify with his unwillingness to accept the injustice that results from that class structure. He believes that women living in poverty should have access to appropriate health care, that children living in poverty should have a chance to attend college, and that certain classes of people should not be written off to, as Woodrow Wilson recommended, "perform specific difficult manual tasks" (para. 7).

Time and again, Loewen cites examples that reveal that the poor are discriminated against by the class structure in the United States not for lack of ability, lack of desire, lack of ambition, or lack of morality, but for no better reason than lack of money—and that such discrimination has been going on for a long time. He expects that his readers also will find such discrimination an unacceptable affront to their values of fair play and democracy and that they will experience the same sense of outrage that he does.

■ Use Illustrations and Examples That Appeal to Readers' Emotions

You can appeal to readers' emotions indirectly through the illustrations and examples you use to support your argument.

For instance, in paragraph 2, Loewen contends that textbook writers share responsibility for high school students' not knowing about the continued relevance of class issues in American life. Loewen's readers—parents, educators, historians—may very well be angered by the omissions he points out. Certainly he would expect them to be angry when they read about the effects of economic class on the health care expectant mothers and then their children receive (para. 6) and on their children's access to quality education (paras. 6–8). In citing the fact that social class "correlates strongly with SAT scores" (para. 8) and so "predicts the rate of college attendance and the type of college chosen" (para. 9), Loewen forces his readers to acknowledge that the educational playing field is far from level.

Finally, he calls attention to the fact that accumulated wealth accounts for deep class divisions in our society—that the inability to save prevents the poor from hiring legal counsel, purchasing a home, or taking advantage of tax shelters. The result, Loewen observes, is that "educational inequality replicates itself in the next generation" (para. 9).

Together, these examples strengthen both Loewen's argument and what he hopes will be readers' outrage that history textbooks do not address class issues. Without that information, Americans cannot fully understand or act to change the existing class structure.

■ Consider How Your Tone May Affect Your Audience

The **tone** of your writing is your use of language that communicates your attitude toward yourself, your material, and your readers. Of course, your tone is important in everything you write, but it is particularly crucial when you are appealing to pathos.

When you are appealing to your readers' emotions, it is tempting to use loaded, exaggerated, and even intemperate language to convey how you feel (and hope your readers will feel) about an issue. Consider these sentences: "The Republican Party has devised the most ignominious means of filling the pockets of corporations." "These wretched children suffer heartrending agonies that can barely be imagined, much less described." "The ethereal beauty of the Brandenburg concertos thrill one to the deepest core of one's being." All of these sentences express strong and probably sincere beliefs and emotions, but some readers might find them overwrought and coercive and question the writer's reasonableness.

Similarly, some writers rely on irony or sarcasm to set the tone of their work. **Irony** is the use of language to say one thing while meaning quite another. **Sarcasm** is the use of heavy-handed irony to ridicule or attack someone or something. Although irony and sarcasm can make for vivid and entertaining writing, they also can backfire and end up alienating readers. The sentence "Liberals will be pleased to hear that the new budget will be making liberal use of their hard-earned dollars" may entertain some readers with its irony and wordplay, but others may assume that the writer's attitude toward liberals is likely to result in an unfairly slanted argument. And the sentence "In my opinion, there's no reason why Christians and Muslims shouldn't rejoice together over the common ground of their both being deluded about the existence of a God" may please some readers, but it risks alienating those who are uncomfortable with breezy comments about religious beliefs. Again, think of your readers and what they value, and weigh the benefits of a clever sentence against its potential to detract from your argument or offend your audience.

You often find colorful wording and irony in op-ed and opinion pieces, where a writer may not have the space to build a compelling argument using evidence and has to resort to shortcuts to readers' emotions. However, in academic writing, where the careful accumulation and presentation of evidence and telling examples are highly valued, the frequent use of loaded language, exaggeration, and sarcasm is looked on with distrust.

Consider Loewen's excerpt. Although his outrage comes through clearly, he never resorts to hectoring. For example, in paragraph 1, he writes that students are "ignorant of the workings of the class structure" and that their opinions are "half-formed and naïve." But he does not imply that students are ignoramuses or that their opinions are foolish. What they lack, he contends, is understanding. They need to be taught something about class structure that they are not now being taught. And paragraph 1 is about as close to name-calling as Loewen comes. Even textbook writers, who are the target of his anger, are not vilified.

Loewen does occasionally make use of irony, for example in paragraph 4, where he points out inconsistencies and omissions in textbooks: "Never mind that the most violent class conflicts in American history— Bacon's Rebellion and Shays's Rebellion—took place in and just after colonial times. Textbooks still say that colonial society was relatively classless and marked by upward mobility. And things have only gotten rosier since." But he doesn't resort to ridicule. Instead, he relies on examples and illustrations to connect with his readers' sense of values and appeal to their emotions.

Steps to Appealing to Pathos

1 **Show that you know what your readers value.** Start from your own values and imagine what assumptions and principles would appeal to your readers. What common ground can you imagine between your values and theirs? How will it need to be adjusted for different kinds of readers?

2 **Use illustrations and examples that appeal to readers' emotions.** Again, start from your own emotional position. What examples and illustrations resonate most with you? How can you present them to have the most emotional impact on your readers? How would you adjust them for different kinds of readers?

3 **Consider how your tone may affect your audience.** Be wary of using loaded, exaggerated, and intemperate language that may put off your readers; and be careful in your use of irony and sarcasm.

A Practice Sequence: Appealing to Ethos and Pathos

Discuss the language and strategies the writers use in the following passages to connect with their audience, in particular their appeals to both ethos and pathos. After reading each excerpt, discuss who you think the implied audience is and whether you think the strategies the writers use to connect with their readers are effective or not.

1   Almost a half century after the U.S. Supreme Court concluded that Southern school segregation was unconstitutional and "inherently unequal," new statistics from the 1998–99 school year show that segregation continued to intensify throughout the 1990s, a period in which there were three major Supreme Court decisions authorizing a return to segregated neighborhood schools and limiting the reach and duration of desegregation orders. For African American students, this trend is particularly apparent in the South, where most blacks live and where the 2000 Census shows a continuing return from the North. From 1988 to 1998, most of the progress of the previous two decades in increasing integration in the region was lost. The South is still much more integrated than it was before the civil rights revolution, but it is moving backward at an accelerating rate.

—Gary Orfield, "Schools More Separate:
Consequences of a Decade of Resegregation"

2   When the judgment day comes for every high school student—that day when a final transcript is issued and sent to the finest institutions, with every sin of class selection written as with a burning chisel on stone—on that day a great cry will go up throughout the land, and there will be weeping, wailing, gnashing of teeth, and considerable grumbling against guidance counselors, and the cry of a certain senior might be, "WHY did no one tell me that Introduction to Social Poker wasn't a solid academic class?" At another, perhaps less wealthy school, a frustrated and under-nurtured sculptress will wonder, "Why can't I read, and why don't I care?" The reason for both of these oversights, as they may eventually discover, is that the idea of the elective course has been seriously mauled, mistreated, and abused under the current middle-class high school system. A significant amount of the blame for producing students who are stunted, both cognitively and morally, can be traced back to this pervasive fact. Elective courses, as shoddily planned and poorly funded as they may be, constitute the only formation that many students get in their own special types of intelligences. Following the model of Howard Gardner, these may

be spatial, musical, or something else. A lack of stimulation to a student's own intelligence directly causes a lack of identification with the intelligence of others. Instead of becoming moderately interested in a subject by noticing the pleasure other people receive from it, the student will be bitter, jealous, and without empathy. These are the common ingredients in many types of tragedy, violent or benign. Schools must take responsibility for speaking in some way to each of the general types of intelligences. Failure to do so will result in students who lack skills, and also the inspiration to comfort, admire, emulate, and aid their fellow humans.

"All tasks that really call upon the power of attention are interesting for the same reason and to an almost equal degree," wrote Simone Weil in her *Reflections on Love and Faith*, her editor having defined attention as "a suspension of one's own self as a center of the world and making oneself available to the reality of another being." In Parker Palmer's *The Courage to Teach*, modern scientific theorist David Bohm describes "a holistic underlying implicate order whose information unfolds into the explicate order of particular fields." Rilke's euphemism for this "holistic . . . implicate order," which Palmer borrows, is "the grace of great things." Weil's term would be "God." However, both agree that eventual perception of this singular grace, or God, is accessible through education of a specific sort, and for both it is doubtless the most necessary experience of a lifetime. Realizing that this contention is raining down from different theorists, and keeping in mind that the most necessary experience of a lifetime should not be wholly irrelevant to the school system, educators should therefore reach the conclusion that this is a matter worth looking into. I assert that the most fruitful and practical results of their attention will be a wider range of electives coupled with a new acknowledgment and handling of them, one that treats each one seriously.

—Erin Meyers,
"The Educational Smorgasbord as Saving Grace"

APPEALING TO LOGOS: USING REASON AND EVIDENCE TO FIT THE SITUATION

To make an argument persuasive, you need to be in dialogue with your readers, using your own character (ethos) to demonstrate that you are a reasonable, credible, and fair person and to appeal to your readers' emotions (pathos), particularly their sense of right and wrong. Both types of appeal go hand in hand with appeals to logos, using converging pieces of evidence—statistics, facts, observations—to advance your claim. Remember that the type of evidence you use is determined by the issue, problem, situation, and readers' expectations. As an author, you should try to anticipate and address readers' beliefs and values. Ethos and pathos are concerned with the content of your argument; logos addresses both form and content.

An argument begins with one or more premises and ends with a conclusion. A **premise** is an assumption that you expect your readers to agree with, a statement that is either true or false—for example, "Alaska is cold in the winter"—that is offered in support of a claim. That claim is the **conclusion** you want your readers to draw from your premises. The conclusion is also a sentence that is either true or false.

For instance, Loewen's major premise is that class is a key factor in Americans' access to health care, education, and wealth. Loewen also offers a second, more specific premise: that textbook writers provide little discussion of the ways class matters. Loewen crafts his argument to help readers draw the following conclusion: "We live in a class system that runs counter to the democratic principles that underlie the founding of the United States, and history textbooks must tell this story. Without this knowledge, citizens will be uninformed."

Whether readers accept this as true depends on how Loewen moves from his initial premises to reach his conclusion—that is, whether we draw the same kinds of inferences, or reasoned judgments, that he does. He must do so in a way that meets readers' expectations of what constitutes relevant and persuasive evidence and guides them one step at a time toward his conclusion.

There are two main forms of argument: deductive and inductive. A **deductive argument** is an argument in which the premises support (or appear to support) the conclusion. If you join two premises to produce a conclusion that is taken to be true, you are stating a **syllogism.** This is the classic example of deductive reasoning through a syllogism:

1. All men are mortal. (First premise)
2. Socrates is a man. (Second premise)
3. Therefore, Socrates is mortal. (Conclusion)

In a deductive argument, it is impossible for both premises to be true and the conclusion to be false. That is, the truth of the premises means that the conclusion must also be true.

By contrast, an **inductive argument** relies on evidence and observation to reach a conclusion. Although readers may accept a writer's premises as true, it is possible for them to reject the writer's conclusion.

Let's consider this for a moment in the context of Loewen's argument. Loewen introduces the premise that class matters, then offers the more specific premise that textbook writers leave class issues out of their narratives of American history, and finally draws the conclusion that citizens need to be informed of this body of knowledge in order to create change:

1. Although class is a key factor in Americans' access to health care, education, and wealth, students know very little about the social structure in the United States.

2. In their textbooks, textbook writers do not address the issue of class, an issue that people need to know about.

3. Therefore, if people had this knowledge, they would understand that poverty cannot be blamed on the poor.

Notice that Loewen's premises are not necessarily true. For example, readers could challenge the premise that "textbook writers do not address issues of class." After all, Loewen examined just eighteen textbooks. What if he had examined a different set of textbooks? Would he have drawn the same conclusion? And even if Loewen's evidence convinces us that the two premises are true, we do not have to accept that the conclusion is true.

The conclusion in an inductive argument is never definitive. That is the nature of any argument that deals with human emotions and actions. Moreover, we have seen throughout history that people tend to disagree much more on the terms of an argument than on its form. Do we agree that Israel's leaders practice apartheid? (What do we mean by *apartheid* in this case?) Do we agree with the need to grant women reproductive rights? (When does life begin?) Do we agree that all people should be treated equally? (Would equality mean equal access to resources or to outcomes?)

Deductive arguments are conclusive. In a deductive argument, the premises are universal truths—laws of nature, if you will—and the conclusion must follow from those premises. That is, a^2 plus b^2 always equals c^2, and humans are always mortal.

By contrast, an inductive argument is never conclusive. The premises may or may not be true; and even if they are true, the conclusion may be false. We might accept that class matters and that high school history textbooks don't address the issue of class structure in the United States; but we still would not know that students who have studied social stratification in America will necessarily understand the nature of poverty. It may be that social class is only one reason for poverty; or it may be that textbooks are only one source of information about social stratification in the United States, that textbook omissions are simply not as serious as Loewen claims. That the premises of an argument are true establishes only that the conclusion is probably true and, perhaps, true only for some readers.

Inductive argument is the basis of academic writing; it is also the basis of any appeal to logos. The process of constructing an inductive argument involves three steps:

1. State the premises of your argument.
2. Use credible evidence to show readers that your argument has merit.
3. Demonstrate that the conclusion follows from the premises.

In following these three steps, you will want to determine the truth of your premises, help readers understand whether or not the inferences you draw are justified, and use word signals to help readers fully grasp the connections between your premises and your conclusion.

■ State the Premises of Your Argument

Stating a premise establishes what you have found to be true and what you want to persuade readers to accept as truth as well. Let's return to Loewen, who asserts his premise at the very outset of the excerpt: "Middle-class students . . . know little about how the American class structure works . . . and nothing at all about how it has changed over time." Loewen elaborates on this initial premise a few sentences later, arguing that students "have no understanding of the ways that opportunity is not equal in America and no notion that the social structure pushes people around, influencing the ideas they hold and the lives they fashion."

Implicit here is the point that class matters. Loewen makes this point explicit several paragraphs later, where he states that "social class is probably the single most important variable in society" (para. 6). He states his second, more specific premise in paragraph 2: "High school history textbooks can take some of the credit for this state of affairs." The burden of demonstrating that these premises are true is on Loewen. If readers find that either of the premises is not true, it will be difficult, if not impossible, for them to accept his conclusion that with more knowledge, people will understand that poverty is not the fault of the poor (para. 10).

■ Use Credible Evidence

The validity of your argument depends on whether the inferences you draw are justified, and whether you can expect a reasonable person to draw the same conclusion from those premises. Loewen has to demonstrate throughout (1) that students do not have much, if any, knowledge about the class structure that exists in the United States and (2) that textbook writers are in large part to blame for this lack of knowledge. He also must help readers understand how this lack of knowledge contributes to (3) his conclusion that greater knowledge would lead Americans to understand that poor people are not responsible for poverty. He can help readers with the order in which he states his premises and by choosing the type and amount of evidence that will enable readers to draw the inferences that he does.

Interestingly, Loewen seems to assume that one group of readers—educators—will accept his first premise as true. He does not elaborate on what students know or do not know. Instead, he moves right to his second premise, which involves first acknowledging what high school history textbooks typically cover, then identifying what he believes are the important events that textbook writers exclude, and ultimately asserting that textbook discussions of events in labor history are never "anchored in any analysis of social class" (para. 3). He supports this point with his own study of eighteen textbooks (paras. 3–5) before returning to his premise that "social class is probably the single most important variable in society" (para. 6). What follows is a series of observations about the rich and references to researchers' findings on inequality (paras. 7–9). Finally, he asserts that "social class determines how people think about social class" (para. 10), implying that fuller knowledge would lead business leaders and conservative voters to think differently about the source of poverty. The question to explore is whether or not Loewen supports this conclusion.

■ Demonstrate That the Conclusion Follows from the Premises

Authors signal their conclusion with words like *consequently*, *finally*, *in sum*, *in the end*, *subsequently*, *therefore*, *thus*, *ultimately*, and *as a result*. Here is how this looks in the structure of Loewen's argument:

1. Although class is a key factor in Americans' access to health care, education, and wealth, students know very little about the social structure in the United States.

2. In their textbooks, textbook writers do not address the issue of class, an issue that people need to know about.

3. Ultimately, if people had this knowledge, they would understand that poverty cannot be blamed on the poor.

We've reprinted much of paragraph 9 of Loewen's excerpt below. Notice how Loewen pulls together what he has been discussing. He again underscores the importance of class and achievement ("All these are among the reasons"). And he points out that access to certain types of colleges puts people in a position to accumulate and sustain wealth. Of course, this is not true of the poor "because affluent families can save some money while poor families must spend what they make." This causal relationship ("Because") heightens readers' awareness of the class structure that exists in the United States.

> All these are among the reasons that social class predicts the rate of college attendance and the type of college chosen more effectively than does any other factor, including intellectual ability, however measured. After college,

most affluent children get white-collar jobs, most working-class children get blue-collar jobs, and the class differences continue. As adults, rich people are more likely to have hired an attorney and to be a member of formal organizations that increase their civic power. Poor people are more likely to watch TV. <u>Because</u> affluent families can save some money while poor families must spend what they make, wealth differences are ten times larger than income differences. <u>Therefore</u> most poor and working-class families cannot accumulate the down payment required to buy a house, which in turn shuts them out from our most important tax shelter, the write-off of home mortgage interest. Working-class parents cannot afford to live in elite subdivisions or hire high-quality day care, so the process of educational inequality replicates itself in the next generation. <u>Finally</u>, affluent Americans also have longer life expectancies than lower- and working-class people, the largest single cause of which is better access to health care. . . .

Once Loewen establishes this causal relationship, he concludes ("Therefore," "Finally") with the argument that poverty persists from one generation to the next.

In paragraph 10, Loewen uses the transition word *ultimately* to make the point that social class matters, so much so that it limits the ways in which people see the world, that it even "determines how people think about social class." (We discuss how to write conclusions in Chapter 11.)

Steps to Appealing to Logos

1 **State the premises of your argument.** Establish what you have found to be true and what you want readers to accept as well.

2 **Use credible evidence.** Lead your readers from one premise to the next, making sure your evidence is sufficient and convincing and your inferences are logical and correct.

3 **Demonstrate that the conclusion follows from the premises.** In particular, use the right words to signal to your readers how the evidence and inferences lead to your conclusion.

RECOGNIZING LOGICAL FALLACIES

We turn now to **logical fallacies**, flaws in the chain of reasoning that lead to a conclusion that does not necessarily follow from the premises, or evidence. Logical fallacies are common in inductive arguments for two reasons: Inductive arguments rely on reasoning about probability, not certainty; and they derive from human beliefs and values, not facts or laws of nature.

Here we list fifteen logical fallacies. In examining them, think about how to guard against the sometimes-faulty logic behind statements you might hear from politicians, advertisers, and the like. That should help you examine the premises on which you base your own assumptions and the logic you use to help readers reach the same conclusions you do.

1. *Erroneous Appeal to Authority.* An authority is someone with expertise in a given subject. An *erroneous authority* is an author who claims to be an authority but is not, or someone an author cites as an authority who is not. In this type of fallacy, the claim might be true, but the fact that an unqualified person is making the claim means there is no reason for readers to accept the claim as true.

Because the issue here is the legitimacy of authority, your concern should be to prove to yourself and your readers that you or the people you are citing have expertise in the subject. An awareness of this type of fallacy has become increasingly important as celebrities offer support for candidates running for office or act as spokespeople for curbing global warming or some other cause. The candidate may be the best person for the office, and there may be very good reasons to control global warming; but we need to question the legitimacy of a nonexpert endorsement.

2. *Ad Hominem.* An ad hominem argument focuses on the person making a claim instead of on the claim itself. (*Ad hominem* is Latin for "to the person.") In most cases, an ad hominem argument does not have a bearing on the truth or the quality of a claim.

Keep in mind that it is always important to address the claim or the reasoning behind it, rather than the person making the claim. "Of course Senator Wiley supports oil drilling in Alaska—he's in the pocket of the oil companies!" is an example of an ad hominem argument. Senator Wiley may have good reasons for supporting oil drilling in Alaska that have nothing to do with his alleged attachment to the oil industry. However, if an individual's character is relevant to the argument, then an ad hominem argument can be valid. If Senator Wiley has been found guilty of accepting bribes from an oil company, it makes sense to question both his credibility and his claims.

3. *Shifting the Issue.* This type of fallacy occurs when an author draws attention away from the issue instead of offering evidence that will enable people to draw their own conclusions about the soundness of an argument. Consider this example:

> Affirmative action proponents accuse me of opposing equal opportunity in the workforce. I think my positions on military expenditures, education, and public health speak for themselves.

The author of this statement does not provide a chain of reasoning that would enable readers to judge his or her stance on the issue of affirmative action.

4. *Either/Or Fallacy.* At times, an author will take two extreme positions to force readers to make a choice between two seemingly contradictory positions. For example:

> Either you support the war, or you are against it.

Although the author has set up an either/or condition, in reality one position does not exclude the other. People can support the troops involved in a war, for example, even if they don't support the reasons for starting the war.

5. *Sweeping Generalizations.* When an author attempts to draw a conclusion without providing sufficient evidence to support the conclusion or examining possible counterarguments, he or she may be making sweeping generalizations. Consider this example:

> Despite the women's movement in the 1960s and 1970s, women still do not receive equal pay for equal work. Obviously, any attempt to change the status quo for women is doomed to failure.

As is the case with many fallacies, the author's position may be reasonable, but we cannot accept the argument at face value. Reading critically entails testing assumptions like this one—that any attempt to create change is doomed to failure because women do not receive equal pay for equal work. We could ask, for example, whether inequities persist in the public sector. And we could point to other areas where the women's movement has had measurable success. Title IX, for example, has reduced the dropout rate among teenage girls; it has also increased the rate at which women earn college and graduate degrees.

6. *Bandwagon.* When an author urges readers to accept an idea because a significant number of people support it, he or she is making a bandwagon argument. This is a fairly common mode of argument in advertising; for example, a commercial might attempt to persuade us to buy a certain product because it's popular.

> Because Harvard, Stanford, and Berkeley have all added a multicultural component to their graduation requirements, other institutions should do so as well.

The growing popularity of an idea is not sufficient reason to accept that it is valid.

7. *Begging the Question.* This fallacy entails advancing a circular argument that asks readers to accept a premise that is also the conclusion readers are expected to draw:

> We could improve the undergraduate experience with coed dorms because both men and women benefit from living with members of the opposite gender.

Here readers are being asked to accept that the conclusion is true despite the fact that the premises—men benefit from living with women, and women benefit from living with men—are essentially the same as the conclusion. Without evidence that a shift in dorm policy could improve on the undergraduate experience, we cannot accept the conclusion as true. Indeed, the conclusion does not necessarily follow from the premise.

8. *False Analogy.* Authors (and others) often try to persuade us that something is true by using a comparison. This approach is not in and of itself a problem, as long as the comparison is reasonable. For example:

> It is ridiculous to have a Gay and Lesbian Program and a Department of African American Culture. We don't have a Straight Studies Program or a Department of Caucasian Culture.

Here the author is urging readers to rethink the need for two academic departments by saying that the school doesn't have two other departments. That, of course, is not a reason for or against the new departments. What's needed is an analysis that compares the costs (economic and otherwise) of starting up and operating the new departments versus the contributions (economic and otherwise) of the new departments.

9. *Technical Jargon.* If you've ever had a salesperson try to persuade you to purchase a television or an entertainment system with capabilities you absolutely *must* have—even if you didn't understand a word the salesperson was saying about alternating currents and circuit splicers—then you're familiar with this type of fallacy. We found this passage in a student's paper:

> You should use this drug because it has been clinically proven that it inhibits the reuptake of serotonin and enhances the dopamine levels of the body's neurotransmitters.

The student's argument may very well be true, but he hasn't presented any substantive evidence to demonstrate that the premises are true and that the conclusion follows from the premises.

10. *Confusing Cause and Effect.* It is challenging to establish that one factor causes another. For example, how can we know for certain that economic class predicts, or is a factor in, academic achievement? How do we know that a new president's policies are the cause of a country's economic well-being? Authors often assume cause and effect when two factors are simply associated with each other:

> The current recession came right after the president was elected.

This fallacy states a fact, but it does not prove that the president's election caused the recession.

11. *Appeal to Fear.* One type of logical fallacy makes an appeal to readers' irrational fears and prejudices, preventing them from dealing squarely with a given issue and often confusing cause and effect:

> We should use whatever means possible to avoid further attack.

The reasoning here is something like this: "If we are soft on defense, we will never end the threat of terrorism." But we need to consider whether there is indeed a threat, and, if so, whether the presence of a threat should lead to action, and, if so, whether that action should include "whatever means possible." (Think of companies that sell alarm systems by pointing to people's vulnerability to harm and property damage.)

12. *Fallacy of Division.* A fallacy of division suggests that what is true of the whole must also be true of its parts:

> Conservatives have always voted against raising the minimum wage, against stem cell research, and for defense spending. Therefore, we can assume that conservative Senator Harrison will vote this way.

The author is urging readers to accept the premise without providing evidence of how the senator has actually voted on the three issues.

13. *Hasty Generalization.* This fallacy is committed when a person draws a conclusion about a group based on a sample that is too small to be representative. Consider this statement:

> Seventy-five percent of the seniors surveyed at the university study just 10 hours a week. We can conclude, then, that students at the university are not studying enough.

What you need to know is how many students were actually surveyed. Seventy-five percent may seem high, but not if the researcher surveyed just 400 of the 2,400 graduating seniors. This sample of students from a total population of 9,600 students at the university is too small to draw the conclusion that students in general are not studying enough.

14. *The Straw Man Argument.* A straw man fallacy makes a generalization about a group's believes without actually citing a specific writer or work:

> Democrats are more interested in running away than in trying to win the war on terrorism.

Here the fallacy is that the author simply ignores someone's actual position and substitutes a distorted, exaggerated, or misrepresented version of that position. This kind of fallacy often goes hand in hand with assuming that what is true of the group is true of the individual, what we call the fallacy of division.

15. *Fallacy of the Middle Ground.* The fallacy of the middle ground assumes that the middle position between two extreme positions must be correct. Although the middle ground may be true, the author must justify this position with evidence.

> E. D. Hirsch argues that cultural literacy is the only sure way to increase test scores, and Jonathan Kozol believes schools will improve only if state legislators increase funding; but I would argue that school reform will occur if we change the curriculum and provide more funding.

This fallacy draws its power from the fact that a moderate or middle position is often the correct one. Again, however, the claim that the moderate or middle position is correct must be supported by legitimate reasoning.

ANALYZING THE APPEALS IN A RESEARCHED ARGUMENT

Now that you have studied the variety of appeals you can make to connect with your audience, we would like you to read an article on urban health problems by Meredith Minkler and analyze her strategies for appealing to her readers. The article is long and carefully argued, so we suggest you take detailed notes about her use of appeals to ethos, pathos, and logos as you read. You may want to refer to the Practice Sequence questions on page 286 to help focus your reading. Ideally, you should work through the text with your classmates, in groups of three or four, appointing one student to record and share each group's analysis of Minkler's argument.

MEREDITH MINKLER

Community-Based Research Partnerships: Challenges and Opportunities

Meredith Minkler is a professor of health and social behavior at the School of Public Health, University of California, Berkeley. She is an activist and researcher whose work explores community partnerships, community organizing, and community-based participatory research. With more than one hundred books and articles to her credit, she is coeditor of the influential *Community Based Participatory Research for Health* (2003). The following article appeared in *The Journal of Urban Health* in 2005.

■ ■ ■

Abstract
The complexity of many urban health problems often makes them ill suited to traditional research approaches and interventions. The resultant frustration, together with community calls for genuine partnership in the research process, has highlighted the importance of an alternative paradigm. Community-based participatory research (CBPR) is presented as a promising collaborative approach that combines systematic inquiry, participation, and action to address urban health problems. Following a brief review of its basic tenets and

historical roots, key ways in which CBPR adds value to urban health research are introduced and illustrated. Case study examples from diverse international settings are used to illustrate some of the difficult ethical challenges that may arise in the course of CBPR partnership approaches. The concepts of partnership synergy and cultural humility, together with protocols such as Green et al.'s guidelines for appraising CBPR projects, are highlighted as useful tools for urban health researchers seeking to apply this collaborative approach and to deal effectively with the difficult ethical challenges it can present.

Keywords
Community-based participatory research, Ethical issues in research, Participatory action research, Partnership, Urban health.

Introduction

The complexity of urban health problems has often made them poorly suited to traditional "outside expert"–driven research and intervention approaches.[1] Together with community demands for authentic partnerships in research that are locally relevant and "community based" rather than merely "community placed," this frustration has led to a burgeoning of interest in an alternative research paradigm.[1,2] Community-based participatory research (CBPR) is an overarching term that increasingly is used to encompass a variety of approaches to research that have as their centerpiece three interrelated elements: participation, research, and action.[3] As defined by Green et al.[4] for the Royal Society of Canada, CBPR may concisely be described as "systematic investigation with the participation of those affected by an issue for purposes of education and action or affecting social change." The approach further has been characterized as

> [A] collaborative process that equitably involves all partners in the research process and recognizes the unique strengths that each brings. CBPR begins with a research topic of importance to the community with the aim of combining knowledge and action for social change to improve community health and eliminate health disparities.[5,6]

This article briefly describes CBPR's roots and core principles and summarizes the value added by this approach to urban health research. Drawing on examples from a variety of urban health settings nationally and internationally, it discusses and illustrates several of the key challenges faced in applying this partnership approach to inquiry and action. The article concludes by suggesting that despite such challenges and the labor-intensive nature of this approach, CBPR offers an exceptional opportunity for partnering with communities in ways that can enhance both the quality of research and its potential for helping address some of our most intractable urban health problems.

Historical Roots and Core Principles

The roots of CBPR may be traced in part to the action research school developed by the social psychologist Kurt Lewin[7] in the 1940s, with its emphasis on the active involvement in the research of those affected by the problem being studied through a cyclical process of fact finding, action, and reflection. But CBPR is most deeply grounded in the more revolutionary approaches to research that emerged, often independently from one another, from work with oppressed communities in South America, Asia, and Africa in the 1970s.[3,8,9] Brazilian adult educator Paulo Freire[9] provided critical grounding for CBPR in his development of a dialogical method accenting co-learning and action based on critical reflection. Freire,[9] Fals-Borda,[10] and other developing countries' scholars developed their alternative approaches to inquiry as a direct counter to the often "colonizing" nature of research to which oppressed communities were subjected, with feminist and postcolonialist scholars adding further conceptual richness.[11,12]

Among the tenets of participatory action approaches to research outlined by McTaggart[13] are that it is a political process, involves lay people in theory-making, is committed to improving social practice by changing it, and establishes "self-critical communities." As Israel et al.[6] adds, other core principles are that CBPR "involves systems development and local community capacity development," is "a co-learning process" to which community members and outside researchers contribute equally, and "achieves a balance between research and action." CBPR reflects a profound belief in "partnership synergy." As described by Lasker et al.[14]:

> [T]he synergy that partners seek to achieve through collaboration is more than a mere exchange of resources. By combining the individual perspectives, resources, and skills of the partners, the group creates something new and valuable together—something that is greater than the sum of its parts.

Moreover, CBPR embodies a deep commitment to what Tervalon and Murray-Garcia[15] have called cultural humility. As they point out, although we can never become truly competent in another's culture, we can demonstrate a "lifelong commitment to self evaluation and self-critique," to redress power imbalances and "develop and maintain mutually respectful and dynamic partnerships with communities."[15] Although the term *cultural humility* was coined primarily in reference to race and ethnicity, it also is of value in helping us understand and address the impacts of professional cultures (which tend to be highly influenced by white, western, patriarchal belief systems), as these help shape interactions between outside researchers and their community partners.[15]

3

4

5

CBPR is not a method per se but an orientation to research that may employ any of a number of qualitative and quantitative methodologies. As Cornwall and Jewkes[16] note, what is distinctive about CBPR is "the attitudes of researchers, which in turn determine how, by and for whom research is conceptualized and conducted [and] the corresponding location of power at every stage of the research process." The accent placed by CBPR on individual, organizational, and community empowerment also is a hallmark of this approach to research.

With the increasing emphasis on partnership approaches to improving urban health, CBPR is experiencing a rebirth of interest and unprecedented new opportunities for both scholarly recognition and financial support. In the United States, for example, the Institute of Medicine[17] recently named "community-based participatory research" as one of eight new areas in which all schools of public health should be offering training.

Although the renewed interest in CBPR provides a welcome contrast to more traditional top-down research approaches, it also increases the dangers of co-optation as this label is loosely applied to include research and intervention efforts in search of funding that do not truly meet the criteria for this approach. The sections below illustrate some of the value added to urban research when authentic partnership approaches are taken seriously and then briefly highlight some of the ethical challenges such work may entail.

The Value Added to Urban Health Research by a CBPR Approach

CBPR can enrich and improve the quality and outcomes of urban health research in a variety of ways. On the basis of the work of many scholars and institutions,[4,6,8,18] and as summarized by the National Institutes of Health (http://grants.nih.gov/grants/guide/pa-files/PAR-05-026.html), some of its primary contributions may be characterized and illustrated as follows.

CBPR Can Support the Development of Research Questions That Reflect Health Issues of Real Concern to Community Members

Ideally, CBPR begins with a research topic or question that comes from the local community, as when the nongovernmental organization (NGO) Alternatives for Community and Environment (ACE) in the low-income Roxbury section of Boston, reached out to Harvard University's School of Public Health and other potential partners to study and address the high rates of asthma in their neighborhood. Collaborative studies using air-monitoring and other approaches yielded data supporting the hypothesis that Roxbury was indeed a hot spot for pollution contributing to asthma. This in turn paved the way for a variety of policy and community education actions and outcomes.[19]

Although having a community partner such as ACE identify an issue and catalyze a research partnership may be the ideal, it is often the privileged outside researcher who initiates a CBPR project. In these instances too, however, a genuine commitment to high-level community involvement in issue selection, with NGOs and formal and informal community leaders engaged as equal partners, can help ensure that the research topic decided upon really is of major concern to the local population.   *11*

CBPR Can Improve Our Ability to Achieve Informed Consent, and to Address Issues of "Costs and Benefits" on the Community, and Not Simply the Individual Level[20]

With its accent on equitable community involvement in all stages of the research process,[6] CBPR often finds creative means of ensuring informed consent. The "One Hand, One Heart" study in urban and rural Tibet, which included a randomized controlled clinical trial of an indigenous medicine to prevent maternal hemorrhaging, actively involved local midwives and other community partners on the research team who played a key role in helping find locally translatable concepts to improve informed consent. Their help in early ethnographic work thus revealed that the concept of disclosing risk was highly problematic, because such disclosure was believed to disturb the wind element responsible for emotions, potentially leading to emotional upset and other adverse outcomes. By reframing risk disclosure as "safety issues," needed information could be conveyed in a far more culturally acceptable manner.[21]   *12*

CBPR also offers an important potential opening for extending the gaze of our ethical review processes such that we examine and address risks and benefits for the community. In Toronto, Travers and Flicker[20] have pioneered in developing such guidelines, pointing out the importance of having us ask such questions as "Will the methods used be sensitive and appropriate to various communities?" "What training or capacity building opportunities will you build in?" and "How will you balance scientific rigor and accessibility?" The strong philosophical fit between questions such as these and CBPR's commitments to equitable partnership and community capacity building reflect another source of value added to urban health research through this approach.   *13*

CBPR Can Improve Cultural Sensitivity and the Reliability and Validity of Measurement Tools through High-Quality Community Participation in Designing and Testing Study Instruments

Particularly in survey research, community advisory boards (CABs) and other partnership structures can improve measurement instruments by making sure that questions are worded in ways that will elicit valid and reliable responses. In a study of urban grandparents raising grandchildren due to the crack cocaine epidemic, the author and her colleagues used validated instruments, such as those for depressive symptomatology. However, they also learned from CAB members how to word other questions about sensitive topics. Rather than asking a standard (and disliked) question about income, for example, the CAB encouraged us to rephrase the question as "How much money is available to help you in raising this child?" When this alternate wording was used, a wealth of detailed income data was obtained, which improved our understanding of the challenges faced by this population.[22]

CBPR Can Uncover Lay Knowledge Critical to Enhancing Understanding of Sensitive Urban Health Problems

Through the cultural humility and partnership synergy involved in deeply valuing lay knowledge and working in partnership with community residents, CBPR can uncover hidden contributors to health and social problems. The high rates of HIV/AIDS in India and the often sensitive nature of this subject among young men led the Deepak Charitable Trust to develop a research committee for a study in the industrial area of Nandesari, in Gujarat, comprised of several male village health workers and other young men from the area. Working closely with a medical anthropologist, the research committee planned the research, including developing a sampling plan and the phrasing of culturally sensitive questions. Their insider knowledge helped reveal that AIDS itself was not perceived as a major problem by the young men in this area. Instead, men who were engaging in high-risk behaviors wanted to find sex partners at least partly to avoid "thinning of the semen" and sexual dysfunction and fatigue, which were believed to be long-term consequences of masturbation and nocturnal emissions. These fears appeared to be contributing to high rates of unprotected intercourse with sex workers at the area's many truck stops and with other sex partners.[23] This insider knowledge both strengthened the research and led to subsequent interventions to help dispel such misinformation.

By Increasing Community Trust and Ownership, CBPR Can Improve Recruitment and Retention Efforts

In a participatory epidemiology project on diabetes in an urban Aboriginal community in Melbourne, Australia, a marked increase in recruitment was experienced following the hiring of a community codi-rector and the changing of the project's name to one chosen by the local community.[24] Similarly, a 69 percent response rate achieved in a CBPR study of the health and working conditions of the largely immigrant hotel room cleaner population (many of them undocumented) in sev-eral of San Francisco's major tourist hotels was heavily attributed to the hiring and training of a core group of twenty-five room cleaners as key project staff. That high response rate, together with the high quality of data collected, made a substantial contribution when results later were presented and used to help negotiate a new contract.[25]

CBPR Can Help Increase Accuracy and Cultural Sensitivity in the Interpretation of Findings

Even highly engaged community members of the research team may   *17*
not wish to be involved in the labor-intensive data analysis phase of a research project,[26] nor do all methodological approaches lend them-selves to such involvement. Yet when applicable and desired, commu-nity involvement in data analysis can make real contributions to our understanding of the themes and findings that emerge. In a U.S. study of and with people with disabilities on the contentious topic of death with dignity legislation in their community, the author and an "insider/outsider" member of the research team met on alternate Saturdays with a subcommittee of the CAB to engage in joint data analysis. Using redacted transcripts, and applying lessons learned in qualitative data interpretation, the diverse CAB members came up with far richer codes and themes than outside researchers could have achieved alone.[27]

CBPR Can Increase the Relevance of Intervention Approaches and Thus the Likelihood of Success

One of the strengths of CBPR is its commitment to action as part of   *18*
the research process. But without strong community input, research-ers not infrequently design interventions that are ill suited to the local context in which they are applied. In the Gujarat case study mentioned above, partnership with local community members helped in the design of culturally relevant interventions, such as street theater performed by locally recruited youth at *melas* (or fairs), and the dissemination of study findings through the fifteen local credit and savings groups that often provided platforms for discussing reproductive health and related issues. Both these approaches provided critical means of information dissemination on this culturally and emotionally charged topic.[23]

Ethical and Other Challenges in Community-Based Participatory Research

Engaging in urban health research with diverse community partners   *19*
can indeed enrich both the quality and the outcomes of such studies.

At the same time, CBPR is fraught with ethical and related challenges, several of which are now highlighted.

"Community Driven" Issue Selection

A key feature of CBPR involves its commitment to ensuring that the research topic comes from the community. Yet many such projects "paradoxically . . . would not occur without the initiative of someone outside the community who has the time, skill, and commitment, and who almost inevitably is a member of a privileged and educated group."[28] In such instances, outside researchers must pay serious attention to community understandings of what the real issue or topic of concern is.

In South Africa, for example, high rates of cervical cancer in the Black and Colored populations led Mosavel et al.[29] to propose an investigation of this problem. In response to community feedback, however, they quickly broadened their initial topic to "cervical health," a concept which "acknowledged the fact that women's health in South Africa extends well beyond the risk of developing cervical cancer, and includes HIV-AIDS and STDs, sexual violence, and multiple other social problems." In other instances, the outside researcher as an initiator of a potential CBPR project needs to determine whether the topic he or she has identified really is of concern to the local community—and whether outsider involvement is welcome. The Oakland, California–based Grandmother Caregiver Study mentioned above grew out of the interests of my colleague and me in studying the strengths of as well as the health and social problems faced by the growing number of urban African American grandmothers who were raising grandchildren in the context of a major drug epidemic. As privileged white women, however, we had to determine first whether this was a topic of local concern and, if so, whether there might be a role for us in working with the community to help study and address it. We began by enlisting the support of an older African American colleague with deep ties in the community, who engaged with us in a frank discussion with two prominent African American NGOs. It was only after getting their strong support for proceeding that we wrote a grant, with funds for these organizations, which in turn helped us pull together an outstanding CAB that was actively involved in many stages of the project.[21,26]

We were lucky in this case that a topic we as outsiders identified turned out to represent a deep concern in the local community. Yet not infrequently "the community" is in fact deeply divided over an issue. Indeed, as Yoshihama and Carr[30] have argued, "communities are not places that researchers enter but are instead a set of negotiations that inherently entail multiple and often conflicting interests." In such situations, outside researchers can play a useful role in helping community partners think through who "the community" in fact is in relation to a proposed project and the pros and cons of undertaking the project to

20

21

22

begin with. The holding of town hall meetings and other forums may then be useful in helping achieve consensus on an issue that is truly of, by, and for the community, however it is defined.[26]

Insider–Outsider Tensions

Urban health researchers in many parts of the world have written poignantly about the power dynamics and other sources of insider–outsider tensions and misunderstandings in CBPR and related partnership efforts. Ugalde[31] points out how in Latin America participants may be exploited as cheap sources of labor or may become alienated from their communities because of their participation. In her work with Native American and other marginalized groups in New Mexico, Wallerstein[32] further illustrates how even outsiders who pride ourselves on being trusted community friends and allies often fail to appreciate the extent of the power that is embedded in our own, often multiple sources of privilege, and how it can affect both process and outcomes in such research.   *23*

One major source of insider–outsider tensions involves the differential reward structures for partners in CBPR. For although a major aim of such research is to benefit the local community, the outside researchers typically stand to gain the most from such collaborations, bringing in grants, getting new publications, and so forth. The common expectation that community partners will work for little or no pay and the fact that receipt of compensation may take months if the funds are coming through a ministry of health or a university are also sources of understandable resentment.[6,26]   *24*

To address these and other sources of insider–outsider tensions in work with indigenous communities in both urban and rural areas, researchers in New Zealand,[33] Australia,[34] the United States,[35] and Canada[36] have worked with their community partners to develop ethical guidelines for their collaborative work, including protocols that address   *25*

1. negotiating with political and spiritual leaders in the community to obtain their input and their approval for the proposed research,

2. ensuring equitable benefits to participants (e.g., appropriate training and hiring of community members) in return for their contributions and resources,

3. developing agreements about the ownership and publication of findings, and the early review of findings by key community leaders.

Although such protocols cannot begin to address all of the conflicts that may arise in CBPR, they can play a critical role in helping pave the way for the continued dialogue and negotiation that must be an integral part of the process.   *26*

Constraints on Community Involvement

Outside researchers committed to a CBPR approach not infrequently express frustration at the difficulty moving from the goal of heavy community partner involvement in the research process to the reality. As Diaz and Simmons[37] found in their Reproductive Health Project in Brazil, despite a strong commitment to involving the most marginalized and vulnerable classes (in this case, women who were users of the public sector services being studied), such individuals often "are least likely to be in a position to donate their time and energy." Further, and even when outside researchers are careful to provide child care and transportation, there are differential costs of participation by gender.[30]   27

Still another set of challenges may arise when community desires with respect to research design and methods clash with what outsider researchers consider to be "good science." In an oft-cited CBPR study with a local Mohawk community in Québec, Chataway[38] describes how community members at first strongly objected to the idea of using a questionnaire approach which they saw as "putting their thoughts in boxes." Through respectful listening on both sides, the value of such an approach was realized and a more qualitative methodology developed, through which community members would then be actively involved in helping analyze and interpret the quantitative findings that emerged. As such case studies illustrate, CBPR does not condone an abandonment of one's own scientific standards and knowledge base. But it does advocate a genuine co-learning process through which lay and professional ways of knowing both are valued and examined for what they can contribute.[26]   28

Dilemmas in the Sharing and Release of Findings

A crucial step in CBPR involves returning data to the community and enabling community leaders and participants to have an authentic role in deciding how that data will be used. As Travers and Flicker[20] suggest, ethical research review processes that ask questions such as "Are there built-in mechanisms for how unflattering results will be dealt with?" should be employed at the front end of our CBPR projects. In addition to the formal IRB process they propose, which offers a critical next step for the field, CBPR partners can look to a variety of formal or informal research protocols and particularly to the detailed guidelines for health promotion research developed by Green et al.,[4,39] which help partnerships decide in advance how potentially difficult issues concerning the sharing and release of findings and other matters will be handled.   29

Challenges in the Action Dimensions of CBPR

Numerous ethical challenges lastly may arise in relation to the critical action component of CBPR. In some instances, community partners   30 may wish to move quickly into action, whereas academic and other outside research partners may want to "put the [brakes] on" until findings have been published or other steps brought to fruition. In other cases, the nature of funding (e.g., from a government body) may constrain action on the policy level that is prohibited or discouraged by the funder. And in still other instances, including the Brazilian Reproductive Health Project[37] cited above, community members may not wish to be associated with a CBPR project that appears connected to a broader political agenda.

Participation in the action phase of CBPR projects may sometimes present risks to community participants, as when immigrant hotel room cleaners in the San Francisco study took part in a Labor Day sit-in and in some cases faced arrest.[25] And for both professionally trained researchers and their community partners, actions that involve challenging powerful corporate or other entrenched interests may have negative consequences for those involved. At the same time, CBPR's fundamental commitment to action and to redressing power imbalances makes this aspect of the work a particularly important contributor to urban health improvement through research.

Conclusion

Difficult ethical challenges may confront urban health researchers who engage in CBPR. Yet this approach can greatly enrich the quality of our research, helping ensure that we address issues of genuine community concern and use methods and approaches that are culturally sensitive and that improve the validity and reliability of our findings. Moreover, through its commitment to action as an integral part of the research process, CBPR can help in translating findings as we work with community partners to help address some of our most intractable urban health problems.

Acknowledgement

Many current and former community and academic partners have contributed to my understanding of the advantages and pitfalls of collaborative urban health research and I am deeply grateful. Particular thanks are extended to Nina Wallerstein, Kathleen M. Roe, Barbara Israel, Lawrence W. Green, and Ronald Labonte, who have greatly stimulated my own thinking and scholarship in this area. I am grateful to former students, Rima Shaw and Caroline Bell, as well as other individuals who have shared some of the cases drawn upon in this paper. My gratitude is extended to Claire Murphy for assistance with manuscript preparation.

References

1. Minkler M, Wallerstein N. Community Based Participatory Research for Health. San Francisco, CA: Jossey-Bass; 2003.

2. Green LW, Mercer SL. Can public health researchers and agencies reconcile the push from funding bodies and the pull from communities? *Am J Public Health.* 2001;91:1926–1929.

3. Hall BL. From margins to center: the development and purpose of participatory action research. *Am Sociol.* 1992;23:15–28.

4. Green LW, George A, Daniel M, et al. *Study of Participatory Research in Health Promotion.* Ottawa, Ontario: Royal Society of Canada; 1995.

5. Community Health Scholars Program. *The Community Health Scholars Program: Stories of Impact.* Ann Arbor, MI; 2002.

6. Israel BA, Schulz AJ, Parker EA, Becker AB. Review of community-based research: assessing partnership approaches to improve public health. *Annu Rev Public Health.* 1998;19:173–202.

7. Lewin K. Action research and minority problems. *J Soc Issues.* 1946;2:34–46.

8. Brown LD, Tandon R. Ideology and political economy in inquiry: action research and participatory research. *J Appl Behav Sci.* 1983;19:277–294.

9. Freire P. *Pedagogy of the Oppressed.* New York, NY: Seabury Press; 1970.

10. Fals-Borda O. The application of participatory action-research in Latin America. *Int Sociol.* 1987;2:329–347.

11. Maguire P. *Doing Participatory Research: A Feminist Approach.* Amherst, MA: Center for International Education; 1987.

12. Duran E, Duran B. *Native American Postcolonial Psychology.* Albany, NY: State University of New York Press; 1995.

13. McTaggart R. Sixteen tenets of participatory action research. In: Wadsworth Y, ed. *Everyday Evaluation on the Run.* Sydney, Australia: Allen & Unwin; 1997:79.

14. Lasker RD, Weiss ES, Miller R. Partnership synergy: a practical framework for studying and strengthening the collaborative advantage. *Milbank Q.* 2001;79:179–205, III–IV.

15. Tervalon M, Murray-Garcia J. Cultural humility vs. cultural competence: a critical distinction in defining physician training outcomes in medical education. *J Health Care Poor Underserved.* 1998;9:117–125.

16. Cornwall A, Jewkes R. What is participatory research? *Soc Sci Med.* 1995;41:1667–1676.

17. Gebbie K, Rosenstock L, Hernandez LM. *Who Will Keep the Public Healthy? Educating Public Health Professionals for the 21st Century.* Washington, DC: Institute of Medicine; 2002.

18. O'Fallon LR, Dearry A. Community-based participatory research as a tool to advance environmental health sciences. *Environ Health Perspect.* 2002;110:155–159.

19. Loh P, Sugerman-Brozan J. Environmental justice organizing for environmental health: case study on asthma and diesel exhaust in Roxbury, Massachusetts. *Environ Health Perspect.* 2002;584: 110–124.

20. Travers R, Flicker S. Ethical issues in community based research. In: *Urban Health Community-Based Research Series Workshop.* Wellesley, MA; 2004.

21. Bell C. *One HEART (Health Education and Research in Tibet) Community Based Participatory Research on Top of the World.* Unpublished manuscript, University of California, Berkeley, School of Public Health; 2004.

22. Roe K M, Minkler M, Saunders FF. Combining research, advocacy and education: the methods of the Grandparent Caregiving Study. *Health Educ Q.* 1995;22:458–475.

23. Shah R. *A Retrospective Analysis of an HIV Prevention Program for Men in Gujarat, India.* Unpublished manuscript, University of California, Berkeley, School of Public Health; 2004.

24. Thompson SJ. Participatory epidemiology: methods of the Living With Diabetes Project. *Intl Q Community Health Educ.* 2000;19: 3–18.

25. Lee P, Krause N, Goetchius C. Participatory action research with hotel room cleaners: from collaborative study to the bargaining table. In: Minkler M, Wallerstein N, eds. *Community Based Participatory Research for Health.* San Francisco, CA: Jossey-Bass; 2003: 390–404.

26. Minkler M. Ethical challenges for the "outside" researcher in community based participatory research. *Health Educ Behav.* 2004;31: 684–701.

27. Fadem P, Minkler M, Perry M, et al. Ethical challenges in community based participatory research: a case study from the San Francisco Bay Area disability community. In: Minkler M, Wallerstein N, eds. *Community Based Participatory Research for Health.* San Francisco, CA: Jossey-Bass; 2003.

28. Reason P. *Participation in Human Inquiry.* London, UK: Sage; 1994.

29. Mosavel M, Simon C, van Stade D, Buchbinder M. *Community Based Participatory Research (CBPR) in South Africa: Engaging Multiple Constituents to Shape the Research Question.* Unpublished manuscript; 2004.

30. Yoshihama M, Carr ES. Community participation reconsidered: feminist participatory action research with Hmong women. *J Community Pract.* 2002;10:85–103.

31. Ugalde A. Ideological dimensions of community participation in Latin American health programs. *Soc Sci Med.* 1985;21:41–53.

32. Wallerstein N. Power between evaluator and community: research relationships within New Mexico's healthier communities. *Soc Sci Med.* 1999;49:39–53.

33. Cram F. Rangahau Maori: Tona tika, tona pono: The validity and integrity of Maori research. In: Tolich M, ed. *Research Ethics in Aotearoa New Zealand.* Longman, Auckland: Pearson Education; 2001:35–52.

34. Anderson I. Ethics and health research in Aboriginal communities. In: Daly J, ed. *Ethical Intersections: Health Research, Methods and Researcher Responsibility.* St. Leonards, New South Wales: Allen & Unwin; 1996:153–165.

35. Turning Point, National Association of County and City Health Officials. Thirteen policy principles for advancing collaborative activity among and between tribal communities and surrounding jurisdictions. In: Minkler M, Wallerstein N, eds. *Community Based Participatory Research for Health.* San Francisco, CA: Jossey-Bass; 2003:436, Appendix E.

36. Stuart CA. Care and concern: an ethical journey in participatory action research. *Can J Couns.* 1998;32:298–314.

37. Diaz M, Simmons R. When is research participatory? Reflections on a Reproductive Health Project in Brazil. *J Women's Health.* 1999;8:175–184.

38. Chataway CJ. Examination of the constraints of mutual inquiry in a participatory action research project. *J Soc Issues.* 1997;53: 747–765.

39. Green LW, George MA, Daniel M, et al. Guidelines for participatory research in health promotion. In: Minkler M, Wallerstein N, eds. *Community Based Participatory Research for Health.* San Francisco, CA: Jossey-Bass; 2003:419, Appendix C.

A Practice Sequence: Analyzing the Appeals in a Researched Argument

1   Make a list of the major premises that inform Minkler's argument, and examine the evidence she uses to support them. To what extent do you find her evidence credible? Do you generally agree or disagree with the conclusions she draws? Be prepared to explain your responses to your class or peer group.

2   Note instances where Minkler appeals to ethos, pathos, and logos. How would you describe the ways she makes these three types of appeals? How does she present herself? What does she seem to assume? How does she help you understand the chain of reasoning by which she moves from premises to conclusion?

3   Working in groups of three or four, compose a letter to Minkler in which you take issue with her argument. This does not mean your group has to disagree with her entire argument, although of course you may. Rather, present your group's own contribution to the conversation in which she is participating. You may want to ask her to further explain one or more of her points, or suggest what she might be leaving out, or add your own take or evidence to her argument. As a group, you will have to agree on your focus. In the letter, include a summary of Minkler's argument or the part of it on which your group is focusing. Pay close attention to your own strategies for appealing to her—how you present yourselves, how you appeal to her values and emotions, and how you present your reasons for your own premises and conclusion.

10

From Image to Text

This chapter focuses on visual rhetoric—that is, the ways images communicate meaning and act upon us as we begin to interpret those images. As you analyze the advertisements in this chapter, for example, it will be important to reflect upon the ways the designers of these ads merge images and text to affect how you feel about issues such as gender, hunger, accommodations for those with disabilities, the role of the environment in our lives, and the like. How do these images make us feel? How do these images do the work of reframing the world as we know it and what we value? Do they make us want to do something to support a cause or challenge an injustice?

We encourage you to "read" these images as you would any text in the role of a writer. After all, in a world that increasingly uses images to affect what we think and believe, you will want to design your own multimodal texts—texts that combine what you have written with photographs, maps, tables, and graphs. Integrating visuals can help you convey a sense of immediacy, if not urgency, in an effort to move readers to understand what you think is important, to emphasize patterns and trends that might otherwise get lost in the data you use, and to appeal to readers' own lived experiences. Images provide readers with what one educator describes as "a vivid presence" that words alone are sometimes too abstract to convey. Actively reading the visuals around you will help you effectively produce and use visuals in your own work.

Pause for a moment to consider the types and forms of argumentation that might benefit from being presented visually as you think about your own work. Visuals can make us aware of the gravity of a given issue and convey the force, strength, and urgency of an issue. But how can an image, for example, encourage an emotional response in readers and motivate them to act? You will want to think about the following questions in developing a visual argument.

- What is your purpose for including an image, such as a chart, map, graph, or photograph? What trends or patterns do you want to emphasize?

- What story does the image help you tell?

- How does this image complement or highlight your written argument?

- How do you want readers to respond to this image? What ideas should they associate with an image? What emotions do you want to evoke?

- What sort of caption should you include to help readers understand the context and meaning of the chart, map, graph, or photograph?

These kinds of questions place rhetoric at the center of your decisions about how to present your argument—whether and in what ways images can help you fulfill your goals as a writer by telling a story about what matters and motivating readers to reframe the ways they see the world and perhaps act to create change.

ANALYZING VISUAL RHETORIC: ADVERTISEMENTS

This section focuses on ways of analyzing visual images as texts, what we have referred to throughout this book as rhetorical analysis or rhetorical reading of how writers construct arguments. In this case, we discuss the ways we can, in our role as readers and writers, begin to understand how images tell stories by conveying values (*ethos*), evoking very specific emotions (*pathos*) in readers, and appealing to readers' sense of reason (*logos*). Images prompt readers to fill in information given their own values, beliefs, and knowledge. Therefore, it might be best to think of images as constructions as opposed to representations of the world. This is to say that most images, especially photographs, are at best generative because they spark our own imagination and cannot really capture the complexity of day-to-day experiences. We fill in that complexity within the context of our own frames of reference.

Imagine, for example, a public service announcement or ad (PSA) that places an image of the earth at the center with minimal text that simply states, "It may not be much, but it's all we got." Some people might associate such an image with the celebration of Earth Day, conservation, sustainability, and climate change. Such associations will influence the conclusions readers draw about what this PSA means and what the ad is asking of its audience. Other readers may make associations that tell a different story—one that the designers of the PSA had not intended or anticipated. Thus it is important to keep in mind the benefits of using images and some of the limitations to convey an argument.

To examine the strategies you can use to understand how images and texts convey meaning, we would like you to analyze a PSA from Feeding America (Figure 10.1), distributed by the Ad Council, a nonprofit institution founded in 1942 for the purpose of bringing attention to social issues. The long, horizontal advertisement shows a blurry group of children in the background playing street hockey. In the foreground to the right is a bright red alarm bell attached to a wooden telephone pole. The text reads, "School may be out for summer but lunch is always in session." A sentence in smaller text below it reads, "If your kids rely on free school meals, call your Feeding America member food bank or visit FeedingAmerica .org/SummerMeals." Examine the advertisement and answer the questions that follow it.

FIGURE 10.1   Feeding America PSA

1. In writing, reflect on the story that the ad is telling us about kids, spaces where kids can be themselves and play, and food insecurity. What does the Ad Council want us to think about this story and what we might do? What appeals does the ad seem to draw on most: appeals based on our cultural relationship to children (*ethos*), on our emotional reaction to the idea of hungry children (*pathos*), or on the ways text and image work together to convey an argument (*logos*)? To what extent do these appeals overlap so that it might be difficult to tease out the differences among *ethos*, *pathos*, and *logos*?

2. Formulate what you think is the ad's argument, whether it's stated explicitly or not. What inferences do you make about the ad's argument when considering its use of text and images? What specific details seem to support the conclusions you draw? Compare your

ideas with those of your classmates. Do they differ significantly? Can you agree on what the argument is?

3. As a class, discuss the extent to which you believe that the following assumptions in the ad are true: When school is in session, policies are in place to ensure federally funded schools feed children in need. Less certain is the extent to which children in need receive sufficient nutrition during the summer when school is out.

Let's begin with the assumption that everything in a public service announcement or ad appears for a specific reason in a particular place to direct your attention in a specific sequence. The economy of the genre and its constraints dictate that the message come across quickly in a limited space.

■ Notice Where the Ad Appears

Analyzing an ad begins with noting where the ad appears. In this case, the Ad Council posted the Feeding America ad on billboards in a wide range of cities across the United States. An ad on a billboard will reach many people whose assumptions about hunger in America will vary, as will their education, age, faith, ethnicity, race, gender, and sexual orientation. Therefore, it's worthwhile to consider how an ad about hunger will connect with such a wide range of possible viewers who will interpret the ad in different ways, create images of children at play given their own experiences, and draw inferences based on their assumptions about hunger in America. The inferences readers draw will not only influence their interpretations but the extent to which they feel compelled to act, if at all. It is also worth considering the Ad Council's choice to post the ad in urban areas, as opposed to rural towns in the United States. Does the Ad Council assume there are greater hunger issues in urban areas? Is this a fair assumption? And equally important, can we assume that the people who should have access to the information on the ad will actually see it and get the support they need?

Imagine for a moment that the ad had appeared in a print issue of *Time* magazine, one of the most widely read magazines in the United States. As a news magazine, not an entertainment magazine such as *People*, *Time* aims to reach a broad, educated, even affluent readership interested in keeping up with current events. Producers of ads always have a target audience in mind when they design and place an ad. They assume that the audience shares certain beliefs and values, and that the ad will move the audience to think and act in particular ways.

As you compare the effects of posting an ad on a billboard versus placing an ad in a widely read magazine, you will inevitably discuss how a particular advertisement will travel from one medium to another. Certainly this Feeding America ad could appear in other popular news magazines such as *Newsweek*. How effective would it be in a weekly tabloid? A fashion magazine? Or someplace more public, such as in a bus terminal or waiting area in a public service office?

■ Identify and Reflect on What Draws Your Attention

Identify what draws your eye when you look at the ad, and think about why that element seems more important or affecting than others. Is it larger or more colorful than other elements? Is it foregrounded? What makes it stand out? Most viewers likely focus first on the central image of four children playing street hockey on a summer day. Does the photograph of children playing evoke your own childhood memories? Is this a familiar scene, one that helps you identify with this particular moment in children's lived experiences? Is there something startling, perhaps even shocking about the situation depicted in the photograph and what the text seems to suggest about hunger in America? Something puzzling that holds your attention? Something about the use of color, the size of the image or text, or the font that catches your eye?

Although the ad was designed to spark our imagination and humanize the problem of hunger in America, the blurred images of individual children also invite us to provide our own images based on our memories, experiences, and relationships. We acknowledge it is reasonable to blur children's faces to protect their identity, but we wonder if it matters that the ad does not specify race and ethnicity. Who are these children? What are they like? How does this reluctance to show race and ethnicity affect or even challenge our assumptions about who is poor in America? Who would personally identify with these children?

We may find ourselves puzzling over the alarm bell in the foreground to the right. (In the full-color ad, the alarm bell is bright red and demands our attention.) If the image of the children provides us with a sense of immediacy in telling a story about growing up, the bell seems to disrupt a sense that this carefree moment will last. What specifically does the designer of the ad want us to understand by juxtaposing children playing during the summer with an image that for many of us represents school? Is there a sense of urgency in the ad that we might easily overlook without this additional image of the bell alongside a scene of children at play? It's difficult to grasp the significance of these juxtapositions without further inquiry, in this case without looking at the text in the foreground of the ad. We assume that the designer intends for readers to look there next, because the writing is large and distinctive—like children's chalk writing on the sidewalk. Finally, our eyes are drawn to the Feeding America logo, and it prompts us to ask *What is Feeding America, and what values does it espouse?*

LaunchPad
macmillan learning
To view this ad in full color, visit LaunchPad for *From Inquiry to Academic Writing*.

■ Consider the Ethos of the Ad

The next step is to evaluate the ethos of the creator or sponsor of the ad. What does the ad say about how the sponsor or creator wishes to be perceived? If you don't recognize a sponsor's logo or brand, it's important to ask, *What is the sponsor's mission? To sell a product or promote a practice? What values does the sponsor espouse? Is the creator or sponsor a nonprofit or commercial enterprise?* You need to know the answers to these questions to assess any underlying bias and to determine how willing you are to believe what the ad promotes. In this case, you might find it helpful to go to the Feeding America Web site (listed in the ad) or to do a simple Internet search to see whether the organization has been discussed by others writing about hunger. Has Feeding America done significant work in the area of hunger? What kind of community organization is it? Is it a reputable organization that benefits those it advocates for? Is there evidence that the organization's past ad campaigns have been successful?

■ Analyze the Pathos in the Ad

Next, analyze the *pathos* in the ad—how images and words appeal to your emotions. An appeal to pathos is meant to evoke emotions such as empathy (which might prompt us to identify with an image) or outrage (which might spur us to act in a certain way). In this case, the image of children playing outdoors with friends on a neighborhood street is likely to appeal to many of us, evoking as it does idyllic childhood memories. Its nostalgic appeal invites us into an apparently calm, innocent world of peaceful play and encourages us to sympathize with the children pictured and described.

■ Understand the Logos of the Ad

We should also consider the composition of the ad as a whole. What is the logic of the ad? What is its appeal to reason? How do the images and text work together to persuade us? What is the takeaway message?

The text in the Feeding America ad helps clarify the meaning of the central images of the children and the alarm bell. The alarm bell ties the image in the background to the foregrounded text: "School may be out for summer, but lunch is always in session." Food insecurity is a problem every day for children in need. But where do these children get their food when school is not in session?

Hunger is not readily visible to many of us. Images of playfulness, even childlike innocence, can mask the deprivation that any of the people surrounding us may experience in their own lives. The text makes the appeal in the ad explicit. Those living in hunger are all around us.

The smaller text answers the question of where children in need can receive the nutrition they require. Children who are eligible for free lunch during the school year are also eligible to receive free meals during the summer.

Translating the discrete images and text into a coherent argument requires inductive reasoning, moving from specific pieces of evidence to a major premise. We would conclude that the argument in the ad goes something like this:

1. Hunger in America is a reality in the lives of many children and families.

2. Food insecurity exists for children year round—whether school is in session or not.

3. Feeding America can help children and families gain access to the nutrition they require.

There are other ways to formulate the argument, and we invite you to discuss these alternatives as a class. Our main point, though, is that visual images present claims to us as viewers in much the same ways as any written text does. Having the tools of visual rhetoric can help you discern how images and text work together to produce an argument.

Steps to Visual Analysis

1 **Notice where the ad appears.** What does the publication space tell you about the ad's target audience? To what extent does the placement of the ad in a magazine or newspaper or on a billboard determine the potential audience of the ad?

2 **Identify and reflect on what draws your attention.** Where does your eye go? To an image, some words, some odd juxtaposition? What elements seem to be given prominence and how? Do color, foregrounding, size, font choice, or other methods of visual emphasis make some elements seem more important than others? Is there something startling or shocking about the images or words—or about the situation depicted? Something puzzling that holds your attention?

3 **Consider the *ethos* of the ad.** Evaluate the legitimacy, or *ethos*, of the ad's creator or sponsor. For example, what do you know about the corporation or institution behind the ad? What values does it espouse? To what extent do you share its values? Is the creator or sponsor a nonprofit or commercial enterprise?

4 Analyze the *pathos* in the ad. How do the images and words appeal to your emotions? What do the images or words make you feel or think about?

5 Understand the *logos* of the ad. What is the logic of the ad? Taken together, what do the cluster of images and words convey? How are the different images and words related to the claim that the ad is making?

A Practice Sequence: Analyzing the Rhetoric of an Advertisement

To practice these strategies, we would like you to analyze the following PSA designed by the American Disability Association (Figure 10.2). First, evaluate the *ethos*, or values, that the PSA tries to project by encouraging us to reframe the experience of climbing stairs to get from one place to another. Some of us may very well take for granted the task of climbing stairs to get to class, to reach a professor's office where there isn't a ramp to ease entry into the building, or reach our seat on a bus to get to work. Those who designed the PSA prompt us to consider that a relatively simple task may seem insurmountable to people with physical disabilities. It would be helpful to do some research into the work of the American Disability Association, especially the work it has done to advocate for people with disabilities. In doing this research, write a brief summary of the company's values. Do you share those values? Do you consider yourself part of the ad's target audience? Why? Is there information available to suggest that the American Disability Association has had success in prior ad campaigns?

Second, reflect on and write about what the images and text make you feel about your own experiences with accessing public spaces. If you don't typically experience physical barriers, in what ways do you identify with those who do not have access to the spaces that you take for granted? Do you find the comparison to scaling Everest effective? If you have struggled with access in spaces without accommodations for physical disabilities, how do you feel about the ad's presentation of that struggle? Is this an adequate representation of the problem, one that might help gain allies in an effort to remedy the problem of access that many people face?

Third, work in small groups to identify the logic of the narrative that the images and words convey. What do you see as the main premise of the ad? What is its goal? How did you arrive at your conclusion? Report your group's findings to the class. Be sure to present the evidence to support your claim.

FIGURE 10.2   American Disability Association PSA

FIGURE 10.3
UN Women PSA

Memac Ogilvy & Mather Dubai, developed for UN Women (2013)

FIGURE 10.4
Ad Council Food Waste PSA

ANALYZING VISUAL RHETORIC: MAPS, PHOTOGRAPHS, TABLES OR CHARTS, AND GRAPHS

Thus far, we have focused on the ways an image can enhance an argument by creating a sense of immediacy (the day-to-day lives of children), urgency (children we see every day may experience the stress of going hungry), and importance (we need to prevent child hunger). An image sparks our imagination, evokes memories, and in many cases adds a human dimension to a problem that in the abstract may not seem to affect us very much. But visualizing the physical challenges that some people face in ascending the stairs to get to a subway platform or the neglect we see when young people face hunger can change the way we feel. We can be more empathic and identify with others. Thus it is important as you write to consider the purpose of what you are trying to accomplish and to use all of the means of persuasion available to you in constructing an argument that moves readers to understand a problem, grasp its immediacy, reframe how they see the world, and perhaps act with a sense of conviction to change the world for the better.

In this section, then, we extend our conversation of integrating images and text to other visuals that can help you support your argument. As always, your purpose, audience, and context are central to the ways you develop an argument. After all, how you establish an argument depends on which conversation you want to enter, who is part of the conversation, and what you want to accomplish. An image of children may be an effective means of conveying a sense of urgency to readers about hunger in America, but using a map can demonstrate to readers where in the United States there is the greatest concentration of children living in poverty and facing the consequences of food insecurity—not knowing when they will get their next meal. A map can offer a different kind of visual representation of a problem that people need to know about or that policy makers need to solve. It can tell a story of where food insecurity exists, how prevalent it is, and perhaps how food insecurity correlates with other problems in different regions of the country, including lack of employment opportunities and residential segregation among different racial and ethnic groups. With numerical data in the form of tables and graphs, you can create a powerful narrative that conveys the sense of immediacy, urgency, and importance that we have described in analyzing an advertisement. Using all of these tools is also what we mean by using the resources available to you—that is, all of the available means of persuasion. At the same time, you'll want to consider the best way to communicate your ideas to make an effective argument.

In the readings that follow, consider the following: the author's purpose, how the author uses maps and other images to frame an argument; what the author assumes about readers' knowledge and values; the source of the data; whether the use of visuals helps establish the importance, urgency, and immediacy of the problem the author identifies; and the extent to which the author integrates visuals into the written argument. These are concerns that you should focus on in reading and interpreting any kind of image, whether it's a map, photograph, table, or graph.

■ Using Maps to Make a Point

Let's now look at a specific use of a map in a 2015 article from the *Washington Post* that examines the relationship between poverty and access to public education. In this case, you might ask if the two maps serve the author well in advancing her purpose or whether she could have represented the problem she identifies in another, perhaps more effective way.

EMILY BADGER

Mapped: The Places Where Most Public School Children Are Poor

Formerly a staff writer at *The Atlantic Cities*, Emily Badger is a regular contributor to the *Washington Post* and writes about politics, race, and urban neighborhoods.

■ ■ ■

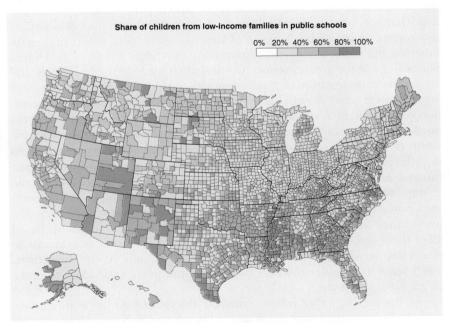

Map: "Share of Children from Low-Income Families in Public Schools," originally from Reed Jordan, "A Closer Look at Income and Race Concentration in Public Schools," Urban Institute, May 13, 2015, http://www.urban.org/features/closer-look-income-and-race-concentration-public-schools

E arlier this year, the Southern Education Foundation reported that America's public schools
had reached a dispiriting milestone: A majority of
children attending them are now low-income. As the
Post's Lyndsey Layton noted at the time, we haven't
seen such demographics in public schools at any
point over the past half-century. And they mean that
teachers must increasingly prioritize combating the
effects of poverty—ensuring children feel safe, fed
and well-clothed—before the learning even begins.

This picture of poverty in the classroom, however,
varies widely across the country, between North and
South, and between urban counties and nearby suburban ones. The Urban Institute on Wednesday released
interactive maps showing that the concentration of poor
children in public schools is remarkably high in some
of these places relative to others—and that these geographic disparities are magnified for children of color.

The above map shows the share of children in public schools in each county who come from low-income
families (low-income is defined here as households
making at or below 185 percent of the federal poverty
line, the cutoff for free and reduced-price lunch programs). Particularly striking is the "belt of rural poverty" across the South, as the Urban Institute puts it.

The share of low-income children is also high in
several metropolitan areas: in Dallas County (73 percent), in Cook County around Chicago (66 percent),
in the District of Columbia (61 percent). In several
Lakota counties in South Dakota, the number of public school children who come from low-income families approaches 100 percent.

This concentration of poverty, which reflects underlying patterns in where the rich and poor live, also
means that a poor child in America is much more
likely than a middle-class or wealthier child to attend
a high-poverty school. About 40 percent of low-income
children attend public schools where 75 percent of the
other students are low-income, too. The same is true of
just 6 percent of non-poor kids. "This is concentrated
disadvantage," writes Urban Institute researcher Reed

Jordan, "the children who need the most are concentrated in schools least likely to have the resources to meet those needs."

Across the country, black children are also about six times more likely to attend high-poverty schools than white children. In many counties in the rural South, nearly all of the black children attend high-poverty schools.

Leads up to a key point that frames the way readers will look at the map that follows.

Disparities in the level of school poverty that white and black children experience often vary as well within the same region. Jordan again:

> In some metropolitan areas, the racial concentration of school poverty is so severe that black and white students effectively attend two different school systems: one for middle- and upper-middle-income white students, and the other for poor students and students of color.

This happens, for example, in Cook County around Chicago. There, 75 percent of black students attend high-poverty schools. For white children, the share is less than 10 percent.

Reaffirms the value of the maps as a way to visualize the problem and create goals that might inform policy.

These maps reflect the importance of better integrating schools, creating environments in which poor children learn alongside upper-income peers. But that's a goal that will be hard to achieve if we don't talk as well about the housing patterns and policies that helped create these maps.

6

7

8

Share of black children in high-poverty schools

0% 20% 40% 60% 80% 100%

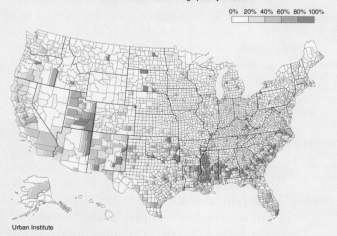

Urban Institute

Map: "Share of Black Children in High-Poverty Schools," originally from Reed Jordan, "A Closer Look at Income and Race Concentration in Public Schools," Urban Institute, May 13, 2015, http://www.urban.org/features/closer-look-income-and-race-concentration-public-schools

■ Using Photographs to Provide Context or Stir Emotions

Of all visuals that appear in multimodal texts, photographs might be the most common. They can serve a wide range of functions in the text and are frequently used to provide context or encourage a particular emotional response—or both. Take online news articles, for example. Most of them, regardless of the topic, include a visual. If the article discusses a statement made by a politician, a photo of the politician usually appears with the writing. This photo provides a visual context for the writer's subject—the politician—but rarely does it capture the exact moment in which the politician made the statement being discussed. The text will usually include a photo that instead reveals something about how the writer wants the politician to be perceived. If the writer questions the validity of the politician's statement, the chosen photo may show the politician wearing a combative or smug expression, for example. These kinds of photos are usually not the subject of overt discussion, but they do connect to the subject and influence most readers' perceptions of the text.

Sometimes photos are at the center of a writer's text. For example, a writer questioning whether the 2017 Women's March in Washington, DC, was inclusive might analyze a photo of the crowd that seems to capture the prevailing mix of genders, races, and ages of the participants. Or in covering the blight of foreclosed, uninhabited homes in low-income neighborhoods in Chicago, a writer might include a photo of one such boarded-up house to characterize the problem and the neighborhood and maybe generate compassion for those living in adjacent properties.

When you encounter photographs in your reading, we encourage you to analyze the photograph by reflecting on your own emotional response to what is depicted and any memories that the photograph helps spark. To what extent does it reflect a world that you know or help reframe what you know and have experienced? What purpose does the photograph serve in the text? That is, what story does the photograph help the author tell? How effective is it in establishing a sense of importance, immediacy, and urgency?

■ Using Tables to Capture the Issue and Present Findings

We now turn to the ways writers use tables as a formal structure to help readers understand the kinds of patterns that complex data represent. Tables tend to be used to present statistics and serve as a starting point for analysis and discussion. You will see that it is a good rule of thumb to summarize and highlight key points in the text you write rather than try to include all of the information that you will include in a table. It's also important to explain what you think readers should pay attention to in a table and offer some context. Don't just include a table without explanation.

In what follows, we provide an excerpt from a 2001 article in which researchers Susan B. Neuman and Donna Celano examine the educational resources that children and their families have access to in two low-income neighborhoods and two middle-class neighborhoods. The excerpt we include describes the methods the researchers used to collect data and some of the results they found. We limit our discussion of results to the quantity and quality of literacy resources available to children.

We encourage you to analyze the way the authors choose to visually represent their findings alongside their discussion of the availability of reading materials for adolescents and adults, where they found these resources, and the differences between quantity and quality of resources in low- and high-income neighborhoods. How effective is their use of tables in establishing a sense of importance, immediacy, and urgency? How do the tables help the authors fulfill their purpose? What story do they tell? And finally, note how the authors have designed the table and used labels to identify the information provided in a given table. Is the information clear? Do the authors integrate the discussion of what is in the tables into the text?

SUSAN B. NEUMAN AND DONNA CELANO

Access to Print in Low-Income and Middle-Income Communities: An Ecological Study of Four Neighborhoods

A former U.S. Assistant Secretary of Elementary and Secondary Education, Dr. Susan B. Neuman is an educator, researcher, and education policy-maker in early childhood and literacy development. Now a professor of education at the University of Michigan, she is director of the Michigan Research Program on Ready to Learn. She has published widely, including her most recent book with Professor Donna Celano, *Giving Our Children a Fighting Chance*. Dr. Celano is a faculty member in the Communication Department at La Salle University, Philadelphia, and has published in *Reading Research Quarterly*, *Phi Delta Kappan*, *Education Week*, and *Educational Leadership*.

■ ■ ■

Our multicultural research team included a project investigator, a project coordinator, and six applied urban anthropology doctoral students. Together, we devised a research strategy to examine literacy resources and opportunities in each community. This strategy recognized that any one variable, or *1*

States the purpose of their study: to identify literacy resources and opportunities from different perspectives (not defined by any one variable or place). The discussion of methods provides some context for analyzing how the authors examine the amount and kinds of literacy materials available in low-income and middle-income neighborhoods.

measure in and of itself, could not explain variations in print access and opportunity. Rather, we hypothesized that each measure operated within a web of relationships, acting simultaneously and in ways that intersected with one another. Initial data collection and analysis were followed by additional data collection and analysis throughout the year.

The research team devised a theory of community influences that might have an impact on children's early literacy development (Connell, Kubisch, Schorr, & Weiss, 1995). On the basis of accumulated evidence from early literacy research, the theory implies that children learn about literacy through contact, experiences, and observations of written language use in their everyday lives (Goodman, 1986; Neuman &

Identifies why the research team looked at the specific factors that influence how children learn.

Roskos, 1997; Teale & Sulzby, 1989). Children construct an understanding of how print works through their independent explorations of print and signs, interactions around books and other print resources, and participation with others engaged in purposeful literacy activities. Accordingly, community access was operationally defined as (a) the quantity and selection of children's books that parents could conceivably purchase in the neighborhood, (b) the environmental print (signs, labels, and logos) in the business area that children might begin to identify, (c) the public areas where children might observe people reading, (d) the quantity and quality of books in the child-care centers they would most likely attend, (e) the quantity and quality of books in the local elementary school libraries, and (f) the collections in the local public library. Although each of these influences most likely plays some role, together they might play a powerful role in children's development as literacy learners.

The authors describe the kinds of reading materials that children in low-income and middle-income neighborhoods have access to.

Survey of reading materials. Using the census boundaries, research assistants walked each block throughout a neighborhood, stopping at every store (i.e., bookstore, grocery store, bodega) likely to have reading resources for purchase: newspapers, magazines, children's books, and teen and adult books. Total number of titles, descriptions of the types of materials, and age distribution for the materials were placed on a spreadsheet. To the degree possible, we also counted newspaper boxes, honor boxes, and newspaper stands by type of newspapers. For the purposes of this study, information on children's resources was then plotted on maps to provide information on proximity to resources across the neighborhood....

The authors explain where these different kinds of reading materials are accessible — if they are accessible at all.

Books in child-care centers. Because increasing numbers of children spend most of their day not around their neighborhood, but in child-care centers within the area in which they live (Children's Defense Fund, 1999), our next step was to focus on access to books in childcare centers. Considering that independent access to books is likely to be particularly important for 3- and 4-year-old children, we randomly selected two classrooms in six not-for-profit child-care centers in each neighborhood (i.e., 48 classrooms).... For the purposes of this study, only two areas of the literacy environment were examined. Children's book displays were rated for availability, according to a scale of 1 (no books accessible to children) to 7 (books available in library corner and other interest areas around the room). Quality was rated from 1 (no attractive books displayed) to 7 (variety of genre and a wide range of age-appropriate selections).... 4

School libraries. We next visited the local school libraries. Many young children were likely to attend prekindergarten and kindergarten in elementary schools and later go on to the middle schools in the neighborhood. We concentrated on public schools, but included several parochial and private ones if they seemed to draw large numbers of children from the local area. Visiting a total of 24 schools, we examined (a) their resources (i.e., number and condition of available books—book count was estimated by multiplying the number of books on a shelf times the number of shelves, and condition was estimated by publication date and condition of the cover on a random selection of books); (b) staffing (i.e., librarian's training and years of work experience); and (c) children's access (i.e., number of days the library 5 was open per week, and whether children could visit independently or needed to go at designated times). Differences in quantity and quality of books and book access were then compared across communities.

Public libraries. Our final analysis focused on the public library branches in each neighborhood.... We limited our analysis to the size of the collection, average number of books per child and adult in the catchment area, and hours of library service for each branch.

6

Results

The authors highlight the extent to which middle-class families have far more access to reading materials than do low-income families and their children.

Results of the data were consistent. There were minor differences in access to print between neighborhoods of similar income, but major and striking differences at almost all levels between neighborhoods of different income. These data indicate that children from middle-income neighborhoods were likely to be deluged with a wide variety of reading materials. However, children from poor neighborhoods would have to aggressively and persistently seek them out....

7

A summary of what the authors found in the four neighborhoods listed at the top in Table 2. On the left side of the table is a list of what the authors examined and which they described earlier in their method for collecting data. Use of a table helps the authors selectively discuss the data presented and emphasize the clear differences in access between low- and middle-class families.

Survey of print resources. Table 2 describes the number of stores in each area that carried children's books and magazines. In Chestnut Hill and Roxborough, 11 and 13 places respectively sold print materials for children. There were seven bookstores with special sections for children in Chestnut Hill and three bookstores, with a large children's selection in one, in Roxborough. In contrast, Kingsessing and Kensington, with a far greater density of children, had 4 places in each community that carried children's print materials. No bookstores were found in either neighborhood.

8

Note that the researchers underscore what they want readers to understand from the table. They stress the "scarcity" of materials they think all children should have access to.

As shown in Table 2, drugstores were the most common source of print materials for children. Young adult materials, defined as chapter books, or magazines more suitable to middle-grade children in all areas were scarce. Apart from the bookstores and a couple of convenience stores in the middle-income areas, these materials were largely absent in any business establishment.

9

Four additional tables further analyze data presented in the summary table. The authors integrate the tables by discussing findings in the text, while offering readers the argument they make about this "disturbing picture."

Looking more closely in each area, Tables 3a through 3d describe an even more disturbing picture and equation. To provide some evidence of choice (not quality), we counted the number of *different* children's titles in each store. Detailing the type of store, number of children's titles, and general type of reading material (e.g., magazines, books, comics), massive differences were reported in print access across community—not only in number, but in type of materials available. Children in Chestnut Hill, for example, had access to literally thousands of book, magazine, and comic-book titles. Roxborough children, though with access to far fewer, still had substantial numbers of book titles to choose from, whereas children in Kensington had only hundreds and in Kingsessing even fewer. No young adult titles were available in either of the two lower-income neighborhoods. *10*

The authors summarize what we find in Tables 3a, b, c, and d. Again, the researchers can be selective in what they write about so as not to overwhelm readers because all of the data appears in the tables they provide.

These data indicate that the equation was dramatically skewed in favor of children from middle-income communities. There were about 13 titles for every 1 child in Chestnut Hill, and 1 book title for about every 3 children in Roxborough. Compare this situation with the low-income communities: There was 1 title for about every 20 children in Kensington and 1, all of which were coloring book titles, for about every 300 children in Kingsessing. *11*

Consequently, even though living in the same city, children's access to print resources was widely differential. In these low-income neighborhoods, children would find it difficult, if not impossible, to purchase a book of any quality in local stores; in the middle-income neighborhoods, children would find it hard to escape them. Such differential access might account for differential print exposure as recorded in research by Stanovich and his colleagues (Stanovich & Cunningham, 1993; Stanovich & West, 1989). *12*

Table 2   Number of Places Selling Children's Reading Resources

STORES	KENSINGTON	KINGSESSING	ROXBOROUGH	CHESTNUT HILL
Children's resources				
Bookstores	0	0	1	3
Drugstores	2	1	5	2
Grocery stores	0	1	3	1
Bargain stores	1	1	2	0
Corner stores	1	0	0	0
Other stores	0	1	1	1
Children's stores	0	0	1	4
Total	4	4	13	11
Young adult				
Bookstores	0	0	1	1
Drugstores	0	0	1	0
Grocery stores	0	0	0	0
Bargain stores	0	0	0	0
Corner stores	0	0	0	0
Other stores	0	0	1	0
Total	0	0	3	1

Table 3a   Reading Resources in Kensington

STORE NAME	TYPE	CHILDREN'S TITLES	YOUNG ADULT TITLES	TYPE
Rite Aid	Drugstore	112	0	Book/magazines (picture, puzzle, comics, activity)
Rite Aid	Drugstore	142	0	Book/magazines (picture, puzzle, comics, activity)
Chico's Cut Rate	Bargain store	95	0	Magazines (comics)
Maria's Candy	Corner store	9	0	Magazines (comics, puzzles)
Total		358	0	

Tables: Republished with permission from John Wiley & Sons, Inc., from "Access to Print in Low-Income and Middle-Income Communities: An Ecological Study of Four Neighborhoods," by Susan B. Neuman and Donna Celano, *Reading Research Quarterly* 36.1 (January/February/March 2001), pp. 8–26; permission conveyed through Copyright Clearance Center, Inc.

Table 3b   Reading Resources in Kingsessing

Store Name	Type	Children's Titles	Young Adult Titles	Type
Pharmacy	Drugstore	15	0	Magazines
Thriftway	Grocery store	5	0	Magazines
Dollar Store	Bargain store	30	0	Books (coloring)
Newstand	Other	5	0	Magazines
Total		55	0	

Table 3c   Reading Resources in Roxborough

Store Name	Type	Children's Titles	Young Adult Titles	Type
Encore Books	Bookstore	1,000	500	Books
CVS	Drugstore	18	0	Books
Rite Aid	Drugstore	34	0	Books/magazines
Eckerd	Drugstore	69	0	Books
Eckerd	Drugstore	55	0	Books/magazines (coloring/activity, easy crossword)
CVS	Drugstore	27	30	Books (picture, coloring/activity, popular teen fiction)
Superfresh	Grocery store	20	0	Books (Golden books, coloring/activity)
Superfresh	Grocery store	27	0	Books/magazines (Disney, Read & Listen, coloring/ activity, comics)
Acme	Grocery store	14	0	Books (bargain)
Dollar Store	Bargain store	35	0	Books (toddler, picture, coloring)
Dollar Store	Bargain store	31	0	Books/magazines (picture, activity, Disney, comics)
World Wide Aquarium	Other store	30	0	Books ("family style" books about pets)
Family Toy Warehouse	Children's store	237	30	Books (toddler, picture, workbooks, Golden books, coloring/activity)
Total		1597	560	

Tables: Republished with permission from John Wiley & Sons, Inc., from "Access to Print in Low-Income and Middle-Income Communities: An Ecological Study of Four Neighborhoods," by Susan B. Neuman and Donna Celano, *Reading Research Quarterly* 36.1 (January/February/ March 2001), pp. 8–26; permission conveyed through Copyright Clearance Center, Inc.

Table 3d   Reading Resources in Chestnut Hill

STORE NAME	TYPE	CHILDREN'S TITLES	YOUNG ADULT TITLES	TYPE
Borders	Bookstore	14,000	Unspecified	Books
Christian Literature Crusade	Bookstore	640	0	Books (toddler, picture, coloring)
Philadelphia Print Shop	Bookstore	1	0	Books (coloring)
CVS	Drugstore	7	0	Books (coloring)
Eckerd	Drugstore	34	0	Books (toddler, workbooks, coloring/ activity)
Superfresh	Grocery store	6	0	Books/magazines
Chris's Store	Children's store	10	0	Unspecified
Benders	Children's store	1,000	0	Unspecified
O'Doodles	Children's store	115	0	Books (toddler, picture, educational coloring, family style art)
Mes Enfants	Toy store	120	0	Books (toddler, picture)
Performing Art Store	Other	520	0	Books (scripts, scores, toddler, stories, multicultural, dance, biography)
Total		16,453	0	

▪ Using Graphs to Present Findings

One final way of presenting data is to use a graph, as Neuman and Celano do to provide a quick summary that gives readers a snapshot of key findings.

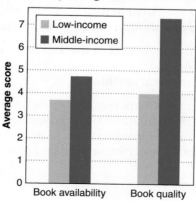

FIGURE 10.5   Book Availability and Book Quality in Preschool Classrooms

They use a bar graph, but you can also use pie charts, scatter plots, and line graphs to emphasize patterns and trends.

Interestingly, Neuman and Celano use tables more frequently to summarize the differences between the types and quantity of literacy resources that low- and middle-income families have access to. Some of the results they present are quite dramatic, especially when we become aware of the tens of thousands of titles in middle-income neighborhoods and the scarcity of books in low-income neighborhoods. They could have easily compiled what they found in a graph like the one on page 309. Why do you think they chose to use a table to represent trends but then use a graph to describe the availability of books in preschools? What differences would you call attention to in using a table versus a graph? What effect do these two different kinds of images have on you? To what extent does the purpose for writing determine the choice? To what extent does either one convey importance, immediacy, or urgency better than the other?

Steps to Using Visuals in Writing an Argument

1 **Identify.** Consider what you want to accomplish—your purpose—in using a visual or a series of visuals. What is the story you want to tell? Are you reframing readers' experiences, sparking their imagination, presenting data, or motivating readers to act?

2 **Analyze.** Conduct some research to understand an audience's values and knowledge base. How might readers respond to your choice of visuals?

3 **Evaluate.** Assess the extent to which a visual will add clarity or create a sense of importance, urgency, and immediacy.

4 **Question.** Examine the source of the data in a map, photograph, table, or graph. Are the data accurate or biased in any way? Does the source of data reveal anything?

5 **Integrate.** Discuss and analyze any visuals you include. Be sure that readers understand the relationship between the text you write and the image(s) you present. What conclusions can readers draw from your maps, photographs, tables, or graphs?

A Practice Sequence: Using Visuals to Enhance an Argument

1   With your own writing in mind, write down how you would follow the steps for integrating visuals in a written argument.

- **Identify** your purpose. What is the story you want to tell?

- **Analyze** your audience's values and knowledge base to determine how they might react to different kinds of media.

- **Evaluate** which kind of visuals will provide support or clarity or create a sense of importance, urgency, and immediacy.

- **Question** the source of the data you want to use. Does the source of data reveal anything?

- **Integrate** the text you have written and the visual(s) you include. What conclusions can readers draw from your discussion of visuals?

2   As a class or in small groups, discuss the strategies that authors use to integrate visuals and discussion in the readings in this section.

- When does using a map make sense? What about a photograph, table, or graph?

- Are there instances when the authors might have combined strategies to fulfill their purpose as writers?

- What are some best practices for integrating visuals that help readers understand the importance, immediacy, and urgency of an argument?

3   Analyze the following editorial as a class or in small groups. The writer collaborated with three other students in an effort to prevent a library from closing in the city where they live and attend a school. The authors were limited to just 700 words and could not include visuals to amplify their argument.

- To what extent could a map have helped readers understand the resources that children and families have access to?

- What would including a photograph add to the story the students wanted to tell?

- Could the writers have added a table with census data or even a graph to advance their argument? Why or why not?

Jindra 1

Nathan Jindra*

Neighbors Need LaSalle Branch

I am writing on behalf of a group of 11 middle and high school students who participated in the Neighborhood Resource Corporation Youth Leadership Workshop, with an enthusiasm for bettering the community. We read with interest the *Tribune* article "Report: Business tax cut to cost county $31.6M," published in January of this year.

The story talked about Governor Pence's efforts to spur economic development in the state and the impact that eliminating the business personal property tax could have on local governments. A total loss to St. Joseph County could be up to $31.6 million in 2015 and $8 million in South Bend alone. The effects can be devastating to public education, transportation, parks, and libraries. We are concerned about all of these, but especially the consequences that tax cuts will have on local libraries. To save money for the library system, Donald Napoli, library director, said he would consider closing the LaSalle Branch, which could save $500,000 a year.

We have met monthly for the past 10 months, and we have been studying and learning about libraries and their place in communities. Looking at the article, we had some shared concerns, particularly the fact that the data only looked at book circulation and not other library uses. It is important to note that libraries have other functions in addition to circulating books, such as Internet use, gathering spaces, and safe environments for learning. Also, in our modern society, not just in South Bend, the use of electronic media is growing rapidly. This is resulting in fewer books being circulated and checked out. It doesn't seem fair to close the LaSalle Branch based just on book circulation.

The LaSalle Library Branch is in a neighborhood that needs it the most. According to ZipSkinny.com, 13 percent of the neighborhood is at or below the poverty line, and 50 percent of residents make $34,000 or less a year. In addition, 20 percent of the neighborhood consists of school-age children, many of whom use the library regularly. A member of our council uses this library frequently and says it provides a good space where she can complete her schoolwork. She will be attending a four-year college in Indianapolis next year. With school cuts being made more and more, closing this library would leave many kids without resources for learning as the other nearest libraries are three miles away. This is a long walk for young children and bicycling is really not an option given the busy roads nearby. Closing the library seems like a counterintuitive way to ensure a successful future for our community. Why take something away from those who need it most?

School resources are a great asset to libraries, but they are not the only one. Libraries are used as shelter in winter and summer when the weather can be extreme. Youth and adults alike use libraries as community centers and much more. Offering programs that community members want is a great way to encourage library use. More programs could include tutoring sessions, activity days, camp, and read-alouds for small children. These could also be alternate sources of revenue. Instead of cutting back on public resources, trying to find other sources of income could be very beneficial for the whole community.

As a community, we need to know more about the people who are using this library. How can we support our community? Are the choices we are making benefiting everyone, or just some? These are points we need to take into consideration. As a council, we feel until all these questions are thoughtfully answered, there has been insufficient planning for the removal of a community asset. We hope the library board and others will take these thoughts into consideration and plan accordingly. As the president of the American Library Association put it so well, "Teens need these kinds of places to find their voices."

*The author wishes to thank Kai Brown, Indonesia Brown, and Julia McKenna for their help in writing this article.

From Introductions to Conclusions
Drafting an Essay

In this chapter, we describe strategies for crafting introductions that set up your argument. We then describe the characteristics of well-formulated paragraphs that will help you build your argument. Finally, we provide you with some strategies for writing conclusions that reinforce what is new about your argument, what is at stake, and what readers should do with the knowledge you convey.

DRAFTING INTRODUCTIONS

The introduction is where you set up your argument. It's where you identify a widely held assumption, challenge that assumption, and state your thesis. Writers use a number of strategies to set up their arguments. In this section we look at five of them:

- Moving from a general topic to a specific thesis (inverted-triangle introduction)
- Introducing the topic with a story (narrative introduction)
- Beginning with a question (interrogative introduction)
- Capturing readers' attention with something unexpected (paradoxical introduction)
- Identifying a gap in knowledge (minding-the-gap introduction)

Remember that an introduction need not be limited to a single paragraph. It may take several paragraphs to effectively set up your argument.

Keep in mind that you have to make these strategies your own. That is, we can suggest models, but you must make them work for your own argument. You must imagine your readers and what will engage them. What tone do you want to take? Playful? Serious? Formal? Urgent? The attitude you want to convey will depend on your purpose, your argument, and the needs of your audience.

▪ The Inverted-Triangle Introduction

An **inverted-triangle introduction**, like an upside-down triangle, is broad at the top and pointed at the base. It begins with a general statement of the topic and then narrows its focus, ending with the point of the paragraph (and the triangle), the writer's thesis. We can see this strategy at work in the following introduction from a student's essay. The student writer (1) begins with a broad description of the problem she will address, (2) then focuses on a set of widely held but troublesome assumptions, and (3) finally, presents her thesis in response to what she sees as a pervasive problem.

The student begins with a general set of assumptions about education that she believes people readily accept.

In today's world, many believe that education's sole purpose is to communicate information for students to store and draw on as necessary. By storing this information, students hope to perform well on tests. Good test scores assure good grades. Good grades eventually lead to acceptances into good colleges, which ultimately guarantee good jobs. Many teachers and students, convinced that education exists as a tool to secure good jobs,

She then cites author bell hooks, to identify an approach that makes use of these assumptions — the "banking system" of education, a term hooks borrows from educator Paulo Freire.

rely on the *banking system*. In her essay "Teaching to Transgress," bell hooks defines the *banking system* as an "approach to learning that is rooted in the notion that all students need to do is consume information fed to them by a professor and be able to memorize and store it" (185). Through the banking system, students focus solely on facts, missing the important themes and life lessons available in classes and school materials. The banking system misdirects the fundamental goals of education.

The student then points to the banking system as the problem. This sets up her thesis about the "true purpose" of education.

Education's true purpose is to prepare students for the real world by allowing them access to pertinent life knowledge available in their studies. Education should then entice students to apply this pertinent life knowledge to daily life struggles through praxis. In addition to her definition of the banking system, hooks offers the idea of praxis from the work of Paulo Freire. When incorporated into education, *praxis,* or "action and reflection upon the world in order to change it" (185), offers an advantageous educational tool that enhances the true purpose of education and overcomes the banking system.

The strategy of writing an introduction as an inverted triangle entails first identifying an idea, an argument, or a concept that people appear to accept as true; next, pointing out the problems with that idea, argument, or concept; and then, in a few sentences, setting out a thesis—how those problems can be resolved.

■ The Narrative Introduction

Opening with a short **narrative**, or story, is a strategy many writers use successfully to draw readers into a topic. A narrative introduction relates a sequence of events and can be especially effective if you think you need to coax indifferent or reluctant readers into taking an interest in the topic. Of course, a narrative introduction delays the declaration of your argument, so it's wise to choose a short story that clearly connects to your argument, and get to the thesis as quickly as possible (within a few paragraphs) before your readers start wondering "What's the point of this story?"

Notice how the student writer uses a narrative introduction to her argument in her essay titled "Throwing a Punch at Gender Roles: How Women's Boxing Empowers Women."

The student's entire first paragraph is a narrative that takes us into the world of women's boxing and foreshadows her thesis.

Glancing at my watch, I ran into the gym, noting to myself that being late to the first day of boxing practice was not the right way to make a good first impression. I flew down the stairs into the basement, to the room the boxers have lovingly dubbed "The Pit." What greeted me when I got there was more than I could ever have imagined. Picture a room filled with boxing gloves of all sizes covering an entire wall, a mirror covering another, a boxing ring in a corner, and an awesome collection of framed newspaper and magazine articles chronicling the boxers whose pictures were hanging on every wall. Now picture that room with seventy-plus girls on the floor doing push-ups, sweat dripping down their faces. I was immediately struck by the discipline this sport would take from me, but I had no idea I would take so much more from it.

With her narrative as a backdrop, the student identifies a problem, using the transition word "yet" to mark her challenge to the conditions she observes in the university's women's boxing program.

The university offers the only nonmilitary-based college-level women's boxing program in America, and it also offers women the chance to push their physical limits in a regulated environment. Yet the program is plagued with disappointments. I have experienced for myself the stereotypes female boxers face and have dealt with the harsh reality that boxing is still widely recognized as only a men's sport. This paper will show that the women's boxing program at Notre Dame serves as a much-needed outlet for females to come face-to-face with

The writer then states her thesis (what her paper "will show"): Despite the problems of stereotyping, women's boxing offers women significant opportunities for growth.	aspects of themselves they would not typically get a chance to explore. It will also examine how viewing this sport as a positive opportunity for women at ND indicates that there is growing hope that very soon more activities similar to women's boxing may be better received by society in general. I will accomplish these goals by analyzing scholarly journals, old *Observer* [the school newspaper] articles, and survey questions answered by the captains of the 20-- women's boxing team of ND.

The student writer uses a visually descriptive narrative to introduce us to the world of women's college boxing; then, in the second paragraph, she steers us toward the purpose of the paper and the methods she will use to develop her argument about what women's boxing offers to young women and to the changing world of sports.

■ The Interrogative Introduction

An **interrogative introduction** invites readers into the conversation of your essay by asking one or more questions, which the essay goes on to answer. You want to think of a question that will pique your readers' interest, enticing them to read on to discover how your insights shed light on the issue. Notice the question Daphne Spain, a professor of urban and environmental planning, uses to open her essay "Spatial Segregation and Gender Stratification in the Workplace."

Spain sets up her argument by asking a question and then tentatively answering it with a reference to a published study.	To what extent do women and men who work in different occupations also work in different space? Baran and Teegarden propose that occupational segregation in the insurance industry is "tantamount to spatial segregation by gender" since managers are overwhelmingly male and
In the third sentence, she states her thesis — that men and women have very little contact in the workplace.	clerical staff are predominantly female. This essay examines the spatial conditions of women's work and men's work and proposes that working women and men come into daily contact with one another very infrequently. Further, women's jobs can be classified as "open floor," but men's jobs are more
Finally, she outlines the effects that this lack of contact has on women.	likely to be "closed door." That is, women work in a more public environment with less control of their space than men. This lack of spatial control both reflects and contributes to women's lower occupational status by limiting opportunities for the transfer of knowledge from men to women.

By the end of this introductory paragraph, Spain has explained some of the terms she will use in her essay (*open floor* and *closed door*) and has offered in her final sentence a clear statement of her thesis.

In "Harry Potter and the Technology of Magic," literature scholar Elizabeth Teare begins by contextualizing the Harry Potter publishing phenomenon. Then she raises a question about what fueled this success story.

In her first four sentences, Teare describes something she is curious about and she hopes readers will be curious about — the popularity of the Harry Potter books.

The July/August 2001 issue of *Book* lists J. K. Rowling as one of the ten most influential people in publishing. She shares space on this list with John Grisham and Oprah Winfrey, along with less famous but equally powerful insiders in the book industry. What these industry leaders have in common is an almost magical power to make books succeed in the marketplace, and this magic, in addition to that performed with wands, Rowling's novels appear to practice. Opening weekend sales charted like those of a blockbuster movie (not to mention the blockbuster movie itself), the reconstruction of the venerable *New York Times* bestseller lists, the creation of a new nation's worth of web sites in the territory of cyberspace, and of course the legendary inspiration of tens of millions of child readers—the Harry Potter books have transformed both the technologies of reading and the way

In the fifth sentence, Teare asks the question she will try to answer in the rest of the essay.

we understand those technologies. What is it that makes these books—about a lonely boy whose first act on learning he is a wizard is to go shopping for a wand—not only an international phenomenon among children and parents and teachers but also a topic of compelling interest to literary,

Finally, in the last sentence, Teare offers a partial answer to her question — her thesis.

social, and cultural critics? I will argue that the stories the books tell, as well as the stories we're telling about them, enact both our fantasies and our fears of children's literature and publishing in the context of twenty-first-century commercial and technological culture.

In the final two sentences of the introduction, Teare raises her question about the root of this "international phenomenon" and then offers her thesis. By the end of the opening paragraph, then, the reader knows exactly what question is driving Teare's essay and the answer she proposes to explain throughout the essay.

■ The Paradoxical Introduction

A **paradoxical introduction** appeals to readers' curiosity by pointing out an aspect of the topic that runs counter to their expectations. Just as an interrogative introduction draws readers in by asking a question, a paradoxical introduction draws readers in by saying, in effect, "Here's something completely surprising and unlikely about this issue, but my essay will go on to show you how it is true." In this passage from "'Holding Back': Negotiating a Glass Ceiling on Women's Muscular Strength," sociologist Shari L. Dworkin points to a paradox in our commonsense understanding of bodies as the product of biology, not culture.

In the first sentence, Dworkin quotes from a study to identify the thinking that she is going to challenge.

Current work in gender studies points to how "when examined closely, much of what we take for granted about gender and its causes and effects either does not hold up, or can be explained differently." These arguments become especially contentious when confronting nature/culture debates on gendered *bodies*. After all, "common

Notice how Dworkin signals her own position "However" relative to commonly held assumptions.

sense" frequently tells us that flesh and blood bodies are about biology. However, bodies are also shaped and constrained through cumulative social practices, structures of opportunity, wider cultural meanings, and more.

Dworkin ends by stating her thesis, noting a paradox that will surprise readers.

Paradoxically, then, when we think that we are "really seeing" naturally sexed bodies, perhaps we are seeing the effect of internalizing gender ideologies—carrying out social practices—and this constructs our vision of "sexed" bodies.

Dworkin's strategy in the first three sentences is to describe common practice, the understanding that bodies are biological. Then, in the sentences beginning "However" and "Paradoxically," she advances the surprising idea that our bodies—not just the clothes we wear, for example—carry cultural gender markers. Her essay then goes on to examine women's weight lifting and the complex motives driving many women to create a body that is perceived as muscular but not masculine.

■ The Minding-the-Gap Introduction

This type of introduction takes its name from the British train system, the voice on the loudspeaker that intones "Mind the gap!" at every stop, to call riders' attention to the gap between the train car and the platform. In a **minding-the-gap introduction**, a writer calls readers' attention to a gap in the research on an issue and then uses the rest of the essay to fill in the "gap." A minding-the-gap introduction says, in effect, "Wait a minute. There's something missing from this conversation, and my research and ideas will fill in this gap."

For example, in the introductory paragraphs to their book *Men's Lives*, Michael S. Kimmel and Michael A. Messner explain how the book is different from other books that discuss men's lives, and how it serves a different purpose.

The authors begin with an assumption and then challenge it. A transition word "but" signals the challenge.

This is a book about men. But, unlike other books about men, which line countless library shelves, this is a book about men as men. It is a book in which men's experiences are not taken for granted as we explore the "real" and significant accomplishments of men, but a book in which those experiences are treated as significant and important in themselves.

The authors follow with a question that provokes readers' interest and points to the gap they summarize in the last sentence.

But what does it mean to examine men "as men"? Most courses in a college curriculum are about men, aren't they?

But these courses routinely deal with men only in their public roles, so we come to know and understand men as scientists, politicians, military figures, writers, and philosophers. Rarely, if ever, are men understood through the prism of gender.

Kimmel and Messner use these opening paragraphs to highlight both what they find problematic about the existing literature on men and to introduce readers to their own approach.

Steps to Drafting Introductions: Five Strategies

1 **Use an inverted triangle.** Begin with a broad situation, concept, or idea, and narrow the focus to your thesis.

2 **Begin with a narrative.** Capture readers' imagination and interest with a story that sets the stage for your argument.

3 **Ask a question that you will answer.** Provoke readers' interest with a question, and then use your thesis to answer the question.

4 **Present a paradox.** Begin with an assumption that readers accept as true, and formulate a thesis that not only challenges that assumption but may very well seem paradoxical.

5 **Mind the gap.** Identify what readers know and then what they don't know (or what you believe they need to know).

A Practice Sequence: Drafting an Introduction

1   Write or rewrite your introduction (which, as you've seen, may involve more than one paragraph), using one of the five drafting strategies discussed in this chapter. Then share your introduction with one of your peers and ask the following questions:

- To what extent did the strategy compel you to want to read further?

- To what extent is my thesis clear?

- How effectively do I draw a distinction between what I believe others assume to be true and my own approach?
- Is there another way that I might have made my introduction more compelling?

After listening to the responses, try a second strategy and then ask your peer which introduction is more effective.

2 If you do not have your own introduction to work on, revise the introduction below from a student's essay, combining two of the five drafting strategies we've discussed in this chapter.

> News correspondent Pauline Frederick once commented, "When a man gets up to speak people listen then look. When a woman gets up, people look; then, if they like what they see, they listen." Ironically, the harsh reality of this statement is given life by the ongoing controversy over America's most recognizable and sometimes notorious toy, Barbie. Celebrating her fortieth birthday this year, Barbie has become this nation's most beleaguered soldier (a woman no less) of idolatry who has been to the front lines and back more times than the average "Joe." This doll, a piece of plastic, a toy, incurs both criticism and praise spanning both ends of the ideological spectrum. Barbie's curvaceous and basically unrealistic body piques the ire of both liberals and conservatives, each contending that Barbie stands for the distinct view of the other. One hundred and eighty degrees south, others praise Barbie's (curves and all) ability to unlock youthful imagination and potential. M. G. Lord explains Barbie best: "To study Barbie, one sometimes has to hold seemingly contradictory ideas in one's head at the same time.... The doll functions like a Rorschach test: people project wildly dissimilar and often opposing meanings on it.... And her meaning, like her face, has not been static over time." In spite of the extreme polarity, a sole unconscious consensus manifests itself about Barbie. Barbie is "the icon" of womanhood and the twentieth century. She is the American dream. Barbie is "us." The question is always the same: What message does Barbie send? Barbie is a toy. She is the image of what we see.

DEVELOPING PARAGRAPHS

In your introduction, you set forth your thesis. Then, in subsequent paragraphs, you have to develop your argument. Remember our metaphor: If your thesis, or main claim, is the skewer that runs through each paragraph in your essay, then these paragraphs are the "meat" of your argument. The paragraphs that follow your introduction carry the burden of evidence in your argument. After all, a claim cannot stand on its own without supporting evidence. Generally speaking, each paragraph should include a topic sentence that brings the main idea of the paragraph into focus, be unified around the main idea of the topic sentence, and adequately develop the idea. At the same time, a paragraph does not stand on its own; as part of your overall argument, it can refer to what you've said earlier, gesture toward where you are heading, and connect to the larger conversation to which you are contributing.

We now ask you to read an excerpt from "Reinventing 'America': Call for a New National Identity," by Elizabeth Martínez, and answer some questions about how you think the author develops her argument, paragraph by paragraph. Then we discuss her work in the context of the three key elements of paragraphs: *topic sentences, unity,* and *adequate development*. As you read, pay attention to how, sentence by sentence, Martínez develops her paragraphs. We also ask that you consider how she makes her argument provocative, impassioned, and urgent for her audience.

ELIZABETH MARTÍNEZ

From Reinventing "America": Call for a New National Identity

Elizabeth Martínez is a Chicana activist who since 1960 has worked in and documented different movements for change, including the civil rights, women's, and Chicano movements. She is the author of six books and numerous articles. Her best-known work is *500 Years of Chicano History in Pictures* (1991), which became the basis of a two-part video she scripted and codirected. Her latest book is *De Colores Means All of Us: Latina Views for a Multi-Colored Century* (1998). In "Reinventing 'America,'" Martínez argues that Americans' willingness to accept a "myth" as "the basis for [the] nation's self-defined identity" has brought the country to a crisis.

▪ ▪ ▪

For some fifteen years, starting in 1940, 85 percent of all U.S. elementary schools used the Dick and Jane series to teach children how to read. The series starred Dick, Jane, their white middle-class parents, their dog Spot, and their life together in a home with a white picket fence. 1

"Look, Jane, look! See Spot run!" chirped the two kids. It was a house full of glorious family values, where Mom cooked while Daddy went to work in a suit and mowed the lawn on weekends. The Dick and Jane books also taught that you should do your job and help others. All this affirmed an equation of middle-class whiteness with virtue. 2

In the mid-1990s, museums, libraries, and eighty Public Broadcasting Service (PBS) stations across the country had exhibits and programs commemorating the series. At one museum, an attendant commented, 3

"When you hear someone crying, you know they are looking at the Dick and Jane books." It seems nostalgia runs rampant among many Euro-Americans: a nostalgia for the days of unchallenged White Supremacy—both moral and material—when life was "simple."

We've seen that nostalgia before in the nation's history. But today it signifies a problem reaching a new intensity. It suggests a national identity crisis that promises to bring in its wake an unprecedented nervous breakdown for the dominant society's psyche.

Nowhere is this more apparent than in California, which has long been on the cutting edge of the nation's present and future reality. Warning sirens have sounded repeatedly in the 1990s, such as the fierce battle over new history textbooks for public schools, Proposition 187's ugly denial of human rights to immigrants, the 1996 assault on affirmative action that culminated in Proposition 209, and the 1997 move to abolish bilingual education. Attempts to copycat these reactionary measures have been seen in other states.

The attack on affirmative action isn't really about affirmative action. Essentially it is another tactic in today's war on the gains of the 1960s, a tactic rooted in Anglo resentment and fear. A major source of that fear: the fact that California will almost surely have a majority of people of color in twenty to thirty years at most, with the nation as a whole not far behind.

Check out the February 3, 1992, issue of *Sports Illustrated* with its double-spread ad for *Time* magazine. The ad showed hundreds of newborn babies in their hospital cribs, all of them Black or brown except for a rare white face here and there. The headline says, "Hey, whitey! It's your turn at the back of the bus!" The ad then tells you, read *Time* magazine to keep up with today's hot issues. That manipulative image could have been published today; its implication of shifting power appears to be the recurrent nightmare of too many potential Anglo allies.

Euro-American anxiety often focuses on the sense of a vanishing national identity. Behind the attacks on immigrants, affirmative action, and multiculturalism, behind the demand for "English Only" laws and the rejection of bilingual education, lies the question: with all these new people, languages, and cultures, what will it mean to be an American? If that question once seemed, to many people, to have an obvious, universally applicable answer, today new definitions must be found. But too often Americans, with supposed scholars in the lead, refuse to face that need and instead nurse a nostalgia for some bygone clarity. They remain trapped in denial.

An array of such ostriches, heads in the sand, began flapping their feathers noisily with the publication of Allan Bloom's 1987 best-selling book, *The Closing of the American Mind.* Bloom bemoaned the decline of our "common values" as a society, meaning the decline of Euro-American cultural centricity (shall we just call it cultural imperialism?). Since then we have seen constant sniping at "diversity" goals across the land. The assault has often focused on how U.S. history is taught. And with reason, for this country's identity rests on a particular narrative about the historical origins of the United States as a nation.

The Great White Origin Myth

Every society has an origin narrative that explains that society to itself and the world with a set of stories and symbols. The origin myth, as scholar-activist Roxanne Dunbar Ortiz has termed it, defines how a society understands its place in the world and its history. The myth provides the basis for a nation's self-defined identity. Most origin narratives can be called myths because they usually present only the most flattering view of a nation's history; they are not distinguished by honesty. *10*

Ours begins with Columbus "discovering" a hemisphere where some 80 million people already lived but didn't really count (in what became the United States, they were just buffalo-chasing "savages" with no grasp of real estate values and therefore doomed to perish). It continues with the brave Pilgrims, a revolution by independence-loving colonists against a decadent English aristocracy, and the birth of an energetic young republic that promised democracy and equality (that is, to white male landowners). In the 1840s, the new nation expanded its size by almost one-third, thanks to a victory over that backward land of little brown people called Mexico. Such has been the basic account of how the nation called the United States of America came into being as presently configured. *11*

The myth's omissions are grotesque. It ignores three major pillars of our nationhood: genocide, enslavement, and imperialist expansion (such nasty words, who wants to hear them?—but that's the problem). The massive extermination of indigenous peoples provided our land base; the enslavement of African labor made our economic growth possible; and the seizure of half of Mexico by war (or threat of renewed war) extended this nation's boundaries north to the Pacific and south to the Rio Grande. Such are the foundation stones of the United States, within an economic system that made this country the first in world history to be born capitalist.... *12*

Racism as Linchpin of the U.S. National Identity

A crucial embellishment of the origin myth and key element of the national identity has been the myth of the frontier, analyzed in Richard Slotkin's *Gunfighter Nation*, the last volume of a fascinating trilogy. He *13* describes Theodore Roosevelt's belief that the West was won thanks to American arms, "the means by which progress and nationality will be achieved." That success, Roosevelt continued, "depends on the heroism of men who impose on the course of events the latent virtues of their 'race.'" Roosevelt saw conflict on the frontier producing a series of virile "fighters and breeders" who would eventually generate a new leadership class. Militarism thus went hand in hand with the racialization of history's protagonists....

The frontier myth embodied the nineteenth-century concept of Manifest Destiny, a doctrine that served to justify expansionist violence by means of intrinsic racial superiority. Manifest Destiny was Yankee conquest as the inevitable result of a confrontation between enterprise and progress (white) versus passivity and backwardness (Indian, Mexican). "Manifest" meant "God-given," and the whole doctrine is profoundly rooted in religious conviction going back to the earliest colonial times. In his short, powerful book *Manifest Destiny: American Expansion and the Empire of Right*, Professor Anders Stephanson tells how the Puritans reinvented the Jewish notion of chosenness and applied it to this hemisphere so that territorial expansion became God's will.... *14*

Manifest Destiny Dies Hard

The concept of Manifest Destiny, with its assertion of racial superiority sustained by military power, has defined U.S. identity for 150 years.... *15*

Today's origin myth and the resulting concept of national identity make for an intellectual prison where it is dangerous to ask big questions about this society's superiority. When otherwise decent people are trapped in such a powerful desire not to feel guilty, self-deception becomes unavoidable. To cease our present falsification of collective memory should, and could, open the doors of that prison. When together we cease equating whiteness with Americanness, a new day can dawn. As David Roediger, the social historian, has said, "[Whiteness] is the empty and therefore terrifying attempt to build an identity on what one isn't, and on whom one can hold back." *16*

Redefining the U.S. origin narrative, and with it this country's national identity, could prove liberating for our collective psyche. It does not mean Euro-Americans should wallow individually in guilt. It does mean accepting collective responsibility to deal with the implications of our real origin. A few apologies, for example, might be a step in the right direction. In 1997, the idea was floated in Congress to apologize for slavery; it encountered opposition from all sides. But to reject the notion because corrective action, not an apology, is needed misses the point. Having defined itself as the all-time best country in the world, the United States fiercely denies the need to make a *17* serious official apology for anything.... To press for any serious, official apology does imply a new origin narrative, a new self-image, an ideo-logical sea-change.

Accepting the implications of a different narrative could also shed   *18*
light on today's struggles. In the affirmative-action struggle, for exam-ple, opponents have said that that policy is no longer needed because racism ended with the Civil Rights Movement. But if we look at slavery as a fundamental pillar of this nation, going back centuries, it becomes obvious that racism could not have been ended by thirty years of mild reforms. If we see how the myth of the frontier idealized the white male adventurer as the central hero of national history, with the woman as sunbonneted helpmate, then we might better understand the dehu-manized ways in which women have continued to be treated. A more truthful origin narrative could also help break down divisions among peoples of color by revealing common experiences and histories of cooperation.

Reading as a Writer

1. To what extent does the narrative Martínez begins with make you want to read further?
2. How does she connect this narrative to the rest of her argument?
3. How does she use repetition to create unity in her essay?
4. What assumptions does Martínez challenge?
5. How does she use questions to engage her readers?

■ Use Topic Sentences to Focus Your Paragraphs

The **topic sentence** states the main point of a paragraph. It should

- provide a partial answer to the question motivating the writer.
- act as an extension of the writer's thesis and the question motivating the writer's argument.
- serve as a guidepost, telling readers what the paragraph is about.
- help create unity and coherence both within the paragraph and within the essay.

Elizabeth Martínez begins by describing how elementary schools in the 1940s and 1950s used the Dick and Jane series not only to teach read-ing but also to foster a particular set of values—values that she believes do not serve all children enrolled in America's schools. In paragraph 4, she states her thesis, explaining that nostalgia in the United States has created "a national identity crisis that promises to bring in its wake an unprecedented nervous breakdown for the dominant society's psyche." This is a point that builds on an observation she makes in paragraph 3: "It seems nostalgia runs rampant among many Euro-Americans: a nostalgia for the days of unchallenged White Supremacy—both moral and material—when life was 'simple.'" Martínez often returns to this notion of nostalgia for a past that seems "simple" to explain what she sees as an impending crisis.

Consider the first sentence of paragraph 5 as a topic sentence. With Martínez's key points in mind, notice how she uses the sentence to make her thesis more specific. Notice too, how she ties in the crisis and breakdown she alludes to in paragraph 4. Essentially, Martínez tells her readers that they can see these problems at play in California, an indicator of "the nation's present and future reality."

> *Nowhere is this more apparent than in California, which has long been on the cutting edge of the nation's present and future reality.* Warning sirens have sounded repeatedly in the 1990s, such as the fierce battle over new history textbooks for public schools, Proposition 187's ugly denial of human rights to immigrants, the 1996 assault on affirmative action that culminated in Proposition 209, and the 1997 move to abolish bilingual education. *Attempts to copycat these reactionary measures have been seen in other states.*

The final sentence of paragraph 5 sets up the remainder of the essay.

As readers, we expect each subsequent paragraph to respond in some way to the issue Martínez has raised. She meets that expectation by formulating a topic sentence that appears at the beginning of the paragraph. The topic sentence is what helps create unity and coherence in the essay.

■ Create Unity in Your Paragraphs

Each paragraph in an essay should focus on the subject suggested by the topic sentence. If a paragraph begins with one focus or major point of discussion, it should not end with another. Several strategies can contribute to the unity of each paragraph.

Use details that follow logically from your topic sentence and maintain a single focus—a focus that is clearly an extension of your thesis. For example, in paragraph 5, Martínez's topic sentence ("Nowhere is this more apparent than in California, which has long been on the cutting edge of the nation's present and future reality") helps to create unity because it refers back to her thesis (*this* refers to the "national identity crisis" mentioned in paragraph 4) and limits the focus of what she includes in the paragraph to "the fierce battle over new history textbooks" and recent pieces of legislation in California that follow directly from and support the claim of the topic sentence.

Repeat key words to guide your readers.   A second strategy for creating unity is to repeat (or use synonyms for) key words within a given paragraph. You can see this at work in paragraph 12 (notice the words we've underscored), where Martínez explains that America's origin narrative omits significant details:

> The myth's omissions are grotesque. It ignores three major pillars of our nationhood: <u>genocide</u>, <u>enslavement</u>, and <u>imperialist expansion</u> (such nasty words, who wants to hear them?—but that's the problem). The massive <u>extermination</u> of indigenous peoples provided our land base; the <u>enslavement</u> of African labor made our economic growth possible; and the <u>seizure</u> of half of Mexico by war (or threat of renewed war) extended this nation's boundaries north to the Pacific and south to the Rio Grande. Such are the foundation stones of the United States, within an economic system that made this country the first in world history to be born capitalist....

Specifically, Martínez tells us that the origin narrative ignores "three major pillars of our nationhood: genocide, enslavement, and imperialist expansion." She then substitutes *extermination* for "genocide," repeats *enslavement*, and substitutes *seizure* for "imperialist expansion." By connecting words in a paragraph, as Martínez does here, you help readers understand that the details you provide are all relevant to the point you want to make.

Use transition words to link ideas from different sentences.   A third strategy for creating unity within paragraphs is to establish a clear relationship among different ideas by using **transition words** or phrases. Transition words or phrases signal to your readers the direction your ideas are taking. Table 11.1 lists common transition words and phrases grouped by function—that is, for adding a new idea, presenting a contrasting idea, or drawing a conclusion about an idea.

Martínez uses transition words and phrases throughout the excerpt here. In several places, she uses the word *but* to make a contrast—to draw a distinction between an idea that many people accept as true and an alternative idea that she wants to pursue. Notice in paragraph 17 how she signals the importance of an official apology for slavery—and by implication genocide and the seizure of land from Mexico:

> ... A few apologies, for example, might be a step in the right direction. In 1997, the idea was floated in Congress to apologize for slavery; it encountered opposition from all sides. <u>But</u> to reject the notion because corrective action, not an apology, is needed misses the point. Having defined itself as the all-time best country in the world, the United States fiercely denies the need to make a serious official apology for anything.... To press for any serious, official apology does imply a new origin narrative, a new self-image, an ideological sea-change.

Similarly, in the last paragraph, Martínez counters the argument that affirmative action is not necessary because racism no longer exists:

TABLE 11.1   Common Transition Words and Phrases

Adding an Idea	Presenting a Contrasting Idea	Drawing a Logical Conclusion
also, and, further, moreover, in addition to, in support of, similarly	although, alternatively, as an alternative, but, by way of contrast, despite, even though, however, in contrast to, nevertheless, nonetheless, rather than, yet	as a result, because of, consequently, finally, in sum, in the end, subsequently, therefore, thus

... In the affirmative-action struggle, for example, opponents have said that that policy is no longer needed because racism ended with the Civil Rights Movement. But if we look at slavery as a fundamental pillar of this nation, going back centuries, it becomes obvious that racism could not have been ended by thirty years of mild reforms. ...

There are a number of ways to rephrase what Martínez is saying in paragraph 18. We could substitute *however* for "but." Or we could combine the two sentences into one to point to the relationship between the two competing ideas: *Although some people oppose affirmative action, believing that racism no longer exists, I would argue that racism remains a fundamental pillar of this nation.* Or we could pull together Martínez's different points to draw a logical conclusion using a transition word like *therefore.* Martínez observes that our country is in crisis as a result of increased immigration. *Therefore, we need to reassess our conceptions of national identity to account for the diversity that increased immigration has created.* We can substitute any of the transition words in Table 11.1 for drawing a logical conclusion.

The list of transition words and phrases in Table 11.1 is hardly exhaustive, but it gives you a sense of the ways to connect ideas so that readers understand how your ideas are related. Are they similar ideas? Do they build on or support one another? Are you challenging accepted ideas? Or are you drawing a logical connection from a number of different ideas?

■ Use Critical Strategies to Develop Your Paragraphs

To develop a paragraph, you can use a range of strategies, depending on what you want to accomplish and what you believe your readers will find persuasive. Among these strategies are using examples and illustrations; citing data (facts, statistics, evidence, details); analyzing texts; telling a story or an anecdote; defining terms; making comparisons; and examining causes and evaluating consequences.

Use examples and illustrations.   Examples make abstract ideas concrete through illustration. Using examples is probably the most common way to develop a piece of writing. Of course, Martínez's essay is full of examples.

In fact, she begins with an example of a series of books—the Dick and Jane books—to show how a generation of schoolchildren were exposed to white middle-class values. She also uses examples in paragraph 5, where she lists several pieces of legislation (Propositions 187 and 209) to develop the claim in her topic sentence.

Cite data.   **Data** are factual pieces of information. They function in an essay as the bases of propositions. In the first few paragraphs of the excerpt, Martínez cites statistics ("85 percent of all U.S. elementary schools used the Dick and Jane series to teach children how to read") and facts ("In the mid-1990s, museums, libraries, and eighty Public Broadcasting Service . . . stations across the country had exhibits and programs commemorating the series") to back up her claim about the popularity of the Dick and Jane series and the nostalgia the books evoke.

Analyze texts.   Analysis is the process of breaking something down into its elements to understand how they work together. When you analyze a text, you point out parts of the text that have particular significance to your argument and explain what they mean. By *texts*, we mean both verbal and visual texts. In paragraph 7, Martínez analyzes a visual text, an advertisement that appeared in *Sports Illustrated*, to reveal "its implication of shifting power"—a demographic power shift from Anglos to people of color.

Provide narratives or anecdotes.   Put simply, a narrative is an account of something that happened. More technically, a narrative relates a sequence of events that are connected in time; and an **anecdote** is a short narrative that recounts a particular incident. An anecdote, like an example, can bring an abstraction into focus. Consider Martínez's third paragraph, where the anecdote about the museum attendant brings her point about racially charged nostalgia among white Americans into memorable focus: The tears of the museum-goers indicate just how profound their nostalgia is.

By contrast, a longer narrative, in setting out its sequence of events, often opens up possibilities for analysis. Why did these events occur? Why did they occur in this sequence? What might they lead to? What are the implications? What is missing?

In paragraph 11, for example, Martínez relates several key events in the origin myth of America. Then, in the next paragraph, she explains what is omitted from the myth, or narrative, and builds her argument about the implications and consequences of those omissions.

Define terms.   A definition is an explanation of what something is and, by implication, what it is not. The simplest kind of definition is a synonym, but for the purpose of developing your argument, a one-word definition is rarely enough.

When you define your terms, you are setting forth meanings that you want your readers to agree on, so that you can continue to build your argument on the foundation of that agreement. You may have to stipulate that your definition is part of a larger whole to develop your argument. For example: "Nostalgia is a bittersweet longing for things of the past; but for the purposes of my essay, I focus on white middle-class nostalgia, which combines a longing for a past that never existed with a hostile anxiety about the present."

In paragraph 10, Martínez defines the term *origin narrative*—a myth that explains "how a society understands its place in the world and its history . . . the basis for a nation's self-defined identity." The "Great White Origin Myth" is an important concept in her developing argument about a national crisis of identity.

Make comparisons.   Technically, a **comparison** shows the similarities between two or more things, and a **contrast** shows the differences. In practice, however, it is very difficult, if not impossible, to develop a comparison that does not make use of contrast. Therefore, we use the term *comparison* to describe the strategy of comparing *and* contrasting.

Doubtless you have written paragraphs or even whole essays that take as a starting point a version of this sentence: "X and Y are similar in some respects and different in others." This neutral formulation is seldom helpful when you are developing an argument. Usually, in making your comparison—in setting forth the points of similarity and difference—you have to take an evaluative or argumentative stance.

Note the comparison in this passage:

> Although there are similarities between the current nostalgias for Dick and Jane books and for rhythm and blues music of the same era — in both cases, the object of nostalgia can move people to tears — the nostalgias spring from emotional responses that are quite different and even contradictory. I will argue that the Dick and Jane books evoke a longing for a past that is colored by a fear of the present, a longing for a time when white middle-class values were dominant and unquestioned. By contrast, the nostalgia for R&B music may indicate a yearning for a past when multicultural musicians provided white folks with a sweaty release on the dance floor from those very same white-bread values of the time.

The writer does more than list similarities and differences; she offers an analysis of what they mean and is prepared to argue for her interpretation.

Certainly Elizabeth Martínez takes an evaluative stance when she compares versions of American history in paragraphs 11 and 12. In paragraph 11, she angrily relates the sanitized story of American history, setting up a contrast in paragraph 12 with the story that does not appear in history textbooks, a story of "genocide, enslavement, and imperialist expansion." Her evaluative stance comes through clearly: She finds the first version repugnant and harmful, its omissions "grotesque."

Examine causes and evaluate consequences. In any academic discipline, questions of cause and consequence are central. Whether you are analyzing the latest election results in a political science course, reading about the causes of the Vietnam War in a history course, or speculating about the long-term consequences of climate change in a science course, questions of why things happened, happen, or will happen are inescapable.

Examining causes and consequences usually involves identifying a phenomenon and asking questions about it until you gather enough information to begin analyzing the relationships among its parts and deciding which are most significant. You can then begin to set forth your own analysis of what happened and why.

Of course, this kind of analysis is rarely straightforward, and any phenomenon worthy of academic study is bound to generate a variety of conversations about its causes and consequences. In your own thinking and research, avoid jumping to conclusions and continue to sift evidence until plausible connections present themselves. Be prepared to revise your thinking—perhaps several times—in light of new evidence.

In your writing, you also want to avoid oversimplifying. A claim like this—"The answer to curbing unemployment in the United States is to restrict immigration"—does not take into account corporate outsourcing of jobs overseas or the many other possible causes of unemployment. At the very least, you may need to explain the basis and specifics of your analysis and qualify your claim: "Recent studies of patterns of immigration and unemployment in the United States suggest that unrestricted immigration is a major factor in the loss of blue-collar job opportunities in the Southwest." Certainly this sentence is less forceful and provocative than the other one, but it does suggest that you have done significant and focused research and respect the complexity of the issue.

Throughout her essay, Martínez analyzes causes and consequences. In paragraph 8, for example, she speculates that the cause of "attacks on immigrants, affirmative action, and multiculturalism" is "Euro-American anxiety," "the sense of a vanishing national identity." In paragraph 13, she concludes that a *consequence* of Theodore Roosevelt's beliefs about race and war was a "militarism [that] went hand in hand with the racialization of history's protagonists." In paragraph 16, the topic sentence itself is a statement about causes and consequences: "Today's origin myth and the resulting concept of national identity make for an intellectual prison where it is dangerous to ask big questions about this society's superiority."

Having shown where and how Martínez uses critical strategies to develop her paragraphs, we must hasten to add that these critical strategies usually work in combination. Although you can easily develop an entire paragraph (or even an entire essay) using comparison, it is almost impossible to do so without relying on one or more of the other strategies. What if you need to tell an anecdote about the two authors you are comparing? What if you have to cite data about different rates of economic growth to clarify the main claim of your comparison? What if you are comparing different causes and consequences?

Our point is that the strategies described here are methods for exploring your issue in writing. How you make use of them, individually or in combination, depends on which can help you best communicate your argument to your readers.

Steps to Developing Paragraphs

1 **Use topic sentences to focus your paragraphs.** Remember that a topic sentence partially answers the question motivating you to write; acts as an extension of your thesis; indicates to your readers what the paragraph is about; and helps create unity both within the paragraph and within the essay.

2 **Create unity in your paragraphs.** The details in your paragraph should follow logically from your topic sentence and maintain a single focus, one tied clearly to your thesis. Repetition and transition words also help create unity in paragraphs.

3 **Use critical strategies to develop your paragraphs.** Use examples and illustrations; cite data; analyze texts; tell stories or anecdotes; define terms; make comparisons; and examine causes and evaluate consequences.

A Practice Sequence: Working with Paragraphs

We would like you to work in pairs on paragraphing. The objective of this exercise is to gauge the effectiveness of your topic sentences and the degree to which your paragraphs are unified and fully developed.

Make a copy of your essay and cut it up into paragraphs. Shuffle the paragraphs to be sure they are no longer in the original order, and then exchange cut-up drafts with your partner. The challenge is to put your partner's essay back together again. When you both have finished, compare your reorderings with the original drafts. Were you able to reproduce the original organization exactly? If not, do the variations make sense? If one or the other of you had trouble putting the essay back together, talk about the adequacy of your topic sentences, ways to revise topic sentences in keeping with the details in a given paragraph, and strategies for making paragraphs more unified and coherent.

DRAFTING CONCLUSIONS

In writing a conclusion to your essay, you are making a final appeal to your audience. You want to convince readers that what you have written is a relevant, meaningful interpretation of a shared issue. You also want to remind them that your argument is reasonable. Rather than summarize all of the points you've made in the essay—assume your readers have carefully read what you've written—pull together the key components of your argument in the service of answering the question "So what?" Establish why your argument is important: What will happen if things stay the same? What will happen if things change? How effective your conclusion is depends on whether or not readers feel that you have adequately addressed "So what?"—that you have made clear what is significant and of value.

In building on the specific details of your argument, you can also place what you have written in a broader context. (What are the sociological implications of your argument? How far-reaching are they? Are there political implications? Economic implications?) Finally, explain again how your ideas contribute something new to the conversation by building on, extending, or even challenging what others have argued.

In her concluding paragraph, Elizabeth Martínez brings together her main points, puts her essay in a broader context, indicates what's new in her argument, and answers the question "So what?":

> Accepting the implications of a different narrative could also shed light on today's struggles. In the affirmative-action struggle, for example, opponents have said that that policy is no longer needed because racism ended with the Civil Rights Movement. But if we look at slavery as a fundamental pillar of this nation, going back centuries, it becomes obvious that racism could not have been ended by thirty years of mild reforms. If we see how the myth of the frontier idealized the white male adventurer as the central hero of national history, with the woman as sunbonneted helpmate, then we might better understand the dehumanized ways in which women have continued to be treated. A more truthful origin narrative could also help break down divisions among peoples of color by revealing common experiences and histories of cooperation.

Let's examine this concluding paragraph:

1. Although Martínez refers back to important events and ideas she has discussed, she does not merely summarize. Instead, she suggests the implications of those important events and ideas in her first sentence (the topic sentence), which crystallizes the main point of her essay: Americans need a different origin narrative.

2. Then she puts those implications in the broader context of contemporary racial and gender issues.

3. She signals what's new in her argument with the word *if* (*if we look at slavery in a new way*; *if we look at the frontier myth in a new way*).

4. Finally, her answers to why this issue matters culminate in the last sentence. This last sentence connects and extends the claim of her topic sentence, by asserting that a "more truthful origin narrative" could help heal divisions among peoples of color who have been misrepresented by the old origin myth. Clearly, she believes the implications of her argument matter: A new national identity has the potential to heal a country in crisis, a country on the verge of a "nervous breakdown" (para. 4).

Martínez also does something else in the last sentence of the concluding paragraph: She looks to the future, suggesting what the future implications of her argument could be. Looking to the future is one of five strategies for shaping a conclusion. The others we discuss are echoing the introduction, challenging the reader, posing questions, and concluding with a quotation. Each of these strategies appeals to readers in different ways; therefore, we suggest you try them all out in writing your own conclusions. Also, remember that some of these strategies can be combined. For example, you can write a conclusion that challenges readers, poses a question, looks to the future, and ends with a quotation.

■ Echo the Introduction

Echoing the introduction in your conclusion helps readers come full circle. It helps them see how you have developed your idea from beginning to end. In the following example, the student writer begins with a voice speaking from behind an Islamic veil, revealing the ways that Western culture misunderstands the symbolic value of wearing the veil. The writer repeats this visual image in her conclusion, quoting from the Koran: "Speak to them from behind a curtain."

Notice that the author begins with "a voice from behind the shrouds of an Islamic veil" and then echoes this quotation in her conclusion: "Speak to them from behind a curtain."

Introduction: A voice from behind the shrouds of an Islamic veil exclaims: "I often wonder whether people see me as a radical, fundamentalist Muslim terrorist packing an AK-47 assault rifle inside my jean jacket. Or maybe they see me as the poster girl for oppressed womanhood everywhere." In American culture where shameless public exposure, particularly of females, epitomizes ultimate freedom, the head-to-toe covering of a Muslim woman seems inherently oppressive. Driven by an autonomous national attitude, the inhabitants of the "land of the free" are quick to equate the veil with indisputable persecution. Yet Muslim women reveal the enslaving hijab as a symbolic display of the Islamic ideals — honor, modesty, and stability. Because of an unfair American assessment, the aura of hijab mystery cannot be removed until the customs and ethics of Muslim culture are genuinely explored. It is this form of enigmatic seclusion that forms the feminist controversy between Western liberals, who perceive the veil as an inhibiting factor against free will, and Islamic disciples, who conceptualize the veil as a sacred symbol of utmost morality.

Conclusion: For those who improperly judge an alien religion, the veil becomes a symbol of oppression and devastation, instead of a representation of pride and piety. Despite Western images, the hijab is a daily revitalization and reminder of the Islamic societal and religious ideals, thereby upholding the conduct and attitudes of the Muslim community. Americans share these ideals yet fail to recognize them in the context of a different culture. By sincerely exploring the custom of Islamic veiling, one will realize the vital role the hijab plays in shaping Muslim culture by sheltering women, and consequently society, from the perils that erupt from indecency. The principles implored in the Koran of modesty, honor, and stability construct a unifying and moral view of the Islamic Middle Eastern society when properly investigated. As it was transcribed from Allah, "Speak to them from behind a curtain. This is purer for your hearts and their hearts."

Notice how the conclusion echoes the introduction in its reference to a voice speaking from behind a curtain.

■ Challenge the Reader

By issuing a challenge to your readers, you create a sense of urgency, provoking them to act to change the status quo. In this example, the student writer explains the unacceptable consequences of preventing young women from educating themselves about AIDS and the spread of a disease that has already reached epidemic proportions.

The changes in AIDS education that I am suggesting are necessary and relatively simple to make. Although the current curriculum in high school health classes is helpful and informative, it simply does not pertain to young women as much as it should. AIDS is killing women at an alarming rate, and many people do not realize this. According to Daniel DeNoon, AIDS is one of the six leading causes of death among women aged 18 to 45, and women "bear the brunt of the worldwide AIDS epidemic." For this reason, DeNoon argues, women are one of the most important new populations that are contracting HIV at a high rate. I challenge young women to be more well-informed about AIDS and their link to the disease; otherwise, many new cases may develop. As the epidemic continues to spread, women need to realize that

Here the author cites a final piece of research to emphasize the extent of the problem.

Here she begins her explicit challenge to readers about what they have to do to protect themselves or their students from infection.

they can stop the spread of the disease and protect themselves from infection and a number of related complications. It is the responsibility of health educators to present this to young women and inform them of the powerful choices that they can make.

■ Look to the Future

Looking to the future is particularly relevant when you are asking readers to take action. To move readers to action, you must establish the persistence of a problem and the consequences of letting a situation continue unchanged. In the concluding paragraph below, the student author points out a number of things that teachers need to do to involve parents in their children's education. She identifies a range of options before identifying what she believes is perhaps the most important action teachers can take.

The second through fifth sentences present an array of options.

First and foremost, teachers must recognize the ways in which some parents are positively contributing to their children's academic endeavors. Teachers must recognize nontraditional methods of participation as legitimate and work toward supporting parents in these tasks. For instance, teachers might send home suggestions for local after-school tutoring programs. Teachers must also try to make urban parents feel welcome and respected in their school. Teachers might call parents to ask their opinion about a certain difficulty their child is having, or invite them to talk about something of interest to them. One parent, for instance, spoke highly of the previous superintendent who had let him use his work as a film producer to help with a show for students during homeroom. If teachers can develop innovative ways to utilize parents' talents and interests rather than just inviting them to be passively involved in an already-in-place curriculum, more parents might respond. Perhaps, most importantly, if teachers want parents to be involved in students' educations, they must make the parents feel as though their opinions and concerns have real weight. When parents such as those interviewed for this study voice concerns and questions over their child's progress, it is imperative that teachers acknowledge and answer them.

In the last two sentences, the writer looks to the future with her recommendations.

■ Pose Questions

Posing questions stimulates readers to think about the implications of your argument and to apply what you argue to other situations. This is the case in the following paragraph, in which the student writer focuses on immigration and then shifts readers' attention to racism and the possibility of hate crimes. It's useful to extrapolate from your argument, to raise questions that test whether what you write can be applied to different situations. These questions can help readers understand what is at issue.

The first question.

Also, my research may apply to a broader spectrum of sociological topics. There has been recent discussion about the increasing trend of immigration. Much of this discussion has involved the distribution of resources to immigrants. Should immigrants have equal access to certain economic and educational resources in America? The decision is split. But it will be interesting to see how this debate will play out. If immigrants are granted more resources, will certain Americans mobilize against the distribution of these resources? Will we see another rise in racist groups such as the Ku Klux Klan in order to prevent immigrants from obtaining more resources? My research can also be used to understand global conflict or war. In general, groups mobilize when their established resources are threatened by an external force. Moreover, groups use framing processes to justify their collective action to others.

Other speculative questions follow from possible responses to the writer's first question.

■ Conclude with a Quotation

A quotation can strengthen your argument, indicating that others in positions of power and authority support your stance. A quotation also can add poignancy to your argument, as it does in the following excerpt, in which the quotation amplifies the idea that people use Barbie to advance their own interests.

The question still remains, what does Barbie mean? Is she the spokeswoman for the empowerment of women, or rather is she performing the dirty work of conservative patriarchy? I do not think we will ever know the answer. Rather, Barbie is the undeniable "American Icon." She is a toy, and she is what we want her to be. A test performed by Albert M. Magro at Fairmont State College titled "Why Barbie Is Perceived as Beautiful" shows that Barbie is the epitome of what we as humans find beautiful. The test sought to find human preferences on evolutionary changes in the human body. Subjects were shown a series of photos comparing different human body parts, such as the size and shape of the eyes, and asked to decide which feature they preferred: the primitive or derived (more evolved traits). The test revealed that the subjects preferred the derived body traits. It is these preferred evolutionary features that are utilized on the body of Barbie. Barbie is truly an extension of what we are and

The writer quotes an authority to amplify the idea that individually and collectively, we project significance on toys.

what we perceive. Juel Best concludes his discourse on Barbie with these words: "Toys do not embody violence or sexism or occult meanings. People must assign toys their meanings." Barbie is whoever we make her out to be. Barbie grabs hold of our imaginations and lets us go wild.

Steps to Drafting Conclusions: Five Strategies

1 **Pull together the main claims of your essay.** Don't simply repeat points you make in the paper. Instead, show readers how the points you make fit together.

2 **Answer the question "So what?"** Show your readers why your stand on the issue is significant.

3 **Place your argument in a larger context.** Discuss the specifics of your argument, but also indicate its broader implications.

4 **Show readers what is new.** As you synthesize the key points of your argument, explain how what you argue builds on, extends, or challenges the thinking of others.

5 **Decide on the best strategy for writing your conclusion.** Will you echo the introduction? Challenge the reader? Look to the future? Pose questions? Conclude with a quotation? Choose the best strategy or strategies to appeal to your readers.

A Practice Sequence: Drafting a Conclusion

1 Write your conclusion, using one of the strategies described in this section. Then share your conclusion with a classmate. Ask this person to address the following questions:

- Did I pull together the key points of the argument?
- Did I answer "So what?" adequately?
- Are the implications I want readers to draw from the essay clear?

After listening to the responses, try a second strategy, and then ask your classmate which conclusion is more effective.

2 If you do not have a conclusion of your own, analyze each example conclusion above to see how well each appears to (1) pull together the main claim of the essay, (2) answer "So what?" (3) place the argument in a larger context, and (4) show readers what is new.

ANALYZING STRATEGIES FOR WRITING: FROM INTRODUCTIONS TO CONCLUSIONS

Now that you have studied the various strategies for writing introductions, developing your ideas in subsequent paragraphs, and drafting conclusions, read Barbara Ehrenreich's essay, "Cultural Baggage," and analyze the strategies she uses for developing her argument about diversity. It may help to refer to the practice sequences for drafting introductions (p. 320) and conclusions (p. 339), as well as Steps to Developing Paragraphs (p. 333). Ideally, you should work with your classmates, in groups of three or four, assigning one person to record your ideas and share with the whole class.

Alternatively, you could put the essays by Ehrenreich and Elizabeth Martínez "in conversation" with one another. How do Martínez and Ehrenreich define the issues around diversity? What is at stake for them in the arguments they develop? What things need to change? How would you compare the way each uses stories and personal anecdotes to develop her ideas? Would you say that either writer is a more effective "conversationalist" or more successful in fulfilling her purpose?

BARBARA EHRENREICH

Cultural Baggage

Barbara Ehrenreich is a social critic, activist, and political essayist. Her book *Nickel and Dimed: On (Not) Getting By in America* (2001) describes her attempt to live on low-wage jobs; it became a national best seller in the United States. Her book, *Bait and Switch: The (Futile) Pursuit of the American Dream* (2005), explores the shadowy world of the white-collar unemployed. Recent books of cultural analysis by Ehrenreich include *Bright-Sided: How the Relentless Promotion of Positive Thinking Has Undermined America* and *This Land Is Their Land: Reports from a Divided Nation* (both published in 2009). Ehrenreich has also written for *Mother Jones, The Atlantic, Ms., The New Republic, In These Times,* Salon.com, and other publications. "Cultural Baggage" was originally published in the *New York Times Magazine* in 1992. Her most recent book is *Living with a Wild God,* a memoir that she published in 2014.

■ ■ ■

An acquaintance was telling me about the joys of rediscovering her ethnic and religious heritage. "I know exactly what my ancestors were doing 2,000 years ago," she said, eyes gleaming with enthusiasm, "and *I can do the same things now.*" Then she leaned forward and inquired politely, "And what is your ethnic background, if I may ask?"   *1*

"None," I said, that being the first word in line to get out of my mouth. Well, not "none," I backtracked. Scottish, English, Irish—that was something, I supposed. Too much Irish to qualify as a WASP; too much of the hated English to warrant a "Kiss Me, I'm Irish" button; plus there are a number of dead ends in the family tree due to adoptions, missing records, failing memories, and the like. I was blushing by this time. Did "none" mean I was rejecting my heritage out of Anglo-Celtic self-hate? Or was I revealing a hidden ethnic chauvinism in which the Britannically derived serve as a kind of neutral standard compared with the ethnic "others"?

Throughout the 1960s and 70s, I watched one group after another— African Americans, Latinos, Native Americans—stand up and proudly reclaim their roots while I just sank back ever deeper into my seat. All this excitement over ethnicity stemmed, I uneasily sensed, from a past in which *their* ancestors had been trampled upon by *my* ancestors, or at least by people who looked very much like them. In addition, it had begun to seem almost un-American not to have some sort of hyphen at hand, linking one to more venerable times and locales.

But the truth is, I was raised with none. We'd eaten ethnic foods in my childhood home, but these were all borrowed, like the pasties, or Cornish meat pies, my father had picked up from his fellow miners in Butte, Montana. If my mother had one rule, it was militant ecumenism in all manners of food and experience. "Try new things," she would say, meaning anything from sweetbreads to clams, with an emphasis on the "new."

As a child, I briefly nourished a craving for tradition and roots. I immersed myself in the works of Sir Walter Scott. I pretended to believe that the bagpipe was a musical instrument. I was fascinated to learn from a grandmother that we were descended from certain Highland clans and longed for a pleated skirt in one of their distinctive tartans.

But in *Ivanhoe*, it was the dark-eyed "Jewess" Rebecca I identified with, not the flaxen-haired bimbo Rowena. As for clans: Why not call them "tribes," those bands of half-clad peasants and warriors whose idea of cuisine was stuffed sheep gut washed down with whiskey? And then there was the sting of Disraeli's remark—which I came across in my early teens—to the effect that his ancestors had been leading orderly, literate lives when my ancestors were still rampaging through the Highlands daubing themselves with blue paint.

Motherhood put the screws on me, ethnicity-wise. I had hoped that by marrying a man of Eastern European Jewish ancestry I would acquire for my descendants the ethnic genes that my own forebears so sadly lacked. At one point, I even subjected the children to a seder of my own design, including a little talk about the flight from Egypt and its relevance to modern social issues. But the kids insisted on buttering their matzos and snickering through my talk. "Give me a break, Mom," the older one said. "You don't even believe in God."

After the tiny pagans had been put to bed, I sat down to brood over Elijah's wine. What had I been thinking? The kids knew that their Jewish grandparents were secular folks who didn't hold seders themselves. And if ethnicity eluded me, how could I expect it to take root in my children, who are not only Scottish English Irish, but Hungarian Polish Russian to boot? *8*

But, then, on the fumes of Manischewitz, a great insight took form in my mind. It was true, as the kids said, that I didn't "believe in God." But this could be taken as something very different from an accusation—a reminder of a genuine heritage. My parents had not believed in God either, nor had my grandparents or any other progenitors going back to the great-great level. They had become disillusioned with Christianity generations ago—just as, on the in-law side, my children's other ancestors had shaken their Orthodox Judaism. This insight did not exactly furnish me with an "identity," but it was at least something to work with: We are the kind of people, I realized—whatever our distant ancestors' religions—who do *not* believe, who do not carry on traditions, who do not do things just because someone has done them before. *9*

The epiphany went on: I recalled that my mother never introduced a procedure for cooking or cleaning by telling me, "Grandma did it this way." What did Grandma know, living in the days before vacuum cleaners and disposable toilet mops? In my parents' general view, new things were better than old, and the very fact that some ritual had been performed in the past was a good reason for abandoning it now. Because what was the past, as our forebears knew it? Nothing but poverty, superstition, and grief. "Think for yourself," Dad used to say. "Always ask why." *10*

In fact, this may have been the ideal cultural heritage for my particular ethnic strain—bounced as it was from the Highlands of Scotland across the sea, out to the Rockies, down into the mines, and finally spewed out into high-tech, suburban America. What better philosophy, for a race of migrants, than "Think for yourself"? What better maxim, for a people whose whole world was rudely inverted every thirty years or so, than "Try new things"? *11*

The more tradition-minded, the newly enthusiastic celebrants of Purim and Kwanzaa and Solstice, may see little point to survival if the survivors carry no cultural freight—religion, for example, or ethnic tradition. To which I would say that skepticism, curiosity, and wide-eyed ecumenical tolerance are also worthy elements of the human tradition and are at least as old as such notions as "Serbian" or "Croatian," "Scottish" or "Jewish." I make no claims for my personal line of progenitors except that they remained loyal to the values that may have *12* induced all of our ancestors, long, long ago, to climb down from the trees and make their way into the open plains.

A few weeks ago, I cleared my throat and asked the children, now mostly grown and fearsomely smart, whether they felt any stirrings of ethnic or religious identity, etc., which might have been, ahem, insufficiently nourished at home. "None," they said, adding firmly, "and the world would be a better place if nobody else did, either." My chest swelled with pride, as would my mother's, to know that the race of "none" marches on.   *13*

12

From Revising to Editing
Working with Peer Groups

Academic writing is a collaborative enterprise. By reading and commenting on your drafts, your peers can support your work as a writer. And you can support the work of your peers by reading their drafts with a critical but constructive eye.

In this chapter, we set out the differences between revising and editing, discuss the peer editing process in terms of the composition pyramid, present a model peer editing session, and then explain the writer's and reader's responsibilities through early drafts, later drafts, and final drafts, providing opportunities for you to practice peer response on three drafts of a student paper.

REVISING VERSUS EDITING

We make a distinction between revising and editing. By **revising**, we mean making changes to a paper to reflect new thinking or conceptualizing. If a reader finds that the real focus of your essay comes at the end of your draft, you need to revise the paper with this new focus in mind. Revising differs from **editing**, which involves minor changes to what will be the final draft of a paper—replacing a word here and there, correcting misspellings, or substituting dashes for commas to create emphasis, for example.

When you're reading a first or second draft, the niceties of style, spelling, and punctuation are not priorities. After all, if the writer had to change the focus of his or her argument, significant changes to words, phrases, and punctuation would be inevitable. Concentrating on editing errors early on, when the writer is still trying to develop an argument with evidence, organize information logically, and anticipate counterarguments, is inefficient and even counterproductive.

Here are some characteristics of revising and editing that can guide how you read your own writing and comment on the writing of others:

REVISING	EDITING
Treats writing as a work in progress	Treats writing as an almost-finished product
Focuses on new possibilities both within and beyond the text	Addresses obvious errors and deficiencies
Focuses on new questions or goals	Focuses on the draft and does not suggest new avenues for discussion
Considers both purpose and readers' needs	Considers grammar, punctuation, spelling, and style
Encourages further discovery	Polishes up the essay

Again, writing is a process, and revising is an integral part of that process. Your best writing will happen in the context of real readers responding to your drafts. Look at the acknowledgments in any academic book, and you will see many people credited with having improved the book through their comments on drafts and ideas. All academic writers rely on conversations with others to strengthen their work.

THE PEER EDITING PROCESS

We emphasize that the different stages of writing—early, later, and final—call for different work from both readers and writers because writers' needs vary with each successive draft. These stages correspond to what has been called the composition pyramid (Figure 12.1).* The composition

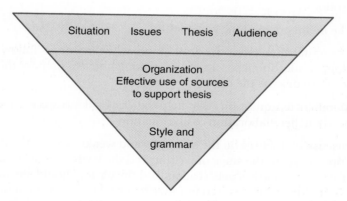

FIGURE 12.1   The Composition Pyramid

*Information from Susannah Brietz-Monta and Anthony Monta.

pyramid represents elements of writing that can help you decide what to pay attention to at different stages of writing.

1. The top of this inverted pyramid corresponds to the early stages of writing. At this point, members of the writing group should identify the situation the writer is responding to (for example, homelessness, inequality, or air pollution), the issue the writer has defined (for example, the economic versus the social costs of homelessness), the thesis or argument the writer advances, and the extent to which the writer addresses a given audience appropriately.

2. The middle portion of the pyramid corresponds to a later stage of the writing process, the point at which members of the group should move on to discuss the writer's organization and use of sources. Is the argument logically organized? Has the writer integrated quotations smoothly into the paper? Is the evidence relevant, recent, and credible?

3. Finally, the bottom of the pyramid corresponds to the final stages of drafting. As the writer's focus shifts to grammar and style, so should the group's. Questions to ask: Is this specific language appropriate to the intended audience? Has the writer presented the argument in ways that will compel readers — even those who disagree — to listen?

Steps in the Peer Editing Process

1 The writer distributes copies of the draft to each member of the writing group. (Ideally, the group should not exceed four students.)

2 The writer distributes a cover letter, setting an agenda for the group.

3 The members read the cover letter.

4 The writer then reads the draft aloud, while members follow along, underlining passages and making notes to prepare themselves to discuss the draft.

5 Members ask questions that help the writer identify concepts that need further elaboration or clarification.

6 Discussion focuses on the strengths and weaknesses of the draft appropriate to the stage of writing and the writer's concerns. (Even in the early stage, readers and the writer should sustain discussion for at least ten minutes before the next student takes a turn as writer.)

PEER GROUPS IN ACTION: A SAMPLE SESSION

Let's take a look at one writing group in action to see the potential of this approach to writing. One student, Rebecca Jegier, worked collaboratively with three other students—Jasmine, Michaela, and Kevin—on a paper about the purpose of education and the extent to which school reforms reflect what she refers to as "a growing culture of impatience." She explained to her group that she struggled to draw a parallel between what she sees as a worn-out factory model of education (students sitting in rows) and the story of Blockbuster, a once-successful movie rental business that failed to respond to customers' changing needs. She also felt that she still needed to sharpen her argument.

> **Rebecca:** I think we are expected to argue what we think the purpose of education should be and to place our argument in the larger context of how others have defined the purpose historically.
>
> **Jasmine:** I am still trying to decide what I think the purpose of education should be. I sort of think that education should prepare people for a job, but we also read that article—you know, the one that said we may not even know what jobs will be available in ten years. The author wrote that schools should prepare people to be creative, innovative, critical thinkers. That other essay explained that school should help people flourish. I haven't decided what that means.
>
> **Michaela:** I think the important thing we need to decide is the issue. I agree that schools don't really prepare us to be very creative or innovative. I guess that's the issue.

Rebecca restated her understanding of the assignment before giving Jasmine, Michaela, and Kevin a copy of her draft. This is a valuable starting point because a writer's interpretation of the writing assignment—the task, the purpose, and the audience—helps readers understand why she is taking a particular approach. If readers disagree with the writer's interpretation, they should discuss their differences before the writer shares the draft and determine an appropriate response to the assignment. Rebecca then read her paper aloud while her group members listened and wrote notes to indicate specific words, phrases, and ideas that they wanted to discuss.

AN ANNOTATED STUDENT DRAFT

Here we reprint the main part of Rebecca's draft, with annotations on passages that elicited comments from her peers. Following the draft, we present their discussion in more detail.

Jegier 1

Rebecca Jegier

Student-Centered Learning: Catering to Students' Impatience

In today's world of high-speed Internet and fast food, Americans have gotten used to receiving instant gratification and immediate results. If a Web site takes four seconds or longer to load, an average of one in four Internet users will get fed up with waiting and abandon the page ("Loading time," 2013). In a survey conducted by the Associated Press, the majority of Americans report losing patience after being kept waiting on the telephone for more than five minutes, and half of those surveyed reported that they have refused to return to a business because of long waits (AP, 2006). This paper is about two hundred times as long as the average tweet—how many teenage students would be willing to read it until the end? With the growing culture of impatience, it comes as no surprise that Americans today are frustrated with recent reforms in education and their lack of immediate results. It is also not a surprising issue that American children have trouble staying focused and engaged in today's standardized and "factory-based" education system driven by worksheets and mandated testing. This outdated system has created an environment that is completely contradictory to the interactive, personalized, and relevant world in which students spend most of their lives.

According to Dr. Martin Luther King Jr. (1947), "Intelligence plus character—that is the goal of true education. The complete education gives one not only power of concentration, but worthy objectives upon which to concentrate." In order for education in America to be "complete" and to reach its full potential of empowering students to concentrate and reach their goals, educators and school reformers might very well explore the issue of impatience. In some cases, such as investing in stocks, the unwillingness to be patient can cause people to make a poor trade-off between immediate, although mediocre, results or receiving something much better after a wait; in the example of the stock market, a larger return on investment usually comes with time. In other circumstances, however, impatience can be largely beneficial if it is handled correctly; successful businesses will improve as they make efforts to become more efficient and provide better customer service to those who do not want to wait.

1

2

Rebecca's group member, Kevin, says he likes the introduction and agrees with the point that we are all becoming impatient. But he worries that the introduction should state the purpose of education more directly since this is the assignment. Jasmine agrees.

Kevin and Michaela both tell Rebecca that they like this phrase, "the culture of impatience."

They all discuss whether or not this is the argument and if Rebecca could restate her key claim.

Rebecca provides one important way that Americans can think about the purpose of education and tries to connect this perspective to her own ideas about impatience.

She anticipates readers' different interpretations of impatience and whether impatience can also be a good thing.

Jegier 2

She goes on to
explain that
school reform-
ers have been
impatient, but
their approach
has been det-
rimental to
learning.

School reformers' impatience belongs in the first category: detrimental and unproductive. Making quality reforms that will be be both effective and enduring is a long-term investment that must be carefully planned instead of hastily implemented. The expectation that coming out with new legislation will immediately change schools for the better is, to put it gently, ludicrous. And it is almost as ridiculous to think that small reforms will be effective when they don't change the underlying problem and allow the system to become relevant to current society.

Rebecca's
peer group is
intrigued by
this analogy
and even its rel-
evance. However,
Jasmine thinks
Rebecca is
beginning to lose
the focus of her
argument.

Take movies, for example. The first Blockbuster store opened in the 1980s, boasting convenience and the ability to customize movie selection to location. By September 2012, however, Blockbuster had filed for bankruptcy and had closed hundreds of stores in a sad attempt to get back on its feet. How did such a successful idea turn into a disaster? The problem with Blockbuster was that it made small improvements to its traditional, formerly successful model and disregarded consumers' changing desires and demands. Netflix had no problem stepping in to fill the gaps with new and innovative methods. In fact, Netflix had been patiently operating and steadily gaining market share for six years before Blockbuster finally came out with its own movie-by-mail service. Albert Einstein once defined insanity as "doing the same thing over and over again and expecting different results." Although schools monopolize the education business, it is still vital for them to adapt and conform to that which is relevant in today's world. Instead of continuing to take a "Blockbuster" attitude towards education — an arguably "insane" route — the U.S. education system needs to examine reforms that have happened in the past as well as reevaluate what its goals are for the children of tomorrow.

In the following
three para-
graphs, Rebecca
shifts the focus
from the pres-
ent to the past,
which is part
of the assign-
ment, to offer
some historical
context for
contemporary
efforts to define
the purpose of
education.

Ever since education began in America with one-room schoolhouses in the nineteenth century, schools have constantly been adapting to meet the needs of the students and those of the country depending on the time period (Tyack, 2007). As the goals of the country have changed, so have the schools. Initially, Thomas

3

4

5

Jegier 3

Jefferson and Noah Webster wanted children to emerge from school as functioning, self-governing citizens who could contribute to the democracy in a new fragile republic. Later, goals were revised due to changes or events in the world such as immigration, the space race, and the *Brown v. Board of Education* decision. When immigrants began to come to America in the late 1800s, the school system had to adapt to find a way to assimilate immigrants into the established education system. In the 1950s when the Supreme Court delivered its *Brown v. Board of Education* decision, schools had to adapt to desegregation and address the effects of opening their doors to those who formerly had no access to education. In 1957, when the Soviets launched the first satellite and effectively "won" the space race, the United States immediately shifted its focus to math and science classes. These reforms were specific to the time, as well as necessary to the relevant situations of that society, and were eventually effective even though they were not seen in this way at first.

In 1983, the National Commission on Excellence in Education published "A Nation at Risk," a report that pointed out flaws in the U.S. education system — flaws that the nation is still addressing today. It recommended that we should raise the standards of high school graduation requirements and college admissions requirements, as well as increase teacher salaries and raise standards for those who wish to teach, in addition to many other suggestions for reform (National Commission on Excellence in Education, 1983). Since this landmark report was produced, school reformers have repeatedly tried to confront the system head-on.

President George W. Bush's No Child Left Behind Act of 2001 (NCLB) is a commonly cited and criticized reform that requires states to assess all students at select grade levels in order for schools to receive federal funding. Intended to increase the quality of education for everyone by requiring schools to improve their performance, NCLB is limited in that it does not address the root of the problem and places the focus on achievement instead of the teaching and learning process. Although some improvement in test scores has

Jegier 4

been reported since its implementation (Dee & Jacob, 2011), frustration with this act has been growing because the tests and the standards sometimes contradict each other and are very often not aligned. NCLB represents an attempt to provide a simple solution for a complex problem. Modern America's "get-rich-quick" attitude toward changes in general and school reforms in particular is a fallacy that must be remedied in order to promote effective reforms in the education system. Although Americans today tend to get frustrated after fifteen minutes of standing in line (AP, 2006), patience is necessary to develop quality reforms that will last in the long term.

In contrast to the detrimental effects of citizens' and reformers' impatience with the current state of education, the "impatience" of our children in schools can actually be beneficial to the American education system, if responded to in the correct way. I place the word "impatience" in quotation marks because the pejorative quality of this word does not fully express what is going on in students' minds when they are categorized in this way by teachers, parents, or doctors. The underlying principle lies in their upbringing; kids are used to alleviating their natural curiosity through googling their questions or by texting a more knowledgeable friend who can respond within the hour (if not within the minute!). There is nothing inherently wrong with wanting to receive instant answers and quick results, especially when today's search engines and mobile apps can easily oblige. Similar to the way businesses constantly strive for better customer service, it is the responsibility of the school system to tailor education to its "impatient" (read: curious) students in relevant and timely ways.

8

Every child has unique talents and skills that are apparent at very early ages. In the 1980s, Harvard psychologist Howard Gardner proposed the theory of multiple intelligences (MI), which argues that intelligence should not be limited to the traditional "school smarts" that can be measured by Binet's IQ test or by the SAT (Gardner, 1987). In addition to the linguistic and logical-mathematical intelligences that are targeted in most school settings, Gardner

9

Jegier 5

proposes that people can be intelligent in other distinct ways. He came up with eight intelligences, including spatial, bodily-kinesthetic, musical, interpersonal, intrapersonal, and naturalist. Besides having different intelligences, students are unique because of their different learning styles (for example, one student might be a visual learner while another learns better from listening to a lecture) and the varying paces which they learn and retain material (Christensen, Horn & Johnson, 2008). This leads us to the question: if all students have different intelligences and learn in different ways, what reasoning do we have to support that standardizing their education would be an effective teaching method for all of them? Is providing the exact same instruction to all students fair, even if such a cookie-cutter method of teaching caters only to those who are "intelligent" in the linguistic and logical-mathematical sense? If the goal is to educate every student, standardization is not an effective way to do it.

Rebecca's group begins with a brief discussion of her introduction and then turns to Rebecca's argument. They ask questions and offer some reflections that they hoped would guide Rebecca toward making a more explicit claim about school reform.

Kevin: I really like your introduction and agree with the idea that we live in a world where we expect instant gratification. I know I get pretty impatient when I have to wait for anything.

Michaela: And you use a great phrase, "a culture of impatience," to describe the problem.

Jasmine: Yes. But isn't the paper supposed to be about the purpose of education? You eventually connect the idea of impatience to the purpose of education, you know, to respond to a generation of students like us who have been brought up on technology. School isn't very responsive to the way we learn. Isn't that what you are arguing?

Rebecca: Okay, I see what you are saying. But I wanted to write an introduction that would capture your attention with something relevant. I'll have to think about that.

Michaela: You do make your argument at the end of the first paragraph. Like Jasmine said, you are arguing that schools need to be more responsive to kids' needs, who they are, and how they learn. I know you are not saying it that way, but is that what you mean to say?

Rebecca: I think so, yes.

Kevin: Could you say that?

Kevin begins with a supportive comment that initiates a more specific conversation about the way Rebecca frames her ideas with the phrase, "a culture of impatience." However, Jasmine asks a pointed question that challenges Rebecca and the others in the group to think about the assignment and the role that an introduction should play. In particular, everyone seems to agree that Rebecca's key claim centers on school's lack of responsiveness to a new generation of students who tend to be impatient. The way that Rebecca states this is different from the way Jasmine and Michaela phrase the argument, and Kevin urges her to restate her claim in keeping with their interpretation. In the course of this conversation, then, peer group members provide support, but also question, even challenge, the way that Rebecca frames her argument. Importantly, the questions and advice are specific enough for Rebecca to use what they suggest to change her approach to writing about the purpose of education. Can or should she lead up to her claim with a story that does not directly address the purpose of education? And should she rephrase her claim? If Rebecca took their advice, this would mean revising an evaluative claim that schools are based on a worn-out factory model of education to a policy-driven claim about what school reform should require.

Group members also extended the conversation to helping Rebecca connect the different ideas that she introduces in her paper: school reforms as a negative example of impatience, the comparison she makes to corporations that fail to recognize "a culture of impatience," and recent research on individual learning styles.

Jasmine: So now I get what you are saying about impatience and the purpose of school, but now you want to compare this to what happened to Blockbuster. The last sentence of your paragraph is good, but it takes you a while to make this point. In the paragraph above it, you say "Take movies, for example. The first Blockbuster store opened in the 1980s, boasting convenience and the ability to customize movie selection to location." But I think you need to connect your two points earlier. Otherwise, I think you are losing focus by introducing the example of Blockbuster.

Michaela: I think the same thing happens when you start to talk about No Child Left Behind. Your last sentence talks about "patience." But you start by summarizing, not making clear that there is a connection here.

Kevin (*interrupting*):	Yeah, I think you keep summarizing different ideas and I get lost in how you are connecting everything.
Michaela:	One way to handle this problem is to say something that connects all the dots and not leave your main points until the end of each paragraph. The same thing happens again when you introduce the idea of learning styles.
Rebecca:	Wow, okay. That's a lot. I am going to have to think about all of this.

Rebecca's draft reflects her first attempt to get her ideas down. It's fine for a first draft to explore ideas. When writers formulate a working thesis (or when they fail to do so), readers in a peer group can offer support, noting strengths or pointing to places of greatest interest to sustain the writer's energy for writing. The more specific the advice, the better the writer will be able to translate that advice into action. Rebecca's group helped her generate a plan for taking some next steps by pointing out how she could define the issue and connect different parts of her paper: " . . . say something that connects all the dots and not leave your main points until the end of each paragraph."

A peer group can also ask questions to help a writer set new goals, so that revision is really a process of reenvisioning or reseeing the key concepts in the writer's draft. As a reader, it is useful to paraphrase particular parts of the draft, so that the writer can hear how you have understood what he or she is trying to say. This is what Michaela did when she explained in a questioning sort of way: "You are arguing that schools need to be more responsive to kids' needs, who they are, and how they learn. I know you are not saying it that way, but is that what you mean to say?"

WORKING WITH EARLY DRAFTS

■ Understand the Writer's Responsibilities

When you present an early draft of your essay to your writing group, you want the group to focus on top-level pyramid concerns—situation, issue, thesis, and audience. You should explain this and any other concerns you have in a cover letter. Use the template in Figure 12.2 as a model for what needs explaining in the letter to your readers.

During the session, it's important to be open to suggestions. Although you don't have to incorporate every suggestion your group makes when you revise your draft, be sure you at least understand the members' comments and concerns. If you don't understand what the members are saying about your draft, ask them to clarify or give you an example.

Finally, if you decide not to take someone's suggestion, have a good reason for doing so. If a suggested change means you won't be addressing the terms of the assignment, for example, it's fine to say no.

---

1. What is your question (or assignment)?
2. What is the issue motivating you to write?
3. How have published writers addressed the issue you discuss?
4. What is your working thesis?
5. Who is your audience, and how do you want them to respond?
6. What do you think is working best?
7. What specific aspect of the essay are you least satisfied with at this time?
8. What kind of feedback do you especially want today?

FIGURE 12.2   The Writer's Cover Letter: Early Drafts

■ Understand the Reader's Responsibilities

Your task as a reader is to follow along as the early draft is read, paying special attention to concerns the writer identifies in the cover letter and focusing on the top of the pyramid: situation, issue, thesis, and audience. Take notes directly on the draft, circling or underlining sections you have questions about, so that you can refer to them specifically in the discussion.

When it's your turn to talk, have a conversation about your reactions to the draft—where the draft amused, confused, or persuaded you, for example. Don't just jump in and start telling the writer what he or she should be doing in the paper. Your role as a reader is to give the writer a live audience: Your responses can help the writer decide what parts of the paper are working and what parts need serious revision. There are times, however, when you should play the role of *deferring reader*, putting off certain comments. You don't want to overwhelm the writer with problems no matter how many questions the essay raises.

Offer both positive and negative remarks. Start by pointing out what is working well in the paper, so the writer knows where he or she is on the right track. This also leaves the writer more open to constructive criticism. But don't shy away from telling the writer what should be working better. It's your job as a reader to offer honest and specific responses to the draft, so the writer can develop it into an effective piece of writing. Figure 12.3 lists key questions you should ask as a reader of an early draft.

1. Are the questions and issues that motivate the writer clear?

2. Has the writer effectively described the conversation that published writers are engaged in?

3. What is at issue?

4. What is the writer's thesis?

5. Is the writer addressing the audience's concerns effectively?

6. What passages of the draft are most effective?

7. What passages of the draft are least effective?

FIGURE 12.3   A Reader's Questions: Early Drafts

▪ Analyze an Early Draft

Keep these questions in mind as you read the following excerpt from a student's early draft. After reading a number of scholarly articles on the Civil Rights Movement, Tasha Taylor decided to address what she sees as the difference between scholars' understanding of the movement and more popular treatments in textbooks and photographs. She also tries to tie in the larger question of historical memory to her analysis of southern blacks' struggle for equality—what people remember about the past and what they forget. In fact, she begins her essay with a quotation she believes summarizes what she wants to argue ("The struggle of man against power is the struggle of memory against forgetting").

As you read Taylor's essay, take detailed notes, and underline passages that concern you. Then write a paragraph or two explaining what she could do to strengthen the draft. Keep in mind that this is an early draft, so focus on the top level of the pyramid: the situation or assignment, the issue, the thesis, and the audience.

Taylor 1

Tasha Taylor
Professor Winters
English 111
October 23, 20—

Memory through Photography

The struggle of man against power is the struggle of memory against forgetting.

—Milan Kundera

Taylor 2

Ask the average American what the key components of the civil rights movement are, and most people will probably recall Martin Luther King Jr. speaking of a dream in front of the Lincoln Memorial, Rosa Parks riding a bus, a few court decisions, and perhaps a photograph of Elizabeth Eckford cowering before an angry mob in front of Central High School in Little Rock. Few people are aware A. Philip Randolph planned the march on Washington. Few could describe Rosa Parks's connection to the civil rights movement (for example, the fact that she had been a member of the NAACP since 1943) before her legendary refusal to give up her seat in December 1955, which led to the Montgomery Bus Boycott. Few recognize the years of struggle that existed between the *Brown v. Board of Education* decision and the actual desegregation of schools. Few consider the fate of Elizabeth Eckford after federal troops were sent to protect her and the other members of the Little Rock Nine had left Central High or the months of abuse (physical and emotional) that they endured in the name of integration. What most people know is limited to textbooks they read in school or the captions under photographs that describe where a particular event occurred.

Why is it that textbooks exclusively feature the stories of larger than life figures like Martin Luther King? Why is it that we remember things the way we do? Historical events "have little meaning without human interpretation, without our speaking about them within the contexts of our lives and our culture, without giving them names and meanings" (Kolker xix). Each person experiencing the exact same event will carry a different memory from that event. Trying to decipher what memories reveal about each person is a fascinating yet difficult endeavor, because each retelling of a memory and each additional memory alters existing ones.

The story that photographs and textbooks tell us does not even begin to describe the depth of the movement or the thousands who risked their lives and the lives of their families to make equality a reality. Embracing this selective memory as a nation prevents understanding and acknowledgment of the harsh reality of other images from the civil rights movement (demonstrators being plowed down by fire hoses, beatings, and the charred bodies of bombing victims) which are key aspects of understanding who we are as a society. The question therefore is why. Why is it that textbook writers and publishers have allowed so much of this history to be skewed and forgotten? How can it be that barely 50 years after these events so many have been forgotten or diluted?

Reading as a Writer

1. What is working well in Taylor's draft?

2. What is Taylor's thesis or argument?

3. To what extent does she connect her analysis of the civil rights movement and historical memory?

4. What parts of her analysis could Taylor explain further? (What do you still need to know?)

5. What would you suggest Taylor do next?

WORKING WITH LATER DRAFTS

■ Understand the Writer's Responsibilities

At a later stage, after you've had the opportunity to take readers' suggestions and do further research, you should be able to state your thesis more definitively than you did in your earlier draft. You also should be able to support your thesis with evidence, anticipating possible counterarguments. Ideally, your readers will still provide constructive criticism, offering their support, as in the first draft, but they will also question and challenge more than before.

Here, too, you want to help readers focus on your main concerns, which you should explain in a cover letter. You may still need to work on one or two top-level pyramid concerns, but your focus will likely be midlevel concerns — organization and the effective use of sources. Use the list of questions in Figure 12.4 to help you write your cover letter.

---

1. What is your research question?

2. What is the issue motivating you to write?

3. What is your thesis?

4. How do you go about identifying a gap in readers' knowledge, modifying other's ideas, or trying to correct readers' misunderstandings?

5. To what extent do you distinguish your argument from the information you quote, summarize, or paraphrase from the sources you have read?

6. To what extent have you organized your ideas in ways that will help readers follow the logic of your argument?

7. To what extent have you anticipated potential counterarguments to your thesis?

8. What do you think is working best?

9. What specific aspect of the essay are you least satisfied with at this time?

FIGURE 12.4   The Writer's Cover Letter: Later Drafts

■ Understand the Reader's Responsibilities

In a later draft, your focus as a reader should be on midlevel concerns in the composition pyramid: places in the writer's text that are confusing, that require better transitions, or that could use sources more effectively. You can challenge writers at this stage of the composing process, perhaps playing the role of *naive reader*, suggesting places in the draft where the writer has left something out or isn't clear. The naive reader's comments tend to take the form of questions: "Do you mean to suggest that everyone who learns to write well succeeds in life? What kind of success are you talking about?" Closely related to the naive reader is the *devil's advocate reader*. This reader's comments also challenge the writer, often taking the form of a question like this: "But why couldn't this be attributed to the effects of socialization rather than heredity?" Figure 12.5 offers questions for reading later drafts.

■ Analyze a Later Draft

Now read the excerpt from Taylor's second draft (pp. 360–62). You will see that she begins with her discussion of historical memory. She also has included an analysis of a book of photographs that Nobel Prize–winning author Toni Morrison compiled. Take notes as you read the draft and write a paragraph in which you describe what you see as some of the strengths of what Taylor has written and what she can do to make other elements stronger. In particular, focus on the middle level of the composition pyramid—on organization and the effective use of sources and evidence to support her thesis.

---

1. To what extent is it clear what questions and issues motivate the writer?

2. What is the writer's thesis?

3. How effectively does the writer establish the conversation—identify a gap in people's knowledge, attempt to modify an existing argument, or try to correct some misunderstanding?

4. How effectively does the writer distinguish between his or her ideas and the ideas he or she summarizes, paraphrases, or quotes?

5. How well does the writer help you follow the logic of his or her argument?

6. To what extent are you persuaded by the writer's argument?

7. To what extent does the writer anticipate possible counterarguments?

8. To what extent does the writer make clear how he or she wants readers to respond?

9. What do you think is working best? Explain by pointing to specific passages in the writer's draft.

10. What specific aspect of the draft is least effective? Explain by pointing to a specific passage in the writer's draft.

FIGURE 12.5   A Reader's Questions: Later Drafts

Taylor 1

Tasha Taylor
Professor Winters
English 111
November 14, 20—

Memory through Photography

The struggle of man against power is the struggle of
memory against forgetting.

—Milan Kundera

Memory is such an integral part of what it is to be human, yet
is something so often taken for granted: People assume that their
memories are accurate to protect themselves from the harsh realities
of the atrocities committed by ordinary people. Even the pictures
used to represent the much-celebrated civil rights movement give
us a false sense of security and innocence. For example, the Ku Klux
Klan is most often depicted by covered faces and burning crosses; the
masks allow us to remove ourselves from responsibility. Few could
describe Rosa Parks's connection to the civil rights movement (for
example, the fact that she had been a member of the NAACP since
1943) before her legendary refusal to give up her seat in December
1955, which led to the Montgomery Bus Boycott. Few recognize
the years of struggle that existed between the *Brown v. Board of
Education* decision and the actual desegregation of schools. Few
consider the fate of Elizabeth Eckford after federal troops were sent
to protect her and the other members of the Little Rock Nine had left
Central High or the months of abuse (physical and emotional) that
they endured in the name of integration. What most people know
is limited to textbooks they read in school or the captions under
photographs that describe where a particular event occurred.

It is important, therefore, to analyze what is remembered and
even more importantly to recognize what is forgotten: to question
why it is that it is forgotten, what that says about society today,
how far it has come and how much it has unwittingly fallen back into
old patterns such as prejudice and ignorance. The discrepancies in
cultural memory are due more to a society's desire to remember itself
in the best light and protect itself from the reality of its brutality
and responsibility. Such selective memory only temporarily heals the
wounds of society; lack of awareness does not cause healing.

Taylor 2

Although there have been many recent moves to increase awareness,
they are tainted by unavoidable biases and therefore continue to
perpetuate a distorted memory.

Images play a central role in the formation of cultural memory   *3*
because people can point to photographs and claim them as concrete
evidence: "Images entrance us because they provide a powerful
illusion of owning reality. If we can photograph reality or paint or
copy it, we have exercised an important kind of power" (Kolker 3).
A picture of black and white children sitting at a table together is
used to reinforce the cultural perception that the problems of racism
are over, that it has all been fixed.

In her book *Remember*, Toni Morrison strives to revitalize   *4*
the memory of school integration through photographs. The book
is dedicated to Denise McNair, Carole Robertson, Addie Mae Collins,
and Cynthia Wesley, the four girls killed in the 16th Street Baptist
Church bombing in 1963. Morrison writes, "Things are better now.
Much, much better. But remember why and please remember us"
(Morrison 72). The pictures are of black and white children happily
eating together, solemnly saluting the flag together, and holding
hands. The photographs of the four murdered girls show them
peacefully and innocently smiling as if everything really is better
now. In reality, according to the United States Bureau of Alcohol,
Tobacco and Firearms, between 1995 and 1997 there were 162
incidents of arson or bombing in African American houses of worship.
There are a few images of people protesting integration, but they
are also consistent with the cultural memory (protesters are shown
simply holding signs and yelling, not beating and killing innocent
children). Finally, the captions are written in a child's voice. Yet it is
not a child's voice at all it is merely a top down view of children that
serves to perpetuate a distorted cultural memory.

The photographs used to suggest how things are much, much   *5*
better now are misleading. For example, the last photograph is of
a black girl and a white girl holding hands through a bus window,
which was transporting them to an integrated school. The caption
reads: "Anything can happen. Anything at all. See?" (71). It is a
very powerful image of how the evil of Jim Crow and segregation
exists in a distant past and the nation has come together and
healed. However, Morrison neglects to point out that the picture

Taylor 3

was taken in Boston, Massachusetts, not the deep south, the heart of racism. Children holding hands in Boston is much less significant than if they were in Birmingham where that action would be concrete evidence of how far we as a nation have come.

Morrison also glorifies Martin Luther King Jr. and Rosa Parks, pointing to them as epitomizing the movement. Unfortunately, she perpetuates the story that one needs to be special or somehow larger than life to affect change. Paul Rogat Loeb writes in *Soul of a Citizen*:

> Once we enshrine our heroes, it becomes hard for mere mortals to measure up in our eyes . . . in our collective amnesia we lose the mechanisms through which grassroots social movements of the past successfully shifted public sentiment and challenged entrenched institutional power. Equally lost are the means by which their participants managed to keep on, sustaining their hope and eventually prevailing in circumstances at least as difficult as those we face today. (Loeb 36, 38)

Placing a select few on pedestals and claiming them as next to divine heroes of the movement does society a disservice; people fail to realize that ordinary people can serve as agents of change.

Morrison's book ignores the thousands of ordinary people who risked their lives for the cause to bring about equality. The caption besides the picture of Rosa Parks in *Remember* reads "because if I ever feel helpless or lonely I just have to remember that all it takes is one person" (Morrison 62). Ironically, Morrison gives credit for the Montgomery Bus Boycott to one person, ignoring the months of planning and dozens of planners involved. Even the photograph presents Rosa Parks in a position of power. It is a low-angle shot up at Parks that makes her appear larger than life and authoritative. The photographs of Martin Luther King Jr. also further the impression of power with a close up shot of his face as he stands above thousands of participants in the March on Washington. Although these photographs were selected to perpetuate the hero illusion, it is more inspiring to remember the ordinary people who took a stand and were able to accomplish extraordinary feats because of their dedication and persistence rather than glorify extraordinary people who were destined for greatness.

6

7

Reading as a Writer

1. What is Taylor's thesis or argument?
2. How well do her transitions help you follow the argument's logic?
3. How effectively does she distinguish between her ideas and the ideas she summarizes, paraphrases, or quotes?
4. To what extent are you persuaded by her argument?
5. What should Taylor do next?

WORKING WITH FINAL DRAFTS

■ Understand the Writer's Responsibilities

Your final draft should require editing, not revising. At this stage, readers should focus on errors in style and grammar in the text, not on the substance of your work. Here, too, indicate your main concerns in a cover letter (Figure 12.6).

---

1. What is your unique perspective on your issue?
2. To what extent do the words and phrases you use reflect who you believe your readers are?
3. Does your style of citation reflect accepted conventions for academic writing?
4. What do you think is working best?
5. What specific aspect of the essay are you least satisfied with at this time?

FIGURE 12.6   The Writer's Cover Letter: Final Drafts

■ Understand the Reader's Responsibilities

Once a writer's ideas are developed and in place, readers should turn their attention to the bottom level of the composition pyramid, to matters of style and grammar. At this stage, details are important: Is this the best word to use? Would this sentence be easier to follow if it were broken into two sentences? Which spelling is correct—*Freedman* or *Friedman*? Are citations handled consistently? Should this question mark precede or follow the quotation mark? The *grammatically correct reader* evaluates and makes judgments about the writer's work. This reader may simply indicate with a mark of some sort that there's a problem in a sentence or paragraph. Figure 12.7 is a list of questions a reader should ask of a final draft.

1. How does the writer go about contributing a unique perspective on the issue?
2. To what extent does the writer use words and phrases that are appropriate for the intended audience?
3. To what extent does the style of citation reflect accepted conventions for academic writing?
4. What do you think is working best?
5. What specific aspect of the essay are you least satisfied with at this time?

FIGURE 12.7　A Reader's Questions: Final Drafts

■ Analyze a Near-Final Draft

Now read Taylor's near-final draft and write a paragraph detailing what she can do to strengthen it. Again, you will see that Taylor has made substantial changes. She compares Morrison's book of photographs to a Spike Lee documentary that she watched with her class. As you read the essay, focus on the bottom level of the composition pyramid: Does the writer use appropriate language? Does she adhere to appropriate conventions for using and citing sources? (See the Appendix for information on MLA and APA formats.)

Taylor 1

Tasha Taylor
Professor Winters
English 111
December 5, 20—

Memory through Photography

Memory is such an integral part of what it is to be human, *1* yet it is something so often taken for granted: people assume that their memories are accurate to protect themselves from the harsh realities of the atrocities committed by ordinary people. Even the pictures used to represent the much-celebrated civil rights movement give us a false sense of security and innocence. For example, the Ku Klux Klan is most often depicted by covered faces and burning crosses; the masks allow us to remove ourselves from responsibility. Few could describe Rosa Parks's connection to the civil rights movement before her legendary refusal to give up her seat in December 1955, which led to the Montgomery Bus Boycott (for example, the fact that she had been a member of the NAACP since 1943). Few recognize the years of struggle that existed between the 1954 *Brown v. Board of Education* decision and the actual desegregation of schools. Few consider the fate of Elizabeth Eckford after the federal troops sent to protect her and the other members of the Little Rock Nine had left Central High or the months of abuse (physical and emotional) that they endured in the name of integration. What most people know is limited to the textbooks they read in school or the captions under photographs that describe where a particular event occurred.

It is important, then, to analyze what is remembered, and even more important to recognize what is forgotten: to question why it is that it is forgotten, what that says about society today, how far it has come and how much it has unwittingly fallen back into old patterns of prejudice and ignorance. The discrepancies in cultural memory are due more to society's desire to remember itself in the best light and protect itself from the reality of its brutality and responsibility. Such selective memory only temporarily heals the wounds of society; lack of awareness does not cause healing. Although there have been many recent moves to increase awareness, they are tainted by unavoidable biases and therefore continue to perpetuate a distorted memory.

Images play a central role in the formation of cultural memory because people can point to photographs and claim them as concrete evidence: "Images entrance us because they provide a powerful illusion of owning reality. If we can photograph reality or paint or copy it, we have exercised an important kind of power" (Kolker 3). A picture of black and white children sitting at a table together is used to reinforce the cultural perception that the problems of racism are over, that they have all been fixed.

In her book *Remember*, Toni Morrison strives to revitalize the memory of school integration through photographs. The book is dedicated to Denise McNair, Carole Robertson, Addie Mae Collins, and Cynthia Wesley, the four girls killed in the 16th Street Baptist Church bombing in 1963. Morrison writes: "Things are better now. Much, much better. But remember why and please remember us" (72).

Taylor 3

The pictures are of black and white children happily eating together, solemnly saluting the flag together, and holding hands. The photographs of the four murdered girls show them peacefully and innocently smiling as if everything really is better now. In reality, according to the United States Bureau of Alcohol, Tobacco and Firearms, between 1995 and 1997 there were 162 incidents of arson or bombing in African American houses of worship. There are a few images of people protesting integration, but they are also consistent with the cultural memory (protesters are shown simply holding signs and yelling, not beating and killing innocent children). Finally, the captions are written in a child's voice. Yet it is not a child's voice at all; it is merely a top-down view of children that serves to perpetuate a distorted cultural memory.

The photographs used to suggest how things are much, much better now are misleading. For example, the last photograph, taken through a bus window, is of a black girl and a white girl holding hands; the bus was transporting them to an integrated school. The caption reads: "Anything can happen. Anything at all. See?" (Morrison 71). It is a very powerful image of how the evil of Jim Crow and segregation exists in a distant past and the nation has come together and healed. However, Morrison neglects to point out that the picture was taken in Boston, not in the Deep South, the heart of racism. Children holding hands in Boston is much less significant than if they were in Birmingham, where that action would be concrete evidence of how far we as a nation have come.

Morrison also glorifies Martin Luther King Jr. and Rosa Parks, pointing to them as epitomizing the movement. Unfortunately, she perpetuates the story that one needs to be special or somehow larger than life to effect change. Paul Rogat Loeb writes in *Soul of a Citizen*:

> Once we enshrine our heroes, it becomes hard for mere mortals to measure up in our eyes. . . . In our collective amnesia we lose the mechanisms through which grassroots social movements of the past successfully shifted public sentiment and challenged entrenched institutional power.

5

6

Taylor 4

Equally lost are the means by which their participants
managed to keep on, sustaining their hope and eventually
prevailing in circumstances at least as difficult as those we
face today. (36, 38)

Placing a select few on pedestals and claiming them as
next-to-divine heroes of the movement does society a disservice;
people fail to realize that ordinary people can serve as agents
of change.

Morrison's book ignores the thousands of ordinary people
who risked their lives for the cause to bring about equality. The
caption beside the picture of Rosa Parks in *Remember* reads "Because
if I ever feel helpless or lonely I just have to remember that all it
takes is one person" (Morrison 62). Ironically, Morrison gives credit
for the Montgomery Bus Boycott to one person, ignoring the months
of planning that involved dozens of planners. Even the photograph
presents Rosa Parks in a position of power. It is a low-angle shot up
at Parks that makes her appear larger than life and authoritative. The
photographs of Martin Luther King Jr. also further the impression of
power with a close-up shot of his face as he stands above thousands
of participants in the March on Washington. Although these
photographs were selected to perpetuate the hero illusion, it is more
inspiring to remember the ordinary people who took a stand and were
able to accomplish extraordinary feats because of their dedication
and persistence rather than to glorify extraordinary people who were
destined for greatness.

In contrast, Spike Lee's 1998 documentary titled *4 Little Girls*
is a stirring depiction of the lives and deaths of the girls who died in
the 1963 16th Street Baptist Church bombing. In his film, Spike Lee
looks behind what some would call "societal amnesia" to disclose
the harsh realities of the civil rights movement. Lee interviews
family members and friends of the murdered girls, revealing the
pain and anger that they grapple with more than forty years after
the tragedy. Lee includes not only images of the bombed church but
also the charred and nearly unrecognizable bodies of the murdered
girls. These disturbing images underscore the reality of their deaths
without appearing sensationalist. The film does an exceptional job

Taylor 5

of reminding the viewer of the suffering and mindless hate that were prevalent during the civil rights movement.

However, the documentary is also biased. For instance, the girls were not little; they were fourteen, not really little girls. Lee chose to describe them as little to elicit emotion and sympathy for their tragic deaths. They were victims. They had not marched through the streets demanding equality; instead, Denise McNair, Carole Robertson, Addie Mae Collins, and Cynthia Wesley were simply attending Sunday school and were ruthlessly murdered. Victimizing Denise, Carole, Addie Mae, and Cynthia is not detrimental to the cultural memory in and of itself. The problem is that the victimization of the four girls is expanded to encompass the entire black community, undermining the power and achievement of the average black citizen. We need to remember the people who struggled to gain employment for blacks in the labor movement of the 1940s and 1950s that initiated the civil rights movement.

9

One can argue that despite the presence of misleading images in Spike Lee's film and Toni Morrison's book, at least some of the story is preserved. Still, it is easy to fall victim to the cliché: Those who do not remember history are doomed to repeat it. Just because a portion of the story is remembered, it does not mean that society is immune to falling back into its old habits. This cultural amnesia not only perpetuates the injustices of the time but leaves open the possibility that these atrocities can occur again. If people believe the government can simply grant black equality, then they may believe that it can also take it away. In essence memory is about power: "The struggle of man against power is the struggle of memory against forgetting" (Kundera). Those who are remembered hold power over the forgotten. Their legacy is lost and so is their ability to inspire future generations through their memory.

10

Taylor 6

Works Cited

4 Little Girls. Directed by Spike Lee, 40 Acres and A Mule Filmworks, 1997.

Kolker, Robert. *Film, Form, and Culture*. McGraw Hill, 1998.

Kundera, Milan. *The Book of Laughter and Forgetting*. Translated by Michael Henry Heim, Penguin Books, 1981.

Loeb, Paul Rogat. *Soul of a Citizen: Living with Conviction in a Cynical Time*. St. Martin's Griffin, 1999.

Morrison, Toni. *Remember: The Journey to School Integration*. Houghton Mifflin, 2004.

United States. Bureau of Alcohol, Tobacco and Firearms. *Arson and Explosives Incidents Report 1994*. US Dept. of the Treasury, 1995.

Reading as a Writer

1. What would you say is Taylor's argument?
2. To what extent does she provide transitions to help you understand how her analysis supports her argument?
3. To what extent does she integrate quotations appropriately into the text of her argument?
4. To what extent does the style of citation reflect accepted conventions for academic writing?
5. If Taylor had more time to revise, what would you suggest she do?

FURTHER SUGGESTIONS FOR PEER EDITING GROUPS

Monitoring your own writing group can help ensure that the group is both providing and receiving the kinds of responses the members need. Here is a list of questions you might ask of one another after a session:

- What topics were discussed?
- Were most questions and comments directed at the level of ideas? Structure? Language?
- Were topics always brought up with a question or a comment?

- Who initiated talk more frequently—the writer or the readers?
- What roles did different group members play?
- Did each author open with specific questions or concerns?
- Did the readers begin by giving specific reactions?

After answering these questions, identify two things that are working well in your group. Then identify two things that you could improve. How would you go about making those improvements?

When we asked our students what they thought contributed to effective conversation in their writing groups, here is what they told us:

- honest and spontaneous expression
- free interaction among members
- high levels of personal involvement
- members' commitment to insight and change
- the sense that self-disclosure is safe and highly valued
- members' willingness to take responsibility for the group's effectiveness
- members' belief that the group is important
- members' belief that they are primary agents of help for one another
- members' focus on communication within the group over other discussions

Other Methods of Inquiry
Interviews and Focus Groups

Sometimes to advance your argument you may need to do original research. By **original research**, we mean using primary sources of evidence you gather yourself. (Another common term for this type of investigation is *field research.*) Remember that primary sources of evidence include firsthand or eyewitness accounts like those found in letters or newspapers, or in research reports in which the researcher explains his or her impressions of a particular phenomenon—for example, gender relations in classroom interactions. (In contrast, a secondary source is an analysis of information contained in primary sources.)

The type of original research we discuss in this chapter relies on people—interviewees and members of focus groups—as primary sources of information. To inquire into gender dynamics in college science classrooms, then, you might conduct interviews with female students to understand their perceptions of how gender affects teaching. Or you might convene a focus group to put a variety of perspectives into play on questions about gendered teaching practices. The pages that follow present strategies for conducting interviews and setting up focus groups that can generate multiple responses to your research questions.

When you conduct research, keep in mind that you are not setting out to prove anything; instead, the process of inquiry will enable you to answer the questions *you* ask, address problems, and move readers to rethink their positions. Good critical readers know that the arguments they produce as writers are influenced by what they choose to discuss and how they construe the evidence they provide.

Although there is really no way to avoid the limitations of writing from one point of view, writers can provide readers with multiple sources of information so that they can make their own judgments about what to believe or not believe. In fact, this is the argument we make on page 371 in studying inequities in education. Relying on a single source of data will inevitably limit your field of vision. Multiple sources of information add complexity and texture to your analysis, conveying to readers the thoroughness of your approach.

WHY DO ORIGINAL RESEARCH?

We can think of four reasons (all of which overlap to some extent) why you might do original research for a writing class.

To increase your ability to read critically.   When you do original research, you learn, at a basic and pragmatic level, how the studies you consult in a researched argument come into being. You're on the ground floor of knowledge making.

As a critical reader, you know it's important to ask questions like these: What is the source of the author's claim? Why should I believe the author? What is the source of the author's authority? What are the possible counterarguments? When you are doing original research, you are in the position of that author, with a real stake in establishing your own authority. By coming to understand what it takes to establish your own authority, you are in a better position to evaluate how effectively other researchers establish theirs.

Let's say your research question concerns gender differences in math education. You might read a study that asserts that girls and young women are being shortchanged in math classes, impeding their ability to go into math-related fields. You would want to ask about the nature of the data used to support this claim. If the author of the study states that 56 percent of the female students interviewed said they were discouraged from going into math-related fields, you might wonder where the figure of 56 percent came from. How many girls and young women were interviewed? How was this sample selected? What were the students asked? Questions like these inform your own use of interviews and focus groups.

To increase your own research skills.   Doing original research broadens your own range of research methods. By developing a repertoire of research methods, you will be better able to explore questions that may be too complex to answer by examining texts alone. One scholar put it this way: "I couldn't see what a text was doing without looking at the worlds in which these texts served as significant activities."* After all, it is one

---

*C. Bazerman, *Shaping Written Knowledge: The Genre and Activity of the Scientific Article in Science* (Madison: University of Wisconsin Press, 1988), p. 4.

thing to read a research report and understand its purpose, its intended audience, the nature of its claims, and the like. But it is quite another to watch scientists at work and begin to understand how they have come to know what they know. The discovery of DNA, for example, was the result of an arduous process that involved much risk, collaboration, chance, error, and competition. The neat structure of a scientific report could mislead you into thinking that science is a linear process that begins with a question, moves on to an experiment, and ends with an answer. Real research is messier than that. Original research takes us behind the words we read, introducing levels of complexity.

To broaden your scope of inquiry.   Doing original research may also broaden the scope of your inquiry. First, it is useful to use different research methods than the ones you are accustomed to using. Learning to interview and run focus groups, at the very least, can give you insight and practice for nonacademic applications—market research, for example. Second, it can make you aware of how people outside your field address the questions you raise. Consider, for example, the different perspectives an educator, a sociologist, and an economist would bring to the question of educational inequities. An educator might study educational inequities as a curricular problem and therefore analyze the content of different curricula within and across schools. A sociologist might visit students' homes, noting the presence or absence of books or asking parents how they go about preparing their children for school. An economist might examine income levels in both wealthy and impoverished neighborhoods. The point is that each field brings its own perspective to a problem, adding complexity and richness to your own discussion of that problem.

To make a unique contribution to a conversation of ideas.   Finally, doing original research affords you the opportunity to make a unique contribution to a conversation of ideas. Instead of relying exclusively on texts others have written as evidence for your claims, you can offer your own data to address a question or problem, data that others do not have available. For instance, if you wanted to examine claims that primary school teachers pay more attention to boys in class than to girls, you could review the relevant literature and then add to that literature a study that systematically analyzes the ways in which teachers in different classrooms treat boys and girls.

GETTING STARTED: WRITING AN IDEA SHEET

The purpose of writing an **idea sheet** is to help you explore not just what you might want to learn by conducting research but why you are interested in a particular topic, issue, or problem. An idea sheet is a form of exploratory writing that can serve as the basis for a more formal research proposal.

We encourage our students to jot down some ideas about the topic they are interested in, why they find the topic of interest, and why it might be compelling to others. Moreover, we want them to answer the kinds of questions we have addressed throughout this book: What's at stake in conducting this research? What other related ideas compete for our attention and limit our ability to see what you think is important, and why?

To compose an idea sheet, you should follow these steps:

Step One: Explain your topic so that others can understand what you want to study.

Step Two: Detail the personal reasons why you are interested in the topic.

Step Three: Identify what is at issue — what is open to dispute for you.

Step Four: Describe any groups for whom this issue might be significant or important.

Step Five: Formulate an issue-based question.

It is important to discuss an issue in the context of a current situation, so that readers will understand why you are raising a particular issue. As a writer, you will need to familiarize yourself with what people are talking and writing about. What is on people's minds? What is at issue for people? What about for you? What do your readers need to know about? In turn, you will need to help readers understand why they are reading your essay and fulfill their expectations that what you are writing about is both relevant and timely.

Formulating an issue-based question can help you think through what you might be interested in writing about and guide your research. As we suggest in Chapter 5, a good question develops out of an issue, some fundamental tension that you identify within a conversation. Your issue-based question should be specific enough to guide inquiry into what others have written and help you accomplish the following:

- Clarify what you know about the issue and what you still need to know.
- Guide your inquiry with a clear focus.
- Organize your inquiry around a specific issue.
- Develop an argument, rather than simply collecting information by asking "how," "why," "should," or "to what extent is it true or not?"
- Consider who your audience is.
- Determine what resources you have, so that you can ask a question that you will be able answer with the resources available to you.

A STUDENT'S ANNOTATED IDEA SHEET

Grace 1

Dan Grace
Professor Greene
English 320
March 10, 20—

Idea Sheet for Parent/Child Autism Study

The student explains the purpose of his research and begins to explain the method he would use to get the information he is interested in.

I would like to study the parent-child home interaction/ dynamic between an individual with autism and his or her parents in the student's home. I would like to research different intervention programs and interview the parents about their own programs with their child, both home- and school-implemented, as well as observe the parent-child interactions in both school work and natural daily activities such as conversations and meals. I would do this by spending at least fifty hours with the student with autism in his or her home, both individually with him or her and also observing his or her parental interactions. I would like to see how these interactions compare with the research performed in this field.

He explains why he is interested in this subject and this provides a rationale for what he will study.

The summer after my freshman year, I worked at a school for children with autism for six weeks. I also worked at a research facility that looked into the effects high vitamin and mineral diets had on individuals with autism. The next summer, and during several breaks in school, I worked at the school for a total of fifteen to twenty weeks. My experiences there have spurred an interest in autism and autism education. I've worked extensively in the classroom setting; however, I've never witnessed the home setting for anyone with autism. Also, I've heard many stories about parents and their different mindsets and levels of involvement with their children, but have never met any parents, except for one at the end of my first summer working at the school. I want to interact with a student outside of the classroom, as well as see the interactions between the student and his or her parents.

Children with autism lack the social, emotional, and cognitive (in many cases) skills that healthy individuals possess/have the potential to have. Early intervention is a very important thing in a child with autism's life, since it has been shown that early intervention can significantly help the child's social, emotional, and cognitive development. Early

Grace 2

He recognizes the importance of early intervention, but he is not altogether sure what that means in a child's everyday life.

intervention includes the parents as well. It is important for parents to interact with their children early and often, and to work with them to help them develop. Though the individual that I will be working with is already at the end of elementary school, it will still be useful to observe the parent-child interactions, as well as question the parents about what measures were taken early in the child's life.

The student provides a broad context for understanding autism and who else might be interested in this topic.

This topic is important/significant for all those working with children with autism, as well as parents of children with autism. Autism is becoming ever more prevalent in this country, and the world, with more than one in every one hundred children being diagnosed with some form of autism spectrum disorder (ASD). The parents need to know how best to interact with, and better understand, their child.

4

Finally, he formulates the topic as a series of questions that need to be answered.

How can parent-child interaction influence the development of a child with autism? This might be a vague question with many different directions in which to take it, but it is still a pertinent question. How might parental interaction in adolescence affect adolescent development? Why should parents work hard to interact with their children with autism? What are the benefits of early intervention? What are the long-term benefits of early intervention programs? What are the effects of good versus poor parental interaction? These questions need to be answered to fully understand the topic and research question.

5

WRITING A PROPOSAL

A **proposal** is a formal plan that outlines your objectives for conducting a research project, specifies the methods you intend to use, and describes the implications of your work. In its most basic form, a proposal is an argument that provides a rationale for conducting research and persuades readers that the research is worth pursuing. It is also a tool that helps guide you through various stages of the project. The most immediate benefit of writing a proposal is that through the act of writing—by setting forth an outline of your project—your thinking will become more focused and precise. And yet your thinking may change as you read more about your topic.

Typically, a research proposal should include four sections: introduction/ purpose, review of relevant research, method, and implications. You may also want to include additional sections with materials that provide concrete support for your proposal—some of the tools that will help you get the job done. You should arrange your plan and use headings so that readers can find information quickly.

■ Describe Your Purpose

In the introduction, you should describe the purpose of your study and establish that the issue you want to study is relevant and timely. Then, briefly summarize how others have treated the issue you are focusing on in order to explain whether you are trying to fill a gap, correct a misconception, build upon and extend others' research, or test a hypothesis. As we point out throughout this book, it is important to help readers understand the context by retracing the conversation. After you provide some context to help readers understand the purpose of your study, you should then formulate the question that is motivating your research.

Finally, you should explain why you are interested in this issue, why it is important, and what is at stake. Ask yourself why others should be interested in your effort to answer the question.

■ Review Relevant Research

Following the introduction, you should provide a review of the relevant research. For a proposal, you should demonstrate that you have a firm grasp of the issue as part of the argument you are making to justify your study. The more effectively you convince readers that you know the issue, the more persuasive your argument. Therefore, you will want to show that you have read widely, that you are aware of the most important studies conducted in your area of research, that you are also aware of current research within the past five years, and that you understand the strengths and limitations of your own approach.

More specifically, you can use your review to accomplish some of the following:

- Define a key term that is central to your study that others may not necessarily agree upon.
- Discuss the history relevant to your research.
- Explain the strengths and limitations of different methodological approaches to answering similar research questions.
- Analyze the different theoretical approaches that authors have used to frame the issue (e.g., psychological, sociological, socioeconomic, racial).
- Identify trends in what researchers are finding or, perhaps, the lack of agreement.
- Point to more comprehensive reviews of research that others have written.

▪ Define Your Method

In your method section, you should first explain how you will answer the research question motivating your study using the tools that are available. Some of the tools and strategies you might use include the following:

- conducting interviews or focus groups;
- taking notes;
- recording particular activities;
- doing background, historical, or archival work, and
- observing or coming to terms with your own impressions.

Since this is a proposal for research you will conduct, you should write this section in the future tense. "To answer the question(s) motivating this study, I will conduct interviews and focus groups and take detailed notes. . . ."

Second, describe how you plan to collect your data. Tell readers whether you will audio-record and transcribe interviews and/or focus groups. If you are taking notes, you will want to explain whether you plan to take notes during or after the session. Be sure to explain where you are conducting the interview or focus group. If you are observing classes, meetings, or some event, you will need to explain how often you will observe, for how long, and whether you will be taking notes or transcribing data.

Third, justify why you are using some methods of collecting data and not others. Discuss the appropriateness of these methods given your research question. Given the objectives you have set for yourself and the constraints of doing the research, are some methods better than others? How will the methods you have chosen to use enable you to answer your question(s)?

Finally, you should have some sense of how you will analyze the data you collect. That is, readers will expect that you have done more than simply read your transcripts from interviews and focus groups to form impressions. Therefore, you will want to explain the principles you will use to analyze the data in light of the research question(s) you are asking.

▪ Discuss Your Implications

It may seem a little premature to talk about what you hope to find in your study, but it is important to address "So what?" to explain what you believe is the significance of your study. Place your argument in the context of the conversation you want to join, and explain how your study can contribute to that conversation. Write about how your study will build upon, challenge, or extend the studies in your area of research. And finally, identify what you believe will be new about your findings.

■ Include Additional Materials That Support Your Research

Depending on your instructor and the level of formality of your proposal, you may be asked to include additional materials that reveal other dimensions of your research. Those materials may include (1) an annotated bibliography, (2) scripts of the questions you plan to ask in interviews and focus groups, (3) the consent forms you will ask participants to sign, and (4) approval from your university's Institutional Review Board (IRB).

Annotated bibliography.   An **annotated bibliography** is a list of sources (arranged alphabetically by author) that you plan to consult and use in your research paper. Typically you provide a citation (author, date, title of source, and publication information) and a short summary of the source. You can present all your sources in one long list or organize them by type of source (books, journals, and so forth). See pages 184–86 in Chapter 7 for a more complete description of how to write an annotated bibliography and an example.

Questions you plan to ask.   Including a list (or lists) of the questions you expect to ask those you plan to interview or survey will help focus your thinking. What personal information do you need to know? What information do you need to know about your issue? What opinions and recommendations would be helpful? Each list should include at least five good questions but can include many more. A sample set of questions, focusing on parents of homeless children, appears in Figure 13.1.

Consent forms.   Whenever you plan to solicit information in an interview or focus group, you need to get permission from the interviewees or participants to use their comments and contributions in your research paper. The Institutional Review Board on your campus probably has a model for writing a consent form that you can use, but we have included a sample consent form for an interview in Figure 13.2.

IRB approval.   Your school's Institutional Review Board ensures that researchers hold high ethical standards in the research they conduct and protect the rights of "human subjects" who participate in a study. It is possible that research conducted for a class will not require IRB approval. You should contact the appropriate office (for example, the Office for Research) on your campus for details and exceptions.

Sample Interview Questions

Parent(s)

1. a. Describe your current living and family situation (parents, siblings, how long homeless, where living, where child attends school).

   b. Describe your child.

   c. Describe your relationship with your child.

2. a. Do you think homelessness is affecting your child's schooling?

   b. If so, tell me how (grades, friends, attendance, transportation).

3. Tell me about enrolling your child in school. What was the process like? Were there any problems? Conditions? Challenges?

4. a. Do you feel that your child's right to an education has been recognized?

   b. Why or why not? Describe any experiences that support your answer.

5. Describe the relationship between your child and his or her teachers.

6. a. What types of support services is your child currently being offered in school and in the community?

   b. How effective are those services?

   c. How supportive of your child's educational and developmental growth do you feel your child's school has been?

   d. What about the Center for the Homeless?

   e. Do you have any recommendations for these sources of help or requests for other types of services for your child that are not currently offered?

7. How do you envision your child's future?

FIGURE 13.1   Sample Interview Questions

■ Establish a Timeline

Draw up a schedule for your research and identify when you expect to complete specific tasks. For example, when will you do the following?

- Submit proposal to Institutional Review Board (if necessary).
- Contact participants and get their commitments.
- Conduct interviews, focus groups, and the like.
- Compile an annotated bibliography.
- Transcribe the data.

Sample Interview Consent Form

You are invited to participate in a study of homelessness and education conducted by Mary Ronan, an undergraduate at the University of Notre Dame, during the next few months. If you decide to participate, you will

1. provide up to two interviews with the researcher
2. allow the researcher to use excerpts from the interviews in publications about research with the understanding that your identity will not be revealed at any time.

Participation is completely voluntary. You may choose to stop participating at any time prior to completion of the project. Should you have any questions at any time, you are welcome to contact the researcher by phone or e-mail. Your decision to participate will have no effect on or prejudice your future relationship with the University of Notre Dame. One possible benefit of participating in the study is that you will have the opportunity to learn about the implications of homelessness on education.

If you are willing to participate in this research, please read and sign the consent form below. You will be given a copy of this form to keep.

CONSENT FORM

I agree to participate in all of the procedures above. I understand that my identity will be protected during the study and that others will not have access to the interviews I provide. I also understand that my name will not be revealed when data from the research are presented in publications. I have read the above and give the researcher, Mary Ronan, permission to use excerpts from transcripts of tapes without identifying me as the writer or speaker.

_____   _____
Date   Signature

_____
[Telephone number]

_____
[E-mail address]

                                                          _____
                                                          Signature of Researcher

FIGURE 13.2   Sample Interview Consent Form

- Analyze the data.
- Draft an introduction, methods, and findings.

Your timeline should include the dates when you expect to finish the proposal, when you will conduct interviews and focus groups, when you expect to have a draft, and when you will complete the project. Be realistic about how long it will actually take to complete the different stages of collecting data and writing. Anticipate that events may prevent things from going exactly as planned. People cannot always meet with you when you would like them to, and you may have to change your own schedule. Therefore, be sure to contact participants well in advance of the time when you would like to speak with them in interviews or focus groups.

Steps to Writing a Proposal

1 **Describe your purpose in the introduction.** Summarize your issue, describing how it has led you to the question motivating your research.

2 **Review relevant research.** Show that you are aware of the most important studies conducted in your area of research, identify points of agreement and disagreement, and define key terms.

3 **Define your method.** What tools and strategies are you planning to use? Why are they appropriate and sufficient for your purposes?

4 **Discuss your implications.** What is the context of the conversation you are entering? What significant information do you expect your study to uncover?

5 **Include additional materials that support your research.** These may include an annotated bibliography, a series of interview questions, and blank consent forms.

AN ANNOTATED STUDENT PROPOSAL

Our student Laura Hartigan submitted a formal proposal for a study of different types of writing. Hartigan's proposal was exceptionally well prepared, thorough, and thoughtful, and she included a number of additional materials: a script of questions for focus groups with students; sample questions for the teacher and students she planned to interview; and consent forms. We reprint only the main part of her proposal—the part that includes a brief overview of the conversation about different modes of writing, her aims for conducting her study, methods, and implications sections—for you to consider as a model for proposal writing. A more complete example would include a separate review of relevant research. Notice how Hartigan summarizes her issue, explains how it motivated the study she proposes, formulates a set of guiding research questions, and helps readers understand why her research is important, particularly in the implications she draws.

 Laura Hartigan's completed paper, along with guidelines for a presentation poster, are available with access to LaunchPad for *From Inquiry to Academic Writing*.

Hartigan 1

Laura Hartigan
Professor Greene
English 385
March 28, 20—

Proposal for Research: The Affordances of Multimodal,
Creative, and Academic Writing

The student retraces the recent, and important, conversation about writing and alternative conceptions that challenge some widely held assumptions.

Researchers (Hughes, 2009; Vasudevan, Schultz & Bateman, 2010) have called attention to the unique ways that writing can foster student learning and have for some time now argued that teachers in elementary and high schools should give students more opportunities to write fiction and poetry using image, music, and text to express themselves. Within the last decade, even more alternative modes of writing have gained prominence. Researchers (Hughes, 2009; Hull & Katz, 2006) argue that "multimodal digital storytelling" provides students with ways to help them engage more deeply with their written work. Digital storytelling in particular enables students to examine their experiences by writing personal narratives in which they confront key turning points in their lives and the challenges they face. In turn, they can use images, music, and voice-over to amplify and give meaning to their written stories. Allowing for what researchers call "new literate spaces" creates the opportunity for multiple modes of learning, understanding, and collaboration that challenge the limited ways that students use writing as a mode of learning in school (Hughes, 2009; Hull & Katz, 2006). Students may learn to write persuasive essays, but they also need opportunities to learn about themselves and use their writing as a way to create changes in their lives. Thus researchers urge educators to reform curricular and pedagogical practices to help students use writing to help them develop a sense of identity and ownership of their writing, to see the decision-making power they have as individuals.

She summarizes recent studies and evidence supporting the value of alternative modes of writing. But she also identifies a gap in the argument researchers make.

When they argue that multimodal, digital literacy practices have a place in the standard curriculum, researchers (Hall, 2011; Hughes, 2009; Hull & Katz, 2006; Ranker, 2007; Vasudevan et al., 2010) provide evidence to show how youth grow and develop, become more confident learners, and use what they learn in and out of school. This is particularly true when youth have opportunities to reflect on their lives and use multiple literacies to give meaning to their experience. They can use image, music, and text to confront how

1

2

Hartigan 2

things in their lives look and feel, to examine the decisions they have made, and to consider the decisions they might make in confronting hardship, discrimination, and loss. However, most research fails to provide a satisfactory or compelling rationale for why new literacies *should* be used in the classroom (Alvermann, Marshall, McLean, Huddleston, Joaquin, 2012; Binder & Kotsopoulos, 2011; Hull and Katz, 2006; Ranker, 2007) or how the seemingly unique gains could be positively integrated into the standard curriculum. The lack of assessment focusing on how academic and new literacies affect one another reveals a flaw in the conclusions drawn from studies that neglect the realities of teaching in K-12 schools. Increased emphasis on standards, testing, and accountability seem to preclude the kind of focus that new literacies seem to require. Thus, if educators are to allow for "new literate spaces," they need to know how to do so within the standard curriculum.

Recognizing this gap, she explores what she sees as a common problem in a number of studies.

Specifically, few researchers explore students' sense of their literate identity in academic and creative writing or how context matters in how students feel about themselves and their writing. While most researchers (Binder & Kotsopoulos, 2011; Hughes, 2009; Hull & Katz, 2006; Vasudevan et al., 2010) refer to what they call "the mono-literacy landscape" of schools, the limits of literate experience to print, none really compare the opportunities that academic writing gives students versus, say, creative writing before, during, and after the study. That is, focusing only on the value of digital storytelling, for example, or creative writing is not sufficient to effect reform in school. Are there really significant differences between different kinds of writing? What are these differences? Such a gap in research seems to necessitate an inquiry into a student's emergent sense of authorship in different forms of composing, even academic writing in and out of school. Therefore, I propose a study that will provide an analysis of both academic and creative writing in an after-school program that helps children develop as learners through tutoring and enrichment. One implication of my research would be to show why educators might expand the types of literate experiences that students have in school.

In turn, this gap serves as a rationale for conducting her own study. She also points to the possible implications for doing the study she proposes.

3

Having defined the problem, she describes the aims of her study.

In order to investigate the possible differences between multimodal, creative, and standardized academic writing, this proposed study aims to explore (a) the unique opportunities afforded by the

4

Hartigan 3

multiple means of expression inherent in digital storytelling, (b) how and if these opportunities create an alternative space for the growth of empowered literate identities and a sense of agency, (c) the extent to which writing supports a student's development of an authorial voice, and (d) why schools should be concerned with the affordances given to the development of a student's written voice and individual identity by including multimodal digital storytelling in the curriculum. The

She reformulates the four aims of her study as questions to guide her inquiry.

study focuses on analyzing the students' sense of authorship in both their academic and creative assignments. To what extent can standard academic and creative multimodal expression help students develop an authorial identity and the skills they need to flourish in and out of school? Considering the current atmosphere of accountability and federal testing (Hull & Katz, 2006), it is important to ask what role multimodal composing can play in the standard and narrow curriculum.

Method

She describes the approach she will take to answer her questions.

To address the aims of my study, I will conduct interviews and focus groups to examine students' attitudes about writing in and out of school at the Crusoe Community Learning Center (CCLC) in a small midwestern city. Interviews and focus groups will enable me to discover student attitudes and feelings about writing across the in-school and out-of-school contexts in order to develop some insight into how writing can enable or disengage students. I will also take field notes taken by a participant-observer in the afterschool creative writing workshop to develop a picture of the after-school classroom dynamics.

Context

To help orient readers, she explains where her study will take place.

The CCLC is an off-campus educational initiative of a nearby private university in partnership with the surrounding neighborhood residents. Serving around 600 participants in the regular programming, the CCLC also partners with the community schools in the surrounding area with program outreach connecting to nearly 8,000 additional youths throughout the year. Located in a high-traffic, low-income neighborhood, the CCLC's mission centers around promoting hospitality, education, partnership, civic engagement, and sustainability in the surrounding area and all the participants. Organized around operating as a learning center and gathering space, the CCLC fosters relationships with the students, the surrounding residents, and the city's universities in a safe,

Hartigan 4

collaborative atmosphere. Classes and programming range from English as a New Language (ENL) to financial literacy, entrepreneurship, basic computing, and one-on-one tutoring for area children conducted by college volunteers.

She identifies the specific class that she will focus on in her research and explains why the context for conducting this study makes sense.

The creative writing class and the CCLC's curricular environment will provide an appropriate population and unique space to explore the possible affordances between creative and academic writing. With the after-school programming divided in weekly, day-by-day activities centered on enrichment, academic tutoring, and creative writing, the CCLC's after-school context is inherently connected to the student's school context. Thus the CCLC's efforts to help students with their day-to-day school work and also offer enrichment unique to an after-school program can enrich my understanding of the way students' contexts (in school and after school) influence how they see themselves as writers.

7

Participants

Importantly, she describes who will participate in the study and why she has chosen this particular teacher and class. Note that at this preliminary stage, she offers a brief sketch of the teacher and her credentials. However, she has not yet met the students.

At the CCLC, I will focus on Ms. Smith's class. Ms. Smith is a former fourth-grade teacher serving the center as a full-time AmeriCorps member. As an AmeriCorps member, Ms. Smith works in a federal program funded by the state of Indiana for a full-time forty-hour week at the CCLC. Taking place every Wednesday, the creative writing class centers around brainstorming, drafting, and publishing the student work for display inside the center and on a developing Web log. I have chosen this specific class and student population because it offered the opportunity to talk to students about their school and after-school writing experiences alongside the physical creative artifacts they created in Ms. Smith's class. Due to the participants' weekly experience of academic tutoring and creative class time, the choice was based on the wide range of writing activities that could be probed by the broad, experience-based focus of the question script.

8

Data Collection Procedure and Analysis

She explains the methods she will use to collect the information she needs to answer her research questions. She notes

I will conduct focus groups and interviews with the students in Ms. Smith's class over the course of three weeks. To obtain parental consent in order to conduct the focus groups and subsequent interviews, I will e-mail consent forms requesting each student's participation in my research. I will do so two weeks

9

Hartigan 5

that she needs the signed informed consent form from each student's parent in the class she is studying. This was stipulated by the Institutional Review Board (IRB).

prior to the study's start in order to provide the necessary time for the forms to be sent home and signed by the parents. (For the complete list of questions, see Appendix A.) Upon receiving confirmation from Ms. Smith that the consent forms had been completed, I can then conduct focus groups and interviews with the participating students.

In keeping with approaches to studies using focus groups and interviews, she plans to transcribe audio recordings. She explains her decision not to take notes during focus groups and interviews.

I will audio-record the focus groups and interviews. Following the end of each session, I will transcribe the recordings. Though I will not take notes during the focus groups and interviews in order to maintain total engagement with the participants, I will type a series of reflections and field notes after the completion of each audio-recorded session. Following the completion of the transcriptions, I will also take more notes to identify the themes that emerge in both interviews with individual children and in the focus groups.

10

Having explained her approach to collecting data, she now indicates what she will look for in her analysis.

After analyzing student responses, I will construct several categories to explore the CCLC participants' sense of self and authorial identity across contexts: safe spaces, expressing interest and meaningful message, and ownership.

11

Implications

In conclusion, she points to some possible implications of her research, but first places her proposed study in the broader context of what other researchers are finding. That is, she brings her study full circle to the ongoing conversation that framed her introduction.

Though many unique and compelling findings support a pedagogical shift toward new literacies, researchers (Vasudevan et al., 2010) tend to ignore the impact of a student's outside knowledge, experience, and contexts for writing. Moreover, without clearly understanding the differences and similarities between academic writing and multimodal writing, educators may not see the importance of including alternative modes of literacy in the standard curriculum. Hughes (2009) notes that the multimodal assignments and digital media in her research helped students engage more deeply with language and their own personal sense of command over their written work. The need to explore the changing materiality of texts figures as Hughes's intriguing concern due to its impact on the ways students construct meaning in what they write. Hughes frames performance "as a vehicle for exploration and learning, rather than as a fixed product to be rehearsed and delivered as a final event" (p. 262) that works in tandem with (not in isolation from)

12

Hartigan 6

She also reminds readers of a significant gap in current research.

literacy practices. Digital media allowed for the students to become what Hughes termed "co-creators," which helped students move beyond simply observing and analyzing poetry as a generally traditional and boring academic topic. However, the shift from print culture to new, performative media has yet to be reflected in classroom culture.

Moreover, after detailing how she will address her research questions above, she justifies the importance of her proposed study.

Sharpening the ideas drawn from the conclusions of Hughes (2009) points to the necessity of documenting the development of a student's voice and presence in multimodal, digital, and academic writing. In essence, research must avoid implying that one form of literacy is somehow more advantageous to the other without also looking at how context influences the ways students feel about themselves and what they write. To address this gap, my study will analyze the differences, and perhaps similarities, in how students develop and perceive their authorial presence and power in both kinds of writing — multimodal and academic — and the influence of context. After all, the mode of writing may not be as significant as the extent to which children feel they have a safe space place to write, where they can take risks without being afraid that their peers and teacher will criticize them. They also need to know that they have ownership of their writing as a means of expression and performance of who they are, who they imagine themselves to be, and what they want for themselves in the future.

13

Hartigan 7

Working Bibliography

Alvermann, D., Marshall, J., McLean, C., Huddleston, A., Joaquin, J., et al. (2012). Adolescents' Web-based literacies, identity construction, and skill development. *Literacy Research and Instruction, 51*(3), 179–195.

Binder, M., & Kotsopoulos, S. (2011). Multimodal literacy narratives: Weaving the threads of young children's identity through the arts. *Journal of Research in Childhood Education, 25*(4), 339–363.

Buckingham, D. (2007). Digital media literacies: Rethinking media education in the age of the Internet. *Research in Comparative and International Education, 2*(1), 43–55.

Hall, T. (2011). Designing from their own social worlds: The digital story of three African American young women. *English Teaching: Practice and Critique, 10*(1), 7–20.

Hughes, J. (2009). New media, new literacies and the adolescent learner. *E-Learning, 6*(3), 259–271.

Hull, G., & Katz, M. (2006). Crafting an agentive self: Case studies of digital storytelling. *Research in the Teaching of English, 41*(1), 43–81.

Ranker, J. (2007). Designing meaning with multiple media sources: A case study of an eight-year-old student's writing processes. *Research in the Teaching of English, 41*(4), 402–434.

Vasudevan, L., Schultz, K., & Bateman, J. (2010). Rethinking composing in a digital age: Authoring literate identities through multimodal storytelling. *Written Communication, 27*(4), 442–468.

INTERVIEWING

An **interview** helps to answer the research question(s) motivating your study by gathering concrete details and stories from various people. In her book *Critical Ethnography: Method, Ethics, and Performance*, D. Soyini Madison offers this advice: "When you first begin to formulate questions, a useful exercise is to reread your research question or problem over several times and then ask yourself, 'If this is what I am to understand, then what is it that I need to know about it to answer the questions or address the problem?' You will then list everything of interest that comes to mind" (p. 31). It's certainly possible to conduct an interview by phone, especially if the interviewee is not local, but a face-to-face conversation, in which you can note physical details and body language, is preferable.

The ways writers incorporate interviews into their writing appears almost seamless, but keep in mind that a finished text hides the process that went into a successful interview. You don't see the planning that occurs. Writers have to make appointments with the people they interview, develop a script or list of questions before the interview, and test the questions beforehand to see if they're likely to lead to the kind of information they're seeking. In other words, the key to a successful interview is preparation. The following information should help you plan your interview and prepare you for writing down your results.

■ Plan the Interview

You'll want to do some preliminary research to identify people who can help you understand more about your topic: What kind of expertise or experience do they have? Then you have to contact them to find out if they are willing to be interviewed. You can send a brief e-mail or letter to initiate a conversation and then follow up with a phone call.

Based on our own experience, it is important to explain the project for participants in plain terms. In fact, when you contact potential participants, we suggest you do so in writing and address the following: Who are you? What are you doing, and why? What will you do with what you find? What are possible benefits and risks? How will you assure confidentiality? How often and how long would you like to meet for interviews?

If you are planning to record the interview—always a wise idea—make sure each individual consents to being recorded. Then make the necessary arrangements. For example, you may need to reserve a room where you can conduct your interview without being disturbed. Try to choose a location that is convenient for the individual(s) you want to interview and familiar, such as a room in a public library.

It's important to set up appointments with people early. To keep on schedule, list the names of people who have agreed to be interviewed:

Interviewee 1:_____   Response? __ yes/no __ date:_____

Interviewee 2:_____   Response? __ yes/no __ date:_____

Interviewee 3:_____   Response? __ yes/no __ date:_____

■ Prepare Your Script

As you prepare the script of questions for your interview, keep coming back to the question motivating your research. To what extent will the questions you want to ask in your interview enable you to answer the broader question motivating your research? That is, what is the story you want to tell in your research? The more specific the questions you ask, the more specific the answers or story that the person you interview will tell.

Build rapport.   In any conversation, you want to build rapport and perhaps establish some common ground. More than getting information from someone, an interview can serve as a means to produce knowledge collaboratively and in ways that are mutually satisfying to you and the people you want to talk to. To create this kind of conversation, you can help the interviewee feel at ease and then move on to the issues you want to learn more about.

Start with nonthreatening questions.   For example, "How long have you been teaching writing?" "When did you start teaching writing in a hybrid classroom?" "What digital tools do you use to teach writing in a hybrid classroom?"

Ask open-ended questions.   Your questions should encourage the person you are interviewing to tell stories that will help you learn about your subject.

This means phrasing questions in ways that avoid simple yes/no answers. For instance, you might ask for an explanation of how children at a homeless center can overcome the obstacles they face as opposed to asking something like this: "Do you think children can overcome the obstacles they face?" Asking for an explanation invites someone to describe the process by which overcoming obstacles is possible. In turn, you can ask specific questions such as the following: "Can you tell me about a specific instance to illustrate the extent to which children can overcome the obstacles they face?" "Can you help me understand what made this possible?"

Avoid leading questions.   It may be tempting to ask leading questions to keep the conversation going in an interview or to fill in something that an individual implies but does not actually say. For example, "Do you think that the food industry has contributed to the problem of obesity?" "So are you saying that the government should formulate policies to regulate the industry?" In each case, the question supplies a possible answer, which is counterproductive. You want to learn from your interviewees, not feed them answers. The questions you ask should allow the person you are interviewing to come to his or her own conclusions. Alternatively, you can ask: "Tell me more about what you are saying about the government's role." Similarly, try not to reinforce or judge the answers that an interviewee gives, such as "That's what I was thinking." "That's great." "You're right." Reinforcing or judging answers may indicate to an interviewee that there is a correct answer to the questions you are asking. Instead, you want this person to explore his or her thoughts in an open, honest way.

Only share experiences occasionally.   Although we have suggested that conducting interviews can be like conversations, you should resist providing your own experiences and stories. Listen to answers and follow up with questions that encourage the person you are interviewing to elaborate.

Rehearse and then revise the script.   After you develop a script of questions, rehearse it with your writing group or a friend who can play the role of the person you want to interview. In doing so, you want to get a sense of how an interviewee is going to respond to your questions. The following questions can serve as a guide for assessing the interview and what you might change:

- What would you point to as an effective exchange?
- What questions helped you get concrete details to tell the story you wanted to tell?
- What would you point to as an example of an exchange that didn't go as well as you had hoped? How would you explain what happened?
- What questions would you rephrase if you were to do the interview again?
- To what extent do you feel that you might have lost some opportunities to follow up?
- Are there follow-up questions you should have asked?

After you answer these questions, revise the script to improve the content, order, and pacing of your questions.

■ Conduct the Interview

On the day before the interview, contact the individual you plan to interview to confirm that he or she remembers the time of the interview and knows how to find the location where the interview will take place. Also, as you prepare for your interview, look over your questions and make sure you know how to use your recording software and device and that your device has sufficient capacity for the interview. Be on time. Have a brief conversation to put the interviewee at ease and then ask this person to read and sign the consent form (see Figure 13.2).

Explain use of technology.   Explain why recording the interview is necessary ("Your responses are really important to me. I will take some notes as you talk, but I don't want to miss anything you have to say. As a result, I will record our conversation so I can revisit the important things you tell me").

Describe the interview process.   Explain what types of questions you will ask in the interview ("Today, I'm going to ask you questions about school and your family"). In addition, explain why you're interested in knowing this information ("I want to learn more about you and your family so I can understand what techniques for school, family, etc. are helpful for you").

Keep the interview conversational.   Use your script as a guide, but be flexible, treating the interview as a conversation. This might mean following the direction that the person you interview takes in answering a question. Listen. Don't interrupt. That is, you might ask what you think is a pointed question and this person might begin to tell a story that may not seem relevant. Let the person finish and patiently return to the questions you would like this person to address. You can also try rephrasing your question(s) to be more specific about the information you need. If you think at some point that the interviewee is implying something of special interest to you, ask for clarification.

Respect silence.   If any interviewee is silent for a while after you ask a question, be patient and don't immediately repeat or ask another question. The interviewee may need time to gather his or her thoughts or understand the question. After some time has passed, you can ask this person the question again or ask another question.

Keep track of important questions.   Toward the end of the interview, check your script for important questions you may have forgotten to ask. If there are several, try to ask only the most important ones in the time remaining. You can also ask to have a follow-up meeting to ensure that you have gotten the information you need.

Follow up after the interview is over.   Continue getting to know the interviewee. Even though the formal interview is done, you still want this person to feel as though he or she matters to you. Just because this person has completed the interview doesn't mean that his or her relationship with the research project is over.

■ Make Sense of the Interview

Conducting an interview is only part of the challenge; you then have to make sense of what was said. That process involves four steps:

1. *Familiarize yourself with the conversation.* If you recorded the interview, listen to it a couple of times to become really familiar with what was said. Read through your notes several times too.

2. *Transcribe the interview.* Transcribing entails listening carefully to and typing up the audio recording of your interview to help you analyze the conversation. A transcript provides a more manageable way to identify key points in the interview, details that you might miss if you only listened to the interview, and stories that you might recount in your research. Transcribing an interview is an important part of doing this kind of research, but it is time-consuming. If you use transcription software to save time, you will still need to compare your transcript to your recording for accuracy. Therefore, you need to plan accordingly. An hour-long interview usually takes about three hours to transcribe.

3. *Analyze the interview.* Read through the interview again. Look for answers to the questions motivating your research, and look for recurring patterns or themes. Make a list of those ideas relevant to the issues you intend to focus on, especially evidence that might support your argument.

4. *Find one good source.* Using the themes you identify in your analysis as a guide, find one good source that relates to your interview in some way. Maybe your subject's story fits into an educational debate (for example, public versus private education). Or maybe your subject's story counters a common conception about education (that inner-city schools are hopelessly inadequate). You're looking for a source you can link to your interview in an interesting and effective way.

■ Turn Your Interview into an Essay

Try to lay out in paragraphs the material you've collected that addresses the question motivating your research and the focus of your paper. In a first draft, you might take these steps:

1. State your argument, or the purpose of your essay. What do you want to teach your readers?

2. Provide evidence to support your thesis. What examples from your reading, observations, or interviews do you want to offer your readers? How do those examples illuminate your claim?

3. Place quotations from more than one source in as many paragraphs as you can, so that you can play the quotations off against one another. What is significant about the ways you see specific quotations "in conversation" with one another? How do these conversations between quotations help you build your own argument?

4. Consider possible counterarguments to the point you want to make.

5. Help readers understand what is at stake in adopting your position.

Steps to Interviewing

1 **Plan the interview.** After you've identified the people you might like to talk to, contact them to explain your project and set up appointments if they are willing to participate.

2 **Prepare your script.** Draft your questions, rehearse them with your classmates or friends, and then make revisions based on their responses.

3 **Conduct the interview.** Be flexible with your script as you go, making sure to take good notes even if you are recording the interview.

4 **Make sense of the interview.** Review the recording and your notes of the interview, transcribe the interview, analyze the transcript, and connect the conversation to at least one good source.

5 **Turn your interview into an essay.** State your argument, organize your evidence, use quotes to make your point, consider counterarguments, and help your readers understand what's at stake.

USING FOCUS GROUPS

Like interviews, focus groups can provide you with an original source of evidence to complement (or complicate, contradict, or extend) the evidence you find in books and articles. According to Bruce L. Berg in *Qualitative Research Methods for the Social Sciences*, a **focus group** "may be defined as an interview style designed for small groups . . . addressing a particular topic of interest or relevance to the group and the researcher." College administrators often speak with groups of students to understand the nature of a problem—for instance, whether writing instruction is as effective as it should be beyond a first-year writing course, or whether technology is used to best effect in classes across the curriculum. One advantage of a focus group, as opposed to an interview, is that once one person starts talking, others join in. It is generally easier to get a conversation going in a focus group than to get an interview started with a single person.

As a method, focus groups provide a supportive environment for discussing an issue that people may feel less comfortable talking about in an interview. The conversations that emerge in focus groups may also prompt individuals to tell stories that they may not have considered relevant or interesting until they hear others telling their stories. Finally, listening to a focus group discussion can give you a pretty good idea of individuals you may want to interview.

A typical focus group session is guided by a facilitator, or moderator. The moderator's job is much like the interviewer's: to draw out information from the participants on topics of importance to a given investigation. The informal atmosphere of the focus group is intended to encourage participants to speak freely and completely about their behaviors, attitudes, and opinions. Interaction among group members often takes the form of brainstorming, generating a larger number of ideas, issues, topics, and solutions to problems than could be produced through individual conversations.

The following are several basic tasks necessary to orchestrating a focus group.

■ Select Participants for the Focus Group

Focus groups should consist of five to seven participants, in addition to you, the moderator. Think carefully about the range of participants you'll need to gather the information you're hoping to find. Depending on your issue, you might choose participants based on gender, ethnicity, major, year in school, living situation, or some other factor. Do you want a wide range of participants? Or do you want to control the focus of the conversation by looking at just one particular group of people? For instance, if you wanted to find out if technology is serving students' needs, would you talk only to people in the sciences? Or would you want a cross section of disciplines represented? Or if your question is whether colleges and universities should take race and ethnicity into consideration when selecting students from the applicant pool, would you limit participation to the admissions staff? Where should you look for input on the purpose of giving preference to minority students or the advantages of a diverse campus?

■ Plan the Focus Group

Planning is as important for a focus group as it is for an interview. Make specific arrangements with participants about the time and place of the focus group session, and be clear about how much time it will take, usually thirty to forty-five minutes. You should audio-record the session and take notes. Jot down important information during the session, and allow yourself time to make more extensive notes as soon as it is over. You will need

Focus Group Consent Form

You are invited to participate in a study of academic writing at the university over the next four years. You were selected from a random sample of all first-year students. If you decide to participate, you will

1. provide the researcher with copies of the writing you complete for every class and the assignment, when available.
2. attend up to four focus group sessions during a given academic year.
3. allow the researcher to use excerpts from the writing you complete and the focus group sessions in publications about research with the understanding that your identity will not be revealed at any time.

In all, out-of-class participation will take no more than four hours during an academic year.

Participation is completely voluntary; you may stop participating at any time prior to completion of the project. Should you have any questions at any time, you are welcome to contact the researcher via phone or e-mail. Your decision to participate or not will have no effect on your grade in any course or prejudice your future relationship with the university. One benefit of participating in the study is that you will have the opportunity to learn important information about writing.

If you are willing to participate in this research, please read and sign the consent form below. You will be given a copy of this form to keep.

CONSENT FORM

I agree to participate in all of the procedures above. I understand that my identity will be protected during the study and that instructors will not have access to the statements I make in focus group sessions. I also understand that my name will not be revealed when data from the research are presented in publications. (Digital files will be kept for five years and then removed from relevant databases.) I have read the above and give the researcher, Stuart Greene, and his coauthors permission to use excerpts from what I write or transcripts of tapes without identifying me as the writer or speaker.

_____   _____
Date   Signature

_____
[Telephone number]

_____
[E-mail address]

                                                             _____
                                                             Signature of Researcher

FIGURE 13.3   Sample Consent Form for a Focus Group

to get permission from respondents to use the information they give you and ensure their anonymity. (In your essay, you can refer to participants by letter, number, or some other designation.) Make a sheet with your signature that spells this out clearly, and make sure all your participants sign it before the session. You should include a statement pointing out that people have the right not to participate. We have included sample consent forms in Figures 13.3 and 13.4.

Alternative Focus Group Consent Form

Should colleges and universities take race and ethnicity into consideration when selecting new freshmen from the applicant pool? What is the purpose of giving preference to minority status in admissions? What does a diverse campus offer its students? These are some of the issues I want to discuss in today's focus group. But before we start, let me tell you about the assignment and your involvement.

The focus group is an interview style designed for small groups of five to seven participants. Focus group interviews are guided discussions that address a particular topic of interest or relevance to the group and the researcher. The informality of the focus group structure is intended to encourage participants to speak freely about their behaviors, attitudes, and opinions. For the purposes of my research, focus groups are a way to include multiple perspectives in my paper.

This session will be recorded so that I can prove my research. No names will be used in any drafts or in my final paper; instead, I will use letters (A, B, C) to identify different speakers. Two focus groups — one for minority students at Notre Dame and another for nonminority students—are being held so that I can obtain opinions and viewpoints from both sides of the issue and discuss their similarities and differences in my report. Some things to keep in mind during the session:

- Because I need to transcribe the dialogue, try not to talk over another person.
- Feel free to agree or disagree with a question, statement, or another person's answer.
- Focus on the discussion, not the question.
- Avoid going off on tangents.
- Be open and honest in all your responses.

Thank you for taking the time to be involved in my research. By signing below you give me permission to use the comments you provide for my paper. You understand that in no way will your identity be revealed, except by your minority or nonminority status. If you would like a copy of the results of the focus groups, please include your e-mail address, and the documents will be sent to you.

Name _____

E-mail address _____

Ethnicity _____   Male / Female   Class of _____
                                        (circle one)

FIGURE 13.4 Alternative Sample Consent Form for a Focus Group

■ Prepare Your Script

Many of the guidelines for designing interview questions (see pp. 390–92) apply equally well to focus group questions. So, for example, you might start by establishing common ground or begin with a couple of nonthreatening questions. For variety, and to keep the discussion moving, use open-ended questions. Consider asking participants in the group for definitions, impressions, examples, their ideas of others' perceptions, and the like. Also, you might quote from key passages in the scholarly research you will be using and ask for the group's responses to these "expert" theories. Not only will this be interesting for them; it also will help you organize and integrate your focus group evidence with evidence from library sources in your essay. Ask a wider range of questions than you think you might need so that you can explore side issues if they arise.

■ Conduct the Focus Group

On the day before you conduct the focus group, contact those who have agreed to participate to remind them of when and where it will happen. Show up ahead of time to set up your recording equipment and make sure that the room has sufficient seating for the participants. And don't forget your script. Here are three other guidelines.

Ask questions that draw people out.   During the focus group, be ready to draw out participants with follow-up questions ("Can you offer an example?" "Where do you think this impression comes from?"). Encourage all participants to speak; don't allow one member to dominate the discussion. (You may need to ask a facilitating question like "Do the rest of you agree with X's statement?" or "How would you extend what X has said?" or "Has anyone had a different experience?")

Limit the time of a focus group session.   It's a good idea to limit the session to thirty to forty-five minutes. When deciding how long the session should last, remember that it will take approximately three times longer to transcribe it manually. Even if you use transcription software, you'll need to spend time checking the transcription against the recording for accuracy. You must transcribe the session so that you can read through the participants' comments and quote them accurately.

Notice nonverbal interactions.   Be sure to notice nonverbal interactions and responses in your session, taking notes of body language, reluctance or eagerness to speak, and dynamics among group members that either open up or shut down conversation. These responses should be part of the data you analyze. For this reason, and also because keeping track of multiple speakers in an audio recording can be challenging, video recording may be more effective than audio recording for focus groups. If filming your group is not an option, you will need to take careful notes about interactions during the session.

■ Interpret the Data from the Focus Group

Once you transcribe your focus group session, remember to refer anonymously to your participants in your analysis. You then need to interpret the significance of the way participants talk about issues, as well as the information they relate. Interpret the nonverbal communication in the group as well as the verbal communication.

In making claims based on focus group data, remember that data from focus group interviews are not the same as data from individual interviews. They reflect collective thinking, ideas shared and negotiated by the group. Also, although you might speculate that data from a focus group are indicative of larger trends, be careful about the kinds of claims you make. One first-year student's idea is not necessarily every first-year student's idea.

The principal aim of doing original research is to make a contribution to a conversation using primary material as evidence to support your argument. For instance, when you conduct interviews or focus group discussions, you are collecting information (or data) that can offer a unique perspective. And doing original research also can enable you to test others' claims or assumptions and broaden your scope of inquiry beyond secondary materials. An effective piece of original research still relies on secondary materials, particularly as you find ways to locate what you discover in the context of what other authors have observed and argued. Moreover, there is the value of using multiple sources of information to support your claims — using your observations and the findings of others to say something about your subject. Also important, the research methods you choose depend on the question you ask. A focus on the types of educational opportunities available to the homeless lends itself more to close observation, interviews, and perhaps focus groups.

■ Important Ethical Considerations

Finally, we want to end with an ethical reminder: *Be fair to your sources.* Throughout this chapter, we have included a number of forms on which you can base your own consent forms when you conduct interviews and focus groups. When people give you their consent to use their words, it is incumbent on you—really it is essential—that you represent as faithfully as possible what people have said. As a researcher, you are given a kind of power over the people you interview and write about, using what they tell you for your own purposes. You cannot abuse the trust they place in you when they consent to be part of your research. It is important that they understand why you're doing the research and how your theories and assumptions will likely figure into your interpretation of the information you gather. You must also be aware of how their words will be construed by those who read what you write.

Steps for Conducting a Focus Group

1 **Select participants for the focus group.** Identify the range of your five to seven participants. Are you looking for diverse perspectives or a more specialized group?

2 **Plan the focus group.** Make sure that you have a specified time and place and that your participants are willing to sign consent forms.

3 **Prepare your script.** Prepare a variety of open-ended questions; consider quoting research you are interested in using in your paper to get participants' responses; and try to rehearse and revise.

4 **Conduct the focus group.** Record the session; ask questions that draw people out; limit the time of the session; and notice nonverbal interactions. And don't forget the consent forms.

5 **Interpret the data from the focus group.** Transcribe and analyze the data, including nonverbal communications; draw conclusions, but be careful not to overgeneralize from your small sample.

APPENDIX:
Citing and Documenting Sources

Y ou must provide a brief citation in the text of your paper for every quotation or idea taken from another writer, and you must list complete information at the end of your paper for the sources you use. This information is essential for readers who want to read the source to understand a quotation or an idea in its original context. How you cite sources in the body of your paper and document them at the end of your paper varies from discipline to discipline, so it is important to ask your instructor what documentation style he or she requires.

Even within academic disciplines, documentation styles can vary. Specific academic journals within disciplines will sometimes have their own set of style guidelines. The important thing is to adhere faithfully to your chosen (or assigned) style throughout your paper, observing all the rules prescribed by the style. You may have noticed small citation style differences among the examples in this text. That's because the examples are taken from the work of a variety of writers, both professionals and students, who had to conform to the documentation requirements of their publication venues or of their teachers.

Here we briefly introduce two common documentation styles that may be useful in your college career: the Modern Language Association (MLA) style, frequently used in the humanities, and the American Psychological Association (APA) style, often used in the social sciences. The information is basic, for use when you begin drafting your paper. In the final stages of writing, you should consult either the *MLA Handbook*, Eighth Edition, or the *Publication Manual of the American Psychological Association*, Sixth Edition.

Although you'll need the manuals or a handbook for complete style information, both the MLA (style.mla.org) and the APA (http://www .apastyle.org/learn/faqs/) maintain Web sites for frequently asked questions. Again, before you start your research, check with your instructor to find out whether you should use either of these styles or if there's another style he or she requires.

MLA and APA styles have many similarities. For example, both require short citations in the body of an essay linked to a list of sources at the end of the essay. But it is their differences, though subtle, that are crucial. To a great extent, these differences reflect the assumptions writers in the humanities and in the social sciences bring to working with sources. In particular, you should understand each style's treatment of the source's author, publication date, and page numbers in in-text citations, as well as verb use in referring to sources.

Author.   MLA style prefers that you give the author's full name on first mention in your paper; APA style uses last names throughout. The humanities emphasize "the human element"—the individual as creative force—so MLA style uses the complete name at first mention to imply the author's importance. Because the social sciences emphasize the primacy of data in studies of human activity, in APA style last names are deemed sufficient for identifying the source.

Publication date.   In-text citations using MLA style leave out the date of publication. The assumption is that the insights of the past may be as useful as those of the present. By contrast, APA in-text citations include the date of the study after the author's name, reflecting a belief in the progress of research, that recent findings may supersede earlier ones.

Verb use.   MLA style uses the present tense of verbs ("the author claims") to introduce cited material, assuming the cited text's timelessness, whether written last week or centuries ago. By contrast, APA style acknowledges the "pastness" of research by requiring past-tense verbs for introducing cited material ("the author claimed" or "the author has claimed"); the underlying assumption is that new data may emerge to challenge older research.

Although it is useful to understand that different citation styles reflect different attitudes toward inquiry and research in different disciplines, for the purposes of your writing, it is mainly important to know the style you have to follow in your paper and to apply it consistently. Whenever you consult a source—even if you don't end up using it in your paper—write down complete citation information so that you can cite it fully and accurately if you need to. Doing so will help you be a responsible researcher and save you the trouble of having to hunt down citation information later. Table A.1 shows the basic information needed to cite books, chapters in books, journal articles, and online sources. You also should note any other

TABLE A.1   Basic Information Needed for Citing Sources

Books	Chapters in Books	Journal Articles	Online Sources
Author(s) or editor(s)	Author(s)	Author(s)	Author(s)
Title and subtitle	Chapter title and subtitle	Article title and subtitle	Document title and subtitle
Edition information	Book editor(s)	Journal title	Print publication information, if any
Place of publication (APA only)	Book title	Volume and issue number	Site publisher or sponsor
Publisher	Edition information	Date of publication	Site title
Year of publication	Place of publication (APA only)	Page numbers	Date of publication or most recent update
	Publisher		URL or DOI
	Year of publication		Date accessed
	Page numbers		

information that could be relevant—a translator's name, for example, or a series title and editor. Being able to cite a source fully without having to go back to it to get more information saves you time.

THE BASICS OF MLA STYLE

In-text citations.   In MLA style, you must provide a brief citation in the body of your essay (1) when you quote directly from a source, (2) when you paraphrase or summarize what someone else has written, and (3) when you use an idea or a concept that originated with someone else.

In the excerpt that follows, the citation tells readers that the student writer's argument about the evolution of Ebonics is rooted in a well-established source of information. Because the writer does not mention the author in the paraphrase of her source in the text, she gives the author's name in the citation:

> The evolution of U.S. Ebonics can be traced from the year 1557 to the present day. In times of great oppression, such as the beginning of the slave codes in 1661, the language of the black community was at its most "ebonified" levels, whereas in times of racial progress, for example during the abolitionist movement, the language as a source of community identity was forsaken for greater assimilation (Smitherman 119).

The parenthetical citation refers to page 119 of Geneva Smitherman's book *Talkin and Testifyin: The Language of Black America* (1977). Smitherman is a recognized authority on Ebonics. Had the student mentioned Smitherman's name in her introduction to the paraphrase, she would not have had to repeat it in the citation. Notice that there is no punctuation within the parentheses and no *p.* before the page number. Also notice that the citation is considered part of the sentence in which it appears, so the period ending the sentence follows the closing parenthesis.

By contrast, in the example that follows, the student quotes directly from Richard Rodriguez's book *Hunger of Memory: The Education of Richard Rodriguez* (1982):

> Many minority cultures in today's society feel that it is more important to maintain cultural bonds than to extend themselves into the larger community. People who do not speak English may feel a similar sense of community and consequently lose some of the individuality and cultural ties that come with speaking their native or home language. This shared language within a home or community also adds to the unity of the community. Richard Rodriguez attests to this fact in his essay "Aria." He then goes on to say that "it is not healthy to distinguish public words from private sounds so easily" (183).

Because the student mentions Rodriguez in her text right before the quotation ("Richard Rodriguez attests"), she does not need to include his name in the parenthetical citation; the page number is sufficient.

Works cited. At the end of your researched essay and starting on a new page, you must provide a list of works cited, a list of all the sources you have used (leaving out sources you consulted but decided not to use). Entries should be listed alphabetically by author's last name or by title if no author is identified. Figure A.1 (p. 406) is a sample Works Cited page in MLA style that illustrates a few of the basic types of documentation.

Steps to Compiling an MLA List of Works Cited

1 Begin your list of works cited on a new page at the end of your paper.

2 Put your last name and page number in the upper-right corner.

3 Double-space throughout.

4 Center the heading ("Works Cited") on the page.

5 Arrange the list of sources alphabetically by author's last name or by title if no author is identified.

6 Begin the first line of each source flush left; second and subsequent lines should be indented ½ inch.

7 Invert the author's name, last name first. In the case of multiple authors, only the first author's name is inverted.

8 Italicize the titles of books, journals, magazines, and newspapers. Put the titles of book chapters and articles in quotation marks. Capitalize each word in all titles except for articles (*a, an, the*), short prepositions (*in, at, of,* for example), and coordinating conjunctions (*and, but, for, so,* for example).

9 For books, list the name of the publisher and the year of publication. For chapters, list the editors of the book, the book title, and the publication information. For articles, list the title of the journal, magazine, or newspaper; the volume and issue numbers (for a journal); and the date of publication.

10 List the relevant page numbers for articles and selections from longer works.

The steps outlined here for compiling a list of works cited apply to printed sources. MLA formats for citing online sources vary, but this is an example of the basic format:

Author. "Title of Work." *Name of Site*, Publisher or Sponsor, publication date/most recent update date, DOI or URL.

Things to remember:

- Invert the author's name (or the first author's name only, when there are multiple authors).
- Italicize the name of the site.
- If the site publisher or sponsor — usually an institution or organization — isn't clear, check the copyright notice at the bottom of the Web page. If the name of the publisher or sponsor is identical to the name of the site, include only the Web site name in your citation.
- Give the publication date or the most recent update date. Use the day-month-year format for dates in the Works Cited list. Abbreviate all months except May, June, and July.
- Notice that there's a comma between the sponsor and the publication date.
- Include the DOI (if available) or URL for the source.
- If a source has no date, give the date of access at the end of the entry.

In addition to books, articles, and Web sites, you may need to cite sources such as films, recordings, television and radio programs, paintings, and photographs. For details on how to format these sources, consult a handbook (if your instructor has assigned one) or the *MLA Handbook*, Eighth Edition, or go to the MLA Style Center (style.mla.org).

Eck 10

Works Cited

For three or more authors, list the first author's name, followed by "et al." — Gutiérrez, Kris D., et al. "English for the Children: The New Literacy of the Old World Order." *Bilingual Review Journal*, vol. 24, no. 1/2, Fall/Winter 2000, pp. 87-112.

Article in an online journal, no author — "History of Bilingual Education." *Rethinking Schools*, vol. 12, no. 3, Spring 1998, www.rethinkingschools.org/restrict .asp?path=archive/12_03/langhst.shtml.

Article in a print journal — Lanehart, Sonja L. "African American Vernacular English and Education." *Journal of English Linguistics*, vol. 26, no. 2, June 1998, pp. 122-36.

Article from a Web site — Pompa, Delia. "Bilingual Success: Why Two-Language Education Is Critical for Latinos." *English for the Children*, One Nation/ One California, 1 Nov. 2000, www.onenation.org/article/ bilingual-success/.

Rawls, John. *Political Liberalism*. Columbia UP, 1993.

Essay in an edited collection; second source by same writer — ---. "Social Unity and Primary Goods." *Utilitarianism and Beyond*, edited by Amartya Sen and Bernard Williams, Cambridge UP, 1982, pp. 159-85.

Rodriguez, Richard. "Aria." *Hunger of Memory: The Education of Richard Rodriguez*, Bantam Books, 1982, pp. 11-40.

Article in a magazine — Schrag, Peter. "Language Barrier." *New Republic*, 9 Mar. 1998, pp. 14-15.

A book — Smitherman, Geneva. *Talkin and Testifyin: The Language of Black America*. Wayne State UP, 1977.

Willis, Arlette Ingram. "Reading the World of School Literacy: Contextualizing the Experience of a Young American Male." *Harvard Educational Review*, vol. 65, no. 1, Spring 1995, pp. 30-49.

FIGURE A.1   Sample List of Works Cited, MLA Format

THE BASICS OF APA STYLE

In-text citations. In APA style, in-text citations identify the author or authors of a source, page or paragraph numbers for the information cited, and the publication date. If the author or authors are mentioned in the text, provide the publication date immediately following the author's name:

> Feingold (1992) documented the fact that males perform much better than females in math and science and other stereotypically masculine areas (p. 92).

APA style does not explicitly require page or paragraph numbers to be included with paraphrased material. It does, however, recommend page or paragraph numbers for all in-text citations, particularly when readers might have trouble finding the material in the original source without that information. If the source is quoted directly, a page number must be included in parentheses following the quotation:

> Feingold (1992) argued that "men scored significantly higher than women in situations designed to test aptitude in mathematics and hard sciences" (p. 92).

APA style uses the abbreviation *p.* or *pp.* before page numbers, which MLA style does not. If the author is not introduced with a signal phrase, the name, year, and page number would be noted parenthetically after the quotation:

> One study found that "men scored significantly higher than women in situations designed to test aptitude in mathematics and hard sciences" (Feingold, 1992, p. 92).

Many studies in the social sciences have multiple authors. In a work with two authors, cite both authors every time:

> Dlugos and Friedlander (2000) wrote that "sustaining passionate commitment to work as a psychotherapist reflects passionate commitment in other areas of life" (p. 298).

Here, too, if you do not identify the authors in a signal phrase, include their names, the year the source was published, and the relevant page number parenthetically after the quotation—but use an ampersand (&) instead of the word *and* between the authors' names:

> Some believe that "sustaining passionate commitment to work as a psychotherapist reflects passionate commitment in other areas of life" (Dlugos & Friedlander, 2000, p. 298).

Use the same principles the first time you cite a work with three to five authors:

> Booth-Butterfield, Anderson, and Williams (2000) tested . . .
> (Booth-Butterfield, Anderson, & Williams, 2000, p. 5)

Thereafter, you can use the name of the first author followed by the abbreviation *et al.* (Latin for "and others") in roman type:

Booth-Butterfield et al. (2000) tested . . .
(Booth-Butterfield et al., 2000, p. 5)

For a work with six or more authors, use *et al.* from the first mention.

These are only some of the most basic examples of APA in-text citation. Consult the APA manual for other guidelines.

References. APA style, like MLA style, requires a separate list of sources at the end of a research paper. In APA style, this list is called "References," not "Works Cited." The list of references starts on a new page at the end of your paper and lists sources alphabetically by author (or title if no author is identified). Figure A.2 shows a sample list of references with sources cited in APA style.

Steps to Compiling an APA List of References

1 Begin your list of references on a new page at the end of your paper.

2 Put a shortened version of the paper's title (not your last name) in all caps in the upper-left corner; put the page number in the upper-right corner.

3 Double-space throughout.

4 Center the heading ("References") on the page.

5 Arrange the list of sources alphabetically by author's last name or by title if no author is identified.

6 Begin the first line of each source flush left; second and subsequent lines should be indented ½ inch.

7 Invert all authors' names. If a source has more than one author, use an ampersand (not *and*) before the last name.

8 Insert the date in parentheses after the last author's name.

9 Italicize the titles of books, capitalizing only the first letter of the title and subtitle and proper nouns.

10 Follow the same capitalization for the titles of book chapters and articles. Do not use quotation marks around chapter and article titles.

11 Italicize the titles of journals, magazines, and newspapers, capitalizing the initial letters of all key words.

12 For books, list the place of publication and the name of the publisher. For chapters, list the book editor(s), the book title, the relevant page numbers, and the place of publication and the name of the publisher. For articles, list the journal title, the volume number, the issue number if each issue of the volume begins on page 1, the relevant pages, and the DOI (digital object identifier) if available. If you retrieve a journal article online and there is no DOI, include the URL of the journal's home page.

GENDER AND TEACHING   15

References

Journal article with no DOI

Campbell, R. J. (1969). Co-education: Attitudes and self-concepts of girls at three schools. *British Journal of Educational Psychology, 39,* 87.

Report, seven authors

Coleman, J., Campbell, E., Hobson, C., McPartland, J., Mood, A., Weinfeld, F., & York, R. (1966). *Equality of educational opportunity (The Coleman Report).* Washington, DC: U.S. Government Printing Office.

Journal article with a DOI

Feingold, A. (1992). Sex differences in variability in intellectual abilities: A new look at an old controversy. *Review of Educational Research, 62,* 61–84. doi:10.3102/00346543062001061

Online source

Haag, P. (2003). *K–12 single-sex education: What does the research say?* Retrieved from http://www.ericdigests .org/2001-2/sex.html

Journal article retrieved online with no DOI

Hallinan, M. T. (1994). Tracking: From theory to practice. *Sociology of Education, 67,* 79–84. Retrieved from http:// www.asanet.org/journals/soe/

Hanson, S. L. (1994). Lost talent: Unrealized educational aspirations and expectations among U.S. youth. *Sociology of Education, 67,* 159–183. Retrieved from http://www .asanet.org/journals/soe/

Jovanovic, J., & King, S. S. (1998). Boys and girls in the performance-based science classroom: Who's doing the performing? *American Educational Research Journal, 35,* 477–496. doi:10.3102/00028312035003477

FIGURE A.2   Sample List of References, APA Format

Lee, V. E., & Marks, H. M. (1990). Sustained effects of the single-sex secondary school experience on attitudes, behaviors, and values in college. *Journal of Educational Psychology, 82*, 578–592.

Mickelson, R. A. (1989). Why does Jane read and write so well? The anomaly of women's achievement. *Sociology of Education, 62*, 47–63. Retrieved from http://www.asanet .org/journals/soe/

Scholarly book   Rosenberg, M. (1965). *Society and the adolescent self-image.* Princeton, NJ: Princeton University Press.

Schneider, F. W., & Coutts, L. M. (1982). The high school environment: A comparison of coeducational and single-sex schools. *Journal of Educational Psychology, 74*, 898–906.

Essay in an edited collection   Spade, J. Z. (2001). Gender education in the United States. In J. H. Ballantine & J. Z. Spade (Eds.), *Schools and society: A sociological approach to education* (pp. 270–278). Belmont, CA: Wadsworth/Thomson Learning.

Streitmatter, J. L. (1999). *For girls ONLY: Making a case for single-sex schooling.* Albany, NY: State University of New York Press.

Dissertation from a database   Winslow, M. A. (1995). *Where the boys are: The educational aspirations and future expectations of working-class girls in an all-female high school* (Doctoral dissertation). University of Arizona. Retrieved from ProQuest Dissertations and Theses database. (AAT 9622975)

The *APA Manual* is your best resource for formatting online sources, but here is an example of a basic reference to an online source:

Author. (Date posted/revised). *Document title.* Retrieved from URL

- Provide the author's name in inverted order: last name first. If no author is identified, alphabetize the entry by its title.
- Capitalize an online document title like an article title and italicize it; don't enclose it in quotation marks.
- Include a retrieval date after the word "Retrieved" only if the content is likely to change.

- Notice that there is no end punctuation after the DOI or URL.
- APA style asks you to break lengthy DOIs or URLs after a slash or before a period, being sure that your composing software doesn't insert a hyphen at the line break.

You should know that some sources you may rely on in your research in the social sciences—interviews and focus groups, for example—do not have to be included in your list of references. Instead, you would cite the person you interviewed or the focus group you conducted in the text of your paper. For example:

(J. Long, personal interview, April 7, 2017)

ACKNOWLEDGMENTS

Emily Badger. "Mapped: The Places Where Most Public School Children Are Poor." From the *Washington Post*, *Wonkblog*, May 13, 2015, https://www.washingtonpost.com/news/wonk/wp/2015/05/13/mapped-the-places-where-most-public-school-children-are-poor/?utm_term=.36097011ca12. Copyright © 2016 The Washington Post. All rights reserved. Used by permission and protected by the Copyright Laws of the United States. The printing, copying, redistribution, or retransmission of this Content without express written permission is prohibited.

Susan D. Blum. "The United States of (Non)Reading: The End of Civilization or a New Era?" From *HuffPost College*, October 8, 2013. Copyright © 2013 by Susan Blum. Reprinted with permission.

Ta-Nehisi Coates. "Between the World and Me." From *Between the World and Me* by Ta-Nehisi Coates. Copyright © 2015 by Ta-Nehisi Coates. Used by permission of Spiegel & Grau, an imprint of Random House, a division of Penguin Random House LLC. All rights reserved. Any third party use of this material, outside of this publication, is prohibited. Interested third parties must apply directly to Penguin Random House LLC for permission.

Anne Colby and Thomas Ehrlich, with Elizabeth Beaumont and Jason Stephens (the Carnegie Foundation for the Advancement of Teaching). Excerpt from "Undergraduate Education and the Development of Moral and Civic Responsibility." From *The Communitarian Network*, www2.gwu.edu/~ccps/Colby.html. Reprinted by permission of the Institute for Communitarian Policy Studies.

William Deresiewicz. "The End of Solitude." From the *Chronicle of Higher Education*, January 2009. Used with the permission of the *Chronicle of Higher Education*. Copyright © 2009. All rights reserved.

John Dickerson. "Don't Fear Twitter." From Nieman Reports, Summer 2008. Nieman Foundation for Journalism at Harvard. Reprinted by permission.

Barbara Ehrenreich. "Cultural Baggage." From the *New York Times Magazine*, April 5, 1992. Copyright © 1992 by Barbara Ehrenreich. Used by permission. All rights reserved.

Gerald Graff. "Hidden Meaning, or Disliking Books at an Early Age" ["Disliking Books"]. From *Beyond the Culture Wars: How Teaching the Conflicts Can Revitalize American Education* by Gerald Graff. Copyright © 1992 by Gerald Graff. Used by permission of W. W. Norton & Company, Inc.

Steve Grove. "YouTube: The Flattening of Politics." From Nieman Reports, Summer 2008. Nieman Foundation for Journalism at Harvard. Reprinted by permission.

Kris Gutiérrez. Excerpt from "Teaching Toward Possibility: Building Cultural Supports for Robust Learning." From *PowerPlay: A Journal of Educational Justice* 3.1 (2011), pp. 22–37. Reprinted by permission.

E. D. Hirsch Jr. "Preface to *Cultural Literacy*." From *Cultural Literacy: What Every American Needs to Know* by E. D. Hirsch Jr. Copyright © 1987 by Houghton Mifflin Harcourt Publishing Company. Reprinted by permission of Houghton Mifflin Harcourt Publishing Company. All rights reserved.

Nathan Jindra. "Keep LaSalle Library Open" ["Neighbors Need LaSalle Branch"]. From the *South Bend Tribune*, June 14, 2014, http://www.southbendtribune.com/news/opinion/viewpoint/viewpoint-neighbors-need-lasalle-branch/article_102711d0-f3ae-11e3-bc42-001a4bcf6878.html. Copyright © 2014. Reprinted by permission. Kai Brown, Indonesia Brown, and Julia McKenna also contributed to the essay.

Dan Kennedy. "Political Blogs: Teaching Us Lessons about Community." From Nieman Reports, Summer 2008. Nieman Foundation for Journalism at Harvard. Reprinted by permission.

Paul Rogat Loeb. "Making Our Lives Count." From *Soul of a Citizen: Living with Conviction in Challenging Times* by Paul Rogat Loeb. Copyright © 1999 by Paul Rogat Loeb. Reprinted by permission of St. Martin's Griffin, an imprint of St. Martin's Press. All Rights Reserved.

James W. Loewen. "The Land of Opportunity." Excerpt from *Lies My Teacher Told Me: Everything Your American History Textbook Got Wrong* by James W. Loewen. Copyright © 1995, 2007 by James W. Loewen. Reprinted by permission of The New Press. www.thenewpress.com.

Elizabeth Martínez. "Reinventing 'America': Call for a New National Identity." From *De Colores Means All of Us: Latina Views for a Multi-Colored Century* by Elizabeth Martínez. Copyright © 1998 by Elizabeth Martínez. Reprinted by permission of the author.

Meredith Minkler. "Community-Based Research Partnerships: Challenges and Opportunities." From *Journal of Urban Health: Bulletin of the New York Academy of Medicine* 82.2, Supplement 2. Copyright © 2005 by Meredith Minkler. Reprinted with permission.

Susan B. Neuman and Donna Celano. "Access to Print in Low-Income and Middle-Income Communities: An Ecological Study of Four Neighborhoods." Republished with permission from John Wiley & Sons, Inc., from *Reading Research Quarterly* 36.1 (January/February/March 2001), pp. 8–26; permission conveyed through Copyright Clearance Center, Inc.

Laurie Ouellette. Excerpt from "Citizen Brand: ABC and the Do Good Turn in US Television." From *Commodity Activism: Cultural Resistance in Neoliberal Times*, edited by Roopali Mukherjee and Sarah Banet-Weiser. Copyright © 2012 New York University. Reprinted by permission.

Phil Primack. "Doesn't Anybody Get a C Anymore?" From the *Boston Globe*, October 5, 2008. Reprinted by permission.

Eugene F. Provenzo Jr. "Hirsch's Desire for a National Curriculum." Excerpt from *Critical Literacy: What Every American Ought to Know* by Eugene F. Provenzo Jr., pp. 53–55. Copyright © 2005 by Paradigm Publishers. Republished with permission of Taylor & Francis Group LLC Books; permission conveyed through Copyright Clearance Center, Inc.

Anna Quindlen. "Doing Nothing Is Something." From *Newsweek*, May 12, 2002. Copyright © 2002 by Anna Quindlen. Used by permission. All rights reserved.

Dana Radcliffe. "Dashed Hopes: Why Aren't Social Media Delivering Democracy?" From the *Huffington Post*, October 21, 2015, http://www.huffingtonpost.com/dana-radcliffe/dashed-hopes-why-arent-so_b_8343082.html. Copyright © 2015. Reprinted by permission of the author.

Richard Rodriguez. "Scholarship Boy." From *Hunger of Memory: The Education of Richard Rodriguez* by Richard Rodriguez. Copyright © 1982 by Richard Rodriguez. Reprinted by permission of David R. Godine, Publisher, Inc.

Stuart Rojstaczer. "Grade Inflation Gone Wild." From the *Christian Science Monitor*, March 24, 2009. Copyright © 2009 by Stuart Rojstaczer. Reprinted with permission.

Tom Standage. Excerpt from "History Retweets Itself," the epilogue to *Writing on the Wall: Social Media—The First 2,000 Years* by Tom Standage. Copyright © 2013. Reprinted by permission of Bloomsbury Publishing Inc.

Index of Authors, Titles, and Key Terms